AN INTRODUCTION TO GLOBAL FINANCIAL MARKETS

An Introduction to Global Financial Markets

An extensively revised edition of

An Introduction to Western Financial Markets

STEPHEN VALDEZ
with
Julian Wood

First published 1993 as *An Introduction to Western Financial Markets*
Reprinted twice
Extensively revised second edition 1997
Reprinted four times
Extensively revised third edition 2000
Reprinted four times
Fourth edition 2003

Published by
PALGRAVE MACMILLAN
Houndmills, Basingstoke, Hampshire RG21 6XS and
175 Fifth Avenue, New York, N.Y. 10010
Companies and representatives throughout the world

PALGRAVE MACMILLAN is the global academic imprint of the Palgrave Macmillan division of St. Martin's Press, LLC and of Palgrave Macmillan Ltd. Macmillan® is a registered trademark in the United States, United Kingdom and other countries. Palgrave is a registered trademark in the European Union and other countries.

ISBN 1–4039–0011–6 hardback
ISBN 1–4039–0012–4 paperback

This book is printed on paper suitable for recycling and made from fully managed and sustained forest sources.

A catalogue record for this book is available from the British Library.

Library of Congress Catalog Card Number: 2003049803

10   9   8   7   6   5
11   10   09   08   07   06   05   04

Printed and bound in Great Britain by
Creative Print & Design (Wales), Ebbw Vale

Contents

Preface   xvii

Acknowledgements   xviii

Introduction   1

1   The Debt Merry-Go-Round   3

   RAISON D'ÊTRE OF THE MARKETS   3
      Lenders   3
      Borrowers   4
      Securities   5
   RAISING CAPITAL   6
      Bank Loans   6
      Bonds   6
      Equity   7
      Gearing   8
   CONCLUSION   9
   SUMMARY   10

Banking   11

2   Banking Background   13

   HISTORY   13
   BANKING SUPERVISION   16
   TYPES OF BANK: DEFINITIONS   17
   OTHER BANKING TERMINOLOGY   25
   A BANK'S BALANCE SHEET   26
   THE CREATION OF CREDIT   28
      Banking Depends on Confidence   29
      The Money Supply   29
      Liquidity Ratios   30
      The Capital Ratio   30
   CAPITAL RATIO   30
      The Basic Concept   30
      The Basle Committee   31
      Increasing Capital Ratio   33
   CENTRAL BANK REPORTING   34

THE SECOND BANKING DIRECTIVE 35

MAJOR WORLD BANKS 36

SUMMARY 39

APPENDIX 1 – MAJOR BANKS ACROSS THE WORLD 41

APPENDIX 2 – INTERNATIONAL AND DOMESTIC
BANKING COOPERATION AND MERGERS 44

3 The Role of the Central Bank **47**

HISTORY OF THE MAJOR CENTRAL BANKS 47
   France 47
   Germany 47
   Japan 48
   UK 48
   US 49
   The European Central Bank 50

CENTRAL BANK ACTIVITIES 50
   Supervision of the Banking System 51
   Monetary Policy 52
   Banknotes 52
   Banker to the Other Banks 53
   Banker to the Government 54
   Raising Money for the Government 55
   Controlling the Nation's Currency Reserves 56
   Acting as Lender of Last Resort 56
   Liaison with International Bodies 57

THE POSITION OF CENTRAL BANKS TODAY 58

SUMMARY 60

4 Commercial Banking **61**

INTRODUCTION 61

RETAIL BANKING 61
   Types of Service 61
   Money Banking – Deposits 62
   The Electronic Purse 66
   Other Services 67
   Delivery Channels 68
   Clearing Systems 70
   Key Retail Banking Issues 72

WHOLESALE BANKING 79

BANK LENDING 79
    Uncommitted Facilities 79
    Committed Facilities 80
    Syndicated Facilities 83
    The Loan Agreement 87
    Wholesale Banking Issues 89
SUMMARY 90

5 Investment Banking **91**

INTRODUCTION 91
INVESTMENT BANKING 91
    Accepting 91
    Corporate Finance 95
    Securities Trading 98
    Investment Management 99
    Loan Arrangement 100
    Foreign Exchange 100
    Miscellaneous Activities 100
REGULATION 101
SUMMARY 103

Securities Markets **105**
6 The Money and Bond Markets **107**

THE RATE OF INTEREST 107
    Risk 107
    Maturity 108
    Expectations 108
    Liquidity 109
    Supply and Demand 109
    Inflation 110
YIELD 110
    Par Values 110
    Interest Yield 111
    Gross Redemption Yield 111
    Accrued Interest 114
CREDIT RATINGS 114
DOMESTIC MONEY MARKETS 117
    Call Money 118
    The Interbank Market 118

Money Market Securities 120
Treasury Bills 120
Local Authority/Public Utility Bills 121
Certificates of Deposit (CDs) 121
Commercial Paper (CP) 121
Bills of Exchange 123
CENTRAL BANK ROLE 124
DOMESTIC BOND MARKETS 125
Introduction 125
Government Bonds 127
Local Authority/Public Sector Bonds 130
Mortgage and Asset-Backed Bonds 131
Corporate Bonds 133
Foreign Bonds 135
Junk Bonds 136
INTERNATIONAL MARKETS 137
Background: Eurocurrencies 137
The Syndicated Loan Market 139
The International Debt Crisis 140
The eurobond Market 142
Coupon Stripping 146
Other Variations 147
Medium-Term Notes (MTNs) 148
The Money Markets 148
Repos 149
Participants and Top Traders 150
SUMMARY 151
APPENDIX 1 – ANNOUNCEMENT OF RESULT OF
A UK BID PRICE AUCTION FOR GOVERNMENT BONDS 153
APPENDIX 2 – RECENT CHANGES TO THE UK GILTS
MARKET 154

7 Stock Exchanges **155**

HISTORY OF ASSOCIATIONS FOR TRADING 155
THE ROLE OF A STOCK EXCHANGE 156
STOCKS AND SHARES 156
INTERNATIONAL EQUITY 159
INDICES 160

WHO OWNS SHARES?   163
    Small Investors vs Institutions   163
    Pension Funds: Funding vs Unfunding   163
    Equity Investment   167
    Mutual Funds   168
    Active vs Passive Management   170
    Custodians   171
DEALING SYSTEMS   171
    Order-Driven Systems   172
    Quote-Driven Systems   175
    Hybrid Systems   178
    Inter Dealer Brokers   179
    Stock Borrowing and Lending   179
    Bought Deals/Block Trades   180
    Share Buy-Backs   180
SETTLEMENT   181
NEW ISSUES   182
RIGHTS ISSUES   184
SCRIP ISSUES AND SPLITS   186
SCRIP DIVIDENDS   187
SECOND MARKETS   187
ANALYSTS' RATIOS   188
US STOCK MARKET – THE NEW PARADIGM
AND THE BURST OF THE DOT.COM BUBBLE   190
EU RULES   191
    Investment Services Directive   191
    Capital Adequacy Directive   191
    Mergers and Acquisitions   192
CHALLENGES TO TRADITIONAL STOCK EXCHANGES   192
SUMMARY   194

Foreign Exchange and International Trade   **197**
8   Foreign Exchange   **199**

INTRODUCTION   199
    The Market   199
    Buyers and Sellers   199
    Bank Profits   200
WHAT DETERMINES EXCHANGE RATES?   200

BRETTON WOODS	203
Exchange Rate Stability	204
International Monetary Fund	204
The World Bank	205
FLOATING RATES	206
EUROPEAN ECONOMIC AND MONETARY UNION	208
FOREIGN EXCHANGE RISK FOR CORPORATES	208
Types of Risk	208
Transaction Risk – Forward Rates	209
Transaction Risk – Options	211
FOREIGN EXCHANGE DEALING	214
Quotations	214
Cross-Rates	216
Foreign Exchange Swaps	216
Brokers	218
Settlement	219
ARBITRAGE	221
CENTRAL BANK SURVEYS	222
WHY LONDON?	224
SUMMARY	224
APPENDIX	226
9 Trade Finance	**227**
GENERAL PROBLEMS	227
PAYMENT SERVICES	227
COLLECTION OF DEBTS	229
EXTENSION OF CREDIT	229
Bill of Exchange	229
Documentary Letter of Credit	230
Types of Documentary Credit	231
Documentary Collection	232
Effect of 1997 Asian Crisis	232
FINANCE FOR THE EXPORTER	233
FOREIGN EXCHANGE	234
TRADING GUARANTEES	234
MISCELLANEOUS SERVICES	236
SUMMARY	237

10   European Economic and Monetary Union   **238**

  INTRODUCTION   238

  HISTORY OF THE EUROPEAN UNION   238
    Early History   238
    1945   239
    The Council of Europe   239
    The European Coal and Steel Community   240
    'All Roads Lead to Rome'   241
    The European Economic Community   241
    Wider Membership   242
    The de Gaulle Stalemate   243
    The European Council   243
    The Single European Act   244
    European Free Trade Area   244
    The Maastricht, Amsterdam and Nice Treaties   245

  THE INSTITUTIONS OF THE EUROPEAN UNION   247
    The European Council   247
    The Council of Ministers   247
    The European Commission   247
    European Parliament   248
    Ecofin   248
    The European Central Bank   248
    The European Court of Justice   251

  HISTORY OF PREVIOUS MONETARY UNIONS   252
    Political Empires   252
    Political Unification   252
    Voluntary Unions   252
    Smaller Unions   252

  HISTORY OF STEPS TO EMU   253
    The Werner Report   253
    European Monetary System   253
    Changes to the ERM   254
    The Delors Plan   254
    The Maastricht Treaty   255
    EMU Begins   256
    Stability and Growth Pact   257
    ERM II   258
    Next Members?   258
    EMU Statistics   259
    Payment Systems   259
    EMU – The Benefits   260

The Counter Arguments 263
The UK Position 267
SUMMARY 268

Derivative Products **271**

11 Traded Options **273**

DERIVATIVE PRODUCTS 273

TRADED OPTIONS: EQUITIES 274
Calls and Puts 274
Option Writers 276
Trading Options 276
Intrinsic Value and Time Value 278
Calculation of the Premium 279
Exercise or Trade? 281
Other Terminology 283
Options on Indices 283

TRADED OPTIONS: OTHER OPTIONS 285
Currencies 285
Bonds 286
Interest Rates 287

OPTION STRATEGIES 289

SUMMARY 291

12 Financial Futures **293**

FUTURES TRADING 293
Background 293
Hedgers vs Speculators 293
Commodity Futures 295
Financial Futures 297
Index Futures 299
Bond Futures 301
Interest Rates 302
Currency Futures 304
Some Problems of Futures Exchanges 304
Open Outcry or Computers? 305
Contract Volumes 306

SUMMARY 307

13 Other Derivative Products   **309**

    INTRODUCTION   309

    FORWARD RATE AGREEMENTS (FRAs)   309

    SWAPS   312
        Comparative Advantage   312
        Interest Rate Swaps   314
        Making a Market in Swaps 314
        Users of Swaps   316
        Swaps and Futures   318
        Other Swaps   319

    CURRENCY SWAPS   319

    CAPS, FLOORS AND COLLARS   320
        Introduction   320
        Caps   321
        Floors   321
        Collars   322

    CREDIT DERIVATIVES   323

    THE MARKET IN DERIVATIVE INSTRUMENTS   324

    SUMMARY   327

Insurance   **329**

14 Insurance   **331**

    BACKGROUND TO THE INSURANCE MARKETS   331
        History   331
        The Insurance Market   332
        Assurance/Insurance   332
        Regulation   333
        Distribution   334
        Self-Insurance   336

    REINSURANCE   336
        Definitions   336
        Proportional and Non-Proportional Reinsurance   337
        Financial Reinsurance   337
        The Reinsurance Market   338

    THE LONDON MARKET   339

    LLOYD'S   340
        Organisation   340
        Early Problems   342
        Commercial Problems   342

THE MARKET TODAY 345

EU REGULATION 347

SUMMARY 348

The Periodic Global Crises **351**

15 Global Financial Crises **353**

INTRODUCTION 353

WHAT HAPPENED? 353

    Mexico 353

    The Far East 353

    Russia 355

    LTCM and Hedge Funds 355

    Japan 356

    China 357

    Brazil 358

    Argentina 358

WHY DID IT ALL HAPPEN? 359

    Short-Term Capital Flows 359

    Paul Volcker's Views 359

    BIS Warning 360

    Short-Term Capital – 'Hot Money' 360

    Transparency 361

    Credit Control and Risk Management 361

    IMF/World Bank Roles 361

THE SOLUTIONS? 362

    Avoiding Fixed Exchange Rates 362

    Exchange Controls 362

    Changes in Short-Term Loans and Capital 363

    Precautionary Credit Line Facility 364

    Greater Private Sector Role 364

    Financial Stability Forum 365

    Self Help 366

SUMMARY 366

Trends in the Global Financial Markets **367**

16 Key Trends **369**

11 SEPTEMBER 369

THE ECONOMIC OUTLOOK 369

THE PENSION TIME BOMB 370

THE INTERNET	371
ELECTRONIC BROKING	371
RISK MANAGEMENT AND DERIVATIVES	372
EXCHANGES	373
ASSET-BACKED SECURITIES	374
SUMMARY	374
Glossary	**375**
Index	**395**

Preface

The idea of a book on global financial markets came to me when I hit the problem of recommended reading for candidates coming from the continent of Europe to one of our courses.

Since the course in question was about the markets in general, books called 'How the City of London Works' (or similar titles) did not exactly answer the problem. This was particularly true when we found ourselves facing audiences from the former Russian republics and from Eastern Europe.

It seemed to me that there was a need for a more general book about the global markets as a whole, as opposed to one about markets in one particular country such as the US or the UK. In any case, the financial world is becoming more integrated and global in its operations. A parochial knowledge of just one country is proving less and less satisfactory. This book attempts to answer this need.

Having said that, the book does not attempt a systematic coverage of the markets in all countries. Such a book would be far bulkier than this one and, probably, unreadable! Instead I have usually concentrated on examples from the US, the UK, Germany, France and Japan. From time to time, illustrations will also be given from markets such as the Netherlands, Spain, Italy and Switzerland. The aim is not only to give a basic idea of how the markets work, but also to show the diversity of customs and practices within a common theme.

The book should prove useful for those preparing for a variety of examinations (MBA, banking, finance, economics and business studies), those working in banking and financial institutions in a support role (computer staff, accountants, personnel, public relations, back office and settlement) and, finally, staff in the many suppliers of information and computer services to the financial markets (computer manufacturers and software houses, Reuters, Telerate and so on).

The second edition saw the addition of a summary at the end of each chapter; the third saw the inclusion of two totally new chapters, one on European Economic and Monetary Union (which started in 1999) and the other on Global Financial Crises, following the crises in the Far East and Russia in 1997 and 1998.

The fourth edition has been fully updated to cover the latest developments in the field. These include the impact of 9/11 and the relative collapse of world stock markets; new capital ratio rules for banks; current retail banking developments; the results of the latest world FX survey; the problems faced by the European Economic Union; attempts to reform Lloyd's of London; and a review of current trends.

Stephen Valdez

Acknowledgements

By the time of this fourth edition, I found myself in part retirement. I, therefore, leaned heavily on my colleague in Profile Financial Training, Julian Wood, who did most of the work to update this edition. He, in turn, was helped by his associates, Malcolm Barnard and Gilbert Williamson. I am grateful to all three for their considerable efforts.

For the chapter on insurance, I am grateful to my friend Richard Bradley, who has knowledge of the industry and provided many helpful comments and suggestions. Others who gave advice and information were Matthew Houston of Proquote Ltd and James Rooney of brokers Redmayne Bentley, who both helped with the specimen computer screens for equity systems; Stephen Haasz for Lloyd's of London's new franchise system; Begonia Roberts of Thomson Investor Relations for the table on top centres of portfolio management; Steve Kelly of Thomson Financial Ltd for the details from the annual Thomson Extel Pan European Survey 2002; and Paul Martin of Swiss Re UK Ltd for the information from Swiss Re Sigma publications on worldwide insurance volumes.

In other cases, I have extracted useful figures found in magazines like *The Banker, Euromoney, Futures Industry* and *IFR Securities Data*.

For Chapter 10, on European Economic and Monetary Union, I am grateful to D. W. Urwin's excellent book '*The Community of Europe. A History of European Integration since 1945*' (Longman) for much of the material on the history of the European Union.

Many organisations gave permission for copyright material to be used, and these were:

Association for Payment Clearing Services
Bank for International Settlements
European Association of Cooperative Banks
London Stock Exchange
Society for Worldwide Interbank Financial Telecommunications
UBS Asset Management

Once again, as with the first three editions, my thanks to Tina Shorter of Firm Focus for her excellent work in preparing the text, including camera-ready copy, and for the patience and tact with which she corrected my many inconsistencies, repetitions and lack of clarity. Those which remain are, of course, my responsibility.

Introduction

1   The Debt Merry-Go-Round

1 The Debt Merry-Go-Round

RAISON D'ÊTRE OF THE MARKETS

The beginning is always a good place to start. Let's go straight to the heart of the matter and ask the most fundamental question of all – what are the financial markets *for*? What is their purpose? What is the raison d'être?

The markets are all about the raising of capital and the matching of those who *want* capital (borrowers) with those who *have* it (lenders).

How do the borrowers find the lenders? Clearly, with difficulty but for the presence of intermediaries, such as banks. Banks take deposits from those who have money to save and bundle it up in various ways so that it can be lent to those who wish to borrow.

More complex transactions than a simple bank deposit require markets in which borrowers and their agents can meet lenders and their agents, and existing commitments to borrow or lend can be sold on to other people. Stock exchanges are a good example. Companies can raise money by selling shares to investors and existing shares can be freely bought and sold.

The money goes round and round, just like a carousel on a fairground (see Table 1.1).

Table 1.1   *The debt merry-go-round*

Lenders	Intermediaries	Markets	Borrowers
Individuals	Banks	Interbank	Individuals
Companies	Insurance companies	Stock Exchange	Companies
	Pension funds	Money market	Central government
	Mutual funds	Bond market	Municipalities
		Foreign exchange	Public corporations

Lenders

Let's have a look at some of those who might be lenders:

Individuals   Individuals may have conscious savings in banks of various kinds. Individuals also may not think of themselves as conscious savers at all but, nevertheless, pay monthly premiums to insurance companies and contributions to pensions. Regarding pensions, there are different traditions. The US, UK, the Netherlands, Switzerland and Japan have a strong tradition of pension funds. They

3

invest the money paid into either private pension plans or employers' pension schemes. In France, the state takes care of most pensions and pays them out of current taxation, not out of a fund. In Germany, company pensions are important but the company decides on the investment, which may be in the company itself. Where pension funds exist, these funds of money, along with those of insurance companies, are key determinants of movements in the markets. They have to look ahead to long-term liabilities, and will assist the borrowers of capital by buying government bonds, corporate bonds, corporate equities and so on. The shortage of such funds in many of the newly emerging economies is a major reason for the slow growth of local securities markets there.

Companies   We think of commercial companies as borrowers of capital. However, even if the company is a borrower, if some of the money is not needed for a short period of time, it will seek to make money by lending in the short-term markets called 'money markets' (that is, transactions of up to one year in duration).

There are also companies whose cash flow is strong and who tend to be lenders rather than borrowers. A major company in the dissemination of financial information is Reuters. On several occasions they have returned surplus liquid funds to shareholders.

Borrowers

Who, then, are the borrowers of capital?

Individuals   Individuals may have bank loans for domestic purchases or longer-term mortgages to fund house purchase.

Companies   Companies need money short-term to fund cash flow. They need money longer-term for growth and expansion.

Governments   Governments are typically voracious borrowers. Their expenditure exceeds their receipts from taxes and they borrow to make up the deficit. They may also borrow on behalf of municipalities, federal states, nationalised industries and public sector bodies generally. The total is usually called the 'Public Sector Borrowing Requirement' (PSBR). The cumulative total for all the borrowing since they started is called the 'National Debt'. The first surprise for many of us is that governments don't pay off the national debt, it just gets bigger. Of this, more in Chapter 3.

Municipalities and similar bodies   Apart from the government borrowing on behalf of various local authorities, these bodies may borrow in their own name. This would cover municipalities like Barcelona, counties like Berkshire in the UK, federal states like Hesse in Germany.

Public corporations   These might include nationalised industries, like SNCF in France or the German railways and post office authorities, or general public sector bodies like Crédit Local de France or the German Unity Fund.

Within an economy, many of the above will not be nationals but foreigners, with implications for the *foreign exchange* market.

Securities

When the money is lent, it may simply be a deposit with a bank. Most of the time, however, the borrower will issue a receipt for the money, a promise to pay back. These pieces of paper are, in the most general sense, what we call *securities*. There are, unfortunately for the beginner, masses of different names – Treasury bills, certificates of deposit, commercial paper, bills of exchange, bonds, convertibles, debentures, preference shares, eurobonds, floating rate notes and so on. At least we can console ourselves with the thought that they are essentially all the same – promises to pay back which show key information:

- ❏ HOW MUCH is owed
- ❏ WHEN it will be paid
- ❏ THE RATE OF INTEREST to reward the lender.

A major characteristic of the markets is that these securities are freely bought and sold. This makes life easier for the lender and helps the borrower to raise the money more easily.

For example, a young American wanting to save for old age spends $5000 on a 30 year government bond which has just been issued. After 5 years, he decides that this was not such a good idea and wants the money now. What does he do? He simply sells the bond to someone else. This is crucially important, as it means that he is more willing to put the money up in the first place, knowing that there is this escape clause. It also gives great velocity to the 'Debt Merry-Go-Round' as the same security is bought and sold many times.

Let's tackle the market jargon here. The first time the money is lent and changes hands, the first time the security is issued, is the *primary market*.

All the buying and selling that takes place thereafter we call the *secondary market*.

The secondary market is very significant as the flexibility it gives makes the primary market work better – it's the oil that helps the wheels to turn round.

Let's look at other terminology used (see Figure 1.1).

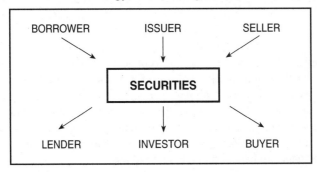

Figure 1.1 *Market terminology*

Suppose the government announces a new bond. We can say the government is *issuing* a new bond. We could just as easily say that the government is *selling* a new bond. We might see it as a sign of the government's need to *borrow* more money.

If you hear of the new bond, you may tell a friend that you've decided to *invest* in it. You might alternatively say you've decided to *buy* the new bond. You probably won't think of it that way, but you are the *lender* of money to a, no doubt ungrateful, government.

It may seem an obvious point, but all those terms might be used. Sometimes newcomers need to be reminded that whoever buys a security is directly or indirectly lending money.

RAISING CAPITAL

Let's look at an example. Suppose a commercial company needs $200m to finance building a new factory. We have just explained that the financial markets are all about the raising of money. What, then, are the choices?

Bank Loans

One obvious source of money when we need it is the *bank*. These days, with large sums of money, it may be a syndicate of banks to spread the risk. The banks are taking deposits lent to them and relending the money to the commercial company. It's their classic role as intermediary. In the international syndicated bank lending market, based in London, the money will not be lent at a fixed rate but at a variable rate according to market rates from time to time. This is called the *floating rate*. The banks may lend at a basic rate (such as the prime rate in the US or the interbank rate in Europe) plus a given margin such as ¾%. The bank will re-adjust the rate, say, every 3 months. The rate is fixed for 3 months but then changed for the next 3 months. Note that this creates *risk*. If rates fall, the lender loses income. If rates rise, the borrower pays more. (Note, however, that in many European domestic markets, the banks' tradition is to lend to corporates at a *fixed* rate.)

Bonds

Another choice would be to issue a *bond*. A bond is just a piece of paper stating the terms on which the money will be paid back. For example, it may be a 10 year bond, paying interest at 7% in two instalments per year. The word 'bond' implies that the rate of interest is fixed. If it's floating, then we have to find another name, such as '*floating rate note*'. The bond may be bought by a bank as another use for depositors' money, or it might be bought directly by an investor who sees the bond notice in the paper and instructs their agent to buy.

There is a strong obligation to meet the interest payments on the bond. If an interest payment is missed, the bond holders acquire certain rights and might even be able to put the company into liquidation.

Equity

A final choice would be to raise the money by selling shares in the company. Shares are called '*equity*'. If it's the first time the company has done this, we call it a '*new issue*'. If the company already has shareholders, it may approach them with the opportunity to buy more shares in the company, called a '*rights issue*'. This is because, under most but not all EU law, the existing shareholders must be approached first if any new shares are to be offered for cash. These rights are not protected as strongly in the US or in Germany.

The reward for the shareholders by way of income is the *dividend*. However, the income is usually poorer than that paid on a bond and the shareholders look to *capital gains* as well, believing that the share price will go up as time goes by.

Our three choices are shown in Figure 1.2.

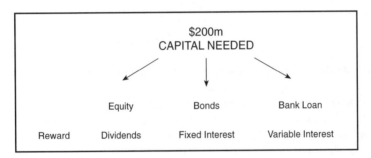

Figure 1.2 *Raising capital*

We must recognise that the equity choice is fundamentally different from the other two. The shareholder is part owner along with the other shareholders. There is, thus, no date for paying the money back (the shares may be sold on a stock exchange to someone else, but that's quite different). The shareholders accept risk – they could prosper if the firm prospers, or lose some or all of their money if the firm goes into liquidation. If the latter sad event happens, the shareholders are the last to receive a share of any money left. In addition, if the firm hits trouble, the dividend can be cut or even missed altogether.

In the case of bonds and bank loans, the money must eventually be paid back and there are strong legal obligations to meet the interest payments – they are *debt* not *equity*. Equity is the exception in the 'Debt Merry-Go-Round' in that it is not debt at all.

Gearing

There's nothing wrong in principle with borrowed money. It enables the company to do more trading than it could on the shareholders' equity alone. The danger comes when too much money is borrowed, especially if boom times are followed (as they usually are) by recession. The firm may be unable to pay the interest out of its reduced profits, apart from the problem of repaying the principal sum itself.

Stock market analysts, therefore, look at firms' balance sheets and look at the ratio of long-term debt to equity. However, let's note here that when we say 'equity', we don't just mean the money raised by selling shares originally and by subsequent rights issues. The firm (we hope) will make profits. Out of the profits it will pay tax to the government and dividends to the shareholders. The remaining profit is retained for growth and expansion. This money also belongs to the shareholders. As a result, the phrase *shareholders' funds* is used for the total equity of the shareholders:

> Original equity
>
> +   Rights issues
> +   Retained profit
> =   Shareholders' funds

Analysts, then, look at the ratio between the long-term debt and the shareholders' funds. The relationship is called *gearing* or *leverage*.

The metaphor is from mechanics. A gear enables more work to be done with a given force. The lever is a similar idea. Remember Archimedes saying 'give me a fulcrum and I will lever the world'? The shareholders are doing more trading than they could with their money alone. How? By borrowing other people's money. The general idea behind gearing or leverage is to make a given sum of money go further. It can be summarised by the popular American expression 'more bang for your buck'! In this context, we do it by borrowing someone else's money. We shall also meet other contexts in this book.

The ratio between long-term debt and shareholders' funds is thus the *gearing ratio*. What ratio is safe? Frankly, this has become a matter of some controversy. Generally, people worry if the ratio reaches 100%, but that's only a crude guideline. For example, if the business is cyclical, analysts will worry more than if it's a steady business from one year to the next. They will also worry less if there are assets that can easily be realised, rather than assets which may not be easy to dispose of, especially during a recession (for example, property). There are, naturally, different national cultures. J P Morgan puts corporate gearing in France at 67%, in the US at 56% and in the UK at 36%. In a low interest rate environment corporate gearing will tend to increase – 2000 and 2001 have seen record volumes of bond issues, for example.

Having looked at the three key choices for new capital – equity, bonds and bank loans – we should also be aware that, in Western financial markets generally, probably 50% of the money needed for growth and expansion comes from retained profits. 'Profit' can be a sensitive topic and, in some people's eyes, a pejorative term – for example, 'they are only in it for the profit'. However, profit provides not only rewards for the shareholders and taxes for the government, but funds for expansion which create further employment and a more secure environment for the employees.

We shall look at the concept of *international* markets in Chapter 6. Briefly, we are talking about equity raised across national boundaries; bonds issued in, say, London in dollars and sold to international investors; international banks getting together to syndicate a large loan. In addition to this would be capital raised in purely *domestic* markets. Equity, bonds and large syndicated loans usually refer to *long-term* capital. There is also the raising of *short-term* capital, for meeting cash flow needs rather than growth and expansion. Equity is not applicable here but there are various securities and types of bank loan which meet this need.

International figures can be misleading, as the emphasis may be quite different in *domestic* markets. Each country has its own traditions. The US is a big market for company bonds, as well as a large equity market. In the 10 years 1988–1998, US non-financial corporate borrowers raised $785bn in the form of bonds – three times their bank loans. German companies, however, have a long tradition of close relationship with banks and use of bank finance. Equity finance is strong in the UK, with a higher proportion of companies publicly quoted than in most other European countries.

CONCLUSION

We have seen that the raison d'être of the financial markets is the raising of capital. Our examination of the choices for finding capital shows us the financial markets in action, and also the themes which we study in this book:

Banking   In Chapters 2–5 we look at banking in all its aspects.

Money and Bond Markets   In Chapter 6 we examine the domestic and international markets. We look at raising money short-term (money markets) and long-term (bond markets).

Foreign Exchange   The international character of the markets today and gradual deregulation create strong demand for foreign currencies. This is considered in Chapter 8.

EMU   European Economic and Monetary Union started on January 1, 1999, as eleven countries moved to a single currency. This key development is discussed in Chapter 10.

Finance for Trade   World trade is, of course, extremely important. The need for capital to back trade transactions and the need to control the risk pose special problems. These are discussed in Chapter 9.

Equities Stock markets, brokers, market makers and institutions are explained in Chapter 7.

Derivative Products Interest rates, currency rates, bond prices and share prices all go up and down, creating *risk*. There are financial products which are, paradoxically, used both to exploit risk and to control risk. These are called *derivative products* and are, possibly, the fastest growing sector of the financial markets today. This complex but fascinating subject is looked at in Chapters 11–13.

Insurance The insurance market is one of the oldest world financial markets. Domestic and business risks create the need for insurance. The premiums paid in advance are a major factor in creating funds for lending to those who need capital, until such time as these funds are required to meet insurance claims. This is explained in Chapter 14.

Global Financial Crises Our global markets have also given rise to global crises in recent years. Why these happened and what (if anything) can be done to prevent them is explained in Chapter 15.

Key Trends Finally, in Chapter 16, we analyse the key trends in the financial markets today.

SUMMARY

The purpose of the markets is to facilitate the raising of capital and match those who want capital (borrowers) with those who have it (lenders).

Typically, the borrower issues a receipt promising to pay the lender back – these are *securities* and may be freely bought and sold.

Money may be raised by a bank loan (commercial banking) or by the issue of a bond or equity (the capital markets). The first two represent debt. The relationship between debt and equity on a balance sheet is known as *gearing*.

There are domestic markets and international (cross-border) markets.

Banking

2 Banking Background

3 The Role of the Central Bank

4 Commercial Banking

5 Investment Banking

2 Banking Background

Money and the use of metal coins as money has a long history – going back at least ten centuries. Banking, certainly in today's sense, is rather more modern.

In many ways, the origins of capitalism as we see it today lie in the operations of Italian merchanting and banking groups in the 13th, 14th and 15th centuries. Italian states, like Lombardy and Florence, were dominant economic powers. The merchants had trading links across borders and used their cash resources for banking purposes.

The bankers sat at formal benches, often in the open air. The Italian for bench is '*banco*', giving us the modern word for bank. (If you happen to be in Prato, Italy, look in the Chapel of San Francisco for a fresco showing the money-changers' *banco,* or counter.) If the bank went into liquidation, the bench would be solemnly broken, giving us the *bancorupto* or bankrupt, as we say today. The early associations were partnerships, as shareholding companies did not begin until 1550. As a result, people might write to the '*Medici e compagni*', the 'Medici and their partners'. It gives us the modern word – the *company*. It is the Italians who claim the oldest bank in the world, Monte dei Paschi of Siena (1472).

For a long period, Florence was a major centre. As a result, many coins ended up with names based on Florence. The UK had a 'florin' until the coinage was decimalised in 1971; the former Dutch guilder had the abbreviation FL – florin; the Hungarian currency is the 'forint'. We also read that, in 1826, Schubert sold his D major piano sonata for '120 florins'. As a result of all this, at the EC Summit in Madrid in December 1996, John Major put forward the florin as the proposed name for Europe's single currency. The meeting finally decided on the rather more boring name, the euro.

Italian bankers had a long relationship with the British crown. The first bankers to lend money in London came from Lombardy and London still has 'Lombard Street' at the heart of the financial area. Bankers lent money to Edward I, Edward II and Edward III (naturally, to finance their various wars). Edward III, however, defaulted on the loan in 1345 and the proud families, the Bardi and the Peruzzi in Florence, crashed into liquidation as a consequence. Presumably this was the world's first (but not last!) international banking crisis.

Those bankers were very advanced for their time. They used bills of exchange (to be explained in Chapter 5), letters of credit, book entry for money instead of physically transporting it and double entry bookkeeping. The first textbook on double entry bookkeeping was published in 1494 by a Franciscan monk, Luca Pacioli. They experimented with marine insurance and evolved a body of mercantile law. The Bardi operated 30 branches in Italy and overseas and employed more than 350 people.

S. D. Chapman, in *The Rise of Merchant Banking* (Allen & Unwin, 1984) shows how the Medici bank helped an Italian firm in Venice sell goods to a firm in London using a bill of exchange. The Medici bank in London would collect the money and the bank would take care of the foreign exchange conversion and risk. The goods were invoiced at £97.18s.4d (in old pounds, shillings and pence). This was the equivalent of about 535 ducats. The Medici branch in Venice paid the local firm 500 ducats on the bill of exchange, making 7% on money they would not receive for 6 months, that is, about 14% p.a. The date? 20 July 1463.

The bill above was not 'discounted' in the modern sense, since this would imply charging interest on money and this was forbidden by the Roman Catholic Church as 'usury'. The bill represented a service to facilitate trade and change foreign money – it could not appear to involve the lending of money. On the deposit side, no formal interest could be paid for the same reason. Depositors received a share of profits paid at discretion. Thus the liabilities side of the balance sheet was headed, '*Discrezione*'. Islamic banking faces similar problems due to the Koran's rejection of the concept of interest as such. Today there are some 60 Islamic banks which follow the principle that the reward for deposits is not fixed but based on the profit from the use of the money.

The one thing the Italians didn't invent was banknotes. For this, we look to goldsmiths in the UK. There, merchants would keep money for safe keeping in the Royal Mint. Charles I had many arguments with Parliament about money and solved one of them by marching down to the Royal Mint and stealing £130,000! Although the money was replaced later, confidence in the Royal Mint had gone. It was good news for goldsmiths who had secure vaults for gold and silver coins and began an era of goldsmiths as bankers for some 150 years. Coutts Bank, still going today, began in 1692 as a goldsmith bank. The goldsmiths found it convenient to give out receipts for a deposit of gold coins made out to 'the bearer' and to issue ten receipts for a deposit of ten coins. In this way, if the bearer owed someone else three gold coins, they could pass on three bearer receipts. Even better, if someone wanted to borrow five gold coins, the goldsmiths could lend them five of these nice pieces of paper and not give gold coins. We are now very much into modern banking traditions, except that today the notes aren't backed by gold or silver anyway! By the end of the 17th century, the goldsmiths' receipts had become banknotes in a formal sense, the first being issued by the Bank of Sweden in 1661.

Internationally, the emphasis in banking, which had been in Florence, moved to Genoa, as gold and silver were flooding in from the New World. Outside Italy, the Fugger family of Augsburg created a financial dynasty comparable to the Italians. They were originally wool merchants, but turned to precious metals and banking. They had gold, silver and copper mines in Hungary and Austria and became principal financiers to the Hapsburg empire in Germany, the Low Countries and Spain (see E. Green, *Banking, an Illustrated History*, Phaidon Press, 1989).

Later still, we have the rise of the two great rivals, the Dutch and British Empires and Amsterdam and London as rival financial centres. Amsterdam, for example, is Europe's oldest stock exchange.

We also see merchant banking (or investment banking) in the modern sense. Francis Baring was a textile merchant from Exeter and started Baring Brothers in 1762. In 1804, Nathan Mayer Rothschild opened up for banking business in London, after a brief spell in textiles in Manchester. In Holland, we had Mees & Hope (1702) and, later, Pierson, Heldring & Pierson – both still in business today as subsidiaries of the Fortis Group under the name Mees Pierson.

The merchant bankers had two key activities – financing trade, using bills of exchange and raising money for governments by selling bonds. Baring Brothers financed the huge reparations imposed on France after the Napoleonic wars with a large international bond issue. (As a consequence, the Duc de Richelieu dubbed them 'Europe's 6th super-power'!) In 1818, Rothschild's raised a large loan for Prussia, to be redeemed after 36 years. They arranged to pay dividends to bondholders in their local currency. The bonds were sold to merchants, private subscribers and the aristocracy. Prussia paid 7½% of which 5% was paid to bondholders and 2½% was used to create a 'sinking fund' to redeem the bond after 36 years (see Chapman, *The Rise of Merchant Banking*). The Dutch Bank Mees, together with Baring Bros, helped the American states finance the purchase of Louisiana from Napoleon in 1803. Later, corporate finance emerged as another investment banking business. In 1886, Baring Bros floated Guinness – police had to hold back the crowds!

In the second half of the 1700s and into the 1800s there was a large growth in Europe's population (from 180 million in 1800 to 450 million by 1914). This period also saw the growth of industrialisation and urbanisation. As a result, the spread of banking followed. While private banks continued to flourish in many cases, the gradual change in legislation to allow joint stock banks (that is, banks with shareholders) paved the way for the growth of larger commercial banks with many branches and a strong deposit-taking function.

In the US, the Bank of New York and the Bank of Boston (later First National Bank of Boston) opened in 1800. The water company, the Manhattan Company, became a bank around about the same time. (It became Chase Manhattan in 1955.) The 'City Bank' opened in 1812, becoming the National City Bank later and merging with First National Bank to form today's Citibank in 1955 (now Citigroup after further acquisitions).

In Europe, we see the Société Générale of Belgium formed in 1822; the Bayerische Hypotheken und Wechsel Bank in 1822; Creditanstalt in Austria in 1856; Crédit Suisse also in 1856; UBS in 1862; Crédit Lyonnais in 1863 and the Société Générale (France) in 1864 (by 1900 they had 200 and 350 branches respectively); Deutsche Bank in 1870 and Banca Commerciale Italiana in 1894.

In the UK, the Bank of England's monopoly of joint stock banking ended in 1826. There were 1700 bank branches in 1850, 3300 by 1875 and nearly 7000 by 1900. The Midland Bank opened in 1836 and the forerunners of National Westminster in 1833–36. Private banks, threatened by the greater resources of the new joint stock banks, were either bought out or merged. One such merger formed the

Barclays we know today. One of the earliest of such private banks was Child & Co, at No. 1 Fleet Street since 1673 and nowadays part of the Royal Bank of Scotland. By 1884, the London Clearing House was clearing cheques worth £6 billion.

There is one interesting point about the UK. Although Rothschild's on the continent had a hand in setting up some of the commercial banks (Creditanstalt and Société Générale of France are examples), in the UK, the merchant banks ignored the new developments and stuck to that which they knew and did best (international bonds and trade finance). As a result, the British tradition has been one of looking at two types of bank – the 'merchant' bank on the one hand and the 'commercial' bank on the other (we shall examine the differences later in this chapter). It was only in the 1960s and later that the large commercial banks thought it necessary to open merchant bank subsidiaries or buy one (for example, Midland Bank buying Samuel Montagu).

On the continent of Europe, especially in Germany, Austria and Switzerland, the pattern became that of banks who did all types of banking – both 'merchant' and 'commercial'. This is the 'universal' bank tradition – banks like Deutsche Bank and UBS.

These developments take us into this century and the age of computers, communications, automated teller machines (ATMs), credit cards, bank mergers and electronic funds transfer at the point of sale (EFT-POS).

BANKING SUPERVISION

Let's start with the question: 'Who is in charge of the banks?' If you were in the Netherlands or Italy, you might reply, 'The Central Bank', and you would be correct. However, this is by no means always the case. Indeed, it is more common to find that the supervisory body is separate. The Bundesbank is not responsible legally for supervision – that is the task of the 'Federal Banking Supervisory Office'. It does, of course, consult the Bundesbank and the latter collects detailed reports from all the country's banks. However, if any action is to be taken, it will be taken by the Federal Banking Supervisory Office.

There is a Banking Commission in France and Belgium and a Federal Banking Commission in Switzerland.

In Japan, the Financial Services Agency is in charge and, in the US, the picture is very mixed with differing roles played by the Federal Reserve, individual states, the Federal Deposit Insurance Corporation (FDIC), the Comptroller of the Currency and the Savings and Loan Associations reporting to the Federal Home Loan Bank System. For example, when Chicago's Continental Illinois Bank hit trouble in 1984, it was rescued by the FDIC and not the Federal Reserve. The US Congress has been promising to simplify this confusion for some time but has, so far, failed to do so.

In the UK, the Bank of England used to be the supervisory body, but in mid 1998, the Labour government transferred powers to the new Financial Services Authority.

Having decided who is in charge, what general rules will they lay down? Usually, the following:

- ❏ Conditions of entry
- ❏ Capital ratios
- ❏ Liquidity rules
- ❏ Large exposure rules
- ❏ Foreign exchange control
- ❏ Rights of inspection.

(The meaning of the more technical terms here will be explained within the banking chapters.)

TYPES OF BANK: DEFINITIONS

There are many different terms used, not all mutually exclusive. Let's examine the following:

- ❏ Central banks
- ❏ Commercial banks
- ❏ Merchant/Investment banks
- ❏ Savings banks
- ❏ Cooperative banks
- ❏ Mortgage banks
- ❏ Giro banks and National Savings banks
- ❏ Credit unions.

Central banks Typically, an economy will have a central bank, like the Federal Reserve in the US or the Bundesbank in Germany. The role of the Central Bank will be examined in detail in Chapter 3.

Commercial banks These are banks in the classic business of taking deposits and lending money. There are two further relevant terms here – *retail* banking and *wholesale* banking. Retail banking involves high street branches, dealing with the general public, shops and very small businesses. The use of cheques and plastic cards is normally of crucial importance; for example, 2500 million cheques were written in the UK in 2001. At the same time, some 3900 million card based transactions took place at point of sale; about two thirds debit cards to one third credit cards. We are talking here of high volume but low value. Wholesale banking involves low volume and high value. It covers dealings with other banks, the central bank, corporates, pension funds and other investment institutions. Cheques and cards are not so important here, but electronic settlement and clearance is – systems like CHIPS (Clearing House Interbank Payments) in New York, CHAPS (Clearing

House Automated Payments) in the UK, SIT (Système Interbancaire de Télécompensation) in France, EAF2 in Germany and TARGET for the euro. The dealings in the money markets which we describe in Chapter 6 are wholesale banking activities. Retail banking and other wholesale activities like corporate loans are discussed in Chapter 4. Foreign exchange may be retail (a member of the public going on holiday) or wholesale (a French corporate wants SFR10m to buy Swiss imports). Foreign exchange is discussed in Chapter 8.

A special subset of retail banking is *private* banking. This involves handling the needs of high net worth individuals – deposits, loans, fund management, investment advice and so on. Historically, it is a key Swiss speciality!

Merchant/Investment banks   *Merchant* bank is a classic UK term; *Investment* bank is the US equivalent and perhaps the more general and modern term. We shall use them interchangeably (but beware use of the term 'merchant banking' in the US, where it is applied to taking an active part with the bank's own capital in takeover/merger activities). If commercial banking is about lending money, merchant banking can be summarised as 'helping people to find the money'. For example, in Chapter 1 we examined three choices for raising capital – bank loan, bond issue or equity. Sometimes the choice is not necessarily clear. For example, in 1989, Sulzer Brothers from Switzerland issued $100m 3 year bonds at 8¾%. The comment in the *Financial Times* was: 'Traders said the terms were very generous and speculated that Sulzer could have borrowed the funds more cheaply by going direct to the banks for a loan' (see *Financial Times*, 28 November 1989). We quote this simply to illustrate that the choice is not necessarily obvious. Equally, in September 1993, an article in London's *Evening Standard* criticised corporates for their fondness that year for rights issues, arguing that bonds would have been better value in the long run. Merchant or investment banks will give advice on this aspect. If the choice is bonds or equities, they will help the issuer to price them, will assist in selling them and, with other associates, *underwrite* the issue, that is, they will buy the securities if the investors do not.

There are other activities of merchant or investment banks and we will cover these in Chapter 5.

In many European countries (France, Germany, Italy, Austria, the Netherlands and Spain) there are banks that do not have outside shareholders but are 'mutually' owned in some way. These are the savings banks and cooperative banks.

Savings banks   What we have to distinguish here is the historical, traditional role of savings banks and their more modern role today. In the modern world they are looking more and more like ordinary commercial banks due to (a) growing mergers of previously autonomous savings banks, (b) deregulation, removing restrictions on their activities and giving them powers to act like commercial banks. In spite of (a) and (b), what might still make them a little different is their ownership structure – usually they are 'mutuals', that is, owned by the members.

There are strong savings bank movements right across Europe with terms like:

- ❏ Sparkasse   Germany/Austria
- ❏ Cassa di Risparmio   Italy
- ❏ Caja de Ahorros   Spain
- ❏ Caisses d'Épargne   France/Belgium.

In the US, they are known as 'Savings and Loan Associations' or 'Thrifts' and in the UK (historically, but not today) – 'Trustee Savings Banks'.

There are about 600 savings banks in Germany with some 19,000 branches. As it is a federal republic, each federal state or county within a state guarantees the deposits and there is a central bank for the savings banks called the *Landesbank*. The biggest of these is the Westdeutsche Landesbank. It is also house bank to the government of North-Rhein Westphalia and Germany's third largest bank. There is also an overall central authority to coordinate activities, the Deutsche Girozentrale Deutsche Kommunalbank. Deregulation means that the Sparkassen have more or less normal banking powers. More than 60% of German citizens have a Sparkasse account. They are said to handle 65% of loans to local authorities, 60% of loans to small businesses and 40% of personal loans. Their numbers have increased since unification with the addition of the savings banks in the former GDR. Federal guarantees given to Landesbanks enable them to raise capital cheaply. Other German banks argue that this is unfair competition and the European Commission is looking at this issue currently.

Having some form of central bank for savings banks is not uncommon. In Austria it's the Girozentrale Vienna (later called GiroCredit Bank and now part of Bank Austria). In Finland, prior to its financial collapse in September 1991, it was the Skopbank. It was reorganised as the Savings Bank of Finland. Widespread mergers are taking place in Spain and Italy and even mergers with other banks. For example, in Italy the Cassa di Risparmio di Roma has merged with Banco di Roma and Banco di Santo Spirito to form a large bank called (curiously) Banca di Roma. In addition, the largest Italian savings bank, Cariplo, has merged with Banco Ambrovenuto and changed the name to Banca Intesa. In Spain the two largest savings banks have merged to form a major force in Spanish banking called La Caixa, using its short Catalan title. In neither Spain nor Italy has deregulation of powers gone as far as in Germany.

In the UK, the movement was started in 1810 in order to accept small deposits (the minimum deposit for a normal bank was quite large). In 1817, the government passed a law that the banks must be run by trustees to protect the depositors, hence 'Trustee Savings Banks'. In 1976, they were deregulated and given normal banking powers. From a large number of distinct autonomous banks, the movement eventually came together as one bank, simply known as 'TSB Bank'. In 1986 the government sold shares to the general public and it lost its mutual status. In April 1991, TSB left the European Association of Savings Banks on the grounds that it was no longer a savings bank in any real sense. This is the most extreme example of a change in status. Finally, in 1996, it was taken over by Lloyds Bank.

In France, too, the movement is coming together and sells and markets itself as 'Caisse Nationale des Caisses d'Épargne et de Prévoyance' (Cencep). This central body has embarked on a programme of mergers leading to a reduction in savings banks from 468 in 1984 to less than 200 today (with over 400 branches). They have normal banking powers, and have expanded into *bancassurance* (see Chapter 4), lending to local authorities, leasing, venture capital, property investment and collective investment sales (UCITs). They account for some 20% of deposits in France and are allowed to run special tax exempt accounts (as is the National Savings Bank). As in Germany, the other banks are complaining that this is unfair competition.

In the US, deregulation of the Savings and Loan Associations in 1981 was a total disaster leading to a mixture of fraud and mismanagement. It created one of America's biggest banking crises.

In Japan, the mutual savings banks are called *sogo* banks and there are 70 of them. They take retail deposits and are important lenders to small businesses.

A list of Europe's top savings banks is shown in Table 2.1.

Table 2.1   *Top European savings banks, 2002*

Bank	Assets $bn
Groupe Caisse d'Épargne	304.1
Sparbanken Sverige	90.0
La Caixa (Barcelona)	77.2
Caixa Geral de Depositos	58.6
Caja de Madrid	58.8
Hamburger Sparkasse	32.5
Stadtsparkasse Köln	18.5
Caja de Mediterráneo	16.7
Cassa di Risparmio di Bologna	15.7
Cassa di Risparmio di Parma e Piacenza	15.4

Source: *The Banker, July 2002.*

Cooperative banks   These are banks which are owned by the members and with maximum profit not necessarily the main objective – they may aim, for example, to give low cost loans to members.

Usually, the membership derives from a trade or profession. Much the most common is agriculture which gives us Crédit Agricole, in France (Europe's ninth largest bank in asset terms), the Rabobank in the Netherlands and the Norinchukin bank in Japan. In Table 2.2 we show the share of deposits in the EU accounted for by cooperatives. From this we see that they are significant in Finland, France, Spain, Austria, the Netherlands, Germany and Italy.

Table 2.2 *Cooperative banks' share of deposits, 2002*

Country	%
France	34.3
Germany	27.2
Italy	17.6
Netherlands	10.6
Austria	4.9
Spain	2.3
Finland	1.2
United Kingdom	0.6
Portugal	0.4
Ireland	0.4
Luxembourg	0.2
Belgium	0.1
Denmark	0.1
Greece	0.0
Sweden	—

Note: — Figures not available.
Source: European Association of Cooperative Banks.

The Crédit Agricole (CA) has 65 local banks and a central Caisse Nationale de Crédit Agricole. The latter was owned by the government, but has since been sold to the whole movement. There are 5700 branches and 67,000 employees. It has 15 million customers and accounts for 25% of all deposits in France. The bank at one time had a monopoly on farm loans. It lost this in 1990, but won the right to lend to corporates. Mortgages are important and CA handles about 30% of the mortgages in France. It bought Banque Indosuez in May 1996 and, as we go to press, it is making a bid for the troubled Crédit Lyonnais.

There are other cooperative organisations in France, although much smaller – Banques Populaires and the Crédit Mutuel.

Germany also has a strong cooperative tradition drawn from all sorts of trades and professions. There is, for example, the 'Chemists and Doctors' Bank' (Apotheker und Ärztebank). There are over 2100 Cooperative banks with some 15,000 branches, although numbers are shrinking and 164 were swallowed up in 1998 by other cooperatives. There exist regional cooperatives and a single central bank acting as a clearing house and using central funds for international activities; this is the Deutsche Genossenschaftsbank or DG Bank. Cooperative banks take 19% of all deposits in Germany. The Rabobank in the Netherlands is the name for the central body which acts for about 800 local agricultural cooperative banks. It is the third biggest bank in Holland. Rabobank was for some years one of the world's few banks with an AAA rating from all three major credit rating organisations (although in September 2002 it was downgraded one notch by Fitch). It has 2500 branches and accounts for 40% of savings deposits and 25% of domestic mortgages. It took control of a Dutch insurance company called Interpolis and later another company called AVCB. It has also entered into a joint venture with the leading Dutch fund management group Robeco. It has 19 offices abroad in ten countries and is active in international banking generally. In 1998, it bought a rival Dutch cooperative, ACHMEA.

In Japan, there are cooperative banks in agricultural fishery and forestry. There is a Central Cooperative bank for Agriculture and Forestry called the Norinchukin Bank. There are also a large number of commercial credit cooperative banks.

In the UK, there is only one cooperative bank, called the Cooperative Bank. It works closely with the general retail cooperative movement and has normal banking facilities. However, its share of total UK bank deposits is about 0.6%.

Finland has many cooperative banks (just under 300) with their own central bank, the Okobank.

Mortgage banks   Some economies have a special sector dealing with mortgages and some do not.

The most obvious example of a special sector is the UK's *Building Societies*. Originally they were associations which came together to build houses and then disbanded. Gradually, they became permanent mutual organisations, collecting small high street savings and using the money to fund domestic mortgages. There were over 2000 in 1900, but only about 65 today in a movement dominated by the larger societies. The Building Societies Act of 1986 deregulated them to the extent of allowing them to offer cheque accounts and unsecured loans as well as a variety of other services. However, the amount of such business that they can do is strictly limited. The Act also allowed them to become a public limited company if the members agreed. Abbey National took advantage of this and went public in 1989, becoming the UK's fifth biggest bank in asset terms. By 1995–96 the movement underwent considerable change. Lloyds Bank acquired the Cheltenham and Gloucester, Abbey National acquired National and Provincial and the merged Halifax/Leeds Societies, along with the Alliance and Leicester, the Woolwich and Northern Rock, all revealed plans to go public and become a bank. Others, like the Britannia, defended the 'mutual' principle and announced loyalty bonuses for their longer term members. However, in late April 1999, one of the largest remaining mutual societies, the Bradford and Bingley, announced its intention to convert to a bank after a vote by its members. This has rekindled the debate and many believe that the remaining large mutuals will end up as banks.

Germany has 35 mortgage banks (Hypothekenbanken), often subsidiaries of other banks, and a few building societies (Bausparkassen). The mortgage banks fund the mortgages with a special bond – the Pfandbriefe. The Netherlands has several mortgage banks which are subsidiaries of other banks (for example, Rabobank) or of insurance companies. Denmark has a small number of Mortgage Credit Associations which sell bonds on the Stock Exchange and hand the proceeds to the borrower whose property is security for the bond.

The specialists in mortgages in the US are the Savings and Loan Associations which were deregulated in 1981. Unlike the UK's 1986 Building Societies Act, however, prudent restrictions on new powers were not imposed and the movement hit serious trouble, as mentioned earlier.

Giro banks   Let's start by considering this word 'Giro'. It comes from the Greek '*Guros*', meaning a wheel or circle. The circle in finance is the passing round of payments between counterparties.

We find references to this term in early Italian banking. In the Middle Ages there were important trade fairs for the cloth industries of France and Flanders. Merchants would incur debts and any not settled could be carried forward to the next fair. Gradually, the merchants who were bankers began to offer a clearing system. One can imagine the circle of debt as – trader *A* owes *B* who owes *C* who owes *D* who also owes *A* (see Figure 2.1).

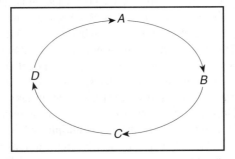

Figure 2.1   *The circle of debt*

The bankers set up a clearing system known as '*giro di partita*' – the giro of ledger entries. In 1619, the state of Venice set up a Banco del Giro to speed up payments to the state's creditors. The bank also issued interest bearing bonds to creditors and a secondary market gradually developed.

In the modern age, the word *giro* crops up in two connections. In the first case, it simply refers to money transfers by which an individual sends a giro slip to their bank instructing them to pay a sum of money to, say, the electricity or gas company. In Germany and Holland this is far more likely than sending a cheque directly to the company.

The second use is in the term *Giro bank* and the use of post offices to help those without a bank account pay their bills. The idea began in Austria in 1883. Those without bank accounts could pay a variety of bills at post offices and the money was then transferred to the payee. There is a Post Office Giro in Belgium and the UK set up a Girobank in 1968 which was sold to a building society in 1990. It is difficult to separate out postal giro from the general concept of a *postal bank*. This itself may be known instead as the *National Savings Bank*. In the UK, the Post Office Savings Bank, which was set up in 1861, became the National Savings Bank in 1969. The general idea is to encourage small savings rather than letting the bank engage in lending. France has a 'Caisse Nationale d'Épargne'; Ireland has a Post Office Savings Bank; in Finland we find the very important Postipankki, which handles much of the government's finances and Spain, too, has a Post Office Savings Bank. In the Netherlands, the Post Office Bank and the National Savings Bank merged to become Postbank, itself later merging with the NMB Bank and now known as ING Bank.

Due to the trend for deregulation, post office banks are flexing their muscles and seeking expanded powers. In May 1992, some German commercial banks took the Postbank to court, accusing it of unfair competition. The Belgian Bankers' Association has claimed that the post offices' financial activities are subsidised and, in France, opposition from the banks has stopped the Post Office from offering a form of current account. However, the Post Office there has sold mutual funds (SICAVs) very successfully. Spain's Caja Postal has gone into leasing, asset management and property consulting. It has now been drawn together with other state-owned financial institutions into a single body called Argentaria.

Credit unions   The idea of credit unions goes back to 1849 in Germany when a local mayor formed a union to help people cope with debt and poverty. By the early 1900s, the idea had spread to Australia, Canada, New Zealand, Ireland, the UK and the US. The general idea is that a local credit union has some common bond – possibly membership of a church or place of work. The members save money and are allowed to borrow a sum of money, usually a multiple of the money saved. There may be tax privileges. For example, in the US, credit unions don't pay federal income tax. There are 15,000 credit unions in that country and 70 million members. The largest, Navy Federal, with assets of $10bn, is bigger than many regional banks. The commercial banks complain of unfair competition and are pursuing a case through the Supreme Court, claiming that the 'common bond' idea is being ignored in some cases. In the UK, there are 700 credit unions with 300,000 members, including British Airways and the London Taxi Drivers, and also community credit unions in deprived areas like Toxteth, Clerkenwell and Strathclyde. The number may reduce over time, as many unions are small and will struggle to comply with new regulation introduced by the FSA in 2002. The Association of British Credit Unions, therefore, expects a number of mergers in the coming years. In Ireland, 23% of the population are members. In Japan, there are some 460 credit associations. They also enjoy tax privileges.

OTHER BANKING TERMINOLOGY

There are one or two other terms which, perhaps, should also be explained.

Clearing banks This term is applied to the banks which are most involved in the system for clearing cheques. They will be the large domestic banks who are heavily into retail banking. Banks which offer cheque book facilities and have smaller volumes will arrange for one of the larger clearing banks to handle clearing of their cheques. Usually, each bank will clear its own cheques, that is, cheques drawn by a customer of the branch in favour of another customer of the same bank. Cheques drawn in favour of other banks are sent to a central clearing system where they can be gathered together and sent to each bank for posting to individual accounts. The customer account number, bank branch code and cheque number are already encoded on the bottom line of the cheque. It only needs the amount to be encoded for the cheques to be sorted using electronic sorting machines.

Electronic clearing is becoming increasingly important for direct debits, standing orders, salary payments, supplier payments and high value payments made electronically by banks for corporate customers.

State or public banks This term is used for banks owned by the state which are not central banks but carry out some public sector activity. State-owned Post Office or National Savings Banks are one example. Sometimes others are set up to lend to industry sectors or local authorities or provide finance for exports and imports. Germany has Kreditanstalt für Wiederaufbau, which was set up in 1948 to help finance reconstruction after the war and is now a general development bank for small to medium size companies. France has Crédit Local de France, which makes loans to local authorities, and Crédit Foncier, which finances house purchase and property development. Italy has Crediop which finances public utilities and makes other industrial loans. In Spain, a major change has taken place which has resulted in the formation of one body from various state banks:

❏ Banco Exterior the finance of foreign trade
❏ Banco Hipotecario subsidised loans for social housing
❏ Banco de Crédito Agrícola loans for agriculture and forestry
❏ Banco de Crédito Local loans for local authorities
❏ Banco de Crédito Industrial loans for industry
❏ Caja Postal de Ahorros post office savings banks.

These were all united in 1991 as Corporación Bancaria de España which operates under the marketing name of 'Argentaria'.

The position regarding state banks is changing somewhat as full or partial privatisation takes place (for example, Crédit Local de France and Argentaria).

Banks which have a role in lending to specialist industries are also known as *industrial banks*.

International banking This involves a variety of activities such as deposits/

loans to nationals in foreign currencies and to non-nationals in the domestic currency. It also covers cross-border operations, trade finance, foreign exchange, correspondent banking, international payments services, international finance with syndicated loans and/or Euromarket instruments, dealing in precious metals, international corporate advice and corporate risk management facilities on an international basis.

Clearly, the terms we have been using are not mutually self-exclusive – they overlap. International banking with a syndicated loan, for example, is commercial wholesale banking. International banking through a eurobond issue is investment banking and largely wholesale, but with sales at times aimed at *retail* investors.

A BANK'S BALANCE SHEET

Before proceeding any further into this chapter, we must look at a bank's balance sheet and the terminology which is used. Then we will be in a position to explain concepts like 'creation of credit', 'liquidity' and 'capital ratio'.

In this section and later, we use the terms 'assets' and 'liabilities'. A liability in accountancy does not have the meaning 'disadvantage' as it does in everyday English. It is money for which the entity concerned is *liable*, for example, if money is borrowed, the borrower is *liable* to repay it, hence it is a liability.

Looking at a bank, the *liabilities* show us where the money comes from. There are three key sources:

❑ Shareholders' equity plus additions from retained profit
❑ Deposits (the largest figure)
❑ Borrowings (for example, a bond issue).

The liabilities, thus, represent claims *against* the bank.

The first category is called 'shareholders' funds' and is the main source for a bank's *capital*. This is the part of the liabilities that can be relied upon because, being the owner's money, there is no date for paying it back. The bank has the indefinite use of the money. If times are hard, even the dividend may be passed. Deposits, on the other hand, can be withdrawn, a large part without notice, and borrowings have to be repaid and interest payments met.

Assets represent how this money has been used, for example:

❑ Notes, coin
❑ Money market funds
❑ Securities
❑ Lending (the largest figure)
❑ Fixed assets, for example, property.

The assets, thus, represent claims by the bank against others. Assets and liabilities will always balance.

Banks list assets in descending order of liquidity:

- ❏ Cash
- ❏ Balances at the central bank
- ❏ Money at call and short notice
- ❏ Bank and trade Bills of Exchange
- ❏ Treasury bills
- ❏ Securities
- ❏ Advances to customers
- ❏ Premises and equipment.

Its liabilities would be:

- ❏ Ordinary share capital
- ❏ Other share capital
- ❏ Reserves
- ❏ Retained profits
- ❏ Provisions against losses
- ❏ Bond issues
- ❏ Customers' deposits
- ❏ Other borrowing
- ❏ Trade creditors
- ❏ Tax.

The balance sheet is laid out with assets on the left and liabilities on the right (see Figure 2.2).

SUMMARY BALANCE SHEET, A. N. OTHER BANK As At 31/12/02

ASSETS	LIABILITIES
(that is, how liabilities have been *used*)	(that is, where the money *comes from*)
Cash	Shareholders' funds
Money market funds	Deposits
Other securities	Borrowings
Lending	

Figure 2.2   Summary balance sheet

The profit and loss account shows how a bank has traded during a particular *period*, such as 1 month, 3 months, or a year – for example: 'Profit and Loss Account for the year ended 31 December 2002'. Note that the balance sheet shows what the bank is worth at a particular *point* in time, for example: 'Balance Sheet as at 31 December 2002'.

Revenue is contrasted with costs and the resulting difference is the profit or loss. After paying dividends and tax, the remaining profit is transferred to the balance sheet and added to the shareholders' funds, thus *increasing capital*. Equally, a loss will *reduce capital*.

One of the assets listed above was 'Balances at the central bank'. Most central banks insist that banks within the country maintain certain reserves with it. Usually, these are substantial sums and help the central bank in its control of monetary policy and what is called the 'money supply'. We shall examine this in more detail in Chapter 3.

Even where the reserves are very tiny (for example, in the UK only 0.15% of eligible liabilities), the main clearing banks have to maintain far higher working balances and *must not fall below these*. These balances are to cover things like the daily settlement for cheque clearing and the daily settlement for Treasury bill and bond purchases for themselves and clients for whom they are acting. There is also the total net payment by the bank's clients of taxes to the government. The government's balance at the central bank will rise – the individual bank's balance will fall.

THE CREATION OF CREDIT

As only a small proportion of deposits is drawn in cash, it follows that banks have considerable facilities to 'create credit'.

Imagine approaching a bank (not your own) to request flexible lending facilities up to $2000. The bank opens an account and sends you a cheque book. You wander down the high street writing cheques to the value of $2000. The recipients pay the cheques into their accounts and the amounts are credited to them 3 days later and debited to you. The bank has created $2000 of expenditure that did not exist 1 week earlier. The suppliers of the goods have $2000 in bank accounts – disposable money. Where did it come from? Not from you, because you didn't have any. It came from the bank that allowed you to overdraw to the value of $2000 – the bank has created money. Bank lending = spending, and excessive spending may mean unacceptable inflation and imports the nation can't afford.

Banks' credit creation has several implications:

1. A reminder that banking depends on confidence
2. Governments and central banks will want to control it in view of the implications for inflation and imports

3. Banks will need internal controls called 'liquidity ratios'
4. An external control enforced by bank supervisors called 'capital ratios' is required.

Banking Depends on Confidence

The system works because we have confidence in it and accept cheques in payment of debt. Where is the gold and silver behind this? Of course, there isn't any. Money is as much an entry on a computer disk as anything else. The economist, Benham, in his well-known text book *Economics*, points out that paper money could be seen as a 'gigantic confidence trick'. It works as long as people believe in it.

The Money Supply

Governments and central bankers will want to control credit and measure the 'money supply'. This figure is a measure of bank deposits as being the best guide to bank lending. The figure for deposits sounds like a motorway – M3 or M4, depending on the country. Another measure is M0 – notes and coin in circulation, plus banks' till money and balances with the central bank. Add to this the private sector's deposits at banks and you have the essential elements of M3 or M4. Control of inflation by controlling these monetary aggregates is part of what is meant by 'monetarism', the economic doctrines of the American economist, Milton Friedman. In the UK, the Conservative government of 1979 used them as a rather rigid instrument of government policy in the early 1980s. (Charles Goodhart, one time economic adviser to the Bank of England, has coined 'Goodhart's Law'. This says that 'when an economic indicator is used as an instrument of government policy, its behaviour then changes'!) Later governments have interpreted the figure more flexibly. Interest rates, however, remain the main economic tool in controlling monetary conditions, being raised to curb inflation or lowered to boost economic activity. The idea is that as interest rates are raised, mortgage payments go up and so does the cost of buying goods on credit. People therefore have less money to spend and the price of goods has to be lowered to attract buyers. Conversely, as we have seen at the start of the new millennium, when economies slow down they can be boosted by lowering interest rates. Mortgage payments come down, the cost of borrowing to buy goods on credit is reduced and, as people go out and spend more, this stimulates and sustains economic activity.

The central bank has a number of weapons – raising mandatory reserves which banks must deposit with it, raising interest rates and general 'open market operations', for example, selling more government paper than it needs to in order to drain credit and keep monetary conditions tight. It may also not be as quick as usual to help banks' liquidity when acting as 'lender of last resort' (see Chapter 3).

Liquidity Ratios

Bankers have internal controls based on 'liquidity ratios'. They know that it would be folly to take their deposits and lend 100% as 3 year personal loans. They have internal rules on what percentage of deposits should be held as cash, what percentage at call and short notice, what percentage as short-term securities (Treasury bills, bills of exchange) and so on. The controls may also be *external* and laid down by the central bank as they are in Spain, where they are called *Coeficientes*. This is why banks list assets in *descending* order of liquidity, that is, the most liquid assets (cash) are first. Cash is particularly important as banks must keep a given percentage to meet cash withdrawals. In the case of the new bank accounts totalling $2000 which we discussed above, if cash withdrawals average 5%, then the bank must have $100 cash to back these accounts.

The Capital Ratio

Capital ratio is the external control imposed by bank supervisors in the interests of prudence. It is a major issue in banking and we need to look at it in more detail.

CAPITAL RATIO

The Basic Concept

The basic concept has been around for hundreds of years. Bankers lend money and some people will default. Does this mean that the banks cannot repay depositors? The buffer, the money the bank can rely on, is its capital. Thus, there should be a prudent relationship between capital and lending – that is the capital ratio.

All this assumes that the bank has not made things worse by an excessive exposure to a few key borrowers. In 1984, for example, it was found that Johnson Matthey Bank in the UK had lent the equivalent of 115% of its own capital to just two borrowers. This loophole was plugged in the 1987 Banking Act. If exposure to one borrower exceeds 10% of capital, the Bank of England must be informed. Before exposure can exceed 25%, Bank of England permission must be obtained. Exposure to industry sectors (for example, textiles) and countries is also monitored. All central banks have 'large exposure' controls.

The older idea of relating capital to *lending* has to be extended to capital to *assets* in the modern age. However, all assets are not the same for this purpose – for example, what is the default risk with cash? Surely the answer is 'none'. Thus we end up with the concept of 'risked weighted assets'. A normal bank loan is, therefore, weighted 100%, that is, a loan of $500,000 counts as $500,000 for this purpose. However, cash is weighted at 0%, and a cash balance of $10m thus becomes $0 for risk weighting purposes. Secured lending has a weight of 50% (see Table 2.3).

The capital ratio is thus determined by applying the ratio to the figure of risk weighted assets. If the agreed ratio were 10%, then, from the figures in Table 2.3, capital must be 10% × $1260m = $126m.

The Basle Committee

However, every central bank had different rules. The Group of 10 nations (see Chapter 3) together with Luxembourg, set up a 'Committee on Banking Regulations and Supervisory Practices' to draw up uniform rules. The Committee meets at Basle in Switzerland under the auspices of the Bank for International Settlements (BIS). It is thus typically (but not accurately) called the 'Basle' Committee or 'BIS' Committee. In 1988, after several years of discussion, the Committee announced agreement on uniform rules for capital ratio.

The first stumbling block was the definition of 'capital'. The Committee came to a compromise – the 'best' capital is called 'Tier 1' and must be at least half the necessary figure. It consists of:

❏ Shareholders' equity
❏ Retained profits
❏ *Non-cumulative* perpetual preference shares.

Table 2.3 *Risk weighting example*

Assets	Value $m	Risk weighting %	Risk weighted value $m
Cash	50	0	—
T. Bills	100	10	10
Mortgages	500	50	250
Loans	1000	100	1000
Total	1650		1260

'Tier 2' capital is the remainder and would include:

❏ *Cumulative* perpetual preference shares
❏ Revaluation reserves
❏ Undisclosed reserves
❏ Subordinated term debt with maturity in excess of 5 years.

(For a discussion of preference shares, see Chapter 6. Subordinated debtors come after other debtors in the event of liquidation.)

The capital ratio itself is 8% and applied from 1 January 1993.

The risk weighting figures were agreed and we gave examples of some of these above. While unsecured loans are 100%, loans to or claims on OECD governments and sometimes other governments as well are weighted 0%. Thus loans to Saudi Arabia have not been given the full 100% weighting, but Kuwait, in raising a large syndicated loan for reconstruction of $5.5bn in Autumn 1991, was weighted 100%.

The risk weightings are not only applied to balance sheet items, but to *off-balance sheet* items that involve risk – loan guarantees, standby letters of credit, documentary letters of credit, derivative products such as options, futures, swaps and FRAs (all explained in later chapters).

The banks are very conscious of capital ratio rules and have tightened up the discipline regarding profit as a return on capital. If a transaction needs capital backing under the new rules, then the profit on the transaction must meet the bank's target for profit on capital employed. Some consultants call this 'RAROC' – 'risk adjusted return on capital'. While there is a capital requirement for off-balance sheet items, it is not as onerous as for on-balance sheet items and thus adds to the attraction of these transactions. For example, documentary letters of credit backed by documents giving title are weighted at 20%. A general standby letter of credit not related to a specific transaction is weighted 100%, but a standby letter of credit which is so related is weighted at 50%. As capital has a cost, the bank will ensure that the charges to the client cover the *cost of capital* as well as any other costs.

For their results for the year ending March 1996, Japanese banks finally recognised their true position regarding bad debts and began to write these off against profit. The three long-term credit banks, the seven trust banks and seven out of the top eleven city banks all declared a loss. As a result, some of the capital ratios were close to the minimum. Despite subsequent restructuring, mergers and a brief return to profit, by 2002 the four largest banks were again reporting substantial losses (totalling $32bn!) and reducing lending to maintain capital ratios.

In September 1998, the Basle Committee under its new chairman, William McDonough, President of the New York Federal Reserve Bank, held the first of a series of meetings to revise the original accord.

There was a general feeling that some of the rules were too crude. In March 1998, the Institute of International Finance, a Washington-based organisation representing commercial and investment banks, called on the Basle Committee to change the formula. For example, lending to banks in the Organisation of Economic Cooperation and Development (OECD) has a ratio of only 1.6%. Thus a loan to General Electric needs a capital ratio of 8% but one to a South Korean bank only 1.6%! Equally, a loan to a AAA rated company is treated the same as a loan to a company of much lower credit quality. In addition, where banks needed 8% capital backing for loans but internal models calculated the risk as far less, they were increasingly selling these loans to the market as securities with a lower weighting. (This is discussed later in this chapter and in Chapter 6.)

The use of credit ratings to make the risk calculation more scientific was discussed, but many European corporates do not have credit ratings – only 70 in Germany and less than a quarter of the UK's FTSE 100 companies. At January 1, 1999, Standard and Poors had issued 2461 long-term debt ratings in the US but only 68 in Europe. The use of statistical credit risk modelling was also discussed, but viewed with scepticism. A BIS committee report in April 1999, *Credit Risk Modelling*, confirmed that regulators were not yet ready to accept them.

In June 1999, the BIS Committee issued a new paper and suggested a ten month consultation period.

In spite of the absence of credit ratings in Europe, to which we have referred, the Committee came down heavily on the use of credit ratings to guide credit risk. Five 'buckets' were suggested, with sovereign governments in the AAA/AA category getting a zero weighting, A grade a 20% weighting and so on, down to 150% for grades of B– or less. Similar rules were drawn up for lending to banks and corporates. More sophisticated banks could use internal ratings as an interim measure, and supervisors could ask for more capital if they thought that banks were taking excessive risks. This has had an effect on pricing for bonds and syndicated loans.

With some reservations, the new proposals were generally welcomed.

All the above relates to *credit risk*. There is also *market risk* and *operational risk*. Market movements in the price of financial instruments may expose the banks to losses. The Capital Adequacy Directive (CAD) addressed this problem and applied from January 1996. In this case, however, use of banks' internal statistical models was accepted subject to monitoring by local central banks. These models are usually called *value at risk* (VAR) models. Operational risk recognises the risk of losses through failure or weaknesses in a bank's internal processes and systems and the Basle II directive requires these risks to be addressed by 2005.

Finally, the CAD introduced the concept of Tier 3 capital – unsecured subordinated debt with a remaining maturity of more than 2 years.

Increasing Capital Ratio

If a bank does not have enough capital to meet the new requirements, what can it do? There are essentially only two possibilities:

(a) Find more capital
(b) Reduce assets.

(a) *Finding more capital* could involve a rights issue, reducing dividends (to increase retained profit), raising money through other forms of capital, for example, *non-cumulative* perpetual preference shares or perpetual variable rate notes. Tier 1 capital must, of course, be 4% and there is a limit to the value of certain Tier 2 items that can be used. Examples of the above include the rights issue by Midland Bank in 1987, followed by selling 14.9% of new shares to the Hongkong and Shanghai Bank. We have also had non-cumulative perpetual preference share issues from National Westminster, the Bank of Scotland and the Royal Bank of Scotland (in dollars). Several German banks have issued their own type of cumulative preference share (genusscheine) to count as Tier 2 capital. National Westminster, NAB, Banco Santander, the Royal Bank of Scotland, Crédit Lyonnais and others have all issued perpetual variable rate notes to count as Tier 2 capital.

(b) *Reducing assets* could involve selling off subsidiaries, selling off loans to other banks or converting assets into securities – *securitisation*.

Examples of selling subsidiaries include Midland Bank selling the Clydesdale in 1987, the British banks owning the Yorkshire Bank selling it in 1990 (they had owned it since 1911!) and Citicorp selling several overseas subsidiaries. We shall meet the word 'securitisation' again in Chapter 6. In that context it means the change in emphasis in international banking markets from 1982, by which borrowers began to borrow on the capital markets by issuing bonds rather than by having a bank loan. The usage in our current context is similar, but here we take an existing loan off the balance sheet by converting it into securities. The best and most common example is selling off mortgage loans as mortgage bonds (pioneered by Salomon Bros – now part of Citigroup – in the US). Other examples include converting car loans into notes or bonds and converting credit card receivables into bonds (frequent issues by Citicorp). Another possibility is simply to bundle bank personal loans together and sell them as bonds or shorter-term notes, with the loans as the assets backing the security. The legalities are difficult, usually involving a special purpose vehicle or SPV to issue. Guarantees from insurance companies or other financial entities are involved and the idea is for the original lender to so weaken the link to the loan that it no longer counts for capital ratio purposes. The issuer usually continues to administer the loan, and will receive a fee for doing so. This is discussed further in Chapter 6.

CENTRAL BANK REPORTING

All banks operating within a country make detailed reports to the central bank as part of its supervisory role, even if any action to be taken will be carried out by a separate supervisory body.

Reports will be sent at varying frequencies – monthly, quarterly, 6 monthly, annually – and will cover the following items:

❏ Maturity of assets, that is, liquidity
❏ Large exposures
❏ Foreign exchange exposure
❏ Capital expenditure
❏ Assets/liabilities for overseas residents
❏ Assets/liabilities in foreign currencies
❏ Balance sheet
❏ Profit and loss.

Foreign banks operating in a country operate as either branches or as legal entities. If only operating as a branch, no reports on capital will be made as the capital is held by the parent company.

THE SECOND BANKING DIRECTIVE

This came into effect on 1 January 1993. The original intention of the Community had been to achieve a full harmonisation of banking legislation throughout the EU. This has now been abandoned. Instead, under the Second Banking Directive, banks in the EU will continue to be authorised and regulated by their own national authority. This will be accepted as adequate for granting them freedom to operate throughout the Community. They will thus acquire a *European Banking Licence* or *Passport*. This will allow them to engage in investment as well as commercial banking, since 'universal banking' has always been the tradition in Europe. In countries where this has not been so, their banks will now be free to engage in activities throughout the Community that they may still be prevented from doing in their own country. (The specific Investment Services Directive is discussed in Chapter 9.)

Third country banks can operate within the EU if 'reciprocal treatment' is afforded in their country to EU member banks. At first this was taken to mean that they must be allowed to engage in the same activities as third country banks are permitted to do within the Community. This led to protest from America (where commercial and investment banks were traditionally separated). In response to this, reciprocity is now defined as equal 'national treatment' – that is, EU banks being treated the same as local banks in third countries. But, in individual cases, the Community may still insist on 'equal/comparable access'.

The EU's Banking Federation has drawn up a list of 26 non-EU countries which impose restrictions on the operation of foreign banks within their country. Should these countries continue to withhold 'equal national treatment' they may find their banks banned from operating within the Community.

MAJOR WORLD BANKS

The UK *Banker* magazine for July 2002 published an analysis of the world's largest banks. Although 'large' was defined by holdings of Tier 1 capital, the asset figures were also disclosed.

We shall, therefore, first look at a 'Top 20' sequence of the world's biggest banks in *asset* terms (Table 2.4).

Table 2.4   *Top 20 world banks, by assets, 2002*

Ranking	Bank	Assets $bn
1	Mizuho Financial Group	1178
2	Citigroup	1051
3	Sumitomo Mitsui Banking Corp	840
4	Deutsche Bank	809
5	Mitsubishi Tokyo Financial Group	751
6	UBS	747
7	BNP Paribas	727
8	HSBC Holdings	696
9	JP Morgan Chase & Co	694
10	Hypovereinsbank	642
11	Bank of America Corp	622
12	UFJ Holding	616
13	Crédit Suisse Group	610
14	ABN Amro	526
15	Industrial and Commercial Bank of China	524
16	Royal Bank of Scotland	520
17	Barclays Bank	505
18	Crédit Agricole Groupe	496
19	Norinchukin Bank	463
20	Société Générale	452

Source: *The Banker* (July 2002).

Looking at *nationality* in the Top 20 we find the following:

Country	Banks
Japan	5
France	3
UK	3
US	3
Germany	2
Switzerland	2
China	1
Netherlands	1

The Japanese provide five of the world's Top 20 (and three out of the top 10). In the 1992 table, however, they provided eleven out of the top 20 and eight out of the top 10. The collapse of the stock exchange index, a serious fall in property values, a prolonged recession and high bank bad debts have all caused a reduction in bank strength (the first four in the table by Tier 1 capital in 1992) and some withdrawal from world markets.

Citicorp was number twenty in 1992, with no other US bank in the table. Now the enlarged Citigroup is number two, the merged JP Morgan and Chase Manhattan at number nine and Bank of America at number eleven.

The other surprise, looking at Table 2.4, is to see the US only providing three banks out of the Top 20. We have to realise that banking is very fragmented in the US where there are no less than about 9000 banks! Unlike Europe, branch banking across the US was unknown. The McFadden Act of 1927 limited banking activities to within a single state; some local state legislation limits it to one branch in one *city* within the state! The Act, however, was repealed in 1994 by the US Interstate Banking and Banking Efficiency Act which permitted full interstate banking by 1997 unless local state laws prevent it. Many states did not wait for Congress but changed their laws and allowed reciprocal banking facilities with other states. This has led to a growth in so-called 'Regional Banks'. A good example is Bank One in Columbus, Ohio, which now operates in twelve states due to a variety of acquisitions and taking advantage of new state laws, and has recently merged with First Chicago. Another example is the NCNB from Carolina which, due to mergers and acquisitions, has become NationsBank and one of the biggest in the US following the merger with Bank of America. The large number of mergers in the US (see Appendix 2 to this chapter) is fast changing the face of American banking. When we look at banks by Tier 1 capital (table 2.7), we see the US with six banks as opposed to three by assets.

Table 2.5   *International banking shares, by nationality of bank, end Q1 2002*

Nationality	%
Other European Banks	27.0
Other Banks	20.6
Germany	18.3
UK	10.5
Japanese	8.9
France	7.7
US	7.0
	———
	100.0

Source: BIS Basle.

Finally, we can look at the original sequence of banks in *The Banker* magazine, that by *capital* (Table 2.6).

The change of sequence to capital (it used to be assets) came about because of the so-called Basle Agreement in 1988. *The Banker* magazine decided that capital was the important thing for the future, and not assets.

There is an interesting change of sequence. Looking at nationality now, we see the following:

Country	Banks
US	6
Japan	4
UK	4
Germany	2
France	2
China	2
Netherlands	—
Switzerland	—

The spate of mergers which has occurred in the last few years is clearly reflected as American, Japanese and British banks dominate the top 20 in terms of size of capital base.

Table 2.6 *Top 20 world banks by capital*

Ranking	Bank	Strength: Tier 1 Capital $bn
1	Citigroup	58.4
2	Bank of America Corp	42.0
3	Mizuho Financial Group	40.5
4	JP Morgan Chase & Co	37.7
5	HSBC Holdings	35.0
6	Sumitomo Mitsui Banking Corp	30.0
7	Crédit Agricole Groupe	28.9
8	Mitsubishi Tokyo Financial Group	25.7
9	UFJ Holding	23.8
10	Industrial and Commercial Bank of China	23.1
11	Bank of China	22.0
12	Deutsche Bank	21.9
13	Royal Bank of Scotland	21.8
14	Bank One Corp	21.7
15	BNP Paribas	21.7
16	HypoVereinsbank	19.1
17	Wachovia Corporation	19.0
18	Wells Fargo & Co	18.2
19	HBOS	18.1
20	Barclays Bank	18.0

Source: *The Banker* (July 2002).

SUMMARY

Supervision of banks may be carried out by the central bank (Netherlands) or other supervisory bodies (France, Germany, Japan, US, UK).

Central banks, commercial banks and investment banks are the main types of bank. There are also savings banks, cooperative banks and mortgage banks but, with increasing deregulation, the differences are generally weakening. Finally, there are credit unions.

On a bank's balance sheet, the *liabilities* are shareholders' equity, deposits and borrowings. The *assets* are cash, money market deposits, securities, loans and fixed assets like buildings.

The shareholders' equity (including retained profits) is at the heart of the bank's *capital*.

Bank regulators have set up a committee (usually called the Basle or BIS Committee) which lays down rules which suggest the capital required not only for the credit risk in bank lending but also the market risk of the financial instruments it holds and the operational risk inherent in a bank's activities.

In an era where money is no longer tied to gold or silver, the ease with which a bank can advance money is called *creation of credit*. It is limited by liquidity rules, capital ratio rules and central bank monetary policy.

The Second European Banking Directive allows banks in the EU to open branches anywhere in the EU under licence from their *home* central bank.

Appendix 1

MAJOR BANKS ACROSS THE WORLD

AUSTRALIA	ANZ
	National Australia Bank
	Westpac
AUSTRIA	Bank Austria
	Erste Bank
	Raiffeisen Zentralbank
BELGIUM	Fortis Banking Group
	KBC Bank
	BBL
BRAZIL	Banco Santander Brasil
	Banco Bradesco
CANADA	Royal Bank of Canada
	Canadian Imperial bank of Commerce
	Toronto-Dominion
DENMARK	Den Danske Bank
	Nykredit Group
FINLAND	Nordea Bank Finland
	Sampo Group
	Okobank
FRANCE	BNP Paribas
	Crédit Agricole
	Société Général
	Crédit Mutuel
GERMANY	Deutsche Bank
	HypoVereinsbank
	Dresdner Bank
	Westdeutsche Landesbank
	Commerzbank

GREECE	National Bank of Greece
	Commercial Bank of Greece
	Agricultural Bank of Greece
HOLLAND	ABN-AMRO
	Rabobank
	ING Bank
IRELAND	Allied Irish
	Bank of Ireland
ITALY	Banco Popolare di Milano
	Banca di Roma
	Banca Monte dei Paschi di Siena
	Banca Intesa
	Unicredito Italiano
JAPAN	Bank of Tokyo/Mitsubishi
	Sumitomo
	Yamaguchi
	Resona
	Bank of Yokohama
LUXEMBOURG	Kredietbank
	Générale du Luxembourg
NORWAY	Nordlandsanken
	Fokus Bank
	Union Bank of Norway
PORTUGAL	Caixa Geral de Depositos
	Banco Comercial Portugues
	Banco Totta e Acores
	Banco Espirito Santo & Commercial
SINGAPORE	DBS
	OCBC
SPAIN	Banco Bilbao Vizcaya
	Banco Santander Central Hispano
	Banco Popular Espanol

SWEDEN	S. E. Banken
	Svenska Handelsbanken
	Sparbanken Sverige
SWITZERLAND	UBS
	Crédit Suisse
TURKEY	Akbank
	TC Ziraat Bankasi
	Turkiye Is Bankasi
	Yapi Kredi Bank
	Garanti Bank
UNITED ARAB EMIRATES	National Bank of Dubai
UNITED KINGDOM	HSBC Holdings
	Royal Bank of Scotland
	Barclays Bank
	Lloyds TSB Group
	Egg
	HBOS
UNITED STATES	Citigroup
	J.P. Morgan Chase
	Bank of America Corp
	Mellon Bank
	Bank One Corp
	State Steet Corp
	Wells Fargo
	Fleet Financial

Appendix 2

INTERNATIONAL AND DOMESTIC BANKING COOPERATION AND
MERGERS

(Some of the following are full-scale mergers; some are merely arrangements to
cooperate. They range over about fifteen years and illustrate the massive changes
that have taken place.)

1. Chemical Bank–Manufacturers Hanover to form Chemical Banking
    Corporation. Later merged with Chase Manhattan, using the Chase name.
    Chase acquired Robert Fleming. JP Morgan and Chase merged to form JP
    Morgan Chase

2. Bank of America–Security Pacific

3. Bank America–NationsBank

4. NationsBank– Barnett Banks–Boatmen's Bancshares–Montgomery
    Securities

5. NCNB–C & S/Sovran to form NationsBank

6. Bank America–Continental

7. Citibank–Salomon Smith Barney (Travellers Group)

8. Morgan Stanley–Dean Witter

9. First Chicago–NBD

10. First Chicago–Bank One

11. Merrill Lynch–Smith New Court

12. Fleet Financial–Shawmut National

13. Fleet Financial–Bank Boston

14. First Bank Systems Inc–US Bancorp Deutsche Bank–Bankers Trust

15. Norwest–Wells Fargo, Wells Fargo–First Security (Wells Fargo)

16. Wells Fargo–First Interstate

17. First Union–First Fidelity

18. First Union–Core States Financial

19. Crédit Lyonnais–BfG Bank

20. CCF/BHF Bank–Charterhouse

21. Crédit Local de France–Crédit Communale de Belgique–BACOB (now Dexia)

22. Deutsche Bank–Morgan Grenfell–Bankers Trust, now Deutsche Bank

23. Dresdner Bank–Kleinwort Benson

24. Bayerische Vereinsbank–Bayerische Hypobank

25. Austria–Österreichische Landerbank and Zentral Sparkasse to form Z-Landerbank (now Bank Austria)

26. Girozentrale–Österreichisches Credit Institut to form GiroCredit Bank

27. Bank Austria–majority holding in Bank GiroCredit

28. Bank Austria–Creditanstalt

29. Kredietbank–CERA

30. ABN–AMRO Bank (acquired Hoare Govett later)

31. ING–Barings–Banque Bruxelles Lambert

32. Fortis–Générale de Banque

33. Cassa di Risparmio di Roma–Banco di Santo Spirito; then a merger with Banco di Roma to form Banca di Roma

34. Bergen Bank–Den Norske Creditbank

35. Den Danske Bank–Copenhagen Handelsbank–Provinsbanken to form the Danske Bank

36. Privatbanken–SDS–Andelsbanken to form UNI Bank, Danmark

37. Svenska Handelsbanken–Skanska Banken

38. Svenska Handelsbanken–Skopbank (Finland)

39. PK Banken–Nordbanken

40. Union Bank of Finland–Kansallis (now Merita Bank, later merged with Nordbanken)

41. Christiana Bank–Fokus–Postbanken

42. Banco de Bilbao–Banco de Vizcaya

43. LaCaixa–Barcelona Savings Bank

44. Banco Central–Banco Hispano Americano

45. Banco Exterior, Caja Postal and Instituto de Crédito Oficial form Corporación Bancaria de España (now trading as Argentaria)

46. Banco Santander–60% of Banesto

47. Banco Santander–Banco Central Hispano Americano

48. Cariplo–Banco Ambrovenuto (now Banca Intesa)

49. Crédit Suisse–Bank Leu

50. Crédit Suisse Group–Swiss Volksbank

51. Swiss Bank Corporation–Banc della Svizzera Italiana

52. Swiss Bank Corporation take over Union Bank of Switzerland and later Warburg Dillon Read – the group now called UBS

53. Mitsui–Taiyo Kobe merged into Sakura, Sakura–Sumitomo merged into Sumitomo Mitsui

54. Dai–Ichi Kangyo–Fuji–IBJ merged into Mizuho Financial Group

55. Bank of Tokyo–Mitsubishi

56. Hongkong and Shanghai Bank–Midland Bank

57. Lloyds Bank–TSB

58. Royal Bank of Scotland–NatWest

59. Halifax–Bank of Scotland (HBOS)

60. National Australia Bank–Yorkshire Bank

3 The Role of the Central Bank

HISTORY OF THE MAJOR CENTRAL BANKS

We shall begin by looking briefly at the historic background of five major central banks – those of France, Germany, Japan, UK and US – and also at the formation of the newest – the European Central Bank.

France

The Bank of France was founded by Napoleon in 1800 to restore stability, especially in banknotes, after the turbulent years of the French Revolution. It was set up as a joint stock company. Napoleon himself was a shareholder and the top 200 shareholders elected the 'Regents', the bank's principal officers.

It was brought more firmly under government control in 1808 and this process was completed in 1836 with the appointment of bank councillors by the government. A monopoly over banknote issue was given in 1848. During the difficult financial years of 1929–30 it intervened to rescue Banque de l'Union Parisienne but allowed Banque Nationale de Crédit to go under. It was nationalised in 1945 and an Act of 1973 redefined its powers and organisation.

The Governor of the bank and two deputy Governors are appointed by executive order of the President of the Republic for an indefinite term. These three head the General Council which consists of ten people appointed for 6 years. The bank was not originally independent of the government but was given independence in 1993 anticipating the proposed European Central Bank. It has about 200 branches. The current governor is Jean-Paul Trichet, expected to be the next president of the European Central Bank.

Germany

The forerunner of the German Bundesbank was the Reichsbank, founded in 1876 to 'regulate the amount of money in circulation, facilitate settlements of payments and ensure that available capital is utilised'. It was a private bank but control was in the hands of the Reich Chancellor.

The terrible experience with inflation in the early 1920s led to a Banking Act of 1924 making the Reichsbank independent of the government.

Unfortunately, as Hitler acquired more power in the 1930s he was impatient with any idea of central bank independence; this was taken away in 1937 and the Bank nationalised in 1939.

After the Second World War, the old currency, the Reichsmark, was replaced by the deutschmark. A two-tier central banking system was set up. Each of the eleven

47

Federal States had a Land Central Bank and between them they owned a central body, the Bank Deutsche Länder. It was responsible for note creation and policy coordination. In particular, it was independent of the government.

This system was abolished by the Act of July 1957 which set up the Deutsche Bundesbank – a unified central bank. The eleven Land Banks became part of it only as regional offices. They carry out the relevant regulations in their own area.

The Central Bank Council consisted of eleven representatives from the Federal States and a central directorate consisting of the President, Deputy President, and up to eight other people appointed by the President of the Republic and the Federal Government. The President is usually appointed for an 8 year term. Unification would have added 5 more Länder representatives to the Council. It was, therefore, decided that from 1 November 1992, the 16 Länder would have 9 representatives between them. There are about 150 branch offices run by the Länder.

The primary task of the Bundesbank in law is to protect the currency. It is independent of government instructions but must support the government's policy unless it conflicts with the primary task. It has clashed with various governments but usually wins. The current President, Ernst Welteke, succeeded Hans Tietmayer in August 1999.

Japan

A central bank, modelled on the Bank of England, was set up in 1885 and by 1889 had become the sole issuer of banknotes. The Governor and assistant Governor are appointed by the Cabinet for a 5 year term. 7 executive directors are appointed by the Ministry of Finance (MoF) on government recommendation. These nine form the Executive Board.

Technically, the Bank is independent of the government. This was prejudiced to some extent by the fact that the MoF appointed so many members of the Executive Board. Also the MoF had the main responsibility for bank regulation and supervision. In April 1996, Mr Yasuo Matsushita, the Governor, urged a review of the central bank's legal status to grant it more independence. As a result, in 1998, as part of Japan's financial market reorganisation, the Ministry of Finance lost its power to order the central bank to delay interest rate rises, and banking supervision was passed to the new Financial Services Agency. The present Governor is Masaru Hayami.

The Zengin system for cheque clearing and electronic payments is run by the Tokyo Bankers Association.

UK

The world's first central bank is said to be the Swedish Riksbank in 1668. However, it was the formation of the Bank of England in 1694 that more clearly showed the potential for a state bank.

The bank was set up to help the government of William and Mary raise money for the wars against the French. Merchants of London and others raised £1.2m and the bank was granted a royal charter. It was the only joint stock bank allowed. From about 1715 onwards the bank was regularly raising money for the government by the sales of government bonds. By the 1826 Banking Act, joint stock banks other than the Bank of England were allowed, which led to a big increase in the numbers of banks. An Act of 1844 effectively gave the bank a monopoly of the note issue. Baring Bros hit trouble in 1890 (after unwise loans in S. America – yes, it's all happened before!) and the Bank of England rescued the bank, using a fund to which it and other banks subscribed.

The powers of the bank were exercised in fact rather than law and the bank was a private bank until 1946. In 1946 it was nationalised and banking legislation confirmed its powers in law in 1979 and 1987. In September 1984, it rescued the Johnson Matthey Bank, buying it for £1 and putting in its own managers to run it. Events during the First World War, rather than legislation, clearly established that the bank was an arm of the government and not independent. This finally changed in 1998.

The Bank of England Act of June 1998 set the statutory basis for the Bank's new Monetary Policy Committee and transfer of supervision to the Financial Services Authority.

The bank is run by a body quaintly called the 'Court'. It is headed by the Governor, two Deputy Governors and 16 non-executive directors. The Governor is appointed by the Prime Minister for a term of 5 years and is usually re-appointed. The current Governor is Eddie George, formerly deputy Governor. He will be replaced in June 2003 by Mervyn King, also a deputy Governor.

US

In the US, the constitution of 1789 put management of the currency firmly in the hands of the Treasury and the Bank of the United States was formed in 1791. As such it pre-dates the setting up of central banks in France and Germany, although its record is not continuous. The bank was responsible for the issue of dollar bills and control of government debt.

Due to opposition, the bank's charter was not renewed in 1811 but it was started again in 1816. Bearing in mind that the US is a federal republic, doubt about the constitutional legality behind the formation of the bank led to a withdrawal of privileges in 1836 and concessions were transferred to individual state banks. As a result, the Bank of the United States went bankrupt in 1841. An Act of 1863 distinguished between banks which were licensed and regulated by the federal government – 'National' banks – and those licensed and regulated by individual states. (This is why banks like Citibank are 'Citibank NA', that is, National Association.) State banks generally gave up their note issues or converted into National banks. By 1880, there were 2000 National banks all issuing banknotes.

It was only in 1913 that the Federal Reserve System was set up with a single central bank controlling note issue and operating it through twelve Federal Reserve Districts. The Board of Governors was appointed by the President, as today. Having been appointed, the Board makes its own decisions on monetary policy without direction from the government, which it does through the Federal Open Market Committee. Alan Greenspan is the Chairman of the Federal Reserve, currently serving his fourth 4 year term.

Of the key central banks we discuss here, the Federal Reserve is the one whose authority as a central body is the least clear cut. As we noted earlier, the individual states can pass laws (and do); there is the role of the Federal Deposit Insurance Corporation (FDIC), as all deposits are insured up to $100,000; the Comptroller of the Currency supervises the national banks and the Federal Home Loan Bank System supervises the Savings and Loan Associations. Finally, credit unions are regulated by the National Credit Union Administrator.

The European Central Bank

The European Central Bank (ECB) was created by the Maastricht Treaty of December 1991. It began operations on 1st June 1998, taking over from its predecessor, the European Monetary Institute. There is an executive board consisting of the president (Wim Duisenberg), the vice-president and four other members, which will carry out policy by issuing instructions to the other central banks. The policy itself is determined by the governing council, consisting of the executive board plus the governors of the twelve central banks of the member countries. This is usually referred to as the 'European System of Central Banks' (ESCB). (Legally, the three non-euro zone central banks are included but take no part in decisions on monetary policy.)

The prime objective of the ECB is price stability and the Maastricht Treaty says that it is also 'to support the EU's general economic policies'. Interest rate decisions are taken by the ECB with majority vote. The national central banks still conduct the bulk of money market operations and foreign exchange intervention but within policy set by the ECB.

CENTRAL BANK ACTIVITIES

We can summarise typical central bank activities as follows:

- ❏ Supervision of the banking system
- ❏ Advising the government on monetary policy
- ❏ Issue of banknotes
- ❏ Acting as banker to the other banks

❏ Acting as banker to the government
❏ Raising money for the government
❏ Controlling the nation's currency reserves
❏ Acting as 'lender of last resort'
❏ Liaison with international bodies.

Supervision of the Banking System

We saw in Chapter 2 that legally the central bank may not be responsible for banking supervision. There may be a separate supervisory body, like the Federal Banking Supervisory Office in Germany. Indeed, this is more often the case than not. Even in these cases, however, the practical day to day supervision and collection of information from the banks will be carried out by the central bank. The amount of information to be submitted (see Chapter 2) is considerable and may often involve several bank employees as a full time job.

Usually, the central bank will issue licences and may have to take decisions about rescues. In 1984, the Bank of England rescued the Johnson Matthey Bank. In the Autumn of 1991, the Bank of Finland had to step in and rescue the ailing Skopbank, the central bank of the savings banks. In March 1992, it was the Bank of Finland which announced a series of measures to bolster confidence in the bank sector, suffering due to the unprecedented recession. On the other hand, when Norway's banking sector was in trouble in 1991, it was the Bank Insurance Fund that set up a fund of state money to support the three major banks – Christiana, Den Norske Bank and Fokus Bank. In Sweden in 1992, the Ministry of Finance carried out rescues of Nordbanken and Forsta Sparbanken and later guaranteed all obligations of the Gota bank. When the Chicago bank, Continental Illinois, was in difficulty in 1984, it was the FDIC who moved in to help, not the Federal Reserve.

Special problems were created in the case of the infamous BCCI which collapsed in 1991. It was active in many countries but registered in Luxembourg, which may not have had the resources to monitor it properly. This problem is potentially more serious now as, in the EU, a 'single passport' policy applies. This says that an EU bank can set up a branch in any EU country with a licence from its *home* bank and not its *host* bank, although supervision will be carried out by the *host* central bank. However, following the BCCI collapse the G10 banking supervision committee met at BIS in Basle and formed some new international rules. In particular, they say that a central bank may refuse a licence if it believes that a bank is not properly supervised by its home authority.

The Bank of England, stung by criticism over its role in the BCCI affair, pointed out that in the 6 years prior to 1992 it had quietly revoked 16 banking licences and obliged 35 banks to recapitalise, change management or merge. However, in mid 1998 its supervisory powers were passed to the new Financial Services Authority.

Monetary Policy

The decisions on monetary policy may be taken by the government if the central bank is not independent, or by the central bank itself if it is. In any case, the central bank will cooperate with the government on economic policy generally and will produce advice on monetary policy and economic matters, including all the statistics.

'Monetary policy' refers to interest rates and money supply which we discussed in Chapter 2. We noted that central banks can use various weapons to control money supply – interest rates, open market operations and changes in banks' reserves held interest free at the central bank. The central bank's role as 'lender of last resort' means that it can control interest rates. The mechanics are discussed in Chapter 6.

The independence of central banks has become a topical issue. In part, this is due to the EU setting up a single currency and central bank. Maastricht decided that it would be independent (even more independent and unaccountable than the mighty Bundesbank had been!). As a result, all eleven central banks of the constituent countries had to be independent too.

What is the argument about? It is whether the fight against inflation should be left to governments influenced by political motives and party political motives. On 11 September 1996, for example, the *London Evening Standard*, discussing a possible fall in interest rates, said 'A party conference cut remains more rather than less likely'. The decision whether to cut interest rates was evidently thought to be influenced by the timing of a political party conference. The Bundesbank would have been horrified at any such possibility in its own market and, indeed, the new UK Labour government in May 1997 decided to give the Bank of England independence in setting interest rates within an inflation target set by government. However, there are, of course, *political* implications as high interest may mean low growth rates and high unemployment. As a result, although the Bundesbank's policies were admired by many, in August 1992, the head of the IG Metall trade union attacked the 'uncontrolled power' of the Bundesbank and said that it paid 'extensive and excessive' attention to inflation and ignored the need for economic growth and increasing employment.

Banknotes

The central bank controls the issue of banknotes and possibly, but not necessarily, coins also. Most payments these days do not involve cash but cheques, standing orders, direct debits, credit cards and so on. Nevertheless, cash is important as banks' cash holdings are a constraint on creation of credit, as we have seen.

Generally, we can say that, if the economy grows at 2%, the central bank will be willing to issue 2% more new banknotes to oil the wheels. On the other hand, less stable central banks may print banknotes to help the government. Usually, they are backed not by gold but securities. The cost of printing is far less than the face value and the securities produce an income. This results in a special profit called *seignorage*. This special profit may go straight to the Treasury and not appear in the bank's books. The central bank will also replace used banknotes with new ones. There are local variations here. The British seem to dislike old banknotes much more than, say, the Germans. As a result, the Bundesbank replaces far fewer notes than the Bank of England.

Each year some 80 billion banknotes are printed by 186 currency issuing authorities in 124 countries. 51 have state printing works and 14 privately owned companies produce notes for the remaining 135.

Banker to the Other Banks

The central bank will act as banker to the other banks in the economy, as well as holding accounts with international bodies like the IMF and the World Bank. It is a common habit for the central bank to insist that the other banks hold non-interest bearing *reserves* with it in proportion to their deposits. Apart from helping the bank to make a profit, these serve as an instrument of control over money supply, as we saw in Chapter 2.

In any case, major banks will have to hold *working balances* for day to day settlement for various activities. Cheque clearing will end each day with a net sum of money owed by one bank to another or due to it. Dealings in government Treasury bills and bonds will be settled through the central bank accounts, and also tax payments. The total of a bank's clients' payments of tax will result in a fall in that bank's balance at the central bank and a rise in the government's balance.

In Germany, prior to European Economic and Monetary Union, the banks had to keep non-interest bearing reserves at the Bundesbank as laid down by the rules which applied. Deposits were divided into sight deposits, time deposits and special savings deposits. For example, under the old rules, 4.95% of time deposits had to be left at the central bank, and 4.15% of savings deposits. For ordinary sight deposits (=current accounts) the percentages varied according to the total amount on deposit. Reserves for residents' deposits were different from those for non-residents' deposits. These rates had been set in 1987 and remained unchanged until 4 February 1993. At the same time as the Bundesbank announced changes to the lombard and discount rates, they announced some relaxation in the rules for reserves. The savings and time deposit rates were cut to an average of 2% but left unchanged for sight deposits. This liberated DM32bn of reserves but, at the same time, the Bundesbank released DM25bn of new 'liquidity paper' in denominations of 3, 6 and 9 months. These securities could also be purchased by non-banks and marked the continuing build up of a money market in Frankfurt. A further relaxation of rules was allowed in March 1994 and August 1995.

(For simplicity, we have talked of 'deposits'. In fact, the reserves are based on 'liabilities' in a more general sense. A bond due to be repaid by the bank is not a deposit but counts as a liability for purposes of reserve requirements.)

The working balances which major domestic banks would need to keep at the

Bundesbank are part of these reserves. The actual figures are averages of the balances held at the Bundesbank during the course of a particular month and the calculation is based on the daily average of the various types of liabilities held. The result is that, at the start of the month, the banks may hold reserves less than the required amount provided they catch up later, so that the overall average is the required figure. This leads to a lot of short-term lending and borrowing in the interbank market.

The whole system has now been reorganised for all twelve countries in Europe's Economic and Monetary Union. The ECB has imposed a minimum reserve requirement (similar to the Bundesbank but paying interest which the Bundesbank did not). Banks must deposit the equivalent of 2% of deposits with their central banks. National central banks will conduct open market operations to keep interest rates within a desired range. All this will be discussed in Chapter 6.

By contrast, the Bank of England abolished reserve requirements of this nature in 1979. The argument is that – as there are no exchange controls – sterling can be exchanged for foreign currencies and vice-versa without constraint. As London is a huge international banking centre, attempts to control money supply by sterling non-interest bearing reserves at the central bank would simply not be effective. The only reserve held is 0.15% of stipulated liabilities – not an instrument of monetary policy but a way of 'joining the UK bank club' and helping the Bank of England to make a profit! However, the main domestic banks must still maintain working balances at the Bank of England.

Banker to the Government

Normally, a central bank acts as the government's banker. It receives revenues for taxes or other income and pays out money for the government's expenditure. Usually, it will not lend to the government but will help the government to borrow money by the sales of its bills and bonds (see next section).

One exception here is Postipankki in Finland. Perhaps because it is owned by the government, it is this bank rather than the central bank which handles the government's money.

As citizens pay taxes, charges are made against their bank accounts and settled through their bank's own account at the central bank. The banks' balances fall and the government's rises. This is one reason why banks must keep working balances at the central bank. Of course, as tax rebates are made, the government's balance falls and the banks' balances rise.

As Treasury bills and bonds are paid for, money is passed to the government's account. As they are redeemed, money flows back to the banks' accounts. If the central bank discounts bills of exchange to help a commercial bank's liquidity, money moves into that bank's account. As the bill is presented for payment, money is credited to the central bank. As a result, there is a constant flow of money from the banks' accounts at the central bank to the government's accounts and vice-versa.

Raising Money for the Government

The government Treasury bill and bond markets are covered in detail in Chapter 6. While sometimes the Treasury or Ministry of Finance handles government issues, it is much more common for the central bank to control this and to settle payments through accounts that banks and financial institutions have with it. This is one of the reasons why these banks must keep working balances at the central bank.

We have seen that, in 1694, the Bank of England was formed specifically for the purpose of raising money for the government (although since 1998 responsibility has been passed to the Treasury's new Debt Management Office).

The cumulative sum of money owed by governments for all their borrowings is called the *national debt*. Over time, the debt grows and is not, in any real sense, ever 'paid off'. Does this matter?

The first point is that, for any individual, how serious debt is depends on their income. Governments are the same. Economists compare the national debt to the national income as a ratio to see if the situation is getting worse or better. For this purpose the figure for Gross Domestic Product (GDP) is used as equivalent to the national income.

In the US, due to heavy government borrowing in the 1980s, the ratio rose from 33% to over 50%, then started to fall in the 1990s as the government was in surplus and able to buy debt back. However, the economic slowdown of 2001–2002 and the falling revenues from President Bush's tax cuts (designed to boost the economy) mean that the US is now back in deficit. In the UK, the figure, which was 100% at the end of the 1960s, has fallen to below 40%.

This relationship of national debt to GDP became an issue in the run up to a possible European single currency and economic union.

The meeting at Maastricht in Holland in December 1991 set out criteria which must be met before a nation could join in the single currency. (This will be examined in detail in Chapter 10.) One of the criteria was that the national debt/GDP ratio should not exceed 60%.

Inflation is also a key factor. As time goes by, inflation simply erodes the value of the debt. A national debt of $100bn in 1960 looks a quite different figure today. Debt servicing costs also play a role. Interest must be paid and this itself may limit further increases in debt. In Italy and Belgium, for example, debt servicing takes no less than 20% of all government tax receipts.

Finally, to whom is the money owed? Often the government bonds and bills are owned by financial institutions and individuals in the domestic market. There will be foreign holders but they will probably not account for more than, say, 20%. This is where the position of the LDC countries is so different – they largely owe the money to foreigners and it is denominated in a foreign currency (see Chapter 6).

Is there a level of national debt that is reasonable or safe? *The Economist* (27 February–4 March 1988) had an interesting article on this subject and this quotation provides a nice summary:

Neither economic theory nor history gives any clue as to what is the critical level of public debt ... The crucial factor is the willingness of investors to hold public debt. If they lose their appetite then, either interest rates must rise sharply or the government has to finance its deficit by printing more money and hence stoking up inflation.

Controlling the Nation's Currency Reserves

Each nation has reserves of gold and foreign currencies held at the central bank. If the bank intervenes in the market to buy the domestic currency, it will do so using foreign currency reserves. If it intervenes to sell the local currency, it will acquire foreign currencies.

The foreign exchange markets are examined in Chapter 8. We shall see that the transactions in major currencies are considerable. The dealing in sterling, to take one example, is so great that the Bank of England alone can't control the exchange rate by its buying and selling. It can, however, influence the rate by careful timing and the knowledge by market operators that the central bank is acting in the market. Under the newer arrangements for European cooperation, several EU central banks may act together. Equally, major countries' central banks may act together as part of the arrangements of the 'Group of seven' countries (G7, see below).

In the ERM crisis of September 1992, the Bank of France is thought to have spent about 40% of its reserves defending the franc – a sum perhaps as high as FFr150bn.

Where a currency is not widely traded, the central bank will have a much better chance of controlling the rate. The central bank of Norway can control the rate for the kroner much more easily than the Bank of England can control that for the pound.

The reserves will usually include gold as well as foreign currencies. The role of gold is itself being considered at the moment. Prices today are at their lowest for 20 years. Many prominent central banks have been selling gold (including the UK, which announced an intention in May 1999 to sell 50% of the nation's gold reserves), and the IMF will almost certainly sell off some 10m ounces of its reserves. The ECB, however, is still holding some 15% of its reserves as gold.

Acting as Lender of Last Resort

This does not only refer to the role of the bank as a periodic rescuer of banks in trouble. It refers to the fact that the central bank will help the other banks temporarily when they meet problems with their liquidity. As we have just seen, tax transactions and settlements for government securities are causing a continuous ebb and flow of money out of and into the accounts of the banks at the central bank. In all cases, they are obliged to keep minimum working balances and in most cases they must keep reserves at the central bank also, although these working balances may be part of the reserves.

The central bank smooths out the peaks and troughs by being prepared to assist the other banks with short-term help. Since the banks are ultimately dependent on the central bank, the rate of interest charged governs other interest rates. How the bank carries out this role is discussed in detail in Chapter 6.

Of course, sometimes a bank does need to be rescued. It is ironic that Baring Bros, which was placed in administration in February 1995, had been in trouble some 100 years earlier and had, on that occasion, been rescued by the Bank of England and other banks. Bad debts in Argentina were three times Baring's capital.

The precise role of the new ECB in rescuing banks in trouble is vague in the Maastricht Treaty. This is discussed later in Chapter 10.

Liaison with International Bodies

Central banks will liaise with other international financial bodies like the International Monetary Fund (IMF) and the International Bank for Reconstruction and Development, usually called the 'World Bank' (see Chapter 8). They also liaise with and take part in discussions at the BIS in Basle. This bank was set up in 1930. By 1929 it was evident that for Germany to pay the massive reparations imposed on it after the First World War was an impossibility and some new arrangement had to be made. The new plan which was devised was called the 'Young Plan' and part of it involved setting up the BIS which would help to transfer reparation payments and other international debts. 84% of the shares were held by 33 central banks and the rest by private shareholders. However, on 9 September 1996, the BIS announced that it was offering membership to nine other central banks, including those in areas like the Far East and Latin America, and these became members in June 1997.

Today, the BIS is used by some 90 central banks and can be regarded as 'the central bankers' central bank'. It handles the payments made between world banks, sponsors cooperation, handles initiatives on key topics and hosts monthly meetings of the world's bankers at its headquarters near Basle's railway station. It also holds 10% of the reserves of major world central banks.

There is far more cooperation on economic matters by the world's major powers than there was 20 years ago. Of key importance here are the periodic meetings of the seven most advanced economic nations, called the 'Group of Seven' or, simply, 'G7'. The seven are US, France, Germany, UK, Canada, Japan and Italy.

G7 members meet periodically to discuss world economic and financial affairs. Central bankers play a key role in preparing for these meetings and briefing the politicians. The world's top powers had realised by early 1985 that the foreign exchange markets were so big that only concerted intervention by all the major central banks could have any effect. Worried about the dollar's inexorable rise, key central bankers led by Paul Volcker, head of the US Federal Reserve, made a secret agreement. On Wednesday morning, 27 February 1985, they struck, selling dollars simultaneously. By the end of the day, the dollar had fallen from DM3.50 to DM3.30. In the process, the foreign exchange markets experienced what can only be called 'pandemonium'.

Later, in September 1985, the predecessor of G7 (G5) called a meeting at the Plaza Hotel in Washington (G5 is G7 minus Canada and Italy). Again the agreement was to force down the dollar, and again it worked. This first international agreement on currencies since Bretton Woods (see Chapter 8) is called the 'Plaza Agreement'. In later years there were other meetings (for example, the 'Louvre Accord' in February 1987). Usually, these were designed to push the dollar *up* and were not as successful.

A wider forum for international meetings is the so called 'Group of Ten' or 'G10'; this is G7 with the addition of Sweden, Belgium, Holland and Switzerland. The reader will not need to be a mathematical genius to see that this is eleven countries, not 10. It's all to do with Swiss neutrality: the Swiss are always there, but officially they aren't there. It's called 'G10' but actually there are eleven countries participating.

Sometimes the G10 members meet with Latin American and Far Eastern representatives on an *ad hoc* basis to form what is usually called G33 (for example to discuss the Far East crisis in 1997).

Another forum is called 'G24'. This consists of eight countries each from Asia, Africa and Latin America, and is used for liaison with the IMF and the World Bank.

THE POSITION OF CENTRAL BANKS TODAY

The last decade has seen a rise in the power and influence of central bankers. Years of high inflation have led to the view that politicians can no longer be trusted with monetary policy. One by one, central banks have become independent, culminating in the formation of the European Central Bank.

Inflation in advanced industrial countries was down to about 1.5% at the start of the millennium, its lowest rate since the 1950s. However, many governments are now concerned at the cost in growth and unemployment. Does low inflation necessarily mean low growth and high unemployment? Alan Greenspan, Chairman of the US Federal Reserve, seems to have delivered 10 years of good growth with low inflation and, despite the 2001–2002 slowdown, he remains confident of the longer term outlook. The position is not as favourable in Europe, where high social costs and labour market rigidities have led to high unemployment (although not in the UK).

If a key role of the central bank is to combat inflation, this raises the question – how do we measure it? There is, for example, consumer inflation and industrial inflation. In particular, price indices do not usually include the prices of financial assets like shares. The collapse of these asset prices could also lead to economic and financial instability, as in Japan. In 1911, Irving Fisher, the economist, argued that a price index should include share and property prices. Joseph Carson, an economist at Deutsche Bank, New York, has constructed just such an index with shares in at

5%. Leading indices, such as the Dow, the Footsie and – most notably – NASDAQ, surged between 1996 and 1999 at a rate not seen since the late 1980s, and people talked of the 'new economy' and 'a new paradigm'. Since the highs of end 1999, the Dow has lost around 30% and the Footsie over 40%, with falls being triggered initially by the burst of the 'dot.com' bubble in Spring 2001, followed by the events of 11 September, and more latterly by concerns over the validity of reported results in the wake of irregularities at Enron, Worldcom and other major corporations. While it is not the role of central banks to maintain stock market growth – and Greenspan warned of the excessive prices of many shares before they collapsed – the knock on economic effect of stock market instability is clearly of concern to central bank governors.

Accountability is another current issue. For all their independence, the Bundesbank and the Federal Reserve are basically accountable to their governments, and the Federal Open Market Committee's minutes are models of openness. There is much concern, however, at the position of the ECB. The Maastricht Treaty prohibits it from taking orders from politicians, and members of the executive are appointed for 8-year, non-renewable terms. The President, Wim Duisenberg, will meet the European Parliament only once a year to explain policy. Outside of this, however, he has stated that no minutes of meetings will be issued. It may be more difficult for the ECB, therefore, to attract public support than the Fed or the Bundesbank.

Finally, what may seem a silly question – do we need a central bank? In 1900, only 18 countries had a central bank, compared to 172 today. Some economists still argue that private banks should issue their own banknotes in competition. This was the position before 1845 in Scotland, where notes were backed by gold but banks competed. Adam Smith admired the system.

But surely we need the role of the lender of last resort? Some argue that the near guarantee of a rescue encourages banks to behave imprudently – an issue called 'moral hazard'.

That wise man, Walter Bagehot, commented on moral hazard in his great work *Lombard St.* (1873):

> *If banks are bad they will certainly continue bad and will probably become worse if the government sustains and encourages them. The cardinal maxim is that any aid to a present bad bank is the surest mode of preventing the establishment of a future good bank.*

Like Adam Smith, Walter Bagehot also favoured the old Scottish system. However, he agreed that a proposal to do away with the Bank of England would be as futile as a proposal to do away with the monarchy. Now that the latter idea is no longer unthinkable in the UK, we may perhaps end up treating central banks with the same lack of reverence!

SUMMARY

The Bank of France was founded in 1800; the Bundesbank in 1957; the Bank of Japan in 1885; the Bank of England in 1694, the Federal Reserve in 1913 and the European Central Bank in 1998.

Central bank activities are:

Supervision of the banking system Where it will play a key role even if legally there is a separate supervisory body.

Monetary policy Controlling interest rates and the money supply. However, some central banks are independent in this respect and others are less so, but central banks all over the world have increasingly been given more independence with respect to monetary policy.

Printing of bank notes and minting of coins This must be linked to the growth in the economy or inflation will follow.

Banker to the other banks Domestic banks must leave sums of money with the central bank for various clearing and settlement systems. In some countries (for example, the euro area) the central bank imposes minimum *reserves* as part of monetary policy.

Banker to the government In raising money for the government, the central bank controls the account into which the money is paid. As taxes are paid, the government balance increases and the commercial banks' balances fall. When the government spends money, the opposite happens.

Raising money for the government This usually involves the sale of short-term Treasury bills and medium- to long-term government bonds. The cumulative sum of money owed for all borrowing not yet repaid is the national debt. It is usually shown as a percentage of Gross Domestic Product to see if the situation is worsening or getting better. Over time, however, inflation erodes the burden of the debt.

Controlling the nation's reserves From time to time, central banks will buy or sell their country's currency to influence the rate. If they buy it, they will use the nation's reserves of gold and foreign currencies to do so.

Acting as lender of last resort Sometimes this refers to the rescue of banks in trouble but, more generally, it is the willingness of the central bank to assist banks with liquidity problems. Usually, this means their inability to meet the necessary balance levels at the central bank (as a direct result of central bank policy!). The rate of interest involved in the transaction gives the central bank control over interest rates.

International liaison This involves cooperation with bodies like the IMF, the World Bank and the BIS, It also involves supporting international meetings called G7 and G10.

4 Commercial Banking

INTRODUCTION

Commercial banks are essentially banks which are in the classic banking business of accepting deposits and making loans. Banks like Citibank, Chase Manhattan, Dai Ichi Kangyo, Barclays and Royal Bank of Scotland are all commercial banks. Other banks, like Deutsche and UBS, would say that they were 'universal' banks: that is, they cover all kinds of banking, including both commercial and investment banking. In the UK, if a commercial bank carries out investment banking, it will do so through a subsidiary, for example, Barclays Bank – Barclays Capital. In Germany and Switzerland (and to a lesser extent France, the Netherlands and Spain) they will do so within the same legal entity. In the US and Japan, commercial banks were prevented until recently from doing investment banking by regulation (see Chapter 5).

As we saw in Chapter 2, commercial banking may be *retail* or *wholesale*. Within their own country, the large commercial banks will carry out both retail and wholesale banking. Abroad, they will concentrate on the wholesale markets.

We shall cover retail banking in this chapter. We shall also explain some areas of wholesale banking, mainly the question of bank lending. Other aspects of wholesale banking will be treated in later chapters – money markets in Chapter 6, foreign exchange in Chapter 8 and finance for trade in Chapter 9.

RETAIL BANKING

Types of Service

Retail commercial banks offer an increasing range of services to their clients. Some relate to the handling of *money* – various forms of deposit accounts and loans. Others relate to *services* – advice, custody, purchase of stocks, shares, insurance and so on. Essentially, these are the two ways banks make their money: taking deposits, that is, borrowing money and lending it out at a profitable rate of interest on the one hand and providing useful services for which they can charge, on the other. The range of products is widening as the banks react to growing competition and falling profits. We hear more and more of the phrase, the 'financial supermarket'.

Retail banking tends to be dominated by a handful of domestic banks. According to figures from Merrill Lynch, the top four banks in the economy control 75% of banking assets in Holland, 60% in France and 28% in the UK.

The one exception is the US where, due to the large number of banks (see Chapter 2), the ten biggest banks only account for 20% of deposits. In Germany and

Italy, savings banks are strong competitors for deposits and, in the UK, the building societies.

Money Banking – Deposits

Current accounts   The principal kind of account offered by the retail bank is the current account, which is seen by the bank as a fundamental way of establishing a relationship with the customer and as a source of cheap money to sustain the various lending activities. The position regarding the charge to the client for providing the current account facility varies. In the present competitive environment, banks either make charges but offset them with interest on credit balances or make no charges but have free use of the credit balances. French banks are not allowed in law to make charges, but many vary the amount of time to clear cheques, which can be as much as 5 days. In the UK and Spain, competition has led to payment of interest on credit balances for the first time. The current account carries with it the obligation to provide a range of payment services – cheques, Automated Teller Machines (ATMs), debit cards and so forth, the costs of which are quite high and consume some of the value of the low cost deposits.

Deposit accounts   These are various forms of interest-bearing accounts which usually do not allow cheques and often severely limit other withdrawal facilities. As a rule, they require a period of notice to be given before withdrawals, for example, 7 days, 1 month or 3 months. The customer is paid interest on the understanding that the appropriate period of notice will be given before drawing out money. Alternatively, the money may be placed on deposit for a fixed term, similar to the above, whereupon it is repaid. Generally, the longer the customer is prepared to commit the funds, and/or the greater the amount, the greater will be the rate paid. The bank has the advantage that it can rely on notice or fixed term money much more than it can with current accounts, where the balances fluctuate.

Payments   Based upon the current account is a range of payment products which manifest themselves in paper or electronic form. Examples of the former are cheques and giro slip payments, while a growing number of electronic payments pass from business to business and business to individuals through computer to computer systems. Thus, in the UK, for example, more than 80% of the workforce receive their salaries by automated transfers from their employers' systems into their current accounts. Equally, Standing Orders and Direct Debits are very widely used to settle recurring payments. Intermixed with electronic payments passing through the current account will be paper-based transactions. People and companies can settle indebtedness by issuing cheques, which give rise to a charge on their account and a credit on the beneficiary's account. Alternatively, a bill may be paid by completing a giro form and sending the form to the beneficiary's bank so that money can be transferred to the creditor's account (very common in the Netherlands, Germany, Austria and Switzerland). Within the banking system, the transmission of payments between banks and the consequent financial settlement is called clearing, and this is discussed later.

Ever increasingly, payment activity is initiated by the use of plastic cards. Details of the account are embedded in a magnetic strip or a microchip, and these, when put together with value information generated at an ATM or at the point of sale, give rise to a current account transaction. There are 500,000 ATMs worldwide with 165,000 in the US and 140,000 in Europe. The UK has nearly 34,000 ATMs, and they are used for 70% of personal cash withdrawals. France, Germany and Italy also have large numbers of ATMs.

The first ATM network in Eastern Europe was set up by the Czech Komercni Bank. There are problems, however, with poor communication links and currency convertibility in many countries, although not the Czech Republic whose currency is convertible.

An alternative to the cheque for payment in a retail shop or similar outlet is the *debit* card, which will usually be also the ATM card of the customer. At the point of sale a machine, sometimes integrated with the till, creates what amounts to an electronic cheque from the information on the card and the amount of the transaction. This data is passed down a telephone line so that the appropriate charge can be made to the customer's account and a credit to the retailer's account. The customer will be called upon to identify themselves at the point of sale in one of two ways. They may put their signature on a paper slip for checking against a specimen on the back of the card by the retailer, or, in some systems, by entering their Personal Identification Number (PIN), as they would at an ATM.

If the customer wants to make a high value purchase, the retailer's machine will seek authorisation from the customer's bank before completing the purchase. Such is the sophistication of the network connecting retailers to the world's banking systems that this takes only a few seconds. In the UK, the growing use of debit cards means that, between 1991 and 2001, the volume of cheques used, which was 3.8 billion, has fallen to 2.5 billion. In the same period, debit card purchases have increased from 0.3 billion to 2.4 billion.

There is a slight variation on the debit card idea in France where they have debit cards which charge transactions a month later. Unlike a credit card, however, this is charged to the current account and the holder is expected to have funds to meet the charge.

When a cheque is used, the same card may serve as a 'cheque guarantee card'. A retailer will accept a cheque up to a given maximum if the card is produced so that its specimen signature can be checked against that written on the cheque. The advantage to the retailer is that the bank guarantees to pay even if the transaction is fraudulent or the cardholder has insufficient funds. In the US, there is no such system and retailers are reluctant to accept cheques ('Don't you have a credit card?'). In France, also, there is no such system, but retailers are happier to accept cheques, as writing a cheque when there are no funds to support it is a criminal offence.

Some interesting figures from BIS on numbers of ATMs and Point of Sale terminals are shown in Table 4.1.

Table 4.1 *Number of cash dispensers, ATMs and EFT POS terminals, end 2000*

	Cash dispensers and ATMs		EFT POS terminals	
	No of machines installed	*No of machines per 1m inhabitants*	*No of terminals installed*	*No of terminals per 1m inhabitants*
Belgium	6808	669	115,558	11,355
Canada	31,434	1034	431,650	14,199
France	27,872	582	664,896	13,884
Germany	47,639	580	591,057	7196
Italy	31,602	549	568,944	9884
Japan	116,295	922	19,551	155
Netherlands	6808	435	152,982	9775
Sweden	2609	295	86,859	9822
Switzerland	4788	675	66,496	9375
UK	33,944	575	727,110	12,317
US	265,446	991	2,723,571	10,168

Source: BIS Statistics on Payment Systems in Eleven Developed Countries (July 2002).

Four types of loan are common in the retail banking sector:

❏ Overdraft
❏ Personal loan
❏ Mortgage
❏ Credit card.

The *overdraft* is a popular method of borrowing in countries where it is permitted. The account holder is allowed to overdraw up to a maximum sum for a given period of time – nominally, perhaps, 6 months, but in practice renewable. Interest is charged on a daily basis (and at a variable rate) on any overdrawn balance.

From the customer's point of view, the overdraft is informal and can be arranged quickly; it is flexible in that the amount 'lent' will vary and can be quite economical in that, when a monthly salary is paid in, the overdrawn balance will be reduced, or even eliminated, at least for a few days.

From the banks' point of view, the overdraft is also informal; the facility is reviewed at the stated time interval and, if necessary, it is repayable on demand – a condition of which many borrowers are happily ignorant!

The overdraft is common in the UK and Germany, not particularly common in France and simply not allowed as a facility in the US.

The *personal loan* is an agreement to borrow a specific amount over a specific period of time with a set sum repaid monthly. $1000 might be borrowed for 2 years. The rate of interest is fixed and charged on the whole amount. If the rate on the above loan was 10%, then 10% p.a. on $1000 for 2 years is $200. This results in 24 monthly repayments of $50. As some of the principal is being repaid every month, the bank is not owed $1000 for 2 years but, on the average, a much smaller sum. The result is that the 10% rate is purely nominal, the actual rate (sometimes termed the 'Annual Percentage Rate' or 'APR') will be nearly twice this.

Mortgages   Although there may be specialised mortgage lenders, the commercial banks may offer mortgages too. The loan is secured on the property and such a loan will bear a much lower rate of interest than an unsecured overdraft or personal loan as the bank is less at risk. In some countries, banks and other mortgage lenders will not lend more than, say, 50% or 60% of the value of the property, but where they do, offering 90% or more, this can fuel a colossal rise in house prices, followed by a subsequent fall as recession strikes. In the UK in the 1990s, it was estimated that 1 million householders were living in houses whose value was actually less than the mortgage loan – a concept called 'negative equity' (The Bank of England's Quarterly Bulletin – August 1992). A recent development in the UK has seen various implementations of the all-in-one account, which works like a hybrid between a current account and a mortgage. The accounts are actually or virtually merged to give the customer the benefit of fluctuations in their overdraft, say after pay day, with the lower interest rates of a mortgage.

Another way of lending money is by a *credit card* account. The major international brand names are Visa, MasterCard and JCB, the Japanese branding organisation. They are offered by banks, retailers and others. The plastic card, with coded information on a magnetic strip or microchip, is offered at the point of sale and the purchase is charged to the credit card account. The method is exactly the same as with a debit card. A statement is sent monthly with a given time to pay, usually two to three weeks. The consumer has the choice of paying the balance in full or paying only part and paying the rest later. It is very flexible in that the card holders can choose how much to borrow (within a pre-arranged limit) and how quickly to repay. Generally, the rate of interest is substantial when borrowing on a credit card account, but competitive pressures and desire for market share often cause the banks to offer very keen introductory or 'balance transfer' rates. Card holders can, of course, choose not to borrow at all but repay in full each month, with perhaps up to seven weeks elapsing between the purchase and the payment, at no cost to them. Most issuing banks seek to make an annual charge for the use of the card, but competitive pressures have, again, forced many to offer cards without fees. Recent years have seen a large increase in card issuers and types of card. Among the issuers are retailers, bodies like AT & T, General Motors, General Electric (US) and mutual funds. In the UK, some 1200 organisations – clubs, societies, unions and common interest groups of many kinds – have cards issued in their names. They contract the banks, or specialist organisations such as MBNA, to manage and operate the accounts, taking an introductory fee and a tiny percentage of the turnover through the accounts. Although not obvious to the card holder, the banks also charge the retailers a percentage of about 1% to 3% of the transaction value for providing the facilities by which the transactions are authorised, collected and cleared.

The familiar green American Express card and the Diners Club card are not credit cards in that they do not offer *credit*. The consumer is expected to pay the balance in full every month. They are usually called 'travel and entertainment' or charge cards.) American Express has introduced a separate credit card called *Optima*.

In general, credit cards are now very widely used. Their acceptability internationally makes them a very useful way of solving foreign currency problems when travelling.

The one country where the use of credit cards was weak is Germany where, at the end of 1995, there were only 6m credit card holders as opposed to, for example, 29m in the UK. This was due to the opposition of the banks. However, things have now changed and we are seeing banks issue credit cards, and also retailers, like Hertie who have 62 stores, and mail order houses, like Quelle who have 30m customers. In part, the move is a response to credit card initiatives in Germany from a foreign bank – Banco Santander, the biggest credit card issuer in Germany. The 6 million credit card holders of 1995 had become 17.7 million by the end of 2000.

The Electronic Purse

Another development using plastic cards which the banks are experimenting with is called 'the electronic purse'. This is based on a 'smart' card which stores information on a microchip. This includes a balance of 'cash' pre-loaded onto the card from an ATM or a suitably equipped telephone terminal. The idea is that the card may be used for a wide range of retail transactions, many of which would be too trivial for a credit card. The card is presented at point of sale and the value loaded in the card is decreased by the amount of the transaction. As with real cash, there is no paperwork. The retailer's equipment has in it a card to which the 'cash' flows and is accumulated. At closing time, the 'cash' can be paid in to the bank using an ATM or telephone terminal in the reverse of the loading procedure.

Perhaps the most advanced development is in Portugal, where the card can be issued by any bank and used to pay for any service anywhere.

In the UK, National Westminster Bank and Midland Bank developed Mondex, an electronic purse which underwent trials in Swindon between 1995 and 1998. The idea was taken up by Midland's new owner HSBC with implementations in Hong Kong and the Far East, and by the Royal Bank of Canada and Canadian Imperial Bank of Commerce for trials in that country. Mondex, now majority owned by Mastercard, is franchised in 53 countries and is being introduced into Japan through Sanwa Bank and LTCB.

While there have been several trials of electronic purses in the US (including one for the Olympic Games in Atlanta), the most ambitious involved cooperation between Citicorp, Chase Manhattan, Visa and MasterCard. A trial was launched for New York's affluent Upper West Side late in 1996 and called off in November 1998.

In general, electronic purses are making slow progress. This is due to several factors: the cost of issue of the cards, the lack of compatible point of sale terminals, conflicting card encoding standards and a general lack of interest by the consumer. The first of these is being addressed by the issue of 'smart', that is, microchip-fitted cards as a counter fraud measure for credit and debit cards; these will be readily capable of carrying an electronic purse application. At the same time, Visa, MasterCard and Europay are cooperating on agreeing global standards for chip cards. This will solve the encoding standard problem. However, the point of sale equipment problem will take longer to solve, as retailers are unwilling to make the very large expenditures necessary. The issue of consumer acceptance of the notion of electronic purses may remain; people are very conservative and the use of real cash is deeply embedded in culture all over the world.

Other Services

There are a number of other services which are typically offered by banks.

Securities purchases In some countries, like Germany and Switzerland, the 'universal' bank tradition has meant that the banks dominate stock markets and the commercial banking branches have been able to offer a full service to clients. Elsewhere, brokers have traditionally had a monopoly of stock exchange transactions and banks would act as an agent for their customers, passing the order to the broker. Today, this might still be the case but all over Europe deregulation has been the rule, starting with the UK's 'Big Bang' in October 1986. As a result, banks have been allowed either to own brokers or set up their own operations and offer their branch customers a securities service.

Securities custody Often bonds and shares are in 'bearer' format and not registered. The share certificate will say that 'the bearer' owns, perhaps, 2000 shares in Daimler Benz. The problem is that, in the event of a burglary, the burglar is now 'the bearer'! Also, since there is no register, interest payments and dividends have to be claimed, voting rights followed up and so on. The banks will, therefore, often hold the certifications for safe-keeping, claim interest payments/dividends for clients, vote by proxy, notify them of AGMs, rights issues, scrip issues and other company events. Needless to say, a fee is charged for this service!

Mutual funds   These are pools of shares run by investment managers and giving the small shareholder a spread of risk. The banks often own these and part of the securities service might be the advice that the client would be better off in a mutual fund than owning shares directly. It would be no surprise to find that the fund recommended is one the bank owns! These are sold in France as SICAVs and FCPs, in the UK as Investment Trusts and Unit Trusts and as Mutual Funds in the US. The idea has spread to Spain where 'Super Fondos' are now being offered by the banks. Following the European single market initiative, the term 'UCITS' may be encountered, and this is covered in Chapter 10.

Advice   The bank manager is available for advice. This may be about investments, trust funds for children, wills and similar issues. Indeed, the manager may end up as the executor for a will and trustee for funds left for children. This position as adviser puts the bank manager in an ideal position to sell the bank's products. This has caused much anguish in the UK due to the operation of the 1986 Financial Services Act. The ruling now is that either the bank manager is an agent for the bank's products or an independent investment adviser. If the former, they must inform the client of this status and are not allowed to give wide ranging advice on a range of products. If an independent adviser, they must also make sure that the client is aware of this. If they recommend the bank's product it must be clear, beyond reasonable doubt, that this is best for the client or criminal prosecution may ensue. All the UK banks and the top ten building societies (except one) have decided that their managers will be agents for the bank's products.

Safe deposits   Banks provide safe deposit boxes to house jewellery, other valuable items and cash. When there is a break in and the boxes are forced open, those clients with large sums, of which the tax authorities are unaware, face a problem when making a claim!

Foreign exchange   Apart from the banks' wholesale foreign exchange operations, they will provide a service for their customers' holiday needs. This will involve supplying travellers' cheques and cash. They may also be involved in requests to transfer sums of money to accounts abroad. The rise of the credit and debit card, now very widely acceptable at point of sale and in ATMs has eroded this business along with the advent of the euro.

Insurance   Most banks are now offering insurance policies either through an association with an insurance company or through their own subsidiary. This is discussed more fully below when we look at key current issues in retail banking.

Delivery Channels

How shall the services of the bank – deposits, loans, payment products and all the other services – be delivered to the customer? Traditionally, there was only one answer; the branch office. Gradually, since the early 1990s, branches have been joined by telephone banking, PC banking and, more recently still, TV and mobile phone delivery.

Branch delivery   still dominates. In the UK, there were 8900 bank branches at the end of 2000, down from over 10,000 in 1996, with some of the reduction being caused by rationalisation from mergers and some from branch closure programmes. However, many people now believe that the new channels are additional services rather than substitutes, with one major bank citing the fact that three out of four customers still regularly visited a branch and another survey suggesting that in the South East 72% of customers depended on branches for at least some of their banking activities. This all suggests that branches are here to stay, at least for the medium term. Branches are convenient for the customer and there is still a demand for face-to-face contact, particularly when discussing more complex financial matters. Branches give the bank high visibility on the streets and are a good base for attracting new customers, dealing with routine transactions and for selling more complex (and profitable) products. There has been a fairly rapid change in how the branches look to the customer. Traditionally, the customer was confined to a public space defined by the imposing barrier of the line of cashiers, behind their security screens. They had to go out of their way to ask to see someone who could open an account or deal with a more complicated transaction. This model of branch is rapidly being supplanted by one in which the space has been opened up and made more welcoming. After encountering some self-service machines – ATMs, deposit machines, statement and enquiry terminals – the customer sees before them desks with people variously described as 'personal bankers' or 'counsellors' awaiting an opportunity to engage them in helpful conversation. The cashiers are relegated to the back of the room. The purpose of all this is to encourage the customers to serve themselves for routine transactions and, as soon as they step beyond this, to expose them to sales opportunities. To make space for this more 'open' setting, something has had to be displaced. This is the clerical processing of payments and correspondence, which was formerly termed the 'back office' function. These activities are still required, but they have been moved out to other units who will, using higher capacity technology, take on the back office work of many branches.

Telephone Banking   Most banks now offer, in parallel with the branches, a service using only the telephone as a means of communication. Staff in call centres offer a service for, perhaps, 12 hours per day (or, as in the case of HSBC's First Direct, 24 hours). Customers' routine enquiries can be satisfied and more complex services, for example bill paying, can be supported. Here, the names and bank account details for regular suppliers (gas, electricity, telephone and so on) are set up on file and, using special security passwords; a whole banking service can be initiated by the customer, using only the telephone. New accounts, loans and mortgages can be negotiated in the same way, with postal confirmation where necessary. Money can be drawn out by using plastic cards in the parent bank's ATMs. The bank has the advantage of not having the cost of a branch network, and will pay a higher than normal rate of interest on credit balances.

Examples of such systems are:

- ❏ Germany   Bank 24 (Deutsche Bank)
- ❏ UK   First Direct (HSBC)
- ❏ Spain   Open Bank (Banco Santander)
- ❏ France   Banque Direct (Paribas).

New entrants to banking, for example supermarkets and insurance companies, almost universally base their operations on telephone call centres.

PC banking   Since the middle to late 1990s there has been a growth in the use of PCs by individuals to access their banks. Initially, special purpose application software and diallers had to be used to provide adequate security, but now the standard Internet browsers are perfectly satisfactory for home banking purposes. Banks have been divided in their approach to Internet banking. Some have set up separately branded operations, distanced from the parent bank, while others have merely added the Internet as a medium for contact, along with their telephone and branch channels. Examples of the separately branded operations are, in the UK, Smile (by Co-operative Bank), Cahoot (by Abbey National Bank) and IF (by HBOS Bank). Again, some new entrants have chosen this route, notably 'egg', an Internet banking offshoot of the Prudential Assurance Company. A totally new Internet startup, First-e, was established in 1999, intended to be international, with an initial presence in the UK, Germany, Italy, France and Spain. It failed to be successful and had closed down by 2001. 'egg', though heavily loss-making since its founding in 1998, finally broke into profit in the final quarter of 2001. It offers a wide range of deposit and loan accounts, credit cards, insurance and investment products as well as a 'shopping zone', where over 250 retailers have space on the 'egg' website to proffer their wares (which can, of course, be paid for using the 'egg' credit card or perhaps with an 'egg' personal loan!)

France has an on-line banking facility which has its roots in a system called 'Videotex', developed much earlier than the Internet. This is commonplace because the government decided to give a boost to communication links by supplying free 'Minitel' terminals using the television set. One early use was to make telephone directory enquiries, but other information services were soon added. There are 5m Minitel subscribers. The banks supply software allowing balance reporting, enquiry of historical data and transfer of funds to creditors' accounts. More advanced software allows portfolio management and various financial calculations.

Clearing Systems

Clearing involves the transmission, exchange and settlement for payments between banks. There are clearing systems for both *paper* (for example, cheques) and *electronic* clearing. Usually, the central bank is involved to provide for inter bank settlement and overall control of the process, but the extent of the involvement differs greatly from country to country.

In the US, the Federal Reserve runs 48 cheque clearing centres. There are also private clearing centres and arrangements made mutually between groups of banks. 30% of cheques are cleared internally by the banks on which they were drawn; 35% are cleared by private centres and mutual arrangements and 35% cleared by the Federal Reserve.

For salaries, standing orders, direct debits and supplier payments, data is encoded electronically and sent to an Automated Clearing House (ACH). For example, having processed salaries by computer and printed payslips for the employees, a corporate will send the data over to an ACH. Here, it will be sorted electronically and passed to the relevant employees' banks so that their salaries can be credited. There are 33 ACHs run by the Federal Reserve and a few are privately operated.

All Federal Reserve System Offices are linked for balance transfers between member banks by a system called *Fedwire*. The New York Clearing Houses Association runs CHIPS, an interbank funds transfer system in New York, and used for large international as opposed to domestic dollar payments.

In France, there are over 100 provincial clearing houses in towns where a branch of the Bank of France is located. If presented within the same catchment area as the bank on which it is drawn, the cheque will usually clear on the second working day after the presentation. Outside the catchment area, the bank will clear on the fifth working day after presentation.

Six banks have their own bilateral clearing arrangements.

Electronic clearing takes place through SIT (Système Interbancaire Télé-compensation). It is run by the Bank of France, which operates nine centres but policy is decided by the Bankers' Association.

In the UK, all clearing has been controlled since 1985 by a body called the 'Association for Payment Clearing Services' (APACS). The Bank of England provides settlement between the banks resulting from the payment flows between them. APACS runs three main systems:

- General Cheque Clearing (usually 3 working days in total)
- CHAPS
- Bankers' Automated Clearing Services (BACS).

CHAPS means 'Clearing Houses Automated Payments Systems' and is a same day interbank clearing system for high value electronic entries in sterling. In January 1999, CHAPS-Euro was added as a parallel system for euro-denominated payments.

BACS is for salaries, standing orders, direct debits and supplier payments just like the ACHs in the US. It is by far the largest such operation in the world, handling some 2.5 billion items in 2001.

Cross-border clearing is a subject attracting a lot of attention. In September 1990, the European Commission published a paper on cross-border cash and electronic payments. It acknowledged that the lack of a single compatible system would be a drawback in the age of the single market.

A group of European cooperative banks have set up a system called TIPA-NET (Transferts Interbancaires de Paiements Automatisés).

Giro clearing organisations in 14 countries have set up a cross-border transfer system called Eurogiro which started in November 1992. European savings banks have set up their own network called Eufiserv with links in ten countries.

Commerzbank, Société Générale, Credito Italiano and National Westminster have started their own cross-border transfer system called Relay.

The Royal Bank of Scotland and Banco Santander have started a joint system – IBOS. This would enable a Royal Bank customer who had pesetas to transfer them to a Spanish customer's account on the same day. The system is on offer to other banks and Crédit Commercial de France and Banco de Comercio e Industria have joined as well as ING Bank and the US merged bank First Union/First Fidelity.

Finally, it might be possible to link national ACH systems like CHAPS (UK), SIT (France), SIS (Switzerland), EAF (Germany), etc.

The plethora of independent and incompatible systems does not instil confidence for the future of an efficient system for cross-border payments, and there is already disappointment that, within Europe's new monetary union, cross-border payments in the euro are neither easier nor cheaper.

Key Retail Banking Issues

Across all the Western financial markets, the commercial banks face a series of key challenges. They are:

1. Growing competition
2. Cost control
3. Sales of non-banking products
4. Use of Information Technology.

Growing competition   Banks face growing competition from:

❑ Other financial institutions
❑ Retailers
❑ Insurance companies
❑ In-house corporate facilities.

Growing deregulation has meant an increase in competition from *other financial institutions* previously precluded from offering a total banking service. This includes the Savings and Loan Associations in the US; building societies in the UK; savings banks generally; post office banks in some sectors; and mutual funds which also offer savings accounts. The competition for deposits has intensified and we see the banks in Spain and the UK offering interest on credit balances for the first time.

Banks and Savings and Loan Associations in the US are estimated to have 28% of the financial services market – half the figure of 20 years ago.

Retailers are increasingly active. In Germany, the huge mail order group, Quelle, is offering a range of financial services, including credit cards. In Italy, Benetton are part of a major financial group, Euromobiliare. In Sweden, the furniture company, Ikea, offers current account facilities. In the UK, Marks and Spencer offer unsecured loans, mutual funds and life insurance. Key supermarkets, like Tesco and Sainsbury's, have offered bank accounts. However, no cheque book facilities are offered, thus avoiding one of the key expenses of retail banking.

Insurance companies are competing vigorously for savings with schemes which link life assurance with a savings product. These often involve the use of mutual funds to improve the return on the fund. While this is not new, pressure has intensified in recent years. Some are forming banks. The Swedish Trygg Hansa launched a bank in mid-October 1995 and merged with Denmark's second largest bank in 1999. The UK's largest life assurance and investment group, the Prudential Corporation, launched its own bank (which transformed itself into 'egg') with loss-making interest rates in late 1998, and within 6 months had 500,000 customers and £5bn in deposits – but losses of £175m! The plan is to sell these customers lots of other financial products. As the loss-leading interest rates were brought into line with the market (though still very competitive), 'egg' lost some of the 'hot' funds and customers, but it seems to have generated a self-sustaining business from a wide set of product offerings as time has gone by, and finally broke into profit in the last quarter of 2001.

In-house corporate 'banks' are now very common – Ford Motor Credit, Renault Crédit International, ICI Finance, Gemina (the Fiat financial services group) and General Electric Financial Services, to mention a few. While the largest effect here is usually on the banks' *wholesale* business, many are active in retail finance also. The General Electric subsidiary, for example, is into consumer loans and credit cards as well as leasing, real estate and corporate finance. It has annual revenues in excess of $30 billion and accounts for 40% of the earnings of its parent.

Cost control Growing competition has made cost control even more important. Increasingly, the banks' annual reports are referring to their success (or lack of it) in cutting the cost/income ratio and increasing the return of capital on equity.

There is room for improvement. US banks' cost/income ratio averages 58%, but is nearer 70% in France, Germany and Italy. Not surprisingly, return on equity in the US is 16% as against less than 10% in France, Germany and Italy. The UK comes out well with an average of about 25%.

In retail banking, a major cost is the branch network. What we have seen in recent years is rationalisation and branch automation. Rationalisation means dividing branches into those which only deal with corporates, full service branches (offering the complete range of products) and local sub-branches, which are largely points for paying in cash and withdrawing it. 'Branch automation' involves withdrawing paperwork to regional centres and making more of the branch a 'front office' for dealing with customers. For example, HSBC in the UK has settled on eight key centres which have cheque sorting machines which can handle 60,000 items per hour. The 1200 people in these centres have replaced 3000 who were in local branches. The UK's Lloyds TSB has taken a slightly different approach, with 70 processing centres for branch paperwork. A more recent development is the out sourcing of parts of these operational activities to special purpose companies independent of the banks. It is believed that these can be more cost effective, often resulting from economies of scale and the application of specialist expertise. However, the banks have to specify very carefully the scope of the services and the expected performance criteria in these arrangements. This is because it has been made clear by the Financial Services Authority that the banks themselves are totally responsible for the smooth and secure operations of the clearing systems. A general response to a fall in business has been a ruthless cutting of staff in those economies where labour laws permit this. It is much harder in continental Europe, where cost-cutting is hampered by restrictive labour laws, combative unions and, in some cases, sympathetic politicians. Things may be changing, albeit slowly. In Switzerland, for example, a fifth of bank branches have been closed since the mid-1990s. On the other hand, in Germany and France the number of bank branches and staff has hardly changed, in spite of several mergers. In Germany, banks have twice as many branches per head as in the US.

In the US, in-store branches now exist in more than 1400 supermarkets. The First National Bank of Chicago is putting ATMs into McDonald's hamburger stores and other outlets. In Finland, Merita has developed a 'Customer Service Centre' which can handle standing orders, giro transfers and bank statements. These are not only being installed in branches but warehouses, supermarkets and kiosks. In Italy, the San Paolo Bank has designed a 'Bancomat' with the aid of Olivetti. This is the automated branch with ATMs and video disc machines selling insurance and giving share quotations. Banca Commerciale Italiana has a similar scheme, the Banca Non-Stop. The UK Co-operative movement plans to install 350 advanced ATM machines in Co-op stores all over Britain, linked by satellites. In the UK, again, the 20,000 bank and building society branches of 1987 were down to 16,500 ten years later.

The UK is still very wedded to expensive cheques and has not made as much progress with electronic banking as many countries. Things are changing, however, and the current projections of the UK clearing body APACS are shown in Figure 4.1.

The question of the future of branches is a major dilemma for the banks. Existing branches and their reorganisation are absorbing large sums of money, but in, say, ten years, how many branches will be needed? How fast will the so-called 'information superhighway' start to have a major impact?

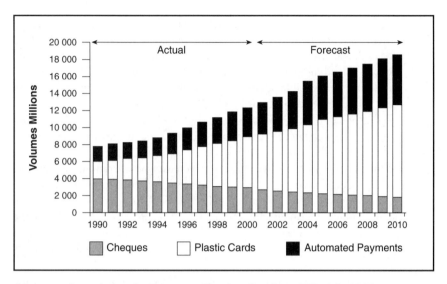

Source: Association for Payment Clearing Services, UK, July 1999.
Figure 4.1 *UK cheque, plastic card and automated transaction volumes, 1990–2010*

Deloitte Consulting did a report in April 1999 projecting that a further 3600 bank branches in the UK will be redundant by 2005, as banks use on-line banking services, telephone banking and other cut-price distribution models. On the other hand, a KPMG survey of 45 banks in six countries published in 1997 found that most expected 'little change' in the number of bank transactions up to 2002. Young people were happy to use PCs, telephone banking and the Internet, but older people were not as ready to change. Amazingly, 25% of customers surveyed used a branch instead of an ATM, and 40% could not see themselves using a PC or any interactive service for banking information.

In the US, a growing number of mergers and repeal of the McFadden Act prohibiting branches in different states has led to a major change. The 14,000 banks of the mid 1980s were down to about 9000 by 15 years later. The top ten now account for two thirds of bank assets, as opposed to half in the 1970s. The merged Bank America–Nationsbank takes 7% of all deposits and is active in 23 states. Banks are now less susceptible to local shocks (for example oil prices in Texas).

Mention of this leads us to the growing trend of mergers or cooperation with other banks. The list in Appendix 2 to Chapter 2 shows the large number of mergers in recent years. Many of these are very large – Dai Ichi Kangyo, Fuji and IBJ; Bank of Tokyo and Mitsubishi; Swiss Bank Corporation and the Union Bank of Switzerland; Chemical Bank and Chase Manhattan, who later merged with JP Morgan; Bank America and Nationsbank; Citicorp and Travellers Group (100 million accounts worldwide!); Deutsche Bank and Bankers Trust; Banco Santander and BCH; BBV and Argentaria; Bayerische Vereinsbank and Bayerische Hypo Bank. After a bitter battle with the Bank of Scotland, the Royal Bank of Scotland succeeded in the takeover of the UK's National Westminster Bank. Subsequently, the Bank of Scotland merged with the Halifax Bank, to make HBOS.

As an example of possible savings in costs, the mergers of Chemical, Manny Hanny and Chase resulted in savings of $2.5bn per annum.

Mergers do not, of course, necessarily go well. Wells Fargo, once a highly rated bank, bought First Interstate. Hit by service problems, many customers left and its share price fell heavily.

In addition to those mergers, we are seeing increasing cooperation. Cooperative banks are arranging for cooperative banks in other countries to offer services to their customers when abroad. A group called 'Unico' links cooperatives in the Netherlands, France, Germany, Finland and Austria. Between them, they have 37,000 branches in these six countries. In 1990, 15 European savings bank institutions jointly launched three mutual funds, covering money markets, bonds and equities.

Banco Santander and the Royal Bank of Scotland have taken a small shareholding in each other's company. They offer mutual services to their client base, have opened a bank in Gibraltar and have set up an electronic money transfer system. Other examples of cooperation include Lloyds TSB Bank and Banco Bilbao-Vizcaya, and Portugal's BCP and Spain's Banco Popular jointly setting up a bank in France (Banco Popular Comercial).

Sales of non-banking products   Another way to reduce the costs of branches is to make them more productive by selling more services. Some of these are products like insurance or mutual funds which might not have been regarded as classic banking products at one time. Other activities include acquisition of travel agencies and estate agencies.

If banking is less profitable and costs are rising, then the banks must increase their selling and marketing skills and promote a wider range of offerings than in the past. Part of the aim of branch automation is to use terminals to give access to all the information needed on the full range of the bank's services. For example, TSB have installed computer terminals with coloured screens which give the details and advantages of all the bank products and will even produce an application form.

Banks now look at their customer base as being divided into social sectors, each with their own needs:

❑ Pre-teens – can we get them used to the bank's brand with piggy bank money boxes?

❑ Teenagers – high spending. Banks offer savings accounts, ATM cards and merchandise discounts.

❑ Young marrieds – no children yet, high joint incomes but a change to come as children arrive.

❏ High net worth – young professionals with high incomes – worth a special approach.
❏ Over 50s – children have now grown up, wives are back at work, houses paid for – but retirement looms!
❏ Retired people – often with high incomes from personal pension plans and savings. This group has special needs.

The above breakdown has preoccupied banks in many countries, resulting in the design of new bank accounts and mail order marketing which was previously associated with consumer products.

Backing up this effort are large customer databases on computer containing not just accounting information but background details to enable the bank to sell new services, either now or later. In retail banking, 'cross-selling' has become the key phrase of the moment.

HBOS in the UK (Bank of Scotland and Halifax, a former building society) claims 77% of business from core mortgages and 23% from life assurance and consumer lending. It plans to reduce mortgages as a share of business to 50% within 10 years. In the US, commissions of one kind or another now account for about 40% of bank revenues.

One product of obvious relevance is insurance – life assurance, endowment policies, assurance products backing mortgages, householder policies, building policies, sickness cover and so on. We are seeing three major trends here. One is full mergers with insurance companies; another is closer cooperation in cross-selling each other's products; and a third is banks setting up full insurance subsidiaries.

In the Netherlands, the ING group merged with NMB-Postbank and later bought BBL and Baring Bros; Trygg Baltica has merged with Unidanmark and SE Banken; Halifax bought Clerical and Medical; Kredietbank/Cera merged with ABB Insurance.

Cooperation includes arrangements for cross-selling between the Swiss Bank Corporation and Zurich Insurance; Dresdner Bank and Allianz; Banco Popular and Allianz; BNP and the French insurer UAP; Banco Santander and Metropolitan Life.

Banks that have set up full insurance subsidiaries include Lloyds TSB, National Westminster, Deutsche, Barclays, Crédit Lyonnais, Banco Bilbao-Vizcaya, Monte dei Paschi di Siena and Crédit Agricole. Crédit Agricole's subsidiary, Predica, has moved into France's top three insurance companies since its formation in 1987. Monte Paschi Vita, set up in mid-1991, collected L200 billion in premium income in the first 6 months. By the end of 1997, it was estimated that French banks had 60% of the life insurance market.

Regarding the cooperative ventures, one element of doubt may be creeping in. The evidence suggests that the banks are much more successful at selling insurance products than the insurance companies are at selling banking services! These links between banks and insurance have led to much use of the French phrase 'Bancassurance' and the German phrase 'Allfinanz'.

The growing effort to sell mutual funds, insurance, stocks, shares and other products has led to a rise in fee and commission income as opposed to interest. The desire to improve profits and control costs has also led to the banks increasingly charging fees for such things as arranging loans/overdrafts, an interview with the bank manager, sending an extra copy of a statement and so on.

Use of Information Technology   Modern banking is unthinkable without the use of Information Technology (IT). Without it, the numbers needing to be employed in banking would have made the expansion of the last 30 years quite impossible. Many of the developments we have discussed above have IT at their heart. Branch automation, new account databases, telephone and home banking, EFT-POS, automated electronic clearing – all are essential to the banks' new strategies and all involve a large investment. Looking at the emerging markets in Central and Eastern Europe and the former Soviet Union, an enormous expenditure on computers and communications infrastructures is required as an essential first step in setting up modern banking systems. As John Reed, Chairman of Citicorp, has put it, 'money is information on the move'.

One area with IT at its heart is, of course, the Internet. Early hopes (by some) for a massive migration to the Internet, with commensurate low costs, appear to be misplaced. It looks more likely that the Internet will take its place as an important delivery method alongside branches and call centres as part of a multi channel strategy for most banks. This would seem to give an advantage to the larger, established banks, who have the financial resources and spread of customers to justify the expenditure in the different systems.

A Booz-Allen & Hamilton survey of comparative transaction costs in the US has estimated the following figures:

PC banking	13¢
Telephone	26¢
Branch	$1.08

The UK building societies have produced similar estimates for the UK:

Internet	8p
Telephone	35p
Branch	70p

Could the threat be exaggerated?   With all that has been written about the problems facing retail banking, could the threat from new entrants be exaggerated? For example, the profit of Marks and Spencer's financial division after some 16 years is about £96m. Tesco, the UK supermarket, is spending £50m on setting up its banking division. Assume a profit of 20% and the result is £10m. Compare these to Lloyds TSB's profit of £4.4bn for 2001. Internet banking will come and may be offered by non-banks (for example, computer and telecommunications companies), but progress is slow. For the present, retail banking still has stability and profitability. Other problems for commercial banks lie in the realm of *wholesale banking*, and that is our next topic.

WHOLESALE BANKING

Wholesale banking includes a bank's wholesale lending, which will be discussed now, and other activities which will be covered in later chapters: money markets, Chapter 6; foreign exchange, Chapter 8; trade finance, Chapter 9.

BANK LENDING

We can begin by breaking bank lending down into uncommitted facilities and committed facilities.

Uncommitted Facilities

Here there is little formal documentation and no network of various fees to be paid to the bank for setting up the facility. The bank agrees to lend money, usually on a short-term basis, but is not committed to renew the loan. The facilities are typically on a 'revolving' basis, that is, the client can repay the loan and then redraw money. There are three types:

Overdrafts This is a great UK favourite with smaller firms. The client is allowed to overdraw up to a given maximum figure. Interest is charged daily on the overdrawn balance, most typically at bank base rates (not LIBOR) plus a given margin. The arrangement may be for, say, 6 months. The bank is not bound to renew the agreement but may well do so. There is no formal arrangement for 'paying back' as there would be with a normal loan. In addition, the overdraft is legally repayable on demand (if necessary).

Lines of credit Here the bank agrees to allow the client to borrow up to a maximum sum for periods such as a month, 3 months or 6 months. The rate of interest will be related to the interbank rate. The client can then repay and reborrow if required.

Bankers' acceptances Here the bank agrees to accept bills of exchange up to a maximum figure – 'acceptance credits'. The bank accepts a bill and may also discount it, or the client may discount it with another bank. If the bill is, say, 1 month, the client is expected to repay but may do so by means of discounting another bill. If the bank discounts the bill, it may keep it on its books or itself sell it in the discount market. The best bills are *bank* or *eligible* bills. These bills:

(a) Are recognised as top quality by the central bank.
(b) Must represent a genuine trade transaction and one of a type not excluded, for example, property and insurance.

Eligible bills are eligible for sale to the central bank in its role of 'lender of last resort'. As a result, they are highly liquid.

There are thus bills signed by a bank *not* on the central bank list and these are 'ineligible bank bills'. There are also bills signed by the trader and, therefore, 'trade bills'. However, the trader may be more creditworthy than some banks on the central bank's list! Nevertheless, the central bank still won't rediscount them.

The above three types of facility are not committed. They are also usually 'self-liquidating'. For example, a bill matures in 1 month and is repaid. The loan is often to support the working capital required for debtors and/or stocks. A swimsuit manufacturer begins producing well before the season – stocks are built up and wages must be paid. As the swimsuits are sold, cash flows in and loans can be repaid.

Committed Facilities

The loan facilities here are typically for 1 year or more. The bank is committed to lend, there are formal loan agreements and a structure of fees. There are three main types and one special case – Project Finance.

Term loans   The term loan is typically up to 5 years but may be up to 7. The loan is amortised over the period, that is, the borrower pays back in stages, although there may be an initial 'grace' period. Sometimes the loan is payable in full at the end of the period – this is 'bullet' repayment. The interest is floating rate, linked to the interbank rate. The money borrowed cannot be relent when part is repaid.

Standby credit   Here, the loan can be drawn down in stages or tranches without losing the availability of the undrawn section. Once repaid, however, the money cannot be reborrowed. It tends to be much shorter term than a term loan and may support other anticipated borrowings, for example, commercial paper. The standby credit may not even be drawn if the 'normal' borrowing method is successful.

The programme will be broken down into the total maximum commitment, the used amount and the unused. Thus, a $200m programme can be drawn down in tranches but repayments cannot be reborrowed. The banker's schedule as time goes by might be as shown in Table 4.2.

Table 4.2   *Drawing banker's commitment down in tranches*

		Total commitment $m	Used $m	Unused $m
1/1	Agreement	200	–	200
2/1	Borrows $75m	200	75	125
31/1	Borrows $25m	200	100	100
12/2	Repays $50m	200	100	100
1/5	Borrows $100m	200	200	–
1/7	Repays $100m	200	200	–
1/10	Repays $50m	200	200	–
1/1	Expiry	–	–	–

Note: Interest is floating rate linked to the interbank rate – LIBOR, EURIBOR, – or, in the US, 'Prime Rate'.

Revolving credit   Here, not only can the loan be drawn in tranches but, if repayments are made, the borrower can repay up to the limit: that is, the funds can be reused. Thus, the commitment is said to 'revolve' – the borrower can continue to request loans provided the committed total is not exceeded. The client gives the bank the appropriate notice and then reborrows within the terms of the agreement. If the amount were $200m, we can see the difference between this and the standby credit when we study a similar loan/repayment schedule in Table 4.3.

Generally these loans are unsecured. If bankers take security, it could well be one of the following: property, accounts receivable, plant/equipment, bonds/shares, bills of lading, inventories.

If the money is raised in the London market, the loans are floating rate 'linked to LIBOR' – but what is LIBOR (London Interbank Offered Rate)? To begin with, LIBOR fluctuates throughout the day. For purposes of loan agreements, LIBOR is that stated by the reference bank(s) at 11.00 a.m. If the loan is bilateral, it may simply be the lending bank's own LIBOR at 11.00 a.m. on the quarterly or 6 monthly day on which the loan is 'rolled over' at a new rate of interest. If it is a syndicated loan, three 'reference' banks may be nominated and LIBOR is the average of the three. It may also be quoted as the 'BBA', or colloquially the 'screen rate'. The British Bankers' Association list 16 reference banks. Telerate omits the four highest and four lowest of the 16 quoted rates and averages the remaining eight. Telerate disseminates this on their dealing screens at 11.00 a.m. each day – hence the reference to the 'screen' rate. LIBOR, of course may be sterling, dollar, yen, or any other currency. If the currency is the euro it is EUROLIBOR, not to be confused with EURIBOR, which is the interbank market in euros of the twelve countries of the monetary union.

Table 4.3   *Loan/repayment schedule*

		Total commitment $m	Used $m	Unused $m
1/1	Agreement	200	—	200
2/1	Borrows $75m	200	75	125
31/1	Borrows $25m	200	100	100
12/2	Repays $50m	200	50	150
1/5	Borrows $100m	200	150	50
1/7	Repays $100m	200	50	150
1/9	Borrows $75m	200	125	75
1/10	Repays $100m	200	25	175

Note: Interest is floating rate linked to the interbank rate.

A term often used in the loan documentation for standby and revolving credit is 'swingline facility'. Sometimes the borrower is due to repay investors in, say, dollars on a particular day and discovers late in the day that they cannot. Swingline is a guarantee of same day dollars in New York to meet this emergency need. (It may not be dollars, but dollars seem to be common.) One banker has described this as 'belt and braces' and reassuring to credit ratings organisations looking at an issuer's loan facilities.

As the bank commits to lend, whether the user draws it all or not and as there is a formal agreement, there are *fees* involved.

There will be a *front end* or *facility fee* for setting up the arrangement. There will also be a *commitment* fee. For example, a bank supports a 3 year standby credit facility for $50m which is never used. The bank has committed some of its loan capacity and used up capital under capital ratio rules. As a result, commitment fees are often charged on the undrawn amount. They are typically 50% of the lending margin. The *margin* is the spread over LIBOR charged on the drawn amount itself, for example, LIBOR + 50 basis points, or bp. (A basis point = $\frac{1}{100}$% or 0.01%.) For example, in April 1999, OTE, the Greek telecommunications operator, arranged a $1bn 5 year revolving credit at 30 bp over LIBOR with a commitment fee of 15 bp.

There are variations for commitment fees by which they may be charged on the whole facility or on the drawn amount *and* the undrawn amount (but at different rates). A recent loan to the Saudi European Petrochemicals Corporation referred to 25 basis points on drawn balances and 12.5 basis points on undrawn balances.

As we have seen in Chapter 3, the central bank may make all banks deposit some of their eligible liabilities with the Bank and pays them no interest. As bankers relend their deposits, they regard this as a cost of lending and will seek to recoup this.

Project finance   This is simply a special case of a term loan. It is 'special' in that the projects are typically of much longer duration than the conventional term loan, and usually much more complex to structure. They are large-scale exploration or construction projects (for example, Eurotunnel, the bridge over the Bosphorus and similar projects) and require complex and time consuming loan arrangements. In particular, a guarantee from a government or parent body may not be available (the banks' recourse is to the flow of funds from the project, called 'limited recourse financing') in which case the banks will want to see a full set of revenue projections to ensure that debt repayments can be met. They may also wish to see firm contracts for the construction project itself and (if possible) firm contracts for the sale of the completed service.

Recent projects include a 10 year $400m facility for Nesté Petroleum, a wholly owned subsidiary of a Finnish state-owned oil company; a $1.1bn facility for oil exploration for BP Norway; $600m for North Sea oil developments for Agip (UK), part of the Italian state-owned oil group and the Teesside Power Station project – £795 million with the loan to continue until 2008.

In the case of Nesté, while there is no explicit guarantee, there is a tacit understanding that the parent will support the subsidiary. The Agip loan will be supported by the parent for 2 years but revert to limited recourse thereafter.

Teesside Power is a huge gas power station being constructed at Wilton, Teesside. Finance was first secured from 14 underwriters and then went out to syndication. The margin over LIBOR is 125 bp up to completion of the station, 112.5 bp after that up to 8 years and 137 bp for the remaining years. However, these margins may be reduced, depending upon hitting performance targets. Semi-annual loan repayments began in April 1994. This is one of the largest and most involved limited recourse projects.

Syndicated Facilities

Syndicated loans arise because a bank does not wish to take on the whole amount of the loan. The task of syndication is also made easier by the fact that there are many banks that will be happy to take on some of the loan exposure at a second stage – banks that may not have a close relationship with major corporates or may not have the resources to compete at the primary stage.

Syndicated loans (sometimes involving as many as 100 banks) were common in the 1970s, when we saw 'petro-dollars' recycled in loans to sovereign borrowers and multinationals. This led to the LDC debt crisis, following Mexico's default in August 1982 (see Chapter 6). The volumes of large international syndicated loans fell somewhat for several years but recovered later. Many banks found that weakened balance sheets and capital ratio constraints made further loan expansion difficult. One result was the rise to popularity after 1982 of new types of syndicated facility – NIFs and RUFs.

NIFs and RUFs   The 1980s became the era of the acronym – NIFs and RUFs, and later MOFs and many others. It was also a time of great competition, especially from Japanese banks. In 1986, the then chairman of Barclays accused the Japanese of 'dumping money', just as people had accused them of dumping goods in the 1920s and 1930s. NIF is 'Note Issuance Facility' and RUF is 'Revolving Underwriting Facility' (ask six bankers what the difference is and you will get six different answers!).

This was also a time in which we saw an increasing use of tender panels of banks, bidding competitively for loan business or bankers' acceptances. For example, a corporate which used bill finance frequently would periodically approach a tender panel to accept bills. This gave us yet another acronym – the RAFT, 'Revolving Acceptance Facility by Tender'.

NIFs and RUFs were facilities by which banks agreed to support note issues by corporates to raise money. The notes were usually called 'Euronotes' and were typically 1, 3 and 6 months. In effect, they were a sort of short-term eurobond. On a revolving basis, the arranging bank would approach a tender panel to buy the client's notes. In the event that the notes could not be sold at or below a given lending rate, a further panel of underwriting banks stood by to lend the money. The facility was thus underwritten. It was, therefore, a mixture of commercial and investment banking techniques. Fees could be earned and US commercial banks could join in without contravening the 1933 Glass-Steagall Act. During the period 1982–86, NIFs, RUFs and Euronotes were all the rage.

Today, the formal 1, 3 and 6 month Euronote has disappeared, its modern equivalent being either Eurocommercial paper or medium-term notes. (The Bank of England uses Euronotes as a generic term for short-term Euro paper, whether ECDs or ECP.)

MOFs   From 1986–87, a more flexible facility – the MOF – appeared. This is 'Multiple Option Facility'. Instead of committing the underwriting banks to support one type of borrowing only (for example, Euronotes), the banks' commitment is to a range of possibilities. The 'multiple options' might be:

❑   Bank loan (multi-currency)
❑   Acceptances
❑   Commercial paper – domestic
❑   Eurocommercial paper.

On a revolving basis, the arranging bank would approach a tender panel of banks for prices for either a bank loan or banker's acceptance to meet the client's need for, say, $10m for 3 months. At the same time, the arranging bank would contact commercial paper dealers to check rates for the same deal. The bank would then report back to the client and use the most attractive option. However, if the best option was above a given borrowing rate, a panel of underwriting banks would agree either to lend the money or sign acceptances at the agreed figure. At first this seemed to be the sort of flexible facility that the market needed and MOFs were all the rage for several years. Later, problems emerged.

To begin with, bank supervisors saw this as a clear off-balance sheet risk and demanded capital cover. Suppose, for example, that the rate at which the underwriting panel would guarantee to lend was LIBOR + 50 bp. The supervisors argued that if the market demanded a higher figure, this might suggest that the client was less creditworthy. The underwriting panel was forced to lend to a client whose credit quality was declining. The Bank of England decided that 50% of the unused capacity must be treated as if the money had actually been lent, for capital ratio purposes. The Bundesbank took a less harsh view. Later, the rules were harmonised through the Basle agreement. The first disadvantage, therefore, was that the banks had to provide capital to back MOFs, although initially they hadn't.

The recession produced other problems. To begin with, the credit quality of many clients did indeed deteriorate, leaving the underwriting banks 'holding the baby'. Secondly, due to poor trading, many clients broke the loan covenants (see later). If covenants are broken, the whole agreement can be renegotiated but *all* the banks must agree the revised terms. Sometimes, one or two banks with the smallest commitment might not agree. In a famous incident in 1989, Laura Ashley was nearly pushed into liquidation in these circumstances.

Finally, the market became less competitive – a lenders' not a borrowers' market. In part, this was due to the departure of the Japanese. The stock market in Tokyo collapsed in January 1990 and property values fell. The Japanese drew in their horns. In 1989, they accounted for 37% of all international bank lending in foreign currencies (BIS figures). In 1998, the figure was 18.5%. The departure of the Japanese, capital ratio constraints and the recession now put the banks into the driving seat. They were no longer willing to be pushed into tender panels and unattractive deals. In London, margins over LIBOR widened as a consequence. Corporates, too, saw the problems. Beating down the banks to tight margins was one thing. Expecting them to be sympathetic when the going got rough was quite another. There was much talk of 'relationship banking' – of this more later. The OECD, in its *Financial Market Trends* for June 1992, commented on the change in the syndicated credit market and the fall in the number of syndicated facilities: 'uncertainties about the creditworthiness of many potential borrowers added to the caution of financial institutions engaged in a process of profit enhancement and asset quality consolidation.'

With the end of the recession in the West, banks were flush with cash again in 1995 and, although the MOF concept had largely disappeared, margins on loans fell again. Then, the 1997/98 global crises led to margins rising yet again! For example, PowerGen of the UK raised a £2.4bn 5 year loan in mid 1998 to purchase East Midlands Electricity at a rate of 50 bp over LIBOR. However, its previous syndicated loan had been at 22.5 bp over LIBOR. Equally, the bid for Inter-Continental Hotels by Bass was funded by a $3bn syndicated loan at a range of margins over LIBOR (depending on the loan term). The range was 22½ bp to 27½ bp; its previous loan – a margin of 15 bp.

It can be seen from the above that many of these loans are for takeover bids. In addition to the above, we have Vodafone looking for $14bn to help take over Air-Touch, Olivetti looking for €22.5bn to fund its bitterly opposed takeover of Telecom Italia, and banks committing €41bn to Elf Aquitaine for its takeover bid for TotalFina.

To make things more flexible, the banks have organised a formal secondary market in which loan commitments may be sold off to other banks. Bank loans are frequently traded in the US, but until recently Europe was well behind. This particularly applies to what is called 'distressed debt'.

A 'Loan Market Association' was set up in London by seven banks in December 1996. It now has 100 banks as full members and 43 institutions as associate members. According to Barclays Capital, trading volume reached $30bn in 1998 compared with $3bn in 1992.

ICI's $8.5bn syndicated loan in 1997 was a watershed, as $1bn was traded within 6 months.

A code of conduct was issued for trading distressed debt in March 1999. This category includes, for example, EuroDisneyland, Eurotunnel and Queens Moat Houses. The risky loan has become just another product!

Syndicated loans are usually more flexible than bond issues. The money can be drawn down as needed, and arrangements may be made more quickly. The latter can be important in takeover bid situations.

Terminology   The facilities we mentioned earlier – term loans, standby credits and revolving credits – are usually syndicated. This leads to a variety of terms being used:

1. *Arranger/Lead manager*   Initially, the 'arranging bank' or 'lead manager' deals with the client and discusses the probable terms on which a loan can be arranged. They advise the borrower on the loan structure, maturity and covenants. The arranger will coordinate the participation of other lenders. It may be, however, that a 'book-runner' is appointed. Their job is to do the 'leg work' of putting a syndicate together. Once the syndicate is together, the book-runner's role is finished. One way or another, once initial discussions with the client are concluded, an invitation is issued to co-managers to participate.

2. *Co-managers*   Along with the arranging bank, they agree to underwrite the loan so that the client is now guaranteed the funds. Each co-manager takes a share – for example, $200m.

3. *Participating banks*   They now join the syndicate. A co-manager will invite, perhaps, four participating banks to take, say, $25m of the loan each.

4. *The agent*   The role of the bank acting as the agent bank is critically important and a special fee is earned. The agency is an administrative role. The agent collects the loan from each participant and passes it to the borrower. Equally, the borrower payments as made are passed to the syndicate in agreed shares. The agent notifies the borrower of the new interest rate related to the interbank rate every 3 or 6 months as agreed. The agent is responsible for the documentation and will notify both borrower and lender of all information relevant to the loan agreement. There is no credit risk but there is still risk. If the agent makes a mistake that loses the syndicate members money, they will be responsible for making this good.

As in the case of a bilateral loan, there will be various fees:

1. *Facility or front end fee*   For agreeing to the arrangement, there will be a front end or facility fee for all involved. This may be a flat fee or a percentage of the money. The arranging bank will also take an extra fee for their special role. This is called a *praecipium*.

2. *Underwriting fees*   These are paid to the group of underwriting banks which took on the initial commitment prior to extending the syndicate. There is a definite risk. In the case of the management buyout of Magnet Joinery, for example, a small group of lead banks led by Bankers Trust found themselves alone as the potential syndicate members withdrew their support, sensing that the risk was unacceptable – very wisely as it happened!

3. *Agent's fee*   This is paid to the agent bank for the role they play, which was described earlier.

4. *Commitment fee*   This was mentioned before in the case of bilateral loans. It is a payment measured in basis points for the commitment to lend which needs to be backed by capital. As we have seen, it may be based on the whole loan, the drawn section, or the undrawn section (or a mixture). Usually the fee is on the undrawn section and typically 50% of the margin (see 5 below).
5. *Loan margin*   This is the actual margin over the interbank rate charged for the borrowed money, for example, LIBOR + 50 bp. It may not be a constant figure but related to loan tranches taken by the syndicate.

While commitment fees are usually 50% of the margin, any variation is possible. For example, the German Thyssen Group arranged a $1.2 billion 7 year revolving credit facility. There was a front end fee of 8 basis points and the margin over LIBOR varies according to how much of the facility is used. For example, 10 basis points if less than 33% of the loan but 20 basis points if more than 66% is used.

The NIFs, RUFs and MOFs were all forms of revolving credit. In general, the term loan, standby credit, revolving credit and project finance are likely to involve syndicates, unless they are of modest size.

The fierce competitive battles of the 1980s, however, have led to much talk of 'relationship banking' and bilateral agreements.

Relationship banking   The inference here is that the corporate encourages a close relationship with a small number of banks and may negotiate bilaterally.

Bilateral agreements, however, can really only be used by corporates with skilled treasury departments with large resources, unless the number of banks is very small. The work done by the agency bank in policing the loan should not be underestimated. A 30 bank syndicate means, for the corporate, one line of communication – the agent bank, which does the rest. 30 bilateral agreements mean 30 lines of communication – one with each bank.

The Loan Agreement

If the loan is syndicated, there will be one loan agreement and one set of terms but the amount owed to each borrower is a separate debt.

The loan agreement will typically have four sections:

1. *Introduction*   This will cover the amount of the loan and its purpose, conditions of drawdown and particulars of the participating banks.
2. *Facilities*   The loan may be drawn down in separate tranches with different terms on interest and repayment. The procedures for drawing down will be covered.
3. *Payment*   This covers the interest calculations, calculation of the interbank rate, repayment arrangements, fees, or any similar charges.
4. *Provisions*   To protect the bank there will be covenants, events of default, procedures if basic circumstances change.

The final documentation is sent to the agent bank prior to drawing the money. The agent must ensure that the documentation embodies that which was agreed.

Covenants These are designed to protect the bank if the 'health' of the borrower changes. If covenants are breached, the banks' commitment will cease. The loan will have to be rescheduled. The usual covenants are:

❑ *Interest cover* This is the relationship between profit (before tax and interest) and interest. This is to ensure that there is a comfortable margin over the loan interest. If there is not, how can the borrower repay the principal? Sometimes cash flow may be used instead of profit. After all, profit is not cash!

❑ *Net worth* Suppose all assets were sold and liabilities paid, what is left? Normally, this should be the figure of share capital and reserves ± current profit/loss, minus goodwill, tax and dividends to be paid. The agreement stipulates a minimum net worth.

❑ *Total borrowing* This will be limited and must cover hire purchase, finance leases and 'puttable' capital instruments (see Chapter 6).

❑ *Gearing* Long-term debt to capital as defined in net worth above – a maximum ratio will be stated.

❑ *Current ratio* A minimum figure will be given for the ratio of current assets to current liabilities – a measure of liquidity.

Events of default This is a list of circumstances in which the loan will be regarded as being in default, for example, insolvency, change of ownership or similar circumstances. A cross-default clause is important. This means that defaults on other loans or bonds will cause this loan to be in default also.

Negative pledge Here the client undertakes not to offer security against a loan from any other party.

Assignment One of the syndicate banks may assign part of its loan commitment to another bank. This cannot be done without the borrower's consent but the loan agreement usually says that 'such consent may not be unreasonably withheld'. However, there may be an initial delay in selling off any of the loan. For example, the $5.5bn Kuwait loan in the Autumn of 1991 had a clause forbidding reassignment to other banks for 180 days.

A *sub-participation* simply means that part of a syndicate bank's loan allotment will be lent to them by another bank and interest payments passed on to this bank. The loan agreement with the client is not affected.

With a *transfer* or *assignment*, the loan documentation changes, the borrower is aware of the change and the assignee is now legally the lender for this portion. Borrowers may worry here about not having a close relationship with the assignee if they hit trouble later.

Why sell part of the loan anyway? Capital ratio rules may make new lending difficult. A transfer would free part of the loan to be lent elsewhere, possibly more profitably. Alternatively, in order to improve capital ratio, the money may not be relent. If capital is no problem, the money may simply be released to take advantage of a more profitable opportunity. With a participation, we may be able to take, say, LIBOR + 22 bp from the client and pass on LIBOR + 20 bp, 'skimming' a little profit.

In the UK, sub-participation and assignment are subject to detailed regulations – BSD 1989/1, 'Loan Transfers and Documentation'.

Wholesale Banking Issues

The key problem for commercial banks is that corporate lending is increasingly unrewarding and becoming a shrinking market. Competition has forced loan charges down to levels which are scarcely profitable. The growth of international capital markets is such that bond and equity issues over the last 10 years have increased their share at the expense of bank loans. The position could be exacerbated by the arrival of the euro. A single market for corporate bonds denominated in the euro for twelve countries is likely to hasten the substitution of bond issues for corporate loans in mainland Europe, which has so far been a market where bank loans have traditionally been a more popular source of finance than bond issues.

One consequence of this has been a move to riskier but potentially more profitable loans. In 1993, 35% of international syndicated loans were for companies below investment grade – by the end of 1998, the figure was 62%. Corporate debt generally is increasing. Attracted by low interest rates, corporates are borrowing to buy back equity – currently all the rage and espoused by financial theorists claiming that debt is cheaper than equity and citing classic financial theory – the Modigliani-Miller work of 1958 onwards – which proves that the post-tax profits of the firm and therefore its share price will increase if it finances itself with debt rather than equity (subject to a few practical assumptions, not least the firm's credit rating). Another consequence of this pressure on profit from lending is to take high quality but low margin loans off the balance sheet and sell them as securities – a process we explain in Chapter 6.

A final consequence is for commercial banks to seek salvation by buying investment banks – Deutsche Bank and Bankers Trust; Swiss Bank Corporation and Warburg/Dillon Read; ING and Barings. These moves have not always met with success. Both Barclays and National Westminster Bank in the UK have lost a great deal of money through their investment banking subsidiaries, and made heavy cuts in their involvement. Commercial banking and investment banking are cultures that are very different, and merging them causes severe problems. The belief seems to be that the bank should offer clients the full range of services, but do clients really care? Clients frequently use one bank for bond issues and another for corporate loans, and fail to see any particular disadvantage.

One of the most profitable banks for its size in the world is Lloyds TSB – a highly focused retail bank.

SUMMARY

Commercial banks are in the classic business of accepting deposits and making loans. The business is both retail (the general public, shops, very small businesses) and wholesale (other banks, corporates and institutions).

Retail banking covers current accounts, cheque facilities, savings accounts, credit cards and loan facilities like overdrafts, personal loans and mortgages. Increasingly, Internet developments are leading to the spread of home banking.

Clearing of payments may involve cheques or electronic payment systems. Cheques are expensive and banks are trying to reduce their use through Internet banking and the use of debit cards.

Key issues in retail banking today are the growing competition, control of costs, sales of non-banking products and the use of Information Technology. In particular, growing links between banks and insurance companies have led to the word *bancassurance*.

Wholesale banking covers bank lending to larger entities than those met in retail banking and activities described in other chapters – money markets, foreign exchange and finance for trade.

Loans may be uncommitted or committed.

Uncommitted facilities include overdrafts, lines of credit and bankers' acceptances.

Committed facilities include term loans, standby credit, revolving credit and project finance.

Syndicated loans are common for large value domestic and cross-border business. There are arranging banks, co-managers, participating banks and agent banks.

Various fees are involved – facility or front end fee, underwriting fees, agents fees and commitment fees. Finally, there is the loan *margin*.

The loan agreement covers the amount of the loan, its purpose, draw down facilities, interest calculations and provisions.

Among the provisions will be covenants. These are designed to protect the bank if the financial position of the borrower worsens. They include interest cover, net worth, total borrowing, gearing and current ratio.

Other provisions cover events of default. There will also be a negative pledge – the client undertakes not to offer security against a loan from another party.

A bank may assign or transfer part of the loan to another bank or it may be a less formal sub-participation.

Falling profit margins on corporate loans have led many commercial banks into riskier lending. Another reaction has been to spread the range of services by moving into investment banking.

5 Investment Banking

INTRODUCTION

We should, perhaps, recognise at the outset that 'commercial' and 'investment' banking do not exist in separate compartments. There are activities which overlap and are carried out by both types of bank, for example, accepting and discounting bills of exchange, foreign exchange and some aspects of trade finance. Nevertheless, there are certain activities which would be regarded as clear 'investment' banking (for example, underwriting share issues) and we shall discuss these in this chapter as well as those which involve a certain amount of overlap.

(The term 'merchant bank' has historically been the UK term for investment bank, but it has a far narrower meaning in the US.)

INVESTMENT BANKING

The range of activities of investment or merchant banks can be summarised as follows:

- ❏ Accepting
- ❏ Corporate finance
- ❏ Securities trading
- ❏ Investment management
- ❏ Loan arrangement
- ❏ Foreign exchange.

Accepting

Although commercial banks accept bills of exchange nowadays, it is a very historic activity for investment banks. Chapter 2 mentioned the Medici bankers helping a Venetian firm to trade with one in London using a bill of exchange in 1463. During the industrial revolution in the UK, enquiries were received from firms all over the world. The role of the British (and Dutch) merchant banks in backing this trade with bills of exchange was of crucial importance. Indeed, until December 1987, the club of top UK merchant banks was called 'The Accepting Houses Committee'.

While bills of exchange can be and are used in connection with inland business, their main use is for export/import business. An exporter sells goods for $100,000 to an importer. Their arrangement is that the goods will be paid for in 3 months, say, on 2 February 2003. The exporter makes out the bill of exchange and sends it to the importer to sign. Its effective message is shown in Figure 5.1.

November 2 2002

You owe me $100,000 for goods received. Please pay on 2 February 2003

Signed: A. N. Exporter

Yes, I agree.

Signed: A. N. Importer

Figure 5.1   *Skeleton bill of exchange*

As you may well imagine, the actual document is rather more formal than this! Nevertheless, it expresses the basic idea. Notice that the *exporter* makes out the bill, that is, *draws* the bill. (There are similar documents used in international trade called *promissory notes*. Here, the *importer* makes out the document and the exporter has less control over the wording.)

The *importer* now has 3 months to put the goods to work before paying. The *exporter* has an internationally acceptable form of debt. True, he has allowed the importer 3 months to pay (not necessary but very common), but his alternative choice might have been to send an invoice, optimistically headed by the words 'Payment Terms – 30 days', with no real assurance that the money will be paid on time.

What if the exporter cannot wait 3 months but needs the money earlier to fund cash flow? The exporter can visit their bank for a loan, armed with a heap of bills proving that cash is on the way. Alternatively, the exporter can sell the bill to a bank. The bank is being asked to put up the money now and to collect it from the importer in 3 months. As the bank is lending $100,000 for 3 months, they are not going to give the exporter all $100,000 but some lower sum reflecting risk and the cost of money – say, $97,000. The bill is sold at a discount and this process is thus called *discounting the bill*.

Let's look at the process in diagrammatic form (Figure 5.2).

The problem is that the bank may be unsure of the credit status of the trader and unwilling to discount the bill. As a result, the practice grew of asking the trader to find a merchant bank to sign the bill in their place. If, in the 19th century, the bill was signed by Baring Bros, Rothschild's or Bank Mees, the bank would have no hesitation in discounting the bill. Naturally, a fee was charged for this service, which is *accepting* the bill. (Whoever signs the bill, promising to pay, is accepting the bill. When people talk of 'acceptances', however, they usually refer to a bank's signature.) In effect, the bank is giving the bill its own credit status and not that of the trader. Hence its importance in the industrial revolution. (The large number of bills in existence in 1890 whose acceptor was Baring Bros led the Bank of England to rescue it that year after unwise investments in Latin America. In 1995, however, there was no second rescue!)

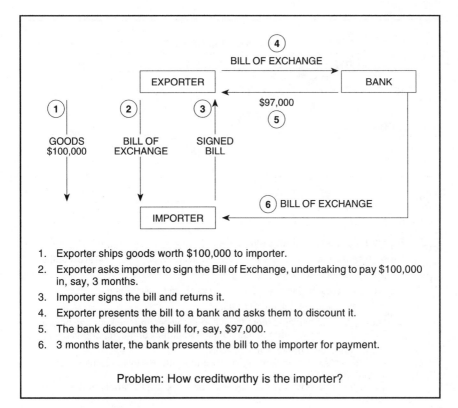

1. Exporter ships goods worth $100,000 to importer.
2. Exporter asks importer to sign the Bill of Exchange, undertaking to pay $100,000 in, say, 3 months.
3. Importer signs the bill and returns it.
4. Exporter presents the bill to a bank and asks them to discount it.
5. The bank discounts the bill for, say, $97,000.
6. 3 months later, the bank presents the bill to the importer for payment.

Problem: How creditworthy is the importer?

Figure 5.2 *The Bill of Exchange: I*

We can find Josiah Wedgewood writing to an Italian customer in 1769,

My foreign correspondents name me a good house, generally in London, to accept my draft for the amount of the goods

or Boulton and Watt in 1795,

We undertake no foreign orders without a guarantee being engineers not merchants.
(Quoted in Chapman *The Rise of Merchant Banking*, Allen & Unwin, 1984)

Our previous diagram is now altered a little (see Figure 5.3).

Today, the whole procedure for trade finance is tied up by arrangements between the importer's bank and the exporter's bank. Usually, a documentary letter of credit is involved. We shall discuss this in Chapter 10.

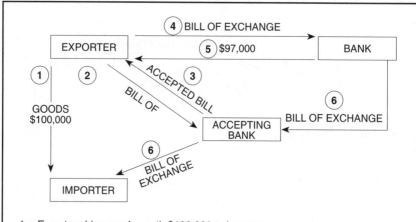

1. Exporter ships goods worth $100,000 to importer.
2. Exporter asks a bank to 'accept' the bill, undertaking to pay $100,000 in 3 months.
3. The bank accepts the bill and returns it.
4. Exporter presents the bill to a bank and asks them to discount it.
5. The bank discounts the bill for $97,000.
6. 3 months later, the bank presents the bill to the accepting bank for payment of $100,000. The latter will recoup this from the importer, or the importer's bank.

N.B.   A bill signed by a trader is a *Trade Bill.*
        A bill accepted by a bank recognised for this purpose by the Central Bank is a *Bank Bill* or *Eligible Bill.*
        The Central Bank will itself discount the bill as part of its 'lender of last resort' role.

Figure 5.3   *The Bill of Exchange: II*

So far, we have discussed the bill in the context of an explicit trade transaction. The market in bankers' acceptances has reached a new level of sophistication today, especially in the London market. Major firms of good credit quality will ask their bank (whether investment or commercial) to accept a bill promising to pay a given sum at a future period of time. The corporate now discounts the bill in the local discount market as a way of borrowing money for trade in general rather than for an explicit transaction. Indeed, in London, firms like Harrods or Marks and Spencer will do this even though they are not selling on credit at all but retailers receiving cash!

Commercial banks are very involved with accepting bills and this is one reason why the UK's 'Accepting Houses Committee' disbanded in 1987. The committee would not include either commercial banks or foreign banks. This was seen to be completely out of date. In any case, accepting had ceased to be a dominant role for UK merchant banks.

Bills of Exchange are used extensively in the UK, quite widely in the continent of Europe generally and very little in the US. They are generally used for exports to the Near and Far East, the Indian continent, Australia and New Zealand.

Corporate Finance

Corporate Finance is likely to be a department of major importance in any investment bank. This department will manage:

❑ New issues – equities/bonds
❑ Rights issues
❑ Mergers and acquisitions
❑ Research.

New issues New issues of either shares or bonds will involve pricing the securities, selling them to investors, underwriting and general advice regarding the regulations that must be followed. Close liaison with firms of lawyers and accountants will be necessary and their fees will be substantial, as well as those of the bankers!

Underwriting is an undertaking to buy any securities that the investors cannot be persuaded to buy. Fees will be charged (of course) and the risk will be spread amongst other merchant banks and investment institutions. One of the most dramatic incidents in modern times occurred when the UK government was selling off its remaining shares in BP to the public. Unfortunately, the market crash of October 1987 occurred after the price was fixed but before the offer closed. The issue was a failure and the underwriters had to buy the shares at a substantial loss.

In the case of equities, the underwriters purchase the shares once it is clear that investors are not taking up their allocation. In the eurobond market, on the other hand, the syndicate of underwriting banks buys the bonds from the issuer and then attempts to sell them to investors.

Rights issues (discussed in Chapter 7) These also need to be priced and underwritten in case the market price falls below the offer price of the rights. Technically, BP was a rights issue as some shares were already quoted but new shares were being created. The government was allowing the public to buy these shares.

The many privatisations in the newly emerging free markets of central and Eastern Europe and the former USSR have created work for US and European investment bankers. Their advice and help are being sought for circumstances which have little precedent. The biggest names tend to be those of the US houses – Merrill Lynch, Salomon Smith Barney, Morgan Stanley Dean Witter and Goldman Sachs.

Mergers and acquisitions Firms planning a takeover will turn to investment banks for help and advice regarding price, timing, tactics and so on. Equally, the object of the takeover will turn to these bankers for help in fending off the predator.

In the UK, Guinness took over the Scottish whisky company Distillers after a long and acrimonious battle. Unhappily, personnel in Guinness and their advisers, Morgan Grenfell, were brought to trial charged with various misdemeanours. In the course of this trial, it was revealed that Morgan Grenfell and associates had been paid £65m and lawyers, Freshfields, paid £2m. The fees involved can be substantial. In a large takeover, like this one, there may be three investment bankers or more on each side.

Nowadays, takeover bids or mergers may be cross-border – Chrysler/Daimler Benz; BP/Amoco; Allianz/AGF; Ford/Volvo; Astra/Zeneca. The biggest takeover in 2002 was the takeover of Pharmacia by Pfizer; the biggest takeover reportedly to date was the takeover of Mannesman by Vodafone for $100bn.

The top M&A houses in the US in 2002 were Goldman Sachs, Salomon Smith Barney and Morgan Stanley. A list of key UK advisers is shown in Table 5.1.

Table 5.1 *Top M&A advisers in UK 2002*

Adviser		*(2001 ranking)*
1	Salomon Smith Barney	(5)
2	UBS Warburg	(3)
3	Morgan Stanley	(8)
4	Merrill Lynch	(2)
5	Rothschild	(7)
6	Deutsche Bank	(12)
7	Credit Suisse First Boston	(4)
8	Goldman Sachs	(6)
9	Lazard	(10)
10	JP Morgan	(11)

Source: Dealogic

In the US, the notorious 'junk bond' era (Chapter 6) saw small companies raising huge sums with bonds to buy much bigger companies. (In the film 'Wall Street', the speech made by Gordon Gecko to shareholders in his planned victim company was said to be based on an actual speech made by Ivan Boesky. He is reported to have coined the infamous phrase, 'greed is good'.)

The fees earned by Drexel Burnham Lambert for bond issues and takeover bids during this era made them quickly one of the highest earning firms on Wall Street (as long as it lasted).

Certain jargon has come to be associated with takeover battles. If a takeover seems inevitable, the merchant bank may find a rival bidder who is preferable to the original predator. This more acceptable bidder is the 'White Knight'. For example, in April 1999, Telecom Italia, facing a hostile bid from Olivetti, turned to Deutsche Telecom as their 'White Knight' (a tactic that did not, however, succeed). Sometimes one or two people can be found who will take a substantial minority holding and block the takeover. These are the 'White Squires'. When Lloyds Bank tried to take over Standard Chartered in 1986, the bid was blocked by holdings taken (separately) by a few entrepreneurs in the Far East and Australia. As it happened, they did Lloyds a good turn as subsequent Standard Chartered problems would have severely weakened a bank with a high reputation for profitability.

Sometimes the 'White Squire' may become a 'Trojan Horse' (to mix our metaphors)! When Britannia Arrow faced a hostile bid in 1985, it found a White Squire in Robert Maxwell. Subsequently, he ousted the board and put in his own nominees.

Those who play computer games may be interested to hear of the Pac-man defence! Here you turn around and gobble up the monster who is chasing you! TotalFina, the Franco-Belgian group, launched a takeover bid for Elf Aquitaine, the French oil group in July 1999. Two weeks later, Elf Aquitaine made a counter-bid for TotalFina!

Sometimes, the bidder may be persuaded to withdraw by the company buying back the shares at a higher price. This is called 'greenmail' (in contrast to blackmail)! In 1986, Sir James Goldsmith, the Anglo-French entrepreneur, made an unpopular bid for the US tyre company, Goodyear Tyre & Rubber Co. In the end, after an acrimonious fight, the firm bought Goldsmith and partners out. They made $93m in the space of a few weeks. However, the incident did damage his reputation in the US, although he always denied the 'greenmail' charge.

A popular defence against hostile takeover bids in the US is the so-called 'poison pill'. This was invented by a top takeover lawyer, Martin Lipton, in 1980 and has been adopted by two thirds of companies in the Standard & Poors 500 Index.

Once one shareholder's stake rises above a given percentage (usually 20%), the poison pill device is triggered. This allows the company to give all shareholders – apart from the 20% holder – the right to buy new shares at a large discount, often 50%. This makes the bid prohibitively expensive.

The poison pill is not unknown in Europe. In 1999, there was a bitterly contested fight between LVMH and Gucci. Gucci sold a 40% stake in the company to Pinault–Printemps–Redoute (PPR), controlled by a 'White Squire', a M. Pinault. This diluted the original LVMH holding of 34.4% (for which it had paid $1.4bn) down to 20%. Gucci is registered in Amsterdam and the Dutch courts rejected complaints by LVMH, although this type of move would not be allowed in most jurisdictions, as trampling on existing shareholders' rights. Finally, in September 2001, LVMH sold their 20% stake in Gucci to PPR, bringing a two-and-a-half year battle to a close.

M&A activity has slowed a little with recent stock market falls, but is buoyed by the continuing trend towards globalisation of industry and commerce and consolidation in specific industry sectors.

General advice   This is always needed by the treasury departments of major firms. They will meet their merchant bankers regularly to discuss the outlook for exchange rates, interest rates, risk management and generally to help them to clarify their policies. Sometimes the client may be a government or quasi-government authority – for example, the Saudi Arabian Monetary Authority (SAMA).

Research capability   This is clearly essential in the corporate finance department if the bank is to be able to give advice and play a major role in raising new capital. The firm may be innovative and invent new variations on standard techniques, for example, convertible capital bonds, perpetual variable rate notes, perpetual auction market preferred stock (AMPS) and similar instruments. Research may uncover potential victims for a takeover or give early identification of potential predators.

It is important to get a good reputation for research. Periodically, surveys are carried out of fund managers, asking them to nominate the best houses for research. One of these is the Thomson–Extel Survey, done each year in the UK. In the latest survey (2002), the top three houses were UBS–Warburg, Schroder–Salomon Smith Barney and Deutschebank. Individual sector analysts are also surveyed, and they and their teams often become the object of poaching by other houses!

Securities Trading

In corporate finance we saw *primary* market activity – new issues and rights issues. Securities trading takes us into the *secondary* market dealing in the same equities and bonds.

The trading will take place in one of the modern dealing rooms with computer terminals and communications giving up to the minute prices and contact with other dealers and investors all over the world.

The dealings will cover domestic bonds and equities and international bonds and equities. International bonds are discussed in Chapter 6. International equities are those of companies outside the domestic market where the investment bank is situated.

The old tradition in many countries (France, Belgium, the UK, Spain, Italy) has been to reserve domestic bond and equities to stock exchange members not allowed to be owned by banks. Change began with London's 'Big Bang' in October 1986 and spread to all the above markets. The result has been to allow banks access to these markets and break the previous monopolies. These banks are either pure investment banks as such, subsidiaries of commercial banks, or 'universal' banks (see Chapter 2).

Alongside these traders will be the experts in the so called 'derivative' products – options, futures, FRAs and so on. We shall discuss these in later chapters, but they enable traders and their clients either to take a view on future price movements with less capital than actually buying/selling the underlying instruments or to hedge their risk. If a commercial bank has an investment bank subsidiary, then the expertise in derivative products will be found in that subsidiary.

The traders in this department carry out a twofold role. They act on behalf of clients (some of whom may be in-house departments) and they take positions of their own – usually called 'proprietary trading'.

Investment Management

The investment funds which these managers are controlling may be the bank's own funds or they may be, in effect, 'looking after other people's money'. These may be:

❑ High net worth individuals
❑ Corporates
❑ Pension funds
❑ Mutual funds.

High net worth individuals   They may approach a commercial bank to handle all their affairs, including investments. In Chapter 2 we called this 'private banking'. They could also approach an investment bank to handle their spare funds (but a minimum sum will be stated). This type of business is also handled by stock-brokers but with lower minimum sums than an investment bank would require.

Corporates   They may either have good cash flow and wish to pay someone else to handle their investments or may build up a large 'war chest', ready for some takeover activity later and, temporarily, pay an investment bank to handle this.

The entity need not be a conventional corporate as such. An excellent example is the Saudi Arabian Monetary Authority (SAMA).

Pension funds   Where economies have pension funds (for example the US, the UK, the Netherlands, Switzerland and Japan), then they may feel that they lack the skill to manage the funds and pay others to do so. In these economies, pension funds will usually be the biggest clients of the investment management department.

Mutual funds   These are discussed in Chapter 7. They are collective investments in money market instruments, bonds or equities. The bank may run its own fund and advertise its attractions to small investors. In addition, it will manage mutual funds for others. Independent organisations provide regular statistics on fund performance and, if the manager has performed less well than comparable funds, they may find themselves being dismissed. This has led to charges of 'short-termism' in their investment decisions. However, as a director of one major fund commented to the author: 'The long run is the sum of the short runs. If we get them right, the long run will be right too.'

Typically, fund managers will charge a small percentage fee for handling the fund and the client will meet costs like broker's commission. Competition for the investment banks comes from firms of independent fund managers, who specialise totally in this business, or large pension funds who will look after the money of smaller funds as well as their own.

The role of fund managers as investment institutions who influence stock market activity will be discussed in Chapter 7.

Loan Arrangement

Where there are complex syndicated loans for special projects, we may often find that the arranger is an investment bank. The bank is using its special skills to decide on the terms of the loan and the cheapest way to find the money. It could involve using the 'swaps' market, for example, which we explain in Chapter 13. Often, several potential teams may be competing for these projects, for example, Eurotunnel, the new Hong Kong airport, the bridge over the Bosphorus. In the case of Teesside Power Station in the UK, a syndicate of banks is putting up the money but the loan arranger is the US investment bank, Goldman Sachs.

Outside of large, complex projects, investment bankers will help clients to raise finance for international trade. In this, there is an overlap with a major commercial bank activity. It may be a question of knowing sources of cheaper finance for exporter or importer (for example, a development bank) or even acting as an agent or middleman – an export house or confirming house. These activities are discussed under 'Finance for Trade' in Chapter 9.

Foreign Exchange

The foreign exchange markets are discussed in Chapter 6. Typically, we regard this as a commercial bank activity. However, investment banks that are permitted commercial bank functions will run a foreign exchange trading desk for their clients and their own proprietary trading and it may be an important source of profit. We make the above comment about being 'permitted commercial bank functions' because of the differing regulatory position in various countries, which we explain before the end of this chapter.

Typically, US and Japanese investment banks have had a modest foreign exchange section, but there are exceptions; Goldman Sachs, for example, have become a major player in foreign exchange dealing. UK merchant banks, fully licensed as banks, will often see foreign exchange dealing as a major activity and will, indeed, have a 'banking' department which will also offer deposit taking functions to clients.

Miscellaneous Activities

There are a range of miscellaneous activities which may be carried out by investment banks, possibly through separate legal subsidiaries. Commodity trading (including derivatives trading), for example, is quite common and one thinks here, for instance, of the links between the US Salomon Bros, Smith Barney and Phibro and also of Goldman's who have a commodity dealing arm. Other activities include insurance broking, life assurance, leasing, factoring (see Chapter 9), property development and venture capital. This latter activity covers finance for new and growing companies which are not well enough established to attract money by equities, bonds or conventional bank loans. The venture capital company puts in a mixture of equity and loans and hopes to make large capital gains later when the firm obtains a flotation on the local Stock Exchange.

Many of these miscellaneous activities overlap with those of commercial banks – for example, leasing, factoring, venture capital and commodity dealing.

REGULATION

We have seen that many commercial banks have investment bank subsidiaries and that universal banks do all kinds of banking anyway. We have also seen that many activities overlap commercial and investment banking and that it is not always possible to draw a clear distinction. As a result, one might conclude that the distinction between the two types of banking is not really significant. However, the two terms are widely used to characterise a bank's activities and culture, and perhaps to compare or contrast it with another bank, or again, to comment on the merits and relevance or 'fit' of an acquisition. Moreover the two types of bank were until recently artificially separated by law in the two biggest markets of the world – the US and Japan!

When the Wall Street crash occurred in 1929, the US authorities concluded that, by engaging in stock market activities, commercial banks might be risking depositors' money. They decided to remove this risk by passing the Glass-Steagall Act of 1933 (named after the Chairmen of the relevant committees of the Senate and House of Representatives). This introduced a deposit protection scheme, gave the Federal Reserve Bank greater powers of supervision and separated commercial and investment banking. A commercial bank could take deposits but could not underwrite any securities. An investment bank could handle underwriting of securities but could not take deposits. As a result, we had US commercial banks on the one hand (Citibank, Chase Manhattan, Chemical, J.P. Morgan) and investment banks on the other (Salomon Bros, Goldman Sachs, Merrill Lynch). J.P. Morgan continued as a commercial bank but passed investment banking to Morgan Stanley, now a separate bank. In London, the already weak links with Morgan Grenfell were then broken.

The whole affair, however, may have been based on a misreading of the position. George Bentson, Professor of Finance at Emory University in Atlanta, has found that allegations that securities trading weakened banks had 'almost no basis in fact'.

As the Americans were in occupation of Japan after the Second World War, they passed the same restrictions into Article 65 of the Japanese Exchange and Securities

Code. As a result, we had the commercial banks (Dai Ichi Kangyo, Mitsubishi, Sumitomo, Sakura) and, quite separate, the securities houses (Nomura, Daiwa and Nikko).

A similar law was passed in Italy in the early 1930s leaving Italy with just one major investment bank, Mediobanca (partly state owned). In 1988, however, the law was repealed.

Several major attempts to repeal Glass-Steagall have been made in recent years. One was the Proxmire-Garn bill introduced in November 1987 and the other was a far-reaching reform bill, introduced by Nicholas Brady, Treasury Secretary, in February 1990, of which Glass-Steagall repeal was part. In the event, both bills failed to obtain the necessary support to pass into law. The new Congress in 1995 was also confidently expected to repeal Glass-Steagall but, once again, no action was taken.

Impatient with this, the Federal Reserve acted on its own. In January 1989, it gave powers to underwrite issues of municipal bonds, mortgage bonds and commercial paper to five banks – J.P. Morgan, Citibank, Chase Manhattan, Security Pacific and Bankers Trust. However, the activities had to be handled by a separate subsidiary and not be more than 5% of the turnover of that subsidiary (later increased to 10%). In June 1989, J.P. Morgan were given permission to underwrite corporate bonds and, in September 1990, permission to underwrite equities (with the same limitations as before). Then, in January 1991, permission to underwrite equities in this limited way was also given to Bankers Trust, Royal Bank of Canada and Canadian Imperial Bank of Commerce. Later, in March 1997, the Fed lifted the 10% limit to 25% and, in April, Bankers Trust bought the investment bank, Alex Brown. The Glass-Steagall Act was crumbling! Then, in 1998, Citibank announced a merger with the Travellers Group which includes Salomon Smith Barney and insurance companies – the latter also forbidden by Glass-Steagall. The Federal authorities approved the merger but stated that unless Glass-Steagall was repealed within 2 years, the merged group must sell all the insurance interests (about 20% of total revenues). There was a provision for increasing the 2 year deadline to 5 if the Fed so chose.

The above merger convinced everyone that Glass-Steagall was on the way out. Although there were bitter disputes in Congress again in 1999 over a new banking bill, these were eventually resolved and Glass-Steagall was finally repealed in November 1999.

In Japan, the Ministry of Finance circulated several papers outlining the possibility of similar deregulation in Japan. 1993 saw the first positive moves here. Some commercial banks were allowed limited operations in bonds and, in November 1994, the list of commercial banks allowed these dealings was widened. As a result, many major banks like Dai-Ichi Kangyo, Bank of Tokyo–Mitsubishi, Fuji, IBJ and LTCB have set up subsidiaries to deal in bonds. The 1993 move also allowed brokers to deal in investment trusts, land trusts and foreign exchange. Nomura, Daiwa, Nikko and Yamaichi all set up subsidiaries to be Trust Banks. Finally, in

June 1997, the Ministry of Finance announced plans for complete deregulation by the year 2001.

This complete deregulation was described as Japan's 'Big Bang'. This was the timetable laid down:

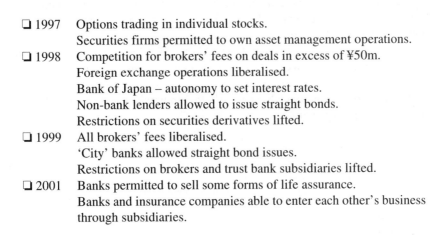

❑ 1997   Options trading in individual stocks.
          Securities firms permitted to own asset management operations.
❑ 1998   Competition for brokers' fees on deals in excess of ¥50m.
          Foreign exchange operations liberalised.
          Bank of Japan – autonomy to set interest rates.
          Non-bank lenders allowed to issue straight bonds.
          Restrictions on securities derivatives lifted.
❑ 1999   All brokers' fees liberalised.
          'City' banks allowed straight bond issues.
          Restrictions on brokers and trust bank subsidiaries lifted.
❑ 2001   Banks permitted to sell some forms of life assurance.
          Banks and insurance companies able to enter each other's business through subsidiaries.

As a result of this, we have seen many new alliances. Travellers Group took a 25% share of Nikko Securities in mid 1988. Merrill Lynch took over 30 offices of the liquidated Yamaichi Securities and recruited 1000 staff. Deutsche Bank has a tie-up with Nippon Life to sell mutual funds. IBJ (now part of Mizuho) and Nomura had a link-up. Sanwa Bank (now part of UFJ) took a 30% stake in Universal Securities and Daiwa Bank took a stake in Cosmo Securities; Sumitomo and Daiwa Securities have set up a joint investment banking operation.

SUMMARY

Investment banking activities can be summarised as:

Accepting   This is putting the bank's signature on a bill of exchange to give it a better credit quality. The bill of exchange is a promise to pay a trade debt. If the bank is one on the central bank's list for this purpose, the bill is a *bank* bill. Others are *trade* bills. The bill is frequently sold at a discount. Commercial banks will accept bills, too, but it is an historic investment bank activity.

Corporate Finance   This covers new issues of equities and bonds, rights issues, mergers and acquisitions and research.

Securities Trading   The trading includes money market instruments, equities, bonds and derivative products.

Investment Management   The funds managed are those of high net worth individuals, corporates, mutual funds and (especially) pension funds.

Loan Arrangement   While the bank may not lend the money, it may help to assemble a syndicate for large-scale financial products.

Foreign Exchange   The large foreign exchange dealers are commercial banks but investment banks will still need to run a foreign exchange section.

In the United States, investment and commercial banks were separated by the Glass-Steagall Act, but actions by the Federal Reserve weakened its provisions, and it has recently been repealed.

The old Japanese restrictions of Article 65 of the Exchange and Securities Code regarding commercial banking, investment banking and insurance have been swept away.

Across Europe, banks which carry out both commercial and investment banking are called *universal* banks.

Securities Markets

6 The Money and Bond Markets

7 Stock Exchanges

6 The Money and Bond Markets

THE RATE OF INTEREST

So far, we have taken the rate of interest involved in borrowing and lending rather for granted. The time has come, however, to look at it more clearly.

The rate of interest is the price of money. We talk casually of *the* rate of interest but, of course, there is no single rate. There are rates appropriate for different borrowers and rates appropriate for different time periods. A middle-sized company making machine tools will expect to pay a higher rate than a government does. A government pays a different rate for borrowing for 3 months than for 10 years.

What affects the rate of interest? We have just touched on two key factors – *risk* and *maturity*.

Risk

Let's take the risk first. Quite simply, a lender will expect a greater reward for lending to the company making machine tools than for lending to a government. After all, the company may go into liquidation and default. We do not expect our government to default, although Mexico's government and those of other Latin American countries caused panic in international markets when they defaulted in the 1980s (more on that later!). Russia's default on its Treasury bills in August 1998 also had widespread repercussions.

So far as the governments of OECD countries are concerned, say, or the US government, the lowest rates of interest in their economies will apply to government transactions since they are regarded as the safest. The government rate thus becomes the benchmark for other rates. For example, an American corporate wishing to borrow for 3 months might be advised to expect to pay 'Treasuries plus 1%', that is, 1% more than the current rate for US government Treasury bills. It is more convenient to express it this way than as an absolute rate because rates vary in wholesale markets, even daily. For example, let's say 3 month Treasury bills pay $3\frac{7}{8}\%$. The rate for our US company is thus $4\frac{7}{8}\%$. However, tomorrow Treasury bills may be $3\frac{3}{4}\%$ and the corporate rate becomes $4\frac{3}{4}\%$. As a result, we find it easier to express the rate as 'Treasuries plus 1%'. Of course, the corporate may become more secure as profits increase and the balance sheet improves. Their investment bankers may express the view that they now see their appropriate rate as 'Treasuries plus 90 bp'. What does this mean? A basis point is very common terminology and is useful for expressing small differences in rates. It is $\frac{1}{100}$ of 1%. Thus, 50 bp is equal to $\frac{1}{2}\%$ and 100 bp is equal to 1%. The difference between any given rate and the benchmark US government rate will be called 'the spread over Treasuries'. In the above case, the corporate has found that its spread over US government Treasury bill rates has fallen from 1% to $\frac{9}{10}\%$.

107

Maturity

Maturity is another important aspect, and it doesn't always make sense in practice. Economic theory tells us that lenders will want a higher rate of interest for lending money for 5 years than for 3 months. This relationship between the rate of interest and time is called the 'yield curve'. If rates for longer-term lending are higher than for shorter-term lending, we would expect the yield curve to look like that in Figure 6.1.

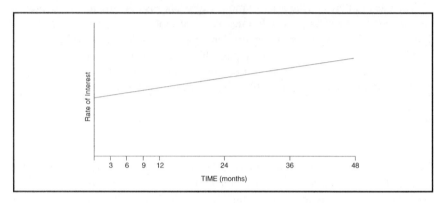

Figure 6.1   *The yield curve*

The yield curve is upward-sloping, or positive. Unfortunately, while this makes complete sense, it often doesn't work that way in real life at all. Sometimes short-term rates are higher than long-term ones and we talk of a 'negative' or downward-sloping yield curve. This may be due to government policy. They change short-term interest rates either to stimulate the economy or to slow it down. For example, from October 1989 to October 1990 in the UK, short-term rates were 15% while the government attempted to slow down a rate of inflation in excess of 10%. Investment in a 10 year government bond, however, only returned about 11%. Conversely, in mid-1992, the US government was desperately trying to 'kick-start' the economy. Short-term rates were only a little over 3%, while the price of a 30 year government bond was such that it yielded about 7½%.

Expectations

Markets are also affected by *expectations*. Suppose everyone believes firmly that the general level of interest rates is due to *fall*. Lots of people will want to lend money for long periods and benefit from higher interest rates. Not many people want to borrow long-term – they would rather wait until rates fall. As a result, long-term rates start to fall in relation to short-term rates. Conversely, if rates are expected to *rise*, then everyone wants to lend short-term, hoping to gain from higher rates later. Borrowers prefer to borrow long-term and lock in to lower rates while they can. Long-term rates will now rise in order to attract funds to meet the demands of the borrowers.

Liquidity

Liquidity also affects the rate of interest – that is, how quickly can the lender get the money back? This is not quite the same as maturity. There may well be one rate for 3 month money and another for 5 year money but another consideration in the case of 5 year money is: can the lender change their mind and get the money back?

A savings bank will pay lower interest on a 'no notice' or 'sight' account than on a '3 months' notice' account. We have to pay (by way of a lower rate of interest) for the flexibility of being able to withdraw our money at any time.

In wholesale markets, if our lending of money is represented by a security, then one way of getting the money back prior to the normal repayment date is to sell the security to someone else.

Supply and Demand

Of course, we cannot ignore the whole question of supply and demand in different market sectors. For example, for over 2 years from 1988 to 1990, the UK government was in surplus and did not need to borrow by issuing bonds. The demand was still there, however, from UK and foreign pension funds, insurance companies and other investors. This contributed to a lowering of interest rates for government bonds. The supply/demand factor can be seen at its best perhaps when one looks at the yield curve for UK government bonds in April 1996 and May 1999 and their most curious 'kinks' (see Figure 6.2). They also show how yields vary from year to year.

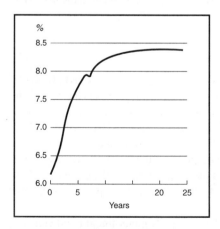
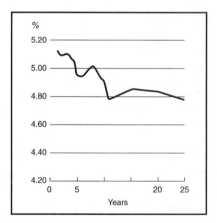

Figure 6.2 *UK gilts yield, 1996 and 1999*

Up to 5 years, there are plenty of lenders, for example banks and UK building societies. Over 10 years, there are plenty of lenders – pension funds and insurance companies. From 5 to 10 years there is a shortage and rates rise a little (if only 10 bp) to attract lenders.

Inflation

Finally, whether a given rate of interest represents good value or not may depend on the rate of inflation. Economists talk of the *real* rate of interest, that is, the nominal rate of interest minus the rate of inflation.

In the UK in 1989/90, interest rates reached 15% while the government desperately tried to curb inflation, which had reached 11%. In 1992, the rate of interest had fallen to 10% but inflation had fallen to less than 4%. Thus, although nominal rates had fallen from 15% to 10%, the *real* rate had risen from 4% to over 6%. In 2002, with nominal rates of 4% and inflation at 2½%, real rates are at a new low of 1½%.

YIELD

Yield is arguably the most important term in the financial markets. 'Yield' is the return to the investor expressed as an annual percentage. As the markets are all about raising capital, the yield is crucially important. Unfortunately, it's not as easy as it seems!

Suppose we have a bond issued in 1996 and maturing in 25 years – 2021. The bond pays a rate of interest of 10% once per year. What is the yield? At first, the answer seems obvious – 10%. 'If I buy the bond', you argue, 'I get 10% – where's the problem?' The problem is that your answer is only true if you paid the full price for the bond.

Par Values

Bonds have a 'par' or 'nominal' value. This is usually taken to be $1000, £100, DM1000 and so on. This is the amount on which the rate of interest is based and the amount which will be repaid at maturity. You buy the 25 year 10% bond and pay the par value of $1000. Your yield is 10%. However, as secondary market trading begins, investors may pay either more or less than $1000 for the bond with a par value of $1000 – this affects the yield. The price of the bond is expressed as a percentage of the par value. For example, if the price is 90, then the price for $1000 par value is $900. In the UK, £100 is taken to be the par value. A price of 90 means that the price for £100 par value is £90.

Suppose the 25 year bond mentioned above is a UK government bond and you buy £5000 worth at issue: after all, government bonds are the safest, aren't they?

2 years later, you need the money and decide to sell. 2 years later, however, the level of interest rates has changed. The yield on long-dated government bonds is now 12½%. As you try to get full price for your 10% bond, no one is interested. Why should they pay you £100 to receive £10, when they could buy a new bond for £100 and get £12.50? They might pay you £80, because your bond pays £10 once per year and £10 for an investment of £80 is 12½%. Therefore, as interest rates went *up*, the price of your bond went *down*. The face rate of interest is 10% but by buying it more cheaply, the yield has increased to 12½% because £10 is 12½% of £80.

Let's say that you refuse to sell. 2 years later, you have lost your job and life is grim. You must sell your bonds, come what may. However, by now things have changed again. The yield on long-dated government bonds is now only 8%. When you attempt to sell your 10% bond you will find no shortage of buyers willing to pay you more than par, because 10% is very attractive if current rates are 8%. As a result, as interest rates went *down*, the price of your bond went *up*. In theory, buyers might pay £125, because the income of £10 returns 8% which is the market rate. That is to say, £10 is 8% of £125.

Interest Yield

Just to cover more market jargon, the face rate of interest on the bond is called the *coupon* (for reasons which will be explained later). The calculation we made above when arriving at the yield was:

$$\frac{\text{Coupon}}{\text{Price}} = \text{Yield}$$

for example

$$\frac{£10}{£80} = 12.5\%$$

or

$$\frac{£10}{£125} = 8\%$$

This calculation of yield is called the interest yield (the terms *simple*, *flat*, *running* and *annual* yield are also used). It's not difficult, but not really helpful either.

Gross Redemption Yield

Let's go back to the illustration above of the effect of yields rising to 12½%. We suggested that someone might buy your bond for £80. We argued:

1. Buy the new 12½% bond for £100 – yield 12½%
2. Buy the existing 10% bond for £80 – yield 12½%.

Unfortunately, we've omitted one crucial factor – redemption, When the bond is redeemed, the government will pay £100. In case 1 above, there is no capital gain. In case 2, there's a capital gain of £20. As a result, the yield is more than 12½% if we throw this factor in. Equally, if anyone paid £125, they would face a loss of £25 at redemption. The market does its calculations on the assumption that the bond is kept until redemption.

We need, therefore, an all-embracing calculation that includes the interest yield and modifies it by any gain or loss at redemption. The resultant figure is the *gross redemption yield* (or *yield to maturity*). ('Gross' means ignoring tax. As we don't know the investor's tax status, we ignore consideration of any tax that might be due on the interest or on any capital gain.) The formula itself is quite complicated, as it's based on discounted cash flow. We are taking the future stream of revenue – interest and redemption – and calculating the yield that would equate this to today's bond price. Alternatively, we could feed into the formula a desired yield and calculate the price to be paid that would achieve that yield. That's why it's so important – it's how bond dealers calculate bond prices.

Suppose, however, that a bond pays 10% and the market yield is 12½%, but redemption is not 2021 but 2 months away. Does this make any difference? Will the bond still only sell for about £80? Surely not – here is a piece of paper that, in 2 months, is worth £100. Why was the bond price so poor in our original example? It was because the bond offered 10% and the market wanted 12½% but, if there's only 2 months' interest payments left, this hardly matters. What matters is that redemption at £100 is quite near.

The result is that the nearer we get to redemption, the nearer the secondary market price moves to £100 and the less important interest rate changes are. Thus, long-dated bonds are highly sensitive to interest rate changes (interest rates *up*, bond prices *down* and vice-versa) but short dates are not.

Consider two 10% bonds. The ultimate reward for the buyer is the interest payments and the redemption value. Suppose one bond has 1 year to run and the other 20 years.

		Interest payments £	+	Redemption £	=	Reward £
1	1 year to go	10	+	100	=	110
2	20 years to go	200	+	100	=	300

In case 1, most of the reward is redemption, not affected by interest rate changes.

In case 2, most of the reward is interest payments. If these don't match the market yield, the effect on price will be very serious.

We could represent this diagrammatically, as shown in Figure 6.3.

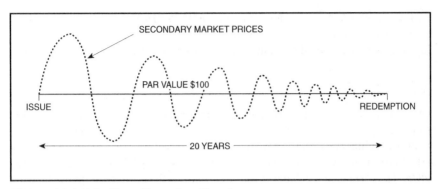

Figure 6.3   *Volatility of long-dated bonds*

Let's verify this against some real prices. These are prices for UK government bonds in February 2002:

Bond				Price
1	Exchequer	10%	2002	100.91
	Treasury	7%	2002	100.94
2	Exchequer	12%	2013/17	161.53
	Treasury	6%	2028	118.49

Notice that in case 1 we have two bonds, one paying 10% and one 7%. It might be thought that the 10% would be much more expensive, when in fact the prices are nearly identical – they are both near redemption.

In case 2, one bond pays 12% and the other 6%, and this is fully reflected in the two prices. Here, redemption is more than 10–20 years away.

(Incidentally, the redemption year shown above of 2013/17 means redemption between 2013 and 2017 at the government's decision. If, in 2013, rates are 10%, we can be quite sure that the government will redeem early and reborrow at 10%. If rates are 14%, however, what would be the point of stopping paying 12% in order to start paying 14%?)

You will still find in US bond markets the use of fractions down to $\frac{1}{32}$. Sensibly, Europe uses decimals. The smallest price movement, in one case $\frac{1}{32}$ and the other 0.01, is called (curiously) a *tick*. Thus, a cry of 'Treasuries are up 5 ticks' in the US would mean $\frac{5}{32}$. A similar cry in Germany would mean 0.05.

You will gather from the above discussion that dealers holding an inventory of long-dated bonds are at risk to interest rate changes. They may seek to hedge this risk using a futures exchange, and we explain this later in Chapter 12. Equally, if you want to buy bonds as a short-term investment, it might be better to buy short-dated bonds, where the risk of market interest rate changes is less.

As an illustration of the dangers, you might like to read Michael Lewis's excellent *Liar's Poker* (Hodder & Stoughton, 1989). He tells the amusing story of how Merrill Lynch trader, Howie Rubin, lost $250m on long-dated bonds in 1987 in one fateful deal. (Well, it's amusing if you're not Howie Rubin!)

Accrued Interest

Unfortunately, there is one other factor to consider before we leave these somewhat technical questions. It is the question of the timing of the interest payments. Suppose the interest is paid twice per year on 16 January and 16 July. You buy a 10% bond in the secondary market on 16 January for £90. You have just missed the interest payment and will have to wait 6 months for the next one. Suppose that you have to sell after 3 months and that prices are unchanged. If you could only sell for £90, this would seem very unfair, as you've held the bond for 3 months and had no reward for your investment. Equally, the buyer would collect 5% although they had only held the bond for 3 months.

Naturally, it doesn't work like that. When you sell your bond you get the *accrued interest* to date. If you held £100 nominal value of the 10% bond for 3 months, you would get half the bi-annual interest, that is, £2.50. (The calculation is simply multiplying the half-yearly interest payments per £100 – £5 in this case – by the number of days the bond is held as a proportion of the days in the half year.) The accrued interest is almost always quoted separately (there are some exceptions in some markets, such as convertible bonds). The price without the accrued interest is the *clean price*. The price you see on a computer screen or in the financial newspapers is always the clean price. If you sell, you will receive the accrued interest in addition. If you buy, you will have to pay it. One reason for accounting for the accrued interest separately is that in many countries any gain in this area is subject to income tax. Gains on the clean price are capital gains.

There is a complication. There must be a cut off point, at which time everyone on the register of holders gets the interest. After this the bond is marked XD (ex dividend). Suppose the half year payment is on 10 June. The bonds may go XD on 3 June. However, the interest accrues from 10 December to 10 June. Anyone selling on 3 June will get the half year interest to 10 June although they did not own the bond in the last 7 days. Anyone buying the bond on 3 June will not accrue any interest until 10 June, even though they have invested their capital 7 days earlier. As a result, when bonds are sold in the XD period, the seller (who gains) *pays* the accrued interest to the buyer (who loses). This is the exception to the way accrued interest is treated.

CREDIT RATINGS

We have seen that the higher the creditworthiness of the borrower, the lower the rate of interest. Some markets (for example, the US) want the credit rating of the borrower officially assessed so as to guide them as to the risk and the appropriate rate of interest. There are several companies in the credit rating business but the two most important are Standard and Poor's (McGraw-Hill) and Moody's Investor Service (Dun and Bradstreet). For banks, there is a UK-based organisation called IBCA. This merged with the French Euronotation in October 1992. In 1997, they merged with the third biggest rating organisation in the US, Fitch Investor Services. Some see this as the first move to a pan-European body to rival Standard and Poor's and Moody's. The credit ratings business began in 1909 when John Moody issued his first-ever ratings of company debt – 200 American railway companies.

These organisations look at bond issues and commercial paper issues (to be covered later) and rate them according to the risk. To quote Standard and Poor's themselves, the ratings are based, in varying degrees, on the following considerations:

1. *Likelihood of default – capacity and willingness of the obligor as to the timely payment of interest and repayment of principal in accordance with the terms of the obligation*
2. *Nature and provisions of the obligation*
3. *Protection afforded to, and relative position of, the obligation in the event of bankruptcy, reorganisation, or other arrangement under the laws of bankruptcy and other laws affecting creditors' rights.*

A bond which is the best risk is rated AAA by Standard and Poor's and Aaa by Moody's. The full list for Standard and Poor's is:
AAA
AA
A
BBB
BB
B
CCC
CC
C
C1
D

A bond rated 'D' is either in default or expected to default.

As a further refinement, the grade may be modified by plus (+) or minus (−), for example, AA+ or AA−. A bond may be issued as AAA but be reduced later to A if the position of the issuer deteriorates. This will increase their borrowing costs. Suppose the appropriate rate for an AAA bond is 10%. The rate for an A might be 10.75%.

Below the BBB rank there is a sort of invisible line. Bonds rated BBB and above are 'investment grade' – top quality if you like. Many investment funds will only invest if the grade is BBB or higher. Below BBB, to quote Standard and Poor's again:

> *Debt rated 'BB', 'B', 'CCC', 'CC' and 'C' is regarded as having predominantly speculative characteristics with respect to capacity to pay interest and repay principal. 'BB' indicates the least degree of speculation and 'C' the highest degree of speculation. While such debt will likely have some quality and protective characteristics, these are outweighed by large uncertainties or major risk exposures to adverse conditions.*

'Junk bonds' are simply bonds which are not investment grade. This is quite a long story and we'll tackle it later.

Moody's have a similar system but use slightly different lettering.

The view of risk for a 3 month loan may be quite different from that for a 5 year loan. As a result, both organisations use a simpler system for the shorter-term commercial paper. For Standard and Poor's this is:

A1
A2
A3
B
C
D

Default could range from simply missing a payment to bankruptcy. A Moody's study shows that over a 15 year period only 1.1% of bonds originally rated with the top grade went into default. For bonds rated CCC (Caa in the case of Moody's) or worse, the default rate was 41.1%. Unfortunately, the fall from grace of top companies in 2002 like Enron, WorldCom and Marconi has led to more defaults from highly rated bonds.

Clearly, non-investment grade will have to pay more than investment grade to compensate for the risk. The interest rate spread over investment grade debt was 300 basis points in 1997, but went much higher as we moved into the Russian-inspired crisis in 1998 (see Chapter 15).

As an example of the way organisations can lose ratings, we have only to look at the banks. In 1990, there were eight banks (not owned by the state) whose bonds were rated AAA by both organisations – Rabobank, Deutsche, Morgan Guaranty, Barclays, Swiss Bank Corporation, Union Bank of Switzerland, Crédit Suisse and Industrial Bank of Japan. Due to commercial bad debts following recession, by mid-1992 the proud band of eight had shrunk to four – Rabobank, Deutsche, Morgan Guaranty and Union Bank of Switzerland and, then, by January 1997 had shrunk to one – Rabobank! (Rabo is still AAA with both these agencies but, as noted earlier, was downgraded in 2002 by Fitch.) In industry and commerce, previously 'blue chip' companies have also been downgraded, with both Corus and Cable & Wireless acquiring junk status in 2002.

Standard and Poor's and Moody's do not always move together. In 1992, for example, Moody's downgraded the Swiss Bank Corporation from AAA. Standard and Poor's did not follow suit until early 1995.

Credit ratings are used extensively in the domestic US market and the Euromarkets (to be explained later). It has not generally been a habit in Europe, but the default of Polly Peck's commercial paper issue in the UK led to an increasing use of ratings in this market. It is likely, in fact, that ratings will be used increasingly in Europe. Ratings are not only applied to corporate issues but also to government issues ('sovereign issues'). In June 1998, for example, Standard and Poor's downgraded Russian debt to B+, a clear sign of the trouble to come!

With the arrival of the Far East crisis in 1997, the rating agencies came in for considerable criticism for not anticipating the problems. The agencies were following the markets, not leading them. South Korea was AA- at January 1st but BBB- by December. The agencies had focused on external debt as a ratio of exports, underestimating the possibility of default. Short-term debt obligations turned out to be much higher than had been previously indicated. Moody's did issue a warning, however, in May 1996 about the gradual build up of short-term debt.

Credit rating agencies, of course, exercise considerable power. Moody's habit of publishing unsolicited ratings has led to criticism. Since this rating will be based on imperfect information, it leads to pressure on the company to pay for a full rating in the hope of getting a better one. (The bond issuers pay, not the investors.) In March 1996, Moody's found itself the subject of an investigation by the US Justice Department into a breach of anti-trust rules.

Discussing the question 'who controls the raters?', the *Economist* in an article on April 6 1996 concluded that:

> *In theory, the agencies have good reason to stick to the straight and narrow. Even more than accountants and lawyers, they must trade on their reputations. If bond investors lose faith in the integrity of the rating agencies' judgements, they will no longer pay attention to their ratings ... companies and governments will not pay their fees.*

DOMESTIC MONEY MARKETS

We have previously mentioned that some markets are *domestic* (that is, transactions are in the local currency and under the control of the local central bank) and some are regarded as *international* (for example, a bond denominated in Japanese yen issued in London through a syndicate of international banks).

There are also *money* markets, which are short-term (that is, borrowing/lending of money for 1 year or less), and *bond* markets, which are markets handling medium- to long-term borrowing/lending.

In this chapter we deal with domestic markets first, covering the various instruments and practices of the money markets, and follow this with bonds.

Then we will look at the international markets, both short- and long-term.

When we look at domestic money markets, we find that there is no single marketplace here, like a stock exchange floor. All over the Western financial markets there are large numbers of people who spend their day buying and selling money in one form and another. Huge sums of money are borrowed or lent, sometimes simply 'overnight'.

Transactions involving the general public and small businesses, like shops, are called the *retail* market.

Transactions between the big players are typically called the *wholesale* market. The players are central banks, other banks, financial institutions, corporates and specialists, like money brokers.

Most of this chapter will be concerned with the wholesale markets.

Call Money

There is a market in money which is borrowed/lent for a very short period of time and is not represented by a marketable instrument or security. Bankers talk of 'call' money and the 'call money market'. Money is lent by one bank to another and may be called back at any time. There is also money lent overnight by one bank to another. 'Overnight' usually means 12.00 p.m. one day to 12.00 p.m. the next day. Sometimes the money may be lent with a right to have the money back with, say, 3 or 7 days' notice. The result, on a bank's balance sheet, becomes 'money at call and short notice'. In most markets, the overnight rate is averaged and used for a variety of purposes. In Paris, for example, this was TMP (Taux Moyen Pondéré) prior to European Monetary Union. Now the rate for the twelve countries is EONIA (Euro Overnight Indexed Average). For example, the French public entity, Crédit Immobilier de France, has issued a 2 year bond where the interest rate is reset every night to EONIA. In London, the equivalent rate (confusingly) is EURONIA, that is the overnight indexed rate for dealings in the euro in London as opposed to the eleven countries. The rate for overnight dealings in London in sterling is SONIA.

The Interbank Market

Apart from the very short-term money mentioned before, there is generally a very strong interbank market in which the banks lend money one to another for periods ranging from several weeks to 1 year.

In our discussions on commercial banking, we concentrated on the idea of banks taking money from deposits and lending it to other people. The banks also top up their funds by borrowing from other banks which have spare liquidity. As this is the marginal cost to the banks for raising new money, their wholesale lending rates are based on the interbank lending rate.

The terms 'bid rate' and 'offer rate' are usually met in securities markets. The bid rate is the dealer's buying rate and the offer rate the dealer's selling rate.

Obviously, the offer is higher than the bid, as the dealers will buy cheaper than they sell. The difference is called the 'spread'.

Curiously, when it comes to wholesale money, the deposit rate offered by a bank is called the bid rate and the lending rate is called the offer rate. Thus, the interbank rates in London are called LIBOR – London Interbank Offered Rate and LIBID – London Interbank Bid Rate. We find TIBOR in Tokyo, and EURIBOR for the twelve countries of the European Monetary Union. One exception is the US, where the interbank rate is called the 'Federal Funds Rate'.

We have already seen that interest rates vary with time and so the interbank rates for 1 month, 3 months, 6 months and 12 months will probably be different. The most common maturity used in the market is 3 months. If someone asks 'What's the £ LIBOR rate today?' they will be referring to 3 month LIBOR. Of course, the interbank market in London deals in dollars, yen, Swiss francs and other currencies and so, although LIBOR refers to London, it doesn't necessarily mean sterling. Again, these wholesale rates vary all the time and each bank's rate could be different. If we say £ LIBOR is 5$\frac{1}{16}$% we mean the average of major banks in the market.

Let's look at rates quoted for 3 month money in currencies in London in September 2002 (Table 6.1).

As London is a huge international market, the rate we hear of most commonly is LIBOR. We have seen that as LIBOR is the marginal cost of new money, then the lending rate in wholesale markets may be quoted as 'LIBOR +$\frac{1}{4}$', 'LIBOR +35 basis points', 'LIBOR +$\frac{1}{2}$'. Equally, floating rate notes issued in London will have the rate reset periodically (typically every 3 or 6 months) as LIBOR plus a given margin. If the rate for a loan or floating rate note is reset every 3 months, but LIBOR is different at different times of the day, then we need to define this precisely. It is usually quoted as the average of the LIBOR rates given by nominated banks at 11.00 a.m. on the relevant day.

Table 6.1 *London Interbank Offered Rate (LIBOR) – 3 month – 6/09/2002*

$	1.77500
£	3.98125
€	3.30575
¥	0.06500
C$	2.88333

Source: British Bankers' Association.

With the arrival of European Monetary Union, we now have the interbank market of the twelve countries in the euro and its reference rate EURIBOR, and we have the interbank market in London in the euro and its reference rate EURO LIBOR. As LIBOR has always been a major reference rate for bond issues, derivatives and other transactions the question arose – which one would win? The answer seems to be EURIBOR. Even London's derivatives exchange LIFFE admitted defeat in February 1999 and changed its contracts to EURIBOR.

Money Market Securities

The markets we have described above – the call money market and the general interbank market – deal with wholesale borrowing and lending amongst banks and financial institutions. The transactions are not represented by any security that can be traded. We will now deal with money market transactions that do result in trading in securities.

Typical instruments are:

❑ Treasury bills
❑ Local authority/Public utility bills
❑ Certificates of deposit
❑ Commercial paper
❑ Bills of Exchange.

Treasury Bills

Governments find that their income from taxes does not come in at a steady rate, nor is their expenditure at a steady rate. Apart from raising money with medium-to long-term government bills, it's convenient and useful to be able to borrow for shorter periods and balance their cash flow. The chosen instrument is the Treasury bill (UK, US); bon du trésor (France); Schatzwechsel (Germany, Austria); GKOs in Russia; or similar terms.

The bills may or may not be offered to the same organisations who buy government bonds. In the US, the bills for 3 or 6 months or 1 year are sold by auction weekly to the same primary dealers who buy federal notes and bonds. In the UK, the 3 and 6 month bills are sold every Friday by auction to banks. In France, anyone who has an account with the central bank can buy the 3 or 6 months or 1 year Treasury bill. They are sold weekly and money market dealers are usually called 'opérateurs principaux du marché' (OPMs). In Germany, the Bundesbank sells 6 month bills called 'Bubills' every quarter.

The payment of interest on an instrument which only lasts 3 months is not necessarily convenient. Most typically, money market instruments are sold *at a discount*. For example, suppose we are talking about a 1 year US Treasury bill, value $100, sold by auction. A dealer may bid $94. If accepted, they pay $94 and 1 year later receive $100 from the government. They discounted the $100 by 6% but now earn $6 for investing $94, which is 6.38%. Thus, the market refers to the *discount rate* and the resulting *yield*.

We have mentioned the term 'sale by auction' (or 'tender'). There are two kinds.

In one, everyone pays the price they bid ('bid price auction'). In the other, everyone pays the same price (often called the 'striking price)'. Anyone bidding at or above the striking price will receive an allocation, but not necessarily all they bid for.

Both types of auction are used in financial markets. For example, the Bank of England sells weekly Treasury bills by tender to the highest bidders – the bid/price technique. Government bonds are also sold on a bid price basis, unless it is index-linked stock and then striking price is used.

Just to make matters worse, a German publication I have in front of me says that the money market instruments are sold by auction on a bid price basis, which it calls 'US style', calling a striking price auction a 'Dutch auction'. A French publication says that money market instruments are sold on a bid price basis which it calls a 'Dutch auction'. For what it matters, I think that the Germans are right. Let's avoid all mention of Dutch auctions and simply say that if everyone pays the price they bid, it is a 'bid price' auction, and if everyone pays the same price, it is a 'striking price' auction. Both methods are used. On balance, the bid price method seems to be the most common, although the Federal Reserve auctions are now using striking price.

Local Authority/Public Utility Bills

These may be offered by municipalities, geographic departments, federal states, or public bodies like railways, electricity, gas. There is a very strong market in public sector bills as well as bonds in France and Germany. There are issues by SNCF or Électricité de France, or by the railways and post offices in Germany (Bundesbahn and Bundespost), as well as by the individual federal states. The market in the UK for local authority/municipal bills is very weak but is quite strong in the US.

Certificates of Deposit (CDs)

These are receipts issued by banks when soliciting wholesale deposits. The lenders may be other banks or corporates or investment institutions. The advantage to the *borrower* is that the money is lent for a specific period of time, for example, 3 months. The advantage to the *lender* is that, if they need the money back earlier, the certificate can be sold to someone else quite easily. There is a very strong CD market in the US and the European economies, with the exception of Germany.

There is usually an active and efficient market in certificates of deposit. As a result, yield rates will be a little less than those for 'sight' deposits, as we must pay for the advantage of liquidity.

Commercial Paper (CP)

So far, we have looked at short-term borrowing by governments, municipalities, public sector bodies and banks. There remains the question of corporates. Commercial companies can borrow in the wholesale markets and offer a security called 'commercial paper' (CP). It's just another promise to pay back. Central banks have to agree, as this is a deposit taking activity and must be controlled. There will be rules on which companies can or cannot borrow using CP. For example, in the UK companies must have a balance sheet capital of £25m and be publicly quoted on a stock exchange (although not necessarily in the UK). The minimum denomination is £100,000.

Commercial paper is an older market in the US (where it is a huge market with outstanding money owed over $1000bn). It has hit Europe in the last 15 years. Germany was the last major market to allow CP issues, in January 1991. Before that it was not practical due to a securities tax and the need for prior notification to the Treasury. Let's have a look at some figures on domestic commercial paper markets in key centres (from the BIS) in Table 6.2.

The market in Germany grew very fast, and the amount outstanding by mid-1992 had reached DM32bn (about $21bn), but later fell in popularity. CP has also reached some of the newer markets, too. In Czechoslovakia, Pilsen did an issue for 100m korunna in November 1991 and VW–Skoda for 300m korunna in January 1992.

Table 6.2 *Domestic markets for commercial paper*

Market	Market opening	Amount outstanding end 2001 $ billion
United States	pre 1960	2452.5
Japan	end 1987	693.2
United Kingdom	1986	220.7
France	end 1985	114.1
Canada	pre 1960	70.9
Australia	mid 1970s	45.8
Spain	1982	42.5
Germany	1991	36.5
Sweden	1983	21.1
Belgium	1990	17.9
Ireland	1986	10.7
Total		3725.9

Source: BIS Basle.

CP issues are, of course, just another way of borrowing money and may provide an alternative to borrowing from the bank. In early 1990, the Bank of Spain was struggling to control the credit explosion and limiting banks' ability to lend. The result was a huge increase in CP ('pagares de empresa') issues, as companies borrowed by selling CP (in some cases to the same banks who couldn't lend them money!).

Deregulation applies here as in other markets. The French now allow non-French entities to issue domestic CP and Germany did so from August 1992. At the end of 1995, outstanding CP in Germany from foreign issuers was higher than that from domestic issuers.

How do the CP issuers find the lenders? They set up a programme (perhaps a 5 year programme) and announce a bank or banks as dealers. If the programme is $500m, then the issuer does not intend to raise $500m *now* (which would be the case if it were a bond issue) but will borrow money from time to time and repay it from time to time, up to the maximum figure. If they wish to borrow $50m for 2 months, they would notify the bank dealer(s), who ring round typical lenders (other corporates, banks and investment institutions) and tie up the deal, all for a small commission. The banks do not *guarantee* to find lenders but if lenders are scarce may buy the CP themselves as a matter of goodwill. The effect of borrowing from the lenders directly, instead of borrowing from the bank, means that the rate may be less than the interbank rate.

Bills of Exchange

Another way in which a corporate might raise money short-term is by selling on a short-term trade debt (we met this in Chapter 5). The seller draws up a bill promising to pay for the goods supplied in, say, 3 months and asks the buyer to sign it. This is the bill of exchange. The seller of the goods can now sell this at a discount to the banks or general money market operators. We have seen that a bank's promise to pay may be better than a trader's and there is always a distinction between bills with the trader's signature (trade bills) and those with a bank's signature (bank or eligible bills). Bills may change hands several times in their short life. There are usually restrictions on the type of transaction that can be represented by a bill and so not all corporates can use bills of exchange. They are not especially popular in the US but widely used in Europe, especially in the UK. In France, the bill is 'lettre de change' and, in Germany, simply 'wechsel'.

We have now already met several ways in which a corporate might raise money short-term – bank overdraft, a general uncommitted bank line of credit, a revolving credit programme, a CP issue or using bill of exchange finance.

CENTRAL BANK ROLE

A key role is played in domestic money markets by central banks. They have a function as 'lender of the last resort', which we met in Chapter 3. They are prepared to help the other banks (especially commercial banks) with their liquidity problems.

Why would banks meet liquidity problems? In the first place, the key commercial banks must maintain working balances at the central bank. Where central banks insist on special reserves being left (Chapter 3), there will be times when the reserves look comfortable and times when they don't. The reserves are usually based on average balances over a month. Until the end of the month, the banks are not sure what the figure will be. Those banks in surplus will lend to other banks; those in deficit will borrow from other banks. At times, all the banks may have problems. This is when heavy tax payments are being made. The government's bank balance is going up; the banks' balances at the central bank are going down. The central bank will relend the money to keep everything on an even basis and to avoid wide fluctuations in money market rates. The rate set for the central bank's help gives it control over interest rates. When interest rates change, it is because the central bank changes the rate for its help to other banks.

There are two ways usually in which a central bank will help: direct assistance at special rates such as the *discount rate* or *lombard rate*; or by what is called *open market operations*.

What are these rates? The *discount rate* is the rate at which the bank will discount eligible bills of exchange (that is, top quality bills) for other banks. (The maturity of the bills must not exceed 3 months.) As this rate is below other rates, there is a quota for each bank, or life would be too easy. If we could discount a bill at $9\frac{1}{2}\%$ and then refinance ourselves at $8\frac{3}{4}\%$ at the central bank we would soon make a lot of money.

The *lombard rate* is an emergency lending rate against top quality securities (eligible bills, bills of exchange or government/federal bonds). Usually, as it is higher than money market rates, no limit to the quantity need be set. At times, however, limits have had to be set for temporary periods because the lombard rate was lower than money market rates.

Open market operations means that the central bank may be prepared to buy bills of exchange, Treasury bills or similar securities to help the banks' liquidity or to sell bills to help drain excess liquidity.

A popular method nowadays is the 'sale and repurchase agreement' (commonly called the *repo*). The central bank will buy nominated securities from the other banks for a stated period, for example, 7 days, 14 days, 28 days. At the end of the period, the banks must be ready to buy them back at a rate which includes the rate of interest on the money. The banks sell the securities to the central bank but must repurchase later. This is a very common method all over Europe. In the UK, the more common method used to be that the Bank of England would simply buy eligible securities outright. Later, repos became much more common.

These operations exist not only to help commercial banks with their liquidity but can also be used to influence money supply and market conditions. The central banks may keep the banks short of liquidity to keep credit scarce and stiffen interest rates.

For example, when a repo falls due, there will normally be another repo to keep the banks funded but the second repo may be for a smaller sum than the first.

With the arrival of monetary union in Europe, the previously separate systems of the twelve countries have been unified into one system. Policy is laid down by the European Central Bank (ECB) but is operated on a decentralised basis by the member central banks. Its rates, as announced on December 22, 1998 were:

- ❏ a fixed rate tender at 3% for the main refinancing operations
- ❏ a marginal lending facility of 4.5% (like the old lombard rate)
- ❏ a deposit facility of 2% for receiving surplus funds from the banking system.

The main refinancing operations are weekly tenders for funds with a 2 week maturity. There are also monthly tenders with a 3 month maturity. These tenders are essentially repos.

By way of contrast, the Bank of England operates on a daily basis using a mixture of repos and outright purchase of securities. (For those with long memories, and who seem to recall that the Bank did all of its refinancing operations through specialists called 'discount houses', this method has now been abandoned.) The decisions are made by the Monetary Policy Committee, consisting of the governor, two deputy governors, two bank executives and four outsiders.

In the US, the Federal Reserve operates by influencing the overnight interbank federal funds rate and also the deposit rate for bank assistance. The rates are announced by the Federal Open Market Committee, consisting of the seven member board of governors and twelve members from regional Federal Reserve Banks.

DOMESTIC BOND MARKETS

Introduction

The term 'bond' applies to instruments which are medium- to longer-term. The term 'note' is also used in some markets. The US, for example, has 2, 5 and 10 year Treasury *notes* and a 30 year Treasury *bond*. In the UK, the same 5 year instrument would be called a bond.

Language here is a problem in that there is no consistency. The French, for example, call instruments up to 5 years (but prior to 1992, up to 7 years) 'bons du trésor' and from 7 years 'obligations du trésor'. The Spanish equally have 'bonos del estado' up to 5 years but after that they are 'obligaciones del estado'. On the other hand, the 10 year issue in Italy is 'buoni del tesoro'.

Let's look at some general characteristics of bonds. As we saw in Chapter 1, they are simply receipts or promises to pay back money lent. We are not, here, talking of short-term money, however, but medium- to long-term borrowings – in excess of 1 year and possibly for 30 or more years.

The general features are:

❑ The name of the bond
❑ The nominal or par value in the currency of denomination
❑ The redemption value – usually the nominal value, but there are other possibilities (index linking, for example)
❑ The rate of interest expressed as a % of nominal value; this is called the 'coupon': the frequency of payment is stated
❑ The redemption date.

The rate of interest is called the coupon because 'bearer' bonds have no register of holders. The bond states that the issuer owes the 'bearer', whoever that may be. The bond therefore has attachments called 'coupons' so that the bearer may detach these as required and claim the interest. Even where bonds are registered and the interest can be posted to the holder's home, the market still refers to the 'coupon' or 'coupon rate'.

The coupon could be variable in cases where the rate of interest is changed periodically in line with market rates. As the word 'bond' implies a fixed rate of interest, instruments like this are usually called *floating rate notes*. If issued in London, the coupon may be defined as 'LIBOR +45 basis points' and reviewed 6 monthly.

Some stocks have no redemption date and are called *undated* or *perpetual*. If the holder needs the capital, they must sell the bond to someone else in the secondary market.

Typically, bonds are classified by remaining maturity. The scale may well be:

❑ *Shorts*   – life of up to 5 years
❑ *Mediums* – life of 5 to 15 years
❑ *Longs*   – life of 15 years or over.

Notice that this is the *remaining* maturity. A 20 year bond is a 'long' at first but 10 years later it's a 'medium' and 6 years later it's a 'short'.

At original issue, bonds may be sold as an open *offer for sale* or sold directly to a smaller number of professional investors and called a *private placing*.

In an offer for sale, a syndicate of banks with one bank as *lead manager* will buy the bonds en bloc from the issuer and resell them to investors. In this way, they underwrite the issue since, if the investors don't buy, the banks will be forced to keep them. Needless to say, they charge fees for this risk.

If the lead bank buys all the bonds and sells them to the syndicate, it's usually called the *bought deal*. The syndicate members may themselves then sell the bonds at varying prices. More commonly these days, the lead manager and syndicate buy the bonds simultaneously and agree to sell at the same price for a period – the *fixed price reoffering*. This is very common in the US and now in the so-called 'euromarkets'. Less frequently (apart from government bonds) there may not be a syndicate but the bonds are sold by competitive *auction*.

There are several types of bond according to the issuer:

❑ Government bonds
❑ Local authority/Public utility bonds
❑ Mortgage and other asset backed bonds
❑ Corporate bonds
❑ Foreign bonds
❑ Junk bonds.

Corporate bonds may also be:

❑ Debentures, or
❑ Convertibles

and there is a hybrid type of instrument, the preference share or participation stock.

Government Bonds

Almost always, these seem to dominate the bond markets. Most modern governments are running a budget deficit and this leads to large-scale issues of bonds. Sometimes the secondary market is run on stock exchanges (France, Germany, UK) and sometimes outside stock exchanges (US).

As regards the types of bonds and method of issue, there are many variations:

❑ The bonds may be issued by the central bank (US, Germany, France) or by the Ministry of Finance (Netherlands, Japan), or general 'Debt Management Offices' (UK, Ireland, Sweden, Portugal, New Zealand).
❑ They may be sold on a regular day per month.
❑ The issue may be to specialist dealers (US, UK, France, Germany, Italy) or to a syndicate of banks in agreed proportions (Switzerland).
❑ Bonds may be 'bearer' status or registered. For example, in the UK, government bonds are registered and the registrar's department handles 5m interest payments per year and 1m changes of ownership. In Germany, the most important government bonds for the wholesale markets are bearer bonds. There are no certificates and buying/selling is entered on the computerised Bundeschuldenbuch.

❑ Some markets pay interest twice per year (US, UK, Italy, Japan), others only once per year (France, Germany, Netherlands, Spain, Belgium).

❑ US government bonds are priced in fractions (down to $\frac{1}{32}$). Elsewhere bonds are priced in decimals.

Let's look at some examples:

In the *US*, 2 year Treasury notes are sold every month, while 5 and 10 year Treasury notes and 30 year Treasury bonds are sold every quarter. They are sold by auction, on regular dates, to some 40 primary dealers.

In *France*, government bonds are called OATS (Obligations Assimilables du Trésor) and are sold on a regular monthly auction basis (on the first Thursday in each month). They are sold to primary dealers who have an obligation to support the auction. They must take up 3% of annual bond issuance and trade 3% of secondary market turnover. The primary dealers are called 'spécialistes en valeurs du trésor' (SVTs). However, at each auction the offerings are usually more of existing bonds rather than offering new ones each time. A point to note is that there are 2 and 5 year issues called Treasury bills rather than bonds. These are known as BTAN (Bons du Trésor à Interêt Annuel). (Short-term Treasury bills are BTF – Bons du Trésor à Taux Fixe.) BTANS are sold on the third Thursday in each month.

In the past, some fixed rate bonds have been issued which are convertible later into floating rate and floating rates convertible into fixed. Also in the past, some zero-coupon bonds (to be explained later) called 'Felins' have been issued (but none in recent years).

After not issuing bonds at floating rate for several years, the Bank of France announced proposals in 1996 to issue new floating rate bonds with the interest paid quarterly and linked to a new benchmark for the yield of 10 year OATS called TEC10 (Taux de l'Échéance Constante).

In *Germany*, there were 2 and 4 year medium-term notes – Bundesschatz-anweisungen, but these maturities were lowered in mid-1996 to 2 years and referred to as 'Schätze'. There are also 5 year government bonds – Bundesobligationen and 10–30 year bonds – Bundesanleihen. The 10 year issues are the popular ones (rather than of longer duration) and most are fixed rate, although there is the occasional Floating Rate Bond.

In Germany, there are bond issues from the Federal States (Länder), the railways and the post office. There are also issues from the German Unity Fund (Fonds Deutsche Einheit). All are issued for them by the Bundesbank.

German government Bundesanleihen issues used to be shared out amongst a syndicate of banks with 20% only reserved for foreign banks. In July 1990, however, part of an issue was sold by auction to the highest bidder. In October 1991 the 20% rule was abolished and, in late 1997, it was announced that the syndicate would be scrapped and replaced by a 'Federal Loan Bidding Group' in 1998. This has 70 members, contrasted with the 40 primary dealers in the US. The Bundes-schatzanweisungen were sold totally by auction but there have been no new issues since mid-1995. They were replaced in late 1996 by a new 2 year Treasury Note.

Bundesobligationen are issued in series. A series is offered continuously for 4–6 weeks 'on tap'. They are aimed at retail buyers, as are the Treasury Financing Notes (Finanzierungschätze). At the end of the period, the unsold bonds are offered for sale by auction. The main retail bond for savers, however, is the Bundesschatz-briefe. These are sold continuously by all banks and financial institutions and are for 6 or 7 years. The bonds can be sold back at par at any time but the longer the holder keeps them, the greater the rate of interest.

All *French* and *German* bonds are now issued in the new currency, the euro, and all outstanding bonds have also been converted to the euro.

In *Japan*, government bonds are sold by auction by the Ministry of Finance. 40% are sold to a bank syndicate in agreed proportions; 60% are sold by the auction method. 2, 4, 5, 6 and 10 year bonds are sold monthly and 20 year bonds are sold quarterly. Interest payments are semi-annual. Government, municipal and public sector bonds are 60% of issuance and dominate the market.

In the *UK*, government bonds are called 'gilts' or 'gilt-edged', meaning a very secure investment (the term came into widespread use in the 1930s). The bonds are issued on regular dates and sold to specialist dealers called 'gilt-edged market makers'. Bonds not taken up at an auction are bought by the Debt Management Office and sold whenever the dealers want them as 'tap stock'. Maturities range typically from 5 to 25 years.

Gilts are divided into three main classes:

1. Dated
2. Undated
3. Index-linked.

New undated gilts are no longer issued but there are eight still in existence. There is no redemption date. In bond markets, bonds with no redemption date may be called undated, perpetual or irredeemable. There is very little trading of undated gilts by the wholesale markets.

Index-linked gilts pay a rate of interest and a redemption value based on the change in the Retail Price Index in the same period. Other governments which offer index-linked bonds are Australia, Canada, Iceland, Israel, New Zealand, Sweden and, more recently, the US and France. The UK index-linked sector is much the biggest of these. Issue began in 1981. In May 1996, the US Treasury Secretary announced that they would issue index-linked Treasury Notes and Bonds for the first time, and began in January 1997. The French government followed suit with its first issue in September 1998.

(In 1973, the French government issued bonds – Giscard bonds – linked to the change in the price of gold between then and 1988. As the price of gold rose, this caused great embarrassment! The bond was used by Tom Wolfe in 'The Bonfire of the Vanities'.)

Why do governments issue index-linked bonds anyway? There are three reasons:

❏　Risk averse investors, such as pension funds and retired people, like the idea.
❏　Monetary policy is more credible – the government has an incentive to keep inflation low.
❏　The yield helps the government and others to estimate market views on further inflation. The difference between the yield on index-linked stock and ordinary stock should equal the expected inflation rate.

The idea is not totally new. In 1780, the State of Massachusetts issued a bond where payment of interest and principal was linked to a commodity basket of corn, beef, wool and leather!

Spanish government bonds are called 'bonos del estado' with maturities of 3 and 5 years but the 10 year maturity is called 'obligaciones del estado'. The central bank sells these on a regular date each month.

Italian government bonds are called BTP (Buoni del Tesoro Poliennali) if fixed rate. These are 2–10 years in maturity. However, there are floating rate bonds of similar maturity called CCT (Certificati Credito del Tesoro). Both are sold by the central bank to 20 primary dealers on fixed dates every month. There are also 6 year bonds which buyers can sell back after 3 years called CTO (Certificati del Tesoro con Opzione).

There seems to be a trend at the moment for some governments to issue longer dated bonds than in the past. In early 1999, Japan and Greece issued their first 30 year bonds, and Switzerland issued a 50 year bond (the first for Switzerland since 1909!).

As explained earlier in this chapter (see *Treasury Bills*), some auctions of government stock are bid price and some striking price. A bid price auction might seem to be the obvious answer. The argument for striking price, however, is that it avoids the problem of the 'winner's curse', that is that some bidders may pay a higher price and end up with bonds that they can't sell. The belief is that striking price may encourage more bidders to participate. Either way, the evidence does not seem to be very strong. The US used to use bid prices, but now uses striking price; the UK, which used to use striking price, now uses bid price (except for index-linked). (An example of the result of a bid price auction is shown as Appendix 1 to this chapter.)

Most government bond markets allow dealing to begin a few days before the auction – the 'grey' or 'when issued' market. Institutions can buy from primary dealers at an agreed price which reduces the dealers' risk.

In early 1999, the outstanding value of government bonds for the then eleven countries of monetary union was the equivalent of $3000bn, compared with $2700bn for the US and $2000bn for Japan.

Local Authority/Public Sector Bonds

We have already mentioned issues in Germany by the railways, post offices, Federal states and the German Unity Fund. Public sector issues are also very common in France. There are the utilities like SNCF, Électricité de France and Gaz de France. There are also public sector bodies like Crédit Foncier (housing credits) and Crédit Local de France (local authority financing). Bonds may, of course, be issued by cities, like New York, or regions, like the Basque Country.

Local authority and public sector issues are very rare in the UK, although some long-dated bonds issued in the 1970s are still traded. Municipal bonds are a big market in the US.

Mortgage and Asset-Backed Bonds

In some markets, there is a big market in mortgage bonds. In the US, for example, it has been the custom for many years to bundle up mortgages and use them as the backing security for mortgage bonds. The mortgages may be guaranteed by bodies with names like Ginnie Mae, Fannie Mae and Sallie Mae. (They, naturally, stand for something much more formal and boring, for example, Government National Mortgage Association – GNMA and hence Ginnie Mae.) The US mortgage bond market is huge – over $1000bn outstanding.

In Germany, some 40 banks, including eight public mortgage banks, have the right to issue mortgage bonds called Pfandbriefe. Banks also issue mortgage bonds in Denmark and Finland. These, however, are not the same as the US mortgage bonds. The latter involve taking the original mortgages off the balance sheet, placing them in a separate *special purpose vehicle* (SPV) and issuing bonds financed by the stream of principal and interest payments of the mortgages (see Figure 6.4). The German Pfandbriefe are simply a way for the banks to raise money to fund their mortgage loans (although they are, of course, a very secure investment).

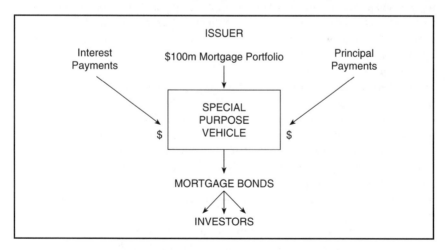

Figure 6.4   *Asset-backed security issue*

The technique involved in the US case is called *securitisation of assets* and we refer to *asset-backed securities* (ABS). You may also see reference to *collaterised mortgage obligations* (CMO). While we have so far only mentioned the US, the technique is also used in Japan and Europe (and is growing).

Again, we have so far only referred to mortgages, but the technique can and has been used to take any stream of income payments (or income and principal payments) and use them to fund an ABS issue. (Why banks and others do this will be explained shortly.) The market is growing in ingenuity, as will be seen from the following list of income streams funding ABS issues:

❏ Auto loans (VW, General Motors and others)
❏ Record royalties (David Bowie, Rod Stewart)
❏ Telephone calls (Telemex, Mexico)
❏ Future export revenues (Brazilian Iron Ore)
❏ Football season tickets (Real Madrid, Lazio, Fiorentina)
❏ Property rentals (British Land and others)
❏ Rolling stock leases (Nomura in the UK)
❏ Credit card receivables (Citibank, MBNA)
❏ Bank corporate loans (National Westminster, Hypovereinsbank)
❏ Non-performing loans (Banca di Roma).

Let's look at two examples.

The National Westminster Bank issue aroused tremendous interest. It was first used in November 1996 and again in 1997 under the acronym 'ROSE' (Repeat Offering Securitised Entity Funding). The first issue was to a value of $5bn and represented as much as one third of NatWest's corporate loan book, being loans to some 300 large corporates in the UK, continental Europe and the US. They were issued as eleven classes of notes – various levels of seniority offering a range of risk/ return ratios. The bank guarantees anonymity and continues to administer the original loans.

The British Land bond was issued in May 1999 and was based on the rental income of twelve properties in London's The Broadgate Centre. At £1.54bn, it was the largest property securitisation in Europe so far. Like NatWest, the issue was made in several tranches of eurobonds varying between medium- and long-term.

To be feasible, all we need is a pool of homogeneous assets like mortgages, trade receivables, motor car loans and so on. The funds are pooled in the same SPV which has a 'firewall' between it and the original issuer. The payments are sometimes (but not always) guaranteed against default, and usually the bonds attract a high credit rating.

What, then, are the attractions of this technique for the issuer?

So far as banks are concerned, it is the ability to lighten the balance sheet and make better use of capital. Basle Committee capital ratio rules make it expensive to keep low profit items on the balance sheet. The money can, when released, be used for more profitable investments. For NatWest this was a major motive in the ROSE case. Low yielding loans were removed from its books without jeopardising client relationships. In the case of British Land, the money was used to pay back more expensive bank debt and get cheaper funding. The average cost of funds was said to have been reduced from 8.49% to 7.4%, saving at least £20m in 1999.

The US market has always been the biggest for ABS, followed by Japan. The market in Europe, however, is now growing fast. It has been helped by regulatory changes in Germany, Spain and Italy (Deutschebank did the first German mortgage-backed bond in May 1998) and also by the arrival of the euro. Merrill Lynch estimate that ABS issues worth $18.9bn were made in the first quarter of 1999, compared to $13.8bn in the same quarter of 1998. The biggest source for ABS in Europe is property, with domestic mortgages accounting for 41% and commercial mortgages another 14%.

Corporate Bonds

There are, of course, bonds issued by corporates and there is a very strong market in the US. In Europe, as a generalisation, the corporate bond market is weaker, being overshadowed by the government and public sector bond market. In Germany there is, anyway, a big tradition of reliance on bank finance as opposed to either bonds or equities. Very large European corporates may, in any case, find it easier to issue the bond in London as a *eurobond* rather than as a domestic bond (see later in this chapter). The largest corporate bond issued so far is one for €9.4bn ($9.78bn) issued by Olivetti in June 1999.

Corporate bonds can, however, be quite long dated. In the UK, a property company (MEPC) issued a bond in 1988 that will redeem in 2032 – 44 years. Also, British Land did a 40 year issue in September 1995. Property companies look far ahead to long-term leases and commitments. Apart from these, we have seen 100 year bonds issued by bodies like Walt Disney, Coca Cola and IBM, although sometimes the issuer has an option to redeem the bond after 30 years. These bonds are so long dated that they are almost equity, but the interest is tax deductible. IBM's 100 year bond only cost them 10 basis points more than their 30 year bond. Who among the investors looks so far ahead? The answer is pension funds and life assurance companies who have to meet long-term liabilities.

There are a number of variations on the theme:

Debentures are corporate bonds which are backed by security, for example, land and buildings. If the issuer goes into liquidation, these assets must be sold to pay the bondholders. Because they are more secure, however, the rate of interest is less. Some investment funds will only invest in corporate bonds which are debentures. Again, language is a problem. The definition given is the UK usage of the term. In the US and Canada, 'debenture' may be used to describe any bond. Just bear in mind that corporate bonds may be unsecured (the majority) or secured on specific assets. Whilst securing a bond gives a corporate cheaper finance, it's also inconvenient to tie up assets in this way. Lengthy and tedious legal procedures must be gone through before these assets can be disposed of and replaced by others. MEPC and British Land (mentioned above) have both unsecured bonds and debentures on the market. The unsecured bonds pay 1.1% more than the debentures in the case of MEPC and 70 basis points in the case of British Land.

A *convertible* is a bond which can be converted later, either into another type of bond (for example, convertible gilts) or into equity. The difference between the implied conversion price of the equity and the market price is called the 'premium'. For example, the bond may confer the right, after 3 years, to convert $100 of bond into 50 shares. The conversion price is $2 per share; if the market price is $1.60 at the time, then the initial premium is 25%. If the conversion price remains above the market price, then the bond will redeem in the normal way.

The attraction to the *investor* is the mix of risk and return – the steady income we associate with a bond with the possible capital gain we associate with a share. For the *issuer*, the finance is cheaper as the interest rate will be less due to its attraction. What if investors wish to convert, where do the shares come from? The issuer creates *new* shares. Suppose the bond is $500m. The issuer hopes that instead of having to find $500m to redeem the bond, they will issue $500m of new shares instead. True, the equity will be diluted but it probably won't be by a large margin. In Europe (but not as clearly in the US), shareholders must give approval for the issue of convertibles because, generally, any new shares issued for cash must be offered to the existing shareholders.

Sometimes convertibles hit unforeseen problems. The general fall in the Japanese stock market since 1990 means that the market price of many shares is below the conversion price. With Japan seen as somewhat risky, re-financing these convertibles will be expensive.

Sometimes the right to convert is into another company's shares (which the issuing company owns). For example, Deutsche Bank issued €1.5bn in early 1999 to help fund its takeover of Bankers Trust. The bonds, however, are exchangeable into Allianz shares, which Deutsche owns. This is a way of Deutsche reducing its holding in Allianz without directly selling the shares and moving the price against it. The premium was 30%. Deutsche had previously done a convertible with the right to convert into shares of Daimler-Benz, which the bank also owned. (The German banks are slowly reducing their shareholdings in large domestic corporates.)

An alternative to a convertible bond is to issue a bond in which the right to buy shares later at a certain price is contained in a separate *warrant*. This is more flexible than the convertible, in that the warrant can be used later to buy shares more cheaply while still keeping the bond. The warrants are often detached from the bonds and sold separately.

Sometimes, an entity which is not the company may issue warrants on the company's shares, for example, Salomon Bros offering warrants on Eurotunnel shares. This is often called the *covered warrants market* because Salomon must cover the risk by owning the shares. If Eurotunnel issued a bond with warrants, it has the right to issue new shares if need be. Naturally, Salomon Bros do not have that right and must obtain the shares conventionally. Warrants may be (and frequently are) offered on a 'basket' of different shares. These covered warrants (very popular these days) are really simply part of the traded options market and priced accordingly (see Chapter 11). For example, in February 1996, James Capel issued a series of basket warrants linking shares tipped as potential takeover victims in 1996 in five different markets – insurance, banking, general finance, utilities and mixed.

Preference shares usually pay dividend as a fixed percentage rate. If there is any shortage of money, their dividends must be paid out before other dividends. In the event of liquidation, preference shareholders have priority over ordinary share-holders. They normally have no voting rights. If the dividend cannot be paid, it is legally owed to them. Hence they are 'cumulative' (normally). On the continent of Europe, these are typically called participation certificates or, in Germany and Switzerland, genusscheine or participationsscheine.

The Americans use the term 'preferred stock' and the French have several variations on this theme:

❏ Certificats d'investissement
❏ Titres participatifs – public sector only and the dividend may be partly fixed and partly linked to profit
❏ Actions à dividende prioritaire (ADP) – the dividend is the ordinary dividend plus a given percentage.

The general features of all the above are non-voting, preference in the event of liquidation and cumulative. They are hybrid instruments with some characteristics of a bond and some of an equity. Banks have done many issues to raise capital to count as Tier 1 Capital (National Westminster Bank, September 1991) or Tier 2. To count as Tier 1 they must be undated and non-cumulative. In April 1996, TB Finance did an issue of ¥100bn preference shares, convertible into common shares of Tokai Bank. As conversion at some point is mandatory, the issue counts as Tier 1 capital.

Foreign Bonds

Foreign bonds are domestic issues by non-residents – 'bulldogs' in the UK, 'yankees' in the US, 'matadors' in Spain, 'samurai' in Tokyo and even 'kangaroo' bonds in Australia! (In April, 1999, Rabobank did an issue of 5 year bonds, A\$350m, in the Australian domestic market.)

Notice that the bonds are domestic bonds in the local currency, it's only the *issuer* who is foreign. They should not be confused with *international* bonds (also called *eurobonds*), which are bonds issued outside their natural market.

Non-US firms seeking dollar funding, for example, have a choice. The bonds may be issued in London as 'eurobonds' or in the US as 'yankee' bonds. The investment community is different in both markets. While the ultimate investors in the US might have a slightly parochial attitude to European firms, the investment institutions themselves have sophisticated credit assessment teams. In the absence of formal credit ratings, they will make up their own minds. The eurobond market might be guided by credit ratings (or their absence) rather more slavishly. In any case, market conditions change from time to time. Sometimes it's easier to raise dollars in New York, sometimes in London. There have been major issues in New York, for example, by well known British corporates such as ICI and Diageo.

In Japan, Asian issues are often better received than in London although the market is not as liquid. In August 1992, the Ministry of Finance relaxed the rules for sovereign borrowers to allow issues rated BBB (previously, they had to be at least A). This proved very attractive to BBB issuers like Hungary, Turkey and Greece as London eurobond issues rated BBB need to carry a higher coupon than samurai. On the other hand, costs are higher than in London. Banks (they must be Japanese) act as custodians and paying/fiscal agents in Europe. As a result, commission fees must be paid. Then, early in 1996, the Ministry of Finance decided to allow non-investment grade issues. This was followed by a spate of samurai issues – ¥2200bn in the first 7 months of 1996 as opposed to ¥1700bn in the whole of 1995.

Foreign bonds may be subject to a different tax regime or other restrictions. For example, 'yankees' can only be sold to qualified institutional buyers in the first 2 years.

Junk Bonds

This was a phenomenon which occurred in the US domestic markets in the 1970s and 1980s. We mentioned earlier, under 'credit ratings' that bonds rated below BBB grade were essentially speculative. As a result, they offered a much higher rate of interest.

A clever researcher at Drexel Burnham Lambert, one Michael Milken, did a study of the behaviour of such bonds in the early 1970s. He proved that an investment in these bonds would return a better yield than investment grade bonds, even deducting the loss due to greater defaults. He was not the first to discover this – other academic studies had come to the same conclusion – but he was the first to do anything about it. At first, his firm dealt in underpriced bonds in this category in the secondary markets. They then began to look at the potential for new issues. At that time, the bonds of 90% of US corporates would, if issued, not be investment grade. Drexels (and Michael Milken) began to do primary issues too, arguing that the judgement of the rating agencies was too harsh.

Then the bonds were used to raise large sums of money for takeover bids. The market began to refer to them as 'junk bonds' (Drexels called them 'high yield bonds', a more respectable title!).

Junk bonds slowly became notorious because huge sums of money were raised with these bonds by entrepreneurs who bought companies much bigger than they were – the 'leveraged' takeover – for example, Nelson Peltz/National Can; Ronald Perelman/Revlon; Carl Icahn/TWA.

Each year at Beverly Hills, Drexels would hold a 'High Yield Bond Conference' at which the wheeler-dealers and the potential investors would sit at the feet of the 'junk bond king' Michael Milken and be entertained in lavish style. The rather less formal name for the conference was the 'Predators' Ball'. (The whole amazing story is told in Connie Bruch, *The Predators' Ball*, Simon & Schuster, 1988.)

Later, the US Securities and Exchange Commission decided that Drexels and Michael Milken had broken the law in various ways during the course of their activities. In addition, banks and other investors realised that they had gone too far, especially with the arrival of the recession. The bubble eventually burst. The firm of Drexel Burnham Lambert collapsed in early 1990 and the 'junk bond king' Michael Milken was jailed for 10 years for infringing various laws, although the sentence was reduced later.

Opinion is still divided between those who believe that Milken revitalised corporate America and those who think that his sentence wasn't nearly long enough!

For a long time there were no junk bond issues in London's 'eurobond' market. In April 1997, however, a UK venture capital company, Doughty Hanson, issued a non-investment grade 10 year bond for DM157m to finance the takeover of a Swiss firm. Other issues followed. Foreseeing monetary union, interest rates in many European countries were falling and investors were anxious to find higher yields, albeit at higher risk. The Far East crisis in 1997 and the Russian default in 1998 dealt the market a severe blow as investors' liking for risk cooled dramatically! Even worse, the collapse of the bonds of many investment grade companies in 2002 has changed the whole perception of risk.

INTERNATIONAL MARKETS

Background: Eurocurrencies

Some markets are called *international* markets or, misleadingly, *Euromarkets*.

We are talking here of dealing outside the natural market of the transaction. For example, December 1996 saw the second biggest privatisation of all time – Deutsche Telekom (the Japanese NTT being the biggest). Shares were offered in tranches to Germany, UK, the rest of Europe, the Americas and Asia.

In late 1991, Kuwait raised a huge dollar loan, $5.5bn, from a syndicate of banks in London to repair the damage caused during the Gulf War. It's an 'international loan'.

Bonds are frequently raised in London by syndicates of banks of all nationalities and in dollars, yen, euros and other major currencies. We call them 'eurobonds' or, more correctly, 'international bonds'. For example, SNCF (the French railways) may decide to issue a bond in London and in dollars, instead of in Paris and in French francs.

How did all this begin? Its origins lie in the period after the Second World War. Russia and so-called 'Iron Curtain' countries which held dollars were worried that the US authorities might seize them for political reasons. The Russians owned a bank in France, Banque Commercial pour l'Europe du Nord, and concentrated their holdings there. This bank lent the dollars to other non-US banks in Europe. Some say that the term *Eurodollars* was used because the telex code of the bank was Eurobank. Others believe that it was a natural name for dollar dealings outside the US.

In the post-war years there were plenty of dollars in the hands of non-Americans. American spending in Europe through the Marshall Plan was one source. 1957 saw the Treaty of Rome and the arrival in Europe of American multinational firms – earning dollars and spending them. A European firm might earn, say, $20m for sales to US firms. The dollars were credited to its account with, perhaps, Banque Nationale de Paris. These were now Eurodollars and could be lent to other entities in Europe. They were dollars outside the control of the US authorities. For years, for example, there was a strict control on interest rates called 'Regulation Q'. It put an upper level on interest rates offered to depositors. If our mythical European firm above chose not to convert the dollars into francs but lend them to BNP on deposit, BNP's interest rate was not constrained by Regulation Q – hence an increase in dealings in dollars held by non-US residents.

(The *Oxford English Dictionary* in 1972 suggested that the first recorded reference to the phrase 'Eurodollar' was in the financial review of *The Times*, 24 October 1960.)

In July 1963, President Kennedy decided to tax 'yankee bonds'. Remember yankees? They are dollar bonds issued in the US by non-residents. The perception was that perhaps these bonds could be issued in Europe, finding the investors amongst those non-US residents who held dollar balances. In 1963, Warburgs lead managed a bond issue in London worth $15m for the Italian motorway authority, Autostrade – generally believed to be the first *eurobond* – a dollar bond issued in Europe and not the US. London, with its non-protectionist policies and its long traditions, became the natural market for this new business. To quote Al Alletzhauser in his interesting history *The House of Nomura* (Bloomsbury, 1990):

Almost overnight the world's financial centre shifted to London. The big four Japanese stockbrokers wasted no time in setting up offices there. If they could not sell Japanese stock to the Americans, they would sell them to the Europeans. Over the years, it proved to be one of the most profitable moves Japan's brokers ever made abroad.

In 1950, there were 140 foreign banks in London; by 1973 the number had risen to 340 and today there over 500. It was a vital shot in the arm for the London financial market which had suffered from the post-war decline of the UK as a major economic power.

We said earlier that the term 'Euro' is misleading. For example, dealings might take place in Tokyo, relending dollars held by Asian organisations. The terms 'euromarkets' and 'eurobonds' are well established, however, although 'international markets' is a more correct term for dealings in a currency outside its natural domestic market (and, thus, outside the *control* of its domestic market). There is now a further confusion between a eurobond and a bond denominated in the euro! Eurocurrencies is a wider term, reminding us that the currency might not be dollars but yen, euros, drachma and so on.

For reasons we shall see below, Eurocurrency dealings grew enormously from an estimated $1bn in 1959 to an estimated $6bn by 1992 (BIS figures).

The irony is that while these markets grew as a result of restrictions in the US, they did not disappear when the restrictions were later abolished.

The Syndicated Loan Market

In 1973–74 came events that led to a large increase in dollars held by non-US residents – the OPEC countries' oil price increases. Oil, which was $3 per barrel in October 1973, was $10.5 per barrel by January 1974. This led to a huge rise in dollar balances held by OPEC countries and a huge reduction in the dollar balances of many sovereign states. The services of international banks were required to recycle these dollars from those with the surpluses to those in deficit, many of whom were underdeveloped countries – largely in Africa and South America.

The original use of the Eurodollars was for the short-term interbank market. Then we saw syndicates of banks getting together to lend the dollar balances as part of, say, a 7 year loan to Mexico. As the source was dependent on what might be short-term balances, the loans were all at floating rate, so that rates could be adjusted according to the new LIBOR rates in London. The banks might argue (as we look back on this period) that they were encouraged to lend by the world's financial and political authorities, worried about a bottleneck in the world's financial system.

To share the risk, the banks spread each loan across a syndicate of banks, perhaps with as many as 100 banks in a syndicate. Notices of these loans would appear in the London *Financial Times* and other relevant publications – 'as a matter of record only'. What was the notice for then? It was an advertisement for the banks concerned – a *tombstone* notice, in the jargon of the trade (some say because financial notices in the last century were placed next to those for births and deaths!).

Whether the banks were encouraged to lend or not, they did so and on a large scale – plenty of dollars, plenty of borrowers and nice rates of interest. To be fair, they must have looked at some borrowers, for example, Mexico or Nigeria and thought 'How can we go wrong, when they have this precious commodity, oil?'

The biggest lender was Citibank, whose chairman, Walter Wriston, encouraged the others with the famous words 'Sovereign borrowers do not go bust.' He meant that governments come and go but countries would always survive and they had assets which could, if necessary, be seized.

The International Debt Crisis

Walter Wriston couldn't have been more wrong. For a time, indeed, 'all went merry as a marriage bell' as the poet Byron says. However, his next line is: 'But hush! hark! a deep sound strikes like a rising knell!'

The deep sound in this case was the voice of the Mexican finance minister telling an audience of bankers in New York, on 20 August 1982, that repayment of principal on bank loans was to be deferred for 3 months. Brazil, Argentina and others quickly followed suit.

Falling oil prices, falling commodity prices generally and a large rise in dollar interest rates (remember, the loans are floating rate) had done the damage. Mexico followed its announcement by imposing total exchange controls and nationalising all the banks.

To understand the banks' reaction to this, we must realise that the three largest South American debtor nations owed commercial banks $150bn, and that Mexican debt alone accounted for 44% of the capital of the nine largest US banks. The very survival of some of the world's largest banks was in question, and that meant that the whole international financial system was in jeopardy.

The banks met in fear and panic at the IMF in Toronto in September 1982. A wit described the meeting as 'rearranging the deckchairs on the Titanic'. The key figures – Jacques de Larosière, IMF managing director, Paul Volcker, chairman of the Federal Reserve Board, Gordon Richardson, governor of the Bank of England and Fritz Leutwiler, chairman of BIS – mapped out a strategy. The essence was to buy time – to ask the debtors to implement economic policies to reduce the deficits that had led to the initial problems and to ask the banks to give the new policies time to work. The loans were to be rescheduled and repayments of interest deferred.

In a sense, it was a cat and mouse game. J.M. Keynes once said 'if you owe the bank £1000 you may be in trouble; if it's £1 million, maybe the bank's in trouble.'

The banks were as much at risk as the debtors. Cut them off from new supplies of money and they can no longer buy Western goods. Drive them into the ground with austere economic programmes and you may provoke a coup d'état and a communist government. America hardly wants a communist government in Mexico, on its doorstep.

Things were not easy. In 1985, the IMF suspended loans to Brazil and Argentina as economic targets were missed. Peru announced a limit on debt repayments. In December, oil halved in price from $30 per barrel to $15 – Mexico's situation worsened.

Everyone called it the 'LDC debt crisis' (LDC, Less Developed Countries). 1987 was a crisis year, as Brazil suspended interest payments and spent all year arguing with the banks.

Up to 1987, banks had had bad debt reserves of only about 5%. Walter Wriston's successor at Citibank, John Reed, decided in May 1987 to grasp the nettle and increased the bad debt charge against profit to $3bn (30%), plunging them into loss.

Other banks followed suit. Of the UK's big four banks, Midland and Lloyds, the two smallest, had the largest exposures and declared in 1987 their first losses of the century. This was followed by their second losses of the century in 1989, as all the banks added to these bad debt reserves, which now ranged in total from 40% at Citibank to 100% in the case of J.P. Morgan's medium- to long-term LDC debt.

The LDC debt crisis was sad news for the ordinary citizens of these countries. It would be nice to think that the money (about $300bn in total) had been spent strengthening the infrastructure of the countries but a great deal was wasted on grandiose prestige projects. Even worse, much has found its way into bank accounts abroad. Meanwhile, at home, the poorer citizen took the consequences – *sunt lacrimae rerum*.

Several attempts to solve the LDC problem have been tried:

❏ Banks sold LDC debt at a large discount to other banks, simply spreading the risk.

❏ Debt for equity swaps – some LDC debt was exchanged (at a discount) for equity in the country concerned. For example, the American Express Bank swapped $100m of its Mexican debt at a discount for equity in Mexican hotels. In a bizarre incident, some Brazilian debt was used to buy a Brazilian centre forward for Eindhoven, the Dutch football team! Other Brazilian debt was purchased at a discount and invested to protect rainforests.

❏ In 1985, US Treasury secretary, James Baker, unveiled the 'Baker Plan' – economic reform to promote growth in LDC countries combined with increased lending by commercial banks.

❏ In 1989, the new US Treasury secretary, Nicholas Brady, launched the 'Brady Plan'. Building on experience gained with the Baker Plan, this envisaged encouraging the creditor banks to allow debt reduction. For example, LDC debt would be exchanged at a heavy discount for 30 year LDC government bonds backed by 30 year zero-coupon US Treasury bonds, thus guaranteeing eventual repayment of principal. Alternatively, banks prepared to lend new money would be rewarded by no write down on the existing debt.

The first case was Mexico in 1989–90. Of the creditor banks, 90% swapped $42bn of debts for bonds on terms implying a discount of 35%. 10% of the banks lent new money. Later, 'Brady Plan' type deals were struck with the Philippines, Uruguay, Venezuela, Costa Rica, Peru, Brazil and Argentina. These bonds, which are still traded in secondary markets, are known as Brady Bonds.

Today, Latin America has reappeared in the world's financial markets and new capital inflows are increasing rapidly. Unfortunately, history has repeated itself. Excessive bank lending led to further crises in 1997 and 1998, and we discuss this fully in a special chapter, Chapter 15.

Whatever the eventual outcome, for the banks concerned the LDC crisis was a disaster. Standard and Poor's and Moody's didn't like what they saw and reduced credit ratings. Not only did this mean that the cost of new money for the banks went up, but often their best customers had a better credit rating than they did. In 1982, banks like Chase, Bank America and Manufacturers Hanover were all of AAA status. By 1990, they were hanging on to single A if they were lucky. Manny Hanny was BBB – almost a junk bond! Yet in June 1986, Marks and Spencer, the famous UK retailer, issued a $150m eurobond rated AAA by both the main organisations. Why should M and S borrow from Lloyds or Midland Bank in 1986? Its credit rating was better than either.

Capital, too, was hit by bad debt reserves and the changed situation. Due to capital ratio constraints, banks found it difficult to expand their lending but still needed to earn money. In Chapter 4, we saw how new techniques were tried – the NIFs, RUFs and RAFTs followed by the MOF. Unfortunately, however, many corporates could avoid the banks by borrowing from other lenders, using the securities market. For example, top quality borrowers could raise money by selling commercial paper to lenders, with the bank role limited to taking a commission. The classic role of the bank is that of intermediary. It takes money from depositors and lends it to borrowers. Cutting out the bank, borrowers meeting lenders directly is often called *disintermediation*. Another term is *securitisation*, that is borrowers borrow by selling a security to lenders rather than borrowing from the bank. The biggest illustration of this process of either disintermediation or securitisation was the rise in the issue of eurobonds from 1982 onwards.

The eurobond Market

From 1982, we see a fall in the size of the international syndicated loan market and a rise in the issue of eurobonds. Banks which could not expand their lending due to capital ratio constraints could make some money by underwriting bond issues. Borrowers found that the holders of eurocurrencies, which provided a short-term deposit market, could now be persuaded to buy bonds denominated in the same currencies and create a longer-term market. As before, London became the major market for these bond issues.

Typical terms for eurobonds were in the range of 3–25 years (the longest so far – 50 years – was issued by British Gas in 1994). A syndicate of banks with a *lead manager* underwrote the issue, sold the bonds to investors and ran secondary markets.

Settlement between the professionals (in the secondary market) is 3 working days: that is, buy the bond on Monday, pay on Thursday; buy the bond Tuesday, pay on Friday and so on. There are two settlement and clearing organisations – Cedel and Euroclear. They are both owned by banks, and the first is in Luxembourg and the second in Brussels. What they do is to ensure that bonds are transferred to the ownership of the buyer and that money is taken from the buyer's account to pay for them. Using another technique, which always seems curious to an outsider, they can arrange to lend bonds to sellers who have sold bonds they don't actually own. The sellers can use these bonds to settle the deal and buy them later in the market in order to return them to the lender. This is *stock lending* and is very common in bond markets everywhere. The lender earns a small fee for their trouble and it makes life easier for the seller.

There is an International Primary Markets Association (IPMA) and an International Securities Markets Association (ISMA) to coordinate issues in the secondary market.

The techniques for selling these bonds are investment banking techniques, as opposed to the commercial banking techniques used for syndicated loans. The rise in eurobond market activities after 1982 led to a big increase internationally in investment banking at the expense of commercial banking.

The *borrowers* in this market are governments, quasi-governments (for example, the EU), international financial organisations (for example, the World Bank), banks and large corporates. As the bonds are not secured, a good credit rating is essential.

The *lenders* are retail investors (that is well-off private individuals), banks and investment institutions.

The interest on the bond is paid gross and, therefore, the onus is on the retail investor to declare this to the local tax authority. On the other hand, the bonds are *bearer* bonds (that is, no one knows who owns them). While it is, of course, wrong to think evil of people it is, unhappily, seldom incorrect. As a result, there is a strong incentive for the retail buyer to indulge in sheer tax evasion and enhance the yield on the bond by not paying any tax. The cliché in the market for the retail buyer is the 'Belgian dentist'. The idea is that they cross the border into Luxembourg (where the paying bank often is), present the coupons and pay the money into a local bank account. (Luxembourg banks have a great tradition of secrecy, like the Swiss.) The European Union is determined to put an end to this and is discussing a uniform withholding tax across all 15 countries.

For professional investors, who will not indulge in tax evasion, there is still a *cash flow* advantage because the interest is paid gross. By the time they come to year end and the auditors agree the tax figures with the authorities, it may be 18 months before the tax is actually paid.

As a result of the tax situation, eurobonds may offer a yield that seems less than general market rates.

An early variation on the theme was the *floating rate note* (FRN). This pays a variable and not a fixed rate of interest. This appeals to financial institutions, which *lend* at floating rate and therefore find it easier to *borrow* at floating rate. If rates fall, their income falls, but so do their costs. Assets and liabilities are nicely matched.

Let's look at some eurobond issues to get the flavour of the market, both for types of issue and types of currency (see Table 6.3).

You may wonder why some of these issuers want a particular currency and why, for example, a financial institution like the UK's Abbey National is borrowing at fixed rate. The curious answer is that perhaps they don't want the currency at all, nor does the Abbey National want a fixed rate commitment. It's all to do with the world of *swaps*, which we discuss fully in Chapter 13. The investment bankers advise you in which currency in the prevailing market conditions it will be easier to raise the money. They then swap it for the currency you really want. They advise you whether a fixed rate bond or FRN will be best received by the market, and then swap the interest rate obligation with you.

Table 6.3   *A selection of eurobond issuers*

Issuer	Maturity years	Currency
Barclays Bank	undated	US dollars
Bank of America	10	US dollars
Federal Home Loan Banks	3	US dollars
CIT Group	5	US dollars
Motiva Enterprises	10	US dollars
ABN Amro	5	euro
BBVA Global Finance	1.5	euro
Hamburgische LB	5	euro
Abbey National	3	Swiss franc
LW Rentenbank	10	Swiss franc
LB Kiel	5	Norwegian kroner

Let's take the Abbey National case. First we have the *currency swap*:

They arrange at the same time to swap back at maturity so that the Abbey National can redeem the bond.

Then we have an interest rate swap for the interest element:

The swap bank passes the Abbey National a stream of money in Swiss francs to pay the interest. The Abbey National passes them a stream of money in sterling at floating rate. The obligations of the Abbey National to the bond holders are unaltered.

Notice that in the above case, we have not only swapped a fixed commitment for a floating one but the fixed is in sterling and the floating is in Swiss francs, that is we have arrived at the CIRCUS (Combined Interest Rate and Currency Swap).

The result is that issuers raise money where it is easiest and cheapest to do so and then the investment banks swap it into the arrangement they really want.

Our real discussion on swaps is in Chapter 13 but it's impossible not to mention them here, as it is estimated that 70% of eurobond issues are swapped one way or another.

The market is very innovative and ingenious. It was noted at an early stage that some professional investors were stripping off all the coupons separately, leaving behind a bond paying no interest. Perhaps they wanted a capital gain rather than income from a tax point of view. As a result, the market invented the *zero coupon bond* in the primary market.

If the bond pays no interest, why buy it? The answer is that the investor buys it at a substantial discount. Suppose market yields for 5 year bonds are 10%. An investor could buy a 10% bond at par. Alternatively, they could buy a zero coupon bond for $62.09 for each $100 nominal. They invest $62.09 and in 5 years receive $100 – also a yield of 10%.

For example, British Gas offered a 30 year zero coupon bond in dollars in 1993. The bonds were sold at $8.77 for each $100 nominal value.

From a tax point of view, it may suit the investor to receive capital gain and not income. In Japan and Italy, for example, the increase in the bond price is taxed as a capital gain, not as income (but this is not the case in the UK). In addition, if the bond is in a foreign currency, the exchange rate risk is limited to the principal not the coupons. These bonds are also even more sensitive to interest rate changes than a normal bond. This might suit a speculator who was convinced that interest rates would fall. Remember – interest rates *down*, bond prices *up*.

Take a conventional 10 year bond paying 10%. The market yield falls to 9% and the price goes up to $106.4 (a rise of 6.4%). Suppose an investor had bought a 10 year zero coupon bond instead. A price of $38.55 per $100 nominal would give a yield of 10%. However, when yields fall to 9%, the price goes up to $42.24 (a rise of 9.6%). This is due to the *gearing* effect. In taking a position on a 10 year bond for $38.55 instead of $100, the investor has increased their exposure to the market. This is another aspect of the term 'gearing', which we met in Chapter 1.

Of course, if bond yields go up and not down, then the loss on the zero coupon bond is even greater. (The unfortunate Merrill Lynch dealer mentioned earlier was not only holding zero coupon bonds but had made them zero coupon by selling the coupons separately!)

In early 1992, the perception was that yields in European bond markets (especially in Spain, Portugal and Italy) would slowly fall to those on DM bonds.

As a result, there were several zero coupon issues to take advantage of later price increases as interest rates fell.

Coupon Stripping

We mentioned earlier that it is not uncommon for innovative investment banks to take an ordinary bond and remove the coupons, making it a zero coupon bond. This is called 'stripping' the bond and is very common with US Treasury issues (see Figure 6.5).

| | *Normal Bond* | *Stripped Bond* | | | | | | |
| | | *Coupons* | | | | | *Principal* | *Total* |
		1	*2*	*3*	*4*	*5*		
Payment now	100	9.09	8.26	7.51	6.83	6.21	62.1	100
Receipt:								
Year 1	10	10						10
Year 2	10		10					10
Year 3	10			10				10
Year 4	10				10			10
Year 5	10					10		10
Year 5	100						100	100
TOTAL	150	10	10	10	10	10	100	150

Figure 6.5   *Coupon stripping*

For example, take a $100m 5 year 10% bond and assume that the market yield is 10%, the bond selling for 100.0. The interest payments are stripped to form five zero coupon bonds of $10m each, maturing one per year in years 1–5. The principal of $100m is itself now a zero coupon bond. Someone needing $10m in 3 years can buy the 3 year zero coupon bond for $7.51m in 3 years. This enables investment institutions to match future assets and liabilities more closely.

The first US government bond was stripped in 1982 and there were some $225bn of US Treasury bonds in stripped form by the end of 1995. Strips began in Canada in 1987, in France in 1991, in the UK and Germany in 1997 and in Italy and Spain in 1998.

Other Variations

There are many, many variations on the theme in the eurobond market – far too many to cover them all here. Let's just look at a few to get some idea of the possibilities:

Callable/Puttable bonds   If *callable*, the issuer can redeem the bond at a stated earlier date if they choose to. The investor is compensated for this disadvantage by a higher coupon. If *puttable*, the investor can sell the bond back at a stated earlier date. The investor has an advantage now and pays for it by receiving a lower coupon. The UK government's huge $4bn FRN issued in 1986 was *both* callable and puttable.

Convertibles   Corporate bonds which can be converted into equity are common, as in domestic markets. However, conversion could be from fixed into floating or floating into fixed.

Warrants   Again, as an alternative to a convertible, separate warrants entitling the investor to buy equity later may be attached. When the Nikkei index in Japan rose strongly up to 1990, Japanese convertibles and bonds with warrants were so popular they accounted for 20% of the market. When the bubble burst as the Nikkei fell, eurobond issues in 1990 fell as a result.

Dual currency   These are bonds which pay interest in one currency but redeem in another.

Rising/Falling coupon   A 10 year bond might be 3% for 5 years and 10% for the last 5 (or some other variation).

Both the above variations were combined in one with an issue by Banca Nazionale del Lavoro. The issue was in yen with 60% of the redemption in yen and 40% in dollars at a fixed rate of ¥163. In addition, the coupon was 4.7% for the first 5 years and 7.5% thereafter!

Collars   In mid-1992, several banks led by Kidder Peabody, issued FRNs with both a lower and upper limit to the interest paid. This idea had been used in 1985 and called 'mini-max'. The revival was due to the unprecedentedly low US interest rates in mid-1992. A *floor* giving a lower limit was attractive, even if there was a maximum upper level to the interest paid.

Reverse FRNs   As the interest rates go *up*, the interest on the FRN goes *down* and vice-versa. In December 1997, the World Bank issued a complex 12 year reverse floater in lira. For the first 4 years, rates were fixed on a falling scale, 12% down to 7%. For the next 7 years, the rate was calculated by a formula: 15.5% – 2×LIBOR. Thus, as LIBOR goes up, rates fall. This expressed the view that Italian rates would fall due to the arrival of the euro. As a further variation of the FRN theme, Aegon, the Dutch insurance company, did a 12 year issue in 1992 which was an FRN for the first 2 years and fixed 8¼ for the remaining 10!

Global bonds   Pioneered by the World Bank in 1989, global bonds are designed to be sold in the eurobond market and the US at the same time, thus increasing liquidity for the bond. The two markets have different conventions – eurobonds are bearer, pay interest gross and annually; US bonds are registered, and pay interest net semi-annually. However, the eurobond issues are registered with the Securities and Exchange Commission (SEC) in the US and can be sold to all classes of US investors. eurobonds cannot be sold into the US initially unless registered under SEC rule 144a, when they can only be sold to qualified institutional investors anyway.

Dragon bonds   A dragon bond is similar to a eurobond but is listed in Asia (typically Singapore or Hong Kong), aimed at investors in the region and launched in the Asian time zone. The first issue was made by the Asian Development Bank at the end of 1991. Other issues were made by the General Electric Capital Corporation and the European Investment Bank, but the really interesting one was the 10 year issue for the People's Republic of China in late 1993. All the issues have been in dollars.

The market is very competitive and each investment bank is seeking ways to score over its rivals with some new innovation. The cliché here is the *rocket scientist* – the highly numerate trader who invents more and more complex instruments.

Medium-Term Notes (MTNs)

These became very popular in the period 1991–92, and have remained popular since. They are very flexible programmes. Within the same programme and legal documentation, the issuer can issue bonds in various quantities, maturities and currencies and either fixed or floating. MTNs were designed in part to meet investor-driven transactions. In other words, an investor might request, say, $10m more of a previously issued bond and the issuer will release more to meet this demand. The issuer can thus issue a new bond, more of an existing bond, or create a bond to a specification suggested by the investor. The structure is particularly useful for issuing small tranches of notes/bonds. Indeed, one investment banker has suggested that issues down to as little as $500,000 are now practical.

For the borrower, the MTN allows them to by-pass the costly and time-consuming documentation associated with issuing a stand-alone bond. The market can then be tapped at very short notice, compared with a delay of several days for a stand-alone offering. They can thus react quickly to a given opportunity.

Amongst those with programmes are IBM International, Abbey National, the European Bank for Reconstruction and Development, GMAC Europe (the finance arm of General Motors), Monte dei Paschi di Siena, Finnish Export Credit and GE Capital, the market's most frequent issuer.

Sometimes the programmes are underwritten, like bond issues, sometimes not.

The Money Markets

We have been looking at syndicated loans and eurobonds. Short-term transactions in Eurocurrencies which are not simply deposits/loans but are represented by securities result in *Eurocertificates of deposit* (ECDs) and *Eurocommercial paper* (ECP). The generic term for these short-term transactions is usually *Euronotes*. The *committed* loan facilities which we mentioned in Chapter 4, like NIFs/RUFs and MOFs, have largely died.

The strong interbank market in London in the Eurocurrencies gives rise to references to Eurodollar LIBOR, Euroyen LIBOR and similar expressions for other currencies.

Repos

Earlier in this chapter, we mentioned that a central bank may use a 'repo' to help out other banks in its role as lender of last resort. A repo is a sale and repurchase agreement. Party *A* may sell stock to *B* and receive a collateral payment. At a later point in time (which may be fixed or variable), Party *A* must buy the stock back and return the collateral plus interest to Party *B* (see Figure 6.6).

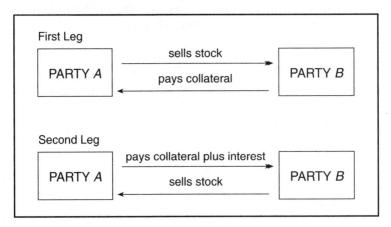

Figure 6.6   *The repo*

The repo technique is used very widely outside its use by central banks. Any dealer may find that they have a short position in stock, that is they have sold stock but not yet purchased it. As an alternative to buying the stock, the dealer can get hold of the stock on a temporary basis using the repo technique. The stock is used to settle the deal and purchased later for its return in the second leg of the repo. Why bother? Maybe the dealer found some difficulty in buying the stock at an attractive price. Perhaps the dealer believed that stock would be cheaper in a few days' time. Sometimes the dealer has actually bought and sold stock but the buy side of the deal fails settlement, and it is the settlement department that uses the repo to fulfil the bank's obligation to deliver. This, of course, gives the market more flexibility and encourages liquidity. For this reason, the technique is often referred to as 'stock lending and borrowing'. (The classic repo is not quite the same as stock borrowing and lending, but let's not get too complicated!)

Often the repo is used for the opposite reason – that is not to get hold of the stock but to get hold of the collateral. A dealer must fund their position. If the bonds which have been purchased are not needed at once, they can be sold via the repo to obtain the cash to fund the purchase. As the borrowing is secured, it will be a cheaper rate than unsecured borrowing. The repo here is simply a technique for borrowing money.

The repo thus suits everyone. The bond dealer can use it either to run a short position or to borrow money at the best rates. An institution which chooses to lend stock earns a small percentage to enhance yield on the portfolio and the deal is secure as collateral has been received.

Repos are widely used in the US Treasury markets; the Bank of England allowed repos in UK gilts in 1996 and the market began properly in Japan in April 1996 after new regulations solved problems with the previous rather weak repo technique (collateral surrender could not be enforced). In June 2002, the ISMA estimated the size of the European repo market to be 3305 bn euros.

Participants and Top Traders

As we have seen, these are large wholesale markets and the transactions involve:

- ❏ Governments
- ❏ Municipalities
- ❏ Public sector bodies
- ❏ International financial institutions
- ❏ Commercial banks
- ❏ Investment banks
- ❏ Investment institutions:
    1. Pension funds
    2. Insurance companies
    3. Mutual funds
- ❏ Large corporates.

There are also brokers who act as intermediaries, displaying anonymously on computer the best prices in the market and putting principals in touch with one another for a small commission (as little as 2 bp).

The top traders for international debt issuance are shown as Table 6.4.

The Euromarkets are the most important financial development of the last 30 years. They have created a vast pool of international money seeking investment in the best place it can, with no especial loyalty to any particular market.

Table 6.4 *Top bookrunners for international debt issuance, 2002*

Rank	Manager or Group
1	Deutsche Bank
2	Salomon Smith Barney
3	Morgan Stanley
4	JP Morgan
5	Lehman Brothers
6	Crédit Suisse First Boston
7	Merrill Lynch & Co.
8	UBS Warburg
9	Barclays Capital
10	Goldman Sachs & Co.

Source: *Euromoney.*

It seems appropriate to close this chapter with a quotation from Citicorp's chairman from 1970 to 1984, Walter Wriston (quoted in Adrian Hamilton, *The Financial Revolution*, Penguin, 1986):

The information standard has replaced the gold standard as the basis of world finance. In place of systems, like the gold standard, based on government established rules, communications now enable and ensure that money moves anywhere around the globe in answer to the latest information or disinformation. Governments can no longer get away with debasing the coinage or controlling the flow of capital. There now exists a new order, a global marketplace for ideas, money, goods and services that knows no national boundaries.

SUMMARY

The rate of interest is the price of money. It varies with risk, maturity and liquidity. There is, finally, supply and demand.

Bonds have a par or nominal value. They may sell at below or above par value and the resulting return to the investor is *yield*. If we ignore the profit or loss at redemption, it is interest yield. If we do not, it is gross redemption yield. As interest rates go up, bond prices go down and vice-versa. This volatility is most marked for long dated bonds. If the bond is sold before going ex dividend, the buyer pays *accrued interest*.

Credit ratings (such as AAA or BB) are assigned to bonds to guide investors as to the risk and, hence, the necessary yield.

Money markets cover transactions whose maturity is 1 year or less. They include:

Money at call and short notice   Liquid funds lent for very short periods.

Interbank market   The rate at which one bank will lend money to another is the offer rate for money, hence London Interbank Offered Rate (LIBOR) or Tokyo Interbank Offered Rate (TIBOR).

Treasury bills, local authority and public sector bills   These represent the short-term borrowing of these entities, say, 3, 6 and 12 months.

Certificates of Deposit   Short-term borrowings by banks.

Commercial paper   Short-term borrowing of corporates, very big in the US.

Bills of Exchange   Discussed in Chapter 5.

Central banks control short-term interest rates using key rates such as lombard rate, discount rate, repo rate and similar terms.

Bonds are transactions in excess of 1 year. The face rate of interest is called the coupon and they may be short, medium or long dated. They may be sold through an offer for sale or a private placing.

Government and public sector bonds are usually the most important. Frequently, they are sold at monthly auctions on set dates to specialist dealers.

Mortgage and other asset-backed bonds use the flows of interest and capital to back bond issues – these are *asset-backed securities* (ABS).

Debentures (in the UK) are corporate bonds secured on assets.

Convertibles   are bonds that may be converted to another bond or equity. The right to buy equity later at a set price may be contained in an attached *warrant*.

Preference shares   usually pay the dividend as a fixed rate of interest. They are preferred to other shareholders for dividends and in the event of liquidation and are non-voting.

Foreign bonds   are those issued in the domestic market by non-residents.

Junk bonds   are bonds below investment grade, offering high yields.

International or *Euromarkets*   refers to primary market activity (loans, bonds or money market instruments) outside the domestic market of that currency, for example, a dollar loan raised in London or a dollar bond issued in Singapore. London is the major centre for these activities.

Coupon stripping   refers to detaching the coupons from a bond and selling the principal and the coupons all separately. They are all now *zero-coupon bonds*.

Medium-term notes   are flexible programmes for issuing paper in any currency, any maturity, any quantity and fixed or floating.

Repos   stands for sale and repurchase agreements. These are used either to borrow bonds for short positions or finance long positions.

Appendix 1

ANNOUNCEMENT OF RESULT OF A UK BID PRICE AUCTION FOR
GOVERNMENT BONDS

◇   **DMO-TAS041/184**

United Kingdom   Eastcheap Court
Debt   11 Philpot Lane
Management   London EC3M 8UD
Office
                                                              Tel. 020 7862 6500
                                                              Fax. 020 7862 6509
31/02
                                                              22 October 2002

PRESS NOTICE

RESULT OF THE SALE BY AUCTION OF £2,750 MILLION OF 5% TREASURY STOCK 2014

The United Kingdom Debt Management Office ("DMO") announces that the auction of £2,750 million of 5%
Treasury Stock 2014 has been allotted in full.

All bids which have been accepted at the lowest accepted price have been allotted
approximately 38.5% of the amount bid for.

1. Competitive bids made at prices above the lowest accepted price have been allotted in full.
   Competitive bids made at prices below the lowest accepted price have been rejected.

2. The range of bids accepted was as follows: **Price   Yield**
   Highest Accepted   £102.18 4.76%

   Non-competitive allotment price
   (i.e. the rounded average acceptance price)   £102.05 4.77%

   Lowest Accepted   £101.97 4.78%

3. The total amounts allotted and bids received were as follows:
   Amount allotted to competitive bids   £2,540.33 million
   Amount allotted to non-competitive bids
                                       Gilt-edged market makers   £206.25 million
                                                            Others   £3.42 million
   Total   £2,750.0 million
   Total bids received   £5,458.99 million
   Times covered   1.99 times

   Cheques may be presented for payment. Refund cheques, where appropriate, will be sent as
   soon as possible by post. Stock allotted to members of CREST will be credited to their
4. accounts by member-to-member deliveries tomorrow if they so requested.

Notes: A non-competitive bid is one in which no bid price is entered and is
             allocated at the rounded average price of the auction.
             CRND – Commissioners for the Reduction of the National Debt.

Appendix 2

RECENT CHANGES TO THE UK GILTS MARKET

❏ Control of the gilts market transferred from the Bank of England to the Debt Management Office, April 1998.

❏ Cedel/Euroclear option for settlement.

❏ XD period reduced from 35 days to 7.

❏ Coupon stripping allowed late 1997.

❏ Dates for regular auctions announced in advance.

❏ Each quarter the gilts to be sold in the next 3 months are announced.

❏ In general, there will be fewer tap issues.

❏ Priced in decimals (not 32nds) from November 1998.

❏ Gilts repos no longer confined only to the gilt-edged market makers (1996).

❏ Bank of England daily assistance to include gilts repos as well as bills of exchange and Treasury bills (1996).

❏ Institutions to pay income tax on capital gains as well as income (1996).

❏ Payments to institutions made gross (1996) – tax to be paid 3 months later.

❏ All gilts eligible for bearer status for recognised foreign buyers, not just selected issues (1996).

❏ Half-yearly interest calculations to be based on precise number of days in the half-year (1998).

❏ Settlement of gilts transferred from the Bank of England's Central Gilts Office to CREST CO (the UK equities settlement body) in May 1999.

7 Stock Exchanges

HISTORY OF ASSOCIATIONS FOR TRADING

The early associations for trading were either sole owners or partnerships. The first modern shareholding enterprise is generally recognised as the proposal by Sebastian Cabot, the British explorer, to set up an enterprise to find a North East trade route to China and the Orient.

In 1553, 250 merchants put up £25 each to equip 3 ships for the voyage. They thus shared the cost and any eventual profit. 2 ships foundered but one reached the port of Archangel and the crew were taken to the court of the so-called Ivan the Terrible. Trade was started between England and Russia and the company's short name was the 'Muscovy Company'. As the shares were held jointly, they were 'joint stock companies'. The famous East India Company was formed in 1600 and was dominant in trading up to about 1850. Of these early trading companies, several are still in existence, the most famous being the Hudson's Bay Company (1668). With the importance of the Dutch Empire, we also see the formation of the United East India Company of the Netherlands in 1602 and the Dutch West India Company in 1621.

Trading began in the shares of these companies. Amsterdam opened a stock exchange in 1611, Europe's oldest. The Austrian Bourse opened in Vienna in 1771, largely to trade government bonds to finance war. By the end of the 19th century it had 2500 equities listed and was one of Europe's most important financial centres. In London, brokers and jobbers (as they were called) met in coffee houses (see Dickens, *Little Dorritt*, Chapter 24 '*Mr Affery went about to other counting-houses and to wharves and docks, and to the Custom House and to Garraway's Coffee House and the Jerusalem Coffee House.*'). To regulate the market, New Jonathan's Coffee House was converted into the 'Stock Exchange' in 1773. Curiously, there seems to be some doubt about the formal start of securities trading in New York. A newspaper, called 'The Diary', indicated in an issue of March 1792 that dealers in stock met each noon at 22 Wall Street (so called because of the building of a wall to keep livestock in and Indians out by early Dutch traders who founded New York). Most trading was in government bonds and bank shares. Inspired by the success of an organisation set up by brokers in Philadelphia, a 'New York Stock Exchange and Board' was set up in 1817 (quoted in F.L. Eames and Thomas G. Hall, *The New York Stock Exchange,* 5th edition, John Wiley, 1987). In 1850, the US actually had 250 stock exchanges, However, by 1900, New York was totally dominant due to the introduction of the telegraph and ticker-tape.

In France, we can trace an early shareholding company, the 'Société des Moulins du Bazacle' in Toulouse with 96 lots or shares which could be bought and sold. Quite logically, this became the local electricity company in the 19th century and was quoted on the Toulouse Stock Exchange until 1946. This was, of course, an earlier example than the Muscovy Company but more of an isolated instance. A form of stock exchange, a 'Bourse', appears in Lyons in 1540 with dealers called, in a decree of 1639, 'agents de change'. A bourse was established in Paris in 1724 but does not seem to have been particularly active. With the revolution, agents de change were abolished in 1791 and the exchange closed in 1793. Under Napoleon, the bourse was officially opened again in 1801 with the agents de change given a monopoly of trading but not allowed the privilege of limited liability.

THE ROLE OF A STOCK EXCHANGE

We should perhaps begin by considering the role of a stock exchange. It provides the regulation of company listings, a price formation mechanism, the supervision of trading, authorisation of members, settlement of transactions and publication of trade data and prices.

However, sometimes listing rules are made by government-sponsored bodies, like the Securities and Exchange Commission in the US. Separate settlement and custody bodies may be taking over this role, as in the UK where CREST Co Ltd (with some 60 shareholders) has taken over settlement from the London Stock Exchange. Some people are questioning the future role of a stock exchange as computerised matching systems outside exchanges are capturing business (like Posit and Island in the US and Tradepoint in London), or trades are handled by broker/dealers like Instinet. With the arrival of the Internet and growth of on-line trading, could Microsoft be the exchange of the future?

STOCKS AND SHARES

We refer to 'stocks and shares' as though there is a clear difference. Strictly speaking, shares are equities in companies, paying (typically) a variable dividend. Stocks are instruments where the payment is by way of interest, such as bonds and similar instruments. Unfortunately, while 'shares' is only used to refer to shares in companies, 'stocks' is a much vaguer term in everyday parlance. In the US, shares are 'common stock' and the shareholders are the stockholders. In the UK, the term 'stocks' is frequently used to mean either shares or bonds, and we shall follow this practice.

Generally, however, exchanges always split turnover between the fixed interest element and equities. Whilst most transactions in number are usually equities, the bond values are high because of the importance here of the professional investors with high value deals. In the UK, for instance, the average domestic equity deal is about £60,000 and the average government bond deal about £3m. In general, bonds are about 55% of turnover in London, 75% in the German exchanges and 80% in

Paris. In New York however, almost all turnover is in equities as few bonds are traded on the exchange.

Figures for the world's largest exchanges are shown in Table 7.1 (the figures have been compiled by the London Stock Exchange and are in sterling). The initials NASDAQ stand for 'National Association of Securities Dealers' Automated Quotations'. They have never had an exchange as such and deal on computer screens. The shares are, therefore, technically 'over the counter' (OTC) but the companies are much larger than one usually finds with OTC trading and include many technology stocks such as Microsoft, Intel and Apple.

Table 7.1 has a note that the turnover has been halved in certain cases. Some exchanges report a deal twice, that is, when bought and when sold. Others record it only once. London's SETS system reports the deal once, but other systems in use in London report it twice.

Table 7.1   *International stock market comparisons, turnover, year ended 31.12.2000*

Exchange	Turnover £bn	Domestic Equity Market Value £bn	Number of Companies Listed at 31.12.00	
			Domestic	Foreign
New York	7313	7659	2035	433
NASDAQ	13,086	2396	4239	487
Tokyo	1404	2113	2055	41
London [1]	2999	1725	2428	501
Germany	1395	850	744	245
Italy	660	514	291	6
Madrid	637	336	1020	16
Paris [2]	707	968	1021	164
Amsterdam [2]	421	429	234	158
Brussels [2]	29	122	161	104
Switzerland	424	530	252	164
Taiwan	587	156	531	—

Notes: * [1] *Turnover has been halved for comparison purposes for non-order book trading*
[2] *Euronext*

Source: London Stock Exchange, *Fact File 2001.*

Looking at Table 7.1, one can see that there is no simple answer to the question: which are the world's biggest stock exchanges? What does 'biggest' mean? It could be market value, total turnover or just equity turnover.

The market value is the number of shares in existence multiplied by the share price. It's also called 'capitalisation' (but beware – it's nothing to do with capital on the balance sheet). Share prices go up and down and the capitalisation is only that at the moment when the calculation is done. That's part of the problem. Had one taken Tokyo at the end of 1989, before their market crashed, Tokyo would have appeared as the world's biggest exchange. The other problem is whether we take an exchange or a country. The German Federation of Stock Exchanges adds the figures for all the eight German exchanges. Frankfurt is perhaps 80% of the value. If we add all Germany's exchanges, should we not also add all those in the US, Japan and Switzerland?

Of the London equity turnover figure of £2999 billion, the claimed foreign equity content is £1767 billion, the highest in the world, and more than the foreign turnover of New York, NASDAQ, Tokyo and Germany combined! This again highlights the international character of the London markets.

Taking capitalisation at the end of 2001 our sequence is:

- ❏ New York
- ❏ NASDAQ
- ❏ Tokyo
- ❏ London
- ❏ Paris
- ❏ Germany.

Taking turnover, the next question is whether we take equities only or total turnover including bonds. If we do the latter, it may not seem fair for exchanges where bonds are traded outside the exchange.

If we take *equity turnover* only, however, our top six become:

- ❏ NASDAQ
- ❏ New York
- ❏ London
- ❏ Tokyo
- ❏ Germany
- ❏ Paris.

We have included NASDAQ, although this is not an exchange and OTC dealings have not been included in other exchanges' figures.

From the above you will see that the question, 'which are the world's biggest stock exchanges?' elicits a somewhat complicated response! The very statistics are themselves controversial. Some exchanges insist that trades handled by local brokers are recorded locally for regulatory reasons even if the trade is actually passed to a foreign exchange. For this reason, London's claim for its foreign equity share has been attacked by many as an exaggeration. A French academic study published in February 1996, for example, said that London's claim to handle 52% of French equity turnover was wrong and that the true figure was only 8%.

INTERNATIONAL EQUITY

In the 1980s and 1990s, it has become common for multinational companies to seek a listing on several foreign stock exchanges. This may be to attract a wider investor market or because the local exchange is a little small for the ambitions of the company (for example, Stockholm and Electrolux). The result has been a large expansion in primary market issues and secondary market trading in non-domestic equities.

For example, although German accounting rules are not as tight as those in the United States, Daimler-Benz has listed in New York and accepted the implications for greater transparency. The French insurance group, Axa, became the first French financial services company to secure a US stock exchange listing in mid-1996. There are still problems, however, as SEC rules require approval for rights issues. Ericsson had to wait three months, during which its share price fell 56%. New legislation following the scandals of Enron and others have also brought in new restrictions.

Large new equities are now offered on an international basis and there have been many involving national telephone companies. The second biggest privatisation of all time was Deutsche Telekom, offered to markets all over the world at the end of 1996. The offering was split as follows:

❏ Germany   462 million shares
❏ Americas   98 million shares
❏ UK   57 million shares
❏ Rest of Europe   38 million shares
❏ Rest of World   34 million shares.

A further slice was offered in June 1999, again on a worldwide basis, leading Deutsche Telekom to claim that they have more shareholders outside their domestic market than any other company.

One key factor here is that US mutual funds and pension funds have gradually become less parochial and are investing more abroad.

INDICES

Share indices are usually based on market capitalisation. If the index is of, say, the top 50 companies, then 'top' means biggest by market capitalisation. Sometimes, the index is described as 'weighted'. This simply means that a 1% change in the price of the largest company in the index will have more impact than a 1% change in the price of the smallest. Since the share price is always changing, it follows that the 'top' shares are not always the same. There is provision for removing some shares and adding others, say, every quarter. For example, in June 1999, Next (retailer) and Sema (software house) dropped out of the UK FTSE 100 and were replaced by Anglo American and Blue Circle. There are rules on this designed to prevent firms moving in and out as they go from 99 to 101 in the index and back. They don't always work. Sema joined the FTSE 100 in September 1998, dropped out in December 1998, joined again in March 1999, left again in June 1999 and joined again in September 1999. Not exactly ideal for an index!

In the modern age, the desire to use an index for purposes of options and futures transactions (see Chapters 11 and 12) has led to the creation of several new indices, which are recalculated every minute of the day.

Strictly speaking, we should distinguish between *averages* and *indices*, although the terms are used as if they were the same. In 1884, for example, Charles Dow (publisher of the *Wall Street Journal*) began publishing share *averages* beginning with an average of eleven railway stocks. The modern Dow Jones industrial average began in 1896 with twelve shares, and was increased to the present 30 in 1928.

As an average, the Dow simply averages the share prices and (but for stock splits, which we explain later) would divide the total of all 30 prices by 30. If, however, a stock split causes a price to fall from $100 to $50, this must be taken into account. The method used is called 'constant divisor'. The Dow used to be calculated hourly but is now done every minute.

In London, the *Financial Times* Ordinary Share Index began in 1935. Its average is even more complicated. The 30 share prices are multiplied together and a thirtieth root of the answer taken.

Modern indices are based on taking the number of shares and multiplying by the price. This gives proper weight to the companies worth the largest capitalisation. In 1957, for example, Standard and Poor's introduced the S&P 500. In 1983, the Chicago Board Options Exchange began trading options on its 100 share index, changing its name to the S&P 100 in July of that year. Both these indices are based on market capitalisation.

Also based on market capitalisation was the New York Stock Exchange index, introduced in 1966 and now consisting of some 1500 stocks. The American Stock Exchange introduced its American Stock Exchange Index in 1973. It is another capitalisation index and is based on about 800 stocks. One interesting and unusual feature is the inclusion of dividends as additions to the index. Thus, the index measures a *total* return (as does the German DAX – see later).

As a competitor to the Dow Jones index, the American Stock Exchange introduced its 'Major Market Index' (MMI) of 20 top stocks in 1980. Its composition and calculation make it similar to the Dow Jones and it has a 90% correlation.

Other important US indices are: the NASDAQ Composite Index (1984); the NASDAQ Industrial Index (1984); the NASDAQ 100 (1985); the Philadelphia Stock Exchange Value Line (1700 stocks – 1985).

In Japan, the main index is the Nikkei Dow 225, an index of 225 shares. It is, however, based on average prices, not capitalisation. As a result, a Nikkei 300 was introduced in 1984. There is another index based on capitalisation, the Tokyo Stock Exchange Price Index (TOPIX), an index of all shares listed in the first section of the TSE.

In London, the need for a more satisfactory measure than the 30 ordinary share index led to the *Financial Times Stock Exchange* 100 index in January 1984. This is the FTSE index and, thus, known locally as the 'Footsie'. It is also based on capitalisation, but only using the 'free float' shares – that is, those freely available for sale and not held by founders or similar entities (this adjustment made in June 2001). It is calculated every fifteen seconds from 8.30 a.m. to 4.30 p.m. (with a pre-index level calculated from 8.00 a.m.). The index began at the level of 1000. It represents 77% of the capitalisation of the whole market.

In October 1992, it was decided to broaden the indices and two new ones were added. The FTSE 250 is the 250 shares after the FTSE 100 and the FTSE Actuaries 350 is the addition of the FTSE 100 and 250. It is calculated every minute and includes figures for market sectors. An older, larger index is the *Financial Times* Actuaries Indices, started in 1962 and widened to include over 800 stocks in December 1992. It covers 97% of the market's capitalisation.

In France, the CAC 40 was started in 1987. It is based on capitalisation and is calculated every 30 seconds. It is 60% of the capitalisation of the whole bourse but the top seven stocks account for 43% of the CAC 40. One interesting point is that the CAC 40 is chosen to represent *all* major market sectors. The FTSE 100 is the top 100 regardless of sector. The older index in Paris is the SBF 240 which is based on opening prices and only calculated once per day. In September 1993 this was replaced by the SBF 250 index which is calculated every minute and integrates dividends as well. At the same time, a new index – the SBF 120 – was introduced. This is based on the 40 shares in the CAC 40 and 80 others. It is calculated every minute. In May 1995, an additional index of middle capitalisation stocks – the MIDCAC – was launched.

The older German indices are the FAZ 100 (from the business newspaper *Frankfurter Allgemeine Zeitung*) and the Commerzbank index of 60 shares on the Dusseldorf exchange. Both these were started in the 1950s and are calculated once per day. The popular new index, however, is the DAX (Deutscher Aktienindex) index of 30 shares introduced in December 1987. This is not only a modern index, calculated continuously, but includes dividends and thus calculates a total return. This makes it especially attractive for some 'swap' transactions of a kind we shall discuss in Chapter 13. It represents 80% of stock market capitalisation and covers all the country's exchanges. The next 70 shares provide the MDAX.

Other prominent indices are:

Amsterdam	AK Share
	AEX
Brussels	General Return Index
	BEL 20
Copenhagen	SE All Share
	KFX 25
Hong Kong	Hang Seng
Madrid	Madrid SE
	IBEX 35
Milan	Comit All Share
	BCI
	MIB 30
Oslo	OBX25
Singapore	Straits Times
Stockholm	Affärsvärlden General
	OMX
Vienna	WBK-Index
	ATX
Zurich	Swiss Market Index
	Swiss Performance Index

With the growth of international equities in investor portfolios, we also have the use of international indices. There are *world* indices, such as the Morgan Stanley World Index, that run by Salomon Bros and Russell and the *Financial Times* Actuaries World Indices.

For *Europe*, there is the FTSE Eurotrack 100 (not including UK shares) and the FTSE Eurotrack 200 (including the UK) – both from the London Stock Exchange, the FTSE 300, a cooperation between Amsterdam and London, the STOXX series of European shares, a cooperation between the Dow Jones company and the French, German and Swiss exchanges, the S&P Euro indices and MSCI Euro indices (Morgan Stanley).

One problem for Europe is, what exactly is meant by Europe? There is the Europe of the twelve countries forming the monetary union but excluding an important market in the UK, the European Union of 15 countries but excluding an important market in Switzerland, and some wider geographical definitions. All this leads to a proliferation of European indices! As if we didn't have enough, in June 1999, FTSE International launched a new index based on the 29 largest and most heavily traded stocks in the euro-zone, like Siemens, Royal Dutch Petroleum and Carrefour. The index is called E Stars and is aimed at the growing body of retail investors.

WHO OWNS SHARES?

Small Investors vs Institutions

The pattern of ownership varies in different world markets. In the US, there is still a strong tradition of equity ownership by private investors who own 50%. In Germany, however, the equivalent figure is only 13%. In between comes France, with 31% and the UK, with 25%.

Germany has lagged behind other markets in the past. It is the largest economy in Europe but its stock exchange capitalisation is less than half of that of London. The German Share Institute, DAI, published figures for the number of new equity issues in Germany in the period 1986–96. The figure was 200 compared with 1947 in the UK and 7179 in the US. However, things are changing and the number of new issues in Germany is strongly on the increase. The above figure of 13% represents shares held directly or through mutual funds. It is a rise on a figure of only 9% in 1997 (figures from the German Share Institute).

Private share ownership is usually contrasted with that of the 'institutions', by which we mean pension funds, insurance funds and mutual funds. In some markets, private pension funds look after the pensions of individuals whether collected by their firms or contributed individually. Life assurance companies collect premiums for years in order to provide a pay out at death. General insurance companies also invest premiums paid in advance but face greater uncertainty with regard to payouts. Storms, hurricanes or oil disasters like the Exxon Valdez lead to unexpectedly large payouts. Mutual funds are explained below.

Sometimes people compare market capitalisation as a percentage of GDP. Figures for leading centres are:

- ❑ London   160%
- ❑ New York   120%
- ❑ Tokyo   55%
- ❑ Paris   50%
- ❑ Frankfurt   39%.

Pension Funds: Funding vs Unfunding

How active the equity market is will usually depend on the activity of the institutions and, especially, pension funds. The precise effect may depend on the asset allocation policy of the pension fund as between equities and bonds.

This brings us to the fundamental question: how are pensions funded? The first point is whether pensions are largely provided by private funds or the state. The second is whether there *is* a fund or whether the pensions are paid out of current taxation and contributions.

Where money contributed by private individuals is invested in funds to provide pensions, the biggest markets are the US, UK, Netherlands, Japan and Switzerland.

Figures for the size of assets at the end of 2000 are in Table 7.2 and provided by UBS Asset Management. In some of these cases, the funds are handled by the state.

In Germany, the employees' pension contributions are handled by the company and held in a *book reserve* in the accounts of the company. The amounts are available for the general purposes of the company and the payments are made from corporate funds. It's interesting that events which caused horror in the UK – Robert Maxwell having access to the pension funds – are the routine in Germany. There are some invested funds but the total is relatively modest, as can be seen from Table 7.2.

In Sweden, pension provision is largely by the state, but the money is invested and the system can be regarded as funded. In France, on the other hand, whilst the state also handles most pension payments through the Caisse de Retraite, they are not funded but paid for out of current taxation. Private pension provision is largely confined to schemes for senior executives.

Table 7.2   *Pension funds, size of assets and percentage of GDP, end 2000*

Country	Pension Fund Assets $bn	Percentage of GDP %
UK	1128	81
Netherlands	417	110
Switzerland	321	128
Germany	294	15
Italy	250	23
Sweden	213	96
Denmark	187	115
France	64	5
Finland	60	50
Norway	50	34
Ireland	46	54
Belgium	33	14
Spain	29	5
Portugal	12	12

Source: UBS Asset Management – *International Pension Fund Indicators 2001*

This 'unfunding' is likely to change due to demographic factors. Right across Europe (and Japan), populations are ageing. With six or seven employees funding each pensioner the older systems may have been satisfactory. The future is likely to see two or three workers for every pensioner. Figure 7.1 shows the incidence of ageing populations.

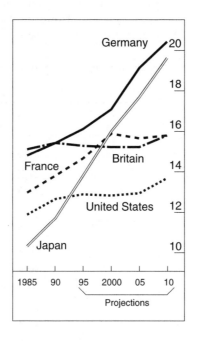

Source: UN.
Figure 7.1 *Ageing populations, % of population aged 65 and over*

The World Bank estimates that, by the year 2030, the number of people over 60 will triple to 1.4 billion. A British think tank, Federal Trust, published a report in early 1996, *The Pensions Time Bomb in Europe*. It calculated a dependency ratio, that is the ratio of people aged 65 and over to the 15 to 64 age group. Over the twelve countries of the EU (prior to 1995), this ratio is expected to increase from 21% in 1990 to 43% in 2040 and 48% in Italy and the Netherlands (see Table 7.3). The Netherlands, at least, have funded pensions; Italy does not. In Germany, by 2030, pension contributions could be 30% of gross income with one worker for every pensioner.

Countries are slow to make progress on this issue. How can we persuade people to pay tax now to fund today's pensioners and put aside extra money for their own retirement at the same time? The French have increased the number of years private sector personnel must work for a full pension from 37.5 to 40. An attempt to do the same for the public sector met with strikes and was withdrawn! This is in spite of the fact that by 2040 France is expected to have 70 people over 60 for every 100 aged between 20 and 59, double the current level. The Germans passed a law in

1992 making it less worthwhile to retire before 65. All this, however, is really only tinkering with the problem, although the announcement by Deutsche Bank, in April 1996, that it would set up its own funded pension scheme was seen as significant.

In Japan, pension funds are big but past protectionist rules have curtailed competition and performance has been poor. However, deregulation from April 1996 opened the markets to foreign investment advisers on a wide scale.

Table 7.3   *Age dependence ratio, persons over 65 as a % of persons aged 15–64*

Country	1990	2040
Belgium	21.9	41.5
Denmark	22.2	43.4
France	21.9	39.2
Germany	23.7	47.1
Greece	20.5	41.7
Ireland	18.4	27.2
Italy	20.4	48.4
Luxembourg	20.4	41.2
Netherlands	17.4	48.5
Portugal	16.4	38.9
Spain	17.0	41.7
UK	23.5	39.1
All EC	21.4	42.8

Source: Federal Trust Report, *The Pensions Time Bomb in Europe.*

The coming of the single market should have resulted in abolition of many restrictions on pension fund investment. For example, Italian funds cannot hold more than 20% in private company equities; Portuguese and Danish funds cannot invest in other countries' securities; German funds cannot hold more than 5% in foreign bonds; and, in Belgium, 15% of the fund must be held in domestic government bonds.

Work was done on a pensions directive which sought to abolish these restrictions or at least modify them. After fierce argument, however, it was withdrawn in 1995.

Brussels is still working on proposals for a directive to liberalise the EU pension fund market. They aim to lift investment restrictions and allow greater competition. Unfortunately, the directive will not tackle the thorny issue of tax at all. Attempts to change taxation require a unanimous vote.

Some multinationals have become impatient. An inaugural meeting, in June 1998, took place between Zeneca (UK, pharmaceuticals), Kvaerner (Anglo/Norwegian, engineering) and British lawyers, Eversheds. Their aim is to provide a test case to challenge the current system which makes cross-border pension systems unworkable due to national tax reliefs and costly bureaucracy. National tax authorities worry about giving tax relief on pensions but not being able to levy it when paid out.

In Britain, Tesco's and a number of other leading companies have decided not to offer guaranteed salary-related pensions to employees, as the cost of doing so becomes prohibitive, and recent accounting rules require this cost to be disclosed as a contingent liability. This is exacerbating the general concerns over pension provision noted earlier in this chapter. The Pension Fund Policy Institute suggested in September 2002 that thought be given to raising the retirement age from 65 to 70.

Equity Investment

The effect of pension fund activity depends, of course, on the attitude to asset allocation. The key choice is between equities and bonds with a further subdivision between domestic and international. Boots, the British retailer, announced in autumn 2001 that it would in future be investing exclusively in bonds and switched funds out of equities. Property is a popular investment in some markets and, clearly, there will also be liquid funds on deposit and invested in money market instruments, like certificates of deposit.

Table 7.4 shows the asset allocation in the four major countries where pensions are funded.

Table 7.4 *International asset allocation, end 2000*

	US %	UK %	Japan %	Netherlands %
Domestic equities	52	49	38	9
International equities	10	22	19	39
Domestic bonds	29	17	31	21
International bonds	1	4	8	23
Cash	5	5	3	3
Property	3	3	1	5
	100	100	100	100

Source: UBS Asset Management – *International Pension Fund Indicators, 2001.*

With pension funds usually the major operators in stock exchanges, their importance for the equity and bond markets can readily be seen. We can also see the current 'cult of equity'. Comparing 1989 with 1998, the US's percentage in equities is up from 39 to 62, Japan's from 29 to 67 and the Netherlands' from 14 to 46. The UK always had a high percentage in equities, partly due to its poor performance on inflation. The general belief is that equities will give better protection than bonds – that is, firms will put their prices up and make more money in nominal if not real terms. However, the equity market prolonged decline in 2001/ 2002 is revising opinions.

The figures also show the rise in global trading. The international content of funds between 1989 and 2000 as a percentage is up in the US from 2 to 11, in Japan from 14 to 27 and in the Netherlands from 10 to 62 – very striking changes, and accounting for the current high level of cross-border trading. The Bundesbank, in its monthly report for June 1999, said that German investors increased their corporate assets abroad by more than a third from the end of 1995 to the end of 1997.

Looking at portfolio management generally and not just that of pension funds, Table 7.5 shows the top centres for portfolio management.

Table 7.5   *Top centres of portfolio management, 2002, ranked by international asset holdings*

City	Equities ($bn)
New York	1767
Boston	1411
London	889
Tokyo	502
San Francisco	493
Los Angeles	392
Paris	272
Chicago	238
Frankfurt	214
Malvern	183

Source: Thomson Financial Ltd.

Mutual Funds

If a small investor has, say, $3000 to spend on equities, there are two choices. The money can be spent on just one or two companies' shares or spread widely over ten companies' shares. In the first case, the risk is great if one company performs badly. In the second case, with $300 spent on each share, the dealing costs are discouragingly high. The answer may be to put the money into *mutual funds*. These are collective investments, run by fund managers. They may be investments in money market instruments, equities or bonds. Indeed, nowadays, there are funds whose investments are in financial futures (see Chapter 12).

In the case of equities, the fund will invest in a wide range of equities; the $3000 is thus spread over a range of shares but without excessive risk. The fund is run by skilled managers and fees must be paid. There are two kinds of fund.

The open-ended fund (Unit Trusts in the UK)   Here the fund raises, say, $50m and spends it on a wide range of shares. Simplifying, the fund is divided into 50m units at $1 each. Later investors can buy units from the managers or sell them back to the managers. If investors with $5m to spend *buy* units, the managers buy more shares and the fund is now $55m. If investors with holdings worth $10m now *sell* the units back to the managers, shares will have to be sold to raise the money and the fund is now only $45m. Hence, we have the term 'open-ended fund'. As the shares grow in value, so do the units and this is how investors make their money. In practice, there are fees to pay and also the basic costs. Units thus have a bid/offer price like an ordinary share.

The closed-ended fund (Investment Trusts in the UK)   Here the fund is a shareholding company, much like any other. It raises $50m and, instead of being in engineering or groceries, invests the money in a portfolio of equities. If, later, investors with $5m to spend want to join in, they buy the shares of the fund on the open market *from someone else who sells them*: that is, the fund doesn't get the money but remains at $50m – hence, 'closed-ended fund'. The idea is that if, in 3 years, the shares double in value, so should the market share of the fund itself. The investors can now sell and take their profit this way. The extent to which the share price may not double but remain at a discount to the asset value per share attracts a lot of attention from analysts and needs to be studied by potential investors. This is because the share price of the closed-ended fund will reflect supply and demand as well as the underlying asset value.

These mutual funds are well established in the US, UK, the Netherlands, France, Germany, Italy and Spain. In France, they are very popular, partly due to tax concessions. The open-ended fund is the SICAV (Société d'Investissement à Capital Variable) and the closed-ended fund, the FCP (Fonds Communs de Placement). As well as equity funds, SICAVs and FCPs for money market instruments are very popular.

As one might expect, the concentration in the UK is on equity investments and in Germany, bonds. Of the UK's £100bn invested in unit trusts, less than £2bn is invested in bonds. Mutual funds were allowed in Italy in 1983 but the equity funds lost popularity after the October 1987 crash. Today, some 55% of the money is invested in Treasury bills.

The US is a huge market for mutual fund investment. By the end of 1998, $4.5

trillion was invested in some 5800 mutual funds and 45% of US households were fund holders. The country's biggest fund group is Fidelity with over $300bn of assets under management. This alone is more than the total UK market! Investment is about 50% equities and 50% bonds and fixed interest. Europe has some $1.5bn in these funds, and the equity content is 30% and growing. The continually rising US stock market has resulted in a phenomenal increase in US mutual funds. The above figure of $4.5 trillion compares with total banking assets of $4.7 trillion.

The defined contribution retirement programmes being introduced and planned will increase mutual fund activity.

UCITS is a term which has arrived due to an EC directive in October 1989. These are 'Undertakings for Collective Investment in Transferable Securities'. The directive sets minimum standards for open-ended funds (not closed-ended). For example, no more than 10% of the investment can be in one security. Investment in commodities, property and money market instruments is excluded. The UCITS managers can take a fund which has domestic authorisation and offer it anywhere within the Community. It must be recognised by regulators in the country where the fund is to be marketed. However, while the marketing regulations are those which are in use locally, investor compensation is from the home country of the fund.

Luxembourg has become a popular centre for UCITS to be sold across Europe. This is because the dividends can be paid gross. A UK UCIT, for example, will deduct tax on dividends at source. While foreigners can reclaim tax, French and German investors, for example, will be reluctant to fill in the forms of the UK Inland Revenue!

Active vs Passive Management

It is beyond the scope of an introductory book of this nature to explain the various theories which exist on asset allocation and pricing of securities. One issue, however, should be mentioned and that is the question of active vs passive management of the funds. Active management can be summarised as 'picking winners', that is, active selection of specific securities with frequent reorganisation of the portfolio. This is often driven by sophisticated computer models and called 'programme trading'. (The same term, however, is used to cover stock index arbitrage and dynamic portfolio insurance strategies.) Passive management, on the other hand, makes an investment in all the stocks in a well known index, such as the S&P 100, and leaves the fund to perform as the S&P 100. The argument for this is that statistics show that less than 50% of funds beat the index anyway and also that 'index tracking' (as it is called) incurs fewer dealing costs. The subject is, naturally, controversial. It appears that in the US, some 50% of pension funds are indexed and in the UK, perhaps 15%–20%.

The first tracker fund was launched by Wells Fargo in 1973, but the idea did not catch on until the mid-1980s. Some 53% of US public sector pension funds are based on tracking. The UK pension performance measurement company, CAPS, pointed out that while the UK's FTSE 100 index rose some 14% in 1998, the median performance of active funds was only 10.4% – the biggest difference in 10 years. Only 21% of the active funds beat the FTSE 100. The UK's National Association of Pension Funds estimates that 39% of private UK pension funds and 49% of public funds use tracking for at least part of their portfolio. On the question of costs, active funds are usually charging fees of some 50 basis points, as opposed to 5 to 10 basis points for tracker funds.

As one might expect, the idea of active vs passive is not completely black and white. Many so-called 'passive' funds are also using quantitative models to add a little to their performance and are not purely tracking.

The activity of the tracker funds is now distorting some of the indices following the mergers of large companies – Vodafone/AirTouch, BP/Amoco, Zeneca/Astra. A small number of companies are becoming more and more dominant. In the UK, the top ten companies accounted for 50% of the total capitalisation of the FTSE 100 in 2000. In 1998, the FTSE 100 index rose 14.5%, but the FTSE 250 (the next 250) rose only 1.4%. In 2000, the FTSE 250 rose 1.6%, whereas the FTSE 100 fell 10.2%. In the US, the Dow Jones was up 12% on March 16 1999, but the Russell 2000 (a much broader index) was down 11%.

When a company drops out of the index, the tracker funds immediately sell it; when one joins the index they immediately buy it. When the Dutch insurance group, Aegon, joined the MSCI pan-European index in early 1999, its price jumped 10% in one day; when Shell left the S&P 500 in June 2002 the opposite occurred.

Custodians

One term we should perhaps mention in this context is that of the *custodian*. Acting for pension funds, mutual funds and the like, the custodian actually looks after the securities, carries out settlement, handles stock lending (if the fund rules permit) and notifies the fund of corporate actions such as rights issues, dividend notification, AGMs and so on. They will also collect and remit dividends and reclaim withholding taxes.

These days this is very big business and dominated by large global custodians like Bank of New York, J.P. Morgan Chase, State Street, Deutsche Bank, Citigroup, Mellon Trust and Northern Trust. The Bank of New York, for example, had $5610bn of assets under management at the end of 1998.

DEALING SYSTEMS

Systems in stock exchanges for buying and selling stock usually follow one of three patterns:

❑ Order-driven systems
❑ Quote-driven systems
❑ A mixture of the two.

Order-Driven Systems

Most systems on the continent of Europe are order-driven. That is to say, an intermediary (usually a broker) matches buy and sell orders at a given price. The broker takes no risk in that shares will not be bought or sold unless there is a counterparty with the equivalent deal on the other side. The broker makes a living by charging commission. The systems in France, Germany, Belgium, Italy. Spain and Switzerland are of this type.

The older type of system saw activity on a physical floor with the broker for a given share surrounded by others calling out buy and sell orders. The broker then matched the orders and declared an official price, which might last until the next session. Today, computer systems are usually used, at least for the major shares. A popular system in Europe is the one taken from the Toronto Exchange, called CATS (Computer Assisted Trading System). Sometimes it is given a different name locally, such as CAC in Paris (Cotation Assistée en Continu).

The French have rewritten the system as Nouveau Système de Cotation (NSC) or Supercac and sold it back to Toronto. It is also used in São Paulo, Brussels, Lisbon and Warsaw.

Let's take Paris as our example. Orders may be keyed into the system directly, fed to member firms, or fed to the CAC system from member firms.

Orders are entered with a price limit, for example, a buyer is prepared to buy 500 shares up to a limit of FFr154 or a seller will sell 400 shares but at a price no lower than FFr151. Some enter an order to be filled at the 'market price'. From 9.00 a.m. to 10.00 a.m., these orders are fed into the system. At 10.00 a.m. the market opens. The computer then calculates the opening price at which the largest number of bids and offers can be matched (see Table 7.6).

Table 7.6   Opening prices

Stock XYZ Buyers		Sellers	
Quantity	Price limits	Price limits	Quantity
500	Market price	Market price	400
200	156	150	250
250	155	151	400
500	154	152	500
750	153	153	600
1000	152	154	1250
3000	151	155	1700

Source: Paris Bourse.

In this example, the market reaches equilibrium at FFr153 with 1700 shares at the offer rate (that is, 200 + 250 + 500 + 750 – all these are prepared to pay at least FFr153) and 1750 shares at the bid rate (that is, 250 + 400 + 500 + 600 – all these are prepared to accept FFr153).

All the orders at the market price are now filled in so far as it is possible. Unfilled orders at the market price are carried forward with FFr153 as the limit price.

From 10.00 a.m. to 5.00 p.m., trading takes place on a continuous basis and the arrival of a new order will trigger a match if matching orders exist on the centralised book. An in-depth display of data on a given security is given at the same time.

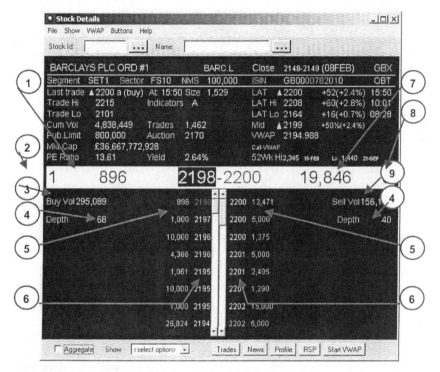

The white strip (yellow in real life) contains the similar information as Level 1 plus four extra values (numbered 1,2,7,8)

Lower left window shows those wanting to buy shares

Lower right window shows those wanting to sell shares

Definitions

NMS = Normal market size

ISIN = Registration number for stock

MQP = Mandatory quote period (i.e. 8:00am - 4:30pm)

OBT = Order book trading

GBX = Great British £

Cum Vol = Total number of shares traded today

Pub.Limit = Publication Limit

Trades = Number of trades actioned today
SET1 = FTSE 100; SET2 = FTSE 250 ; SET3 = FTSE 350
LAT = Last automatic trade
Mid = Calculated mid price
VWAP = Volume weighted average price (Total volume of shares traded divided by the total number of shares that have been traded)
Key
1. Total number of shares available at best price at bid
2. Number of orders in order book at the current best price at bid (i.e. how many 'best buyers')
3. Total number of shares awaiting 'buy' transaction
4. Number of orders (bid or offer) placed/queued at current time
5. Green for share volume
6. Share price. Note that the most recent Order is displayed in the user-selected 'down' colour, the second most-recent Order is displayed in the user-selected 'up' colour, and the third most recent Order is displayed in green.
7. Total number of shares available at best price at offer
8. Number of orders in order book at the current best price at offer (i.e. how many 'best sellers')
9. Total number of shares available at offer

Source: Proquote.
Figure 7.2   SETS screen

London's SETS system (Stock Exchange Electronic Trading System) is used for FTSE 100 stocks, stocks in the Eurotop 30 index and stocks with traded options on LIFFE. It was introduced in October 1997 and is an order matching system like the French NSC. Orders can be placed at a limit price or simply 'at best'. Further options allow the user to decide if a part-match is acceptable and whether any unmatched order is to remain on the order book. The information shown on a screen once continuous order input takes place is shown as Figure 7.2. On the left, we can see that the best 'buy' price for Barclays is £21.98 and the best 'sell' is £22.00. Total buy orders are 896 and total sell orders are 19,846. Stock exchange members, however, can still do deals outside the SETS system, reporting them through the system. This is why some prices reported are AT (automatic trading) and some are not.

Very large orders present a problem. They may wait quite a long time until they can be matched and their very presence will tend either to raise or lower the price. Block trades between institutions can be matched by brokers if there is a matching price but stamp duty (amongst other things) prevents a *market maker* in Paris (*teneur du marché*) either buying a large block (not knowing to whom they will sell them) or selling a large block they will now have to buy. The liquidity in trading for large orders attracts business to London from Paris, Frankfurt, Milan, Brussels and Madrid because London's traders are used to taking risks, because previously the only system used involved *market making*, which will be discussed shortly.

In Germany, on the official market there are official price fixers (Amtliche Kursmakler), on the second market there are independent brokers (Freimakler). The whole system is dominated by the banks handling their own and client orders. As a result of conflicts of interest, there have been three rival computer systems – the banks with IBIS, the Kursmakler with MATIS and the Freimakler with MIDAS. However, IBIS eventually became the sole system for top shares and was itself replaced by Xetra in December 1997. The Vienna exchange will also use Xetra.

In Japan, there are eight stock exchanges: Tokyo, Osaka and six others. The Tokyo exchange trades the shares of about 1800 companies and accounts for 70% of Japan's trading, with Osaka doing 18%. (Osaka, on the other hand, is very strong in derivatives.) Investors place their orders with stock exchange members. Specialists – *saitori* – match orders through an open outcry system. The details are circulated on computer screens.

Quote-Driven Systems

In quote-driven systems there is someone called a *market maker*. They quote continuously bid and offer prices at which they will buy or sell shares. The difference is the *spread*, that is their profit margin.

As a result, they will buy shares at the bid price, not knowing to whom these shares will be sold. They also agree from time to time to sell *short*, that is, to sell stock that they don't actually own but will now have to go out and buy. This clearly involves risk and needs capital (not to mention strong nerves!).

The systems, therefore, tend to be driven by the quotations. The prices, especially first thing in the morning, do not necessarily reflect the prices at which deals have taken place, as the market makers can change the quotations whenever they wish. Usually these prices are firm for a given quantity of shares and may be shown thus:

Share XYZ	*Bid*	*Offer*	*Bid quantity*	*Offer quantity*
	100	102	50	50

Seen on a computer screen in the UK, this would indicate that the market maker will buy shares at say £1.00 or sell them at £1.02 for any quantity up to 50,000 shares. For higher quantities, brokers will then negotiate on behalf of clients.

The main quotation driven systems are NASDAQ (in the US) and London's SEAQ (Stock Exchange Automated Quotations), which was heavily modelled on NASDAQ. Although the top 100 shares in London are traded on the SETS system previously discussed, other shares are still handled by SEAQ, which was used for all shares until October 1997. Where there are such systems, there are now two types of trader – the *broker* and the *market maker*.

The broker approaches market makers on behalf of clients and buys shares from them for the clients or sells the clients' shares to them. They make a living by charging a commission and do not take risk. In London, a broker may match buy/ sell orders from a client provided the price is better than that available from a market maker. This is a slight complication and leads to the term *broker dealer*. Generally, however, the role of the broker is that of an agent, especially for smaller clients.

Large clients, like the investment institutions, don't have to use a broker but may approach a market maker directly. If they do use a broker, it will be on a *quid pro quo* basis – that is, the broker in return for the business will make available equity research reports free of charge. As a result, providing top quality equity research is essential to attract business.

The market is very competitive and there may be 15–20 market makers competing in a particular share with the prices freely available to all. This ability to take risk is useful for large deals as the market maker will buy and sell and keep liquidity going. Very large deals hit problems with order-driven systems. On the other hand, market makers are reluctant to handle small company shares in which there is little trading. The spreads are very wide and this further discourages trading!

To combat this, the London Stock Exchange launched a new system in October 1992 called SEATS – Stock Exchange Alternative Trading System. This is a hybrid system, similar to those in New York which we discuss below. A single market maker is appointed for illiquid stocks and will be obliged to make continuous two way prices. At the same time investors will be able to post buy and sell orders at limit prices. When market makers trade they must fulfil orders that are posted first if they are at the same price or better than a proposed trade. In addition, any orders to be matched in brokers' offices must first be offered to the official market maker who may trade at a better price on their own account or by matching the posted orders.

The NASDAQ and SEAQ systems are very similar. Let's examine the SEAQ type of display for a major share, such as Babcock International, in Figure 7.3.

Normal market size is the minimum quantity of shares for which a firm quotation is given. (Smaller market makers can register as 'reduced size market makers' and post half this figure.) We can see that for Babcock International, there are 11 market makers competing for the business. The main display shows the market makers' initials, the bid/offer price and the bid/offer quantity. For example, on left towards the bottom we see that CSFB are quoting a price of 100p bid and 104p offered for quantities of 15,000 shares bid and offered.

We don't even need to search for the best prices as the panel halfway up shows us the best bid and offer, 101–104. These are called the 'touch prices'. The spread at the touch is usually measured and a record kept as an indication of the market's efficiency. Above these figures are shown the cumulative volume of shares traded so far and the latest price and trading history. All prices must be entered within 3 minutes of the conclusion of the deal.

Note that the trading itself is not automated. If the broker wishes to deal, the arrangement is concluded on the telephone. Only the SETS system is automated.

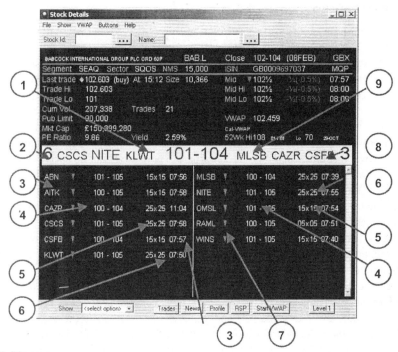

Definitions

NMS = Normal market size

ISIN = Registration number for stock

MQP = Mandatory quote period (i.e. 8:00am – 4:30pm)

OBT = Order book trading

GBX = Great British £

Cum Vol = Total number of shares traded today

Trades = No of trades actioned today

VWAP = Volume weighted average price (Total volume of shares traded divided by the total number of shares that have been traded)

Key

1. Market maker's identification at the best price at bid.
2. Number of quotes at the current best price at bid
3. Blue (cyan) – Market maker's ID
4. Yellow – Bid spread
5. Yellow – Number of shares at bid/offer (see below)
6. Grey –Time the order was placed
7. Arrow and colour indicates direction of last price change for market maker (red for down, cyan for up)
8. Number of quotes at the current best price at offer
9. Market makers identification at the best price at offer.

Source: Proquote.

Figure 7.3   *SEAQ screen*

Hybrid Systems

Hybrid systems, with both order-driven and quote-driven characteristics, are found in New York and Amsterdam.

In New York, each share is allocated to a *specialist*. The specialist acts as a broker, executing orders for other brokers on a commission basis. However, they may act for their own account (like a market maker) by buying from the public when there are no other buyers and selling to the public when there are no other sellers, all at or near the price of the last transaction. In other words, they match buyers and sellers when there are plenty of them but will keep the market going, by buying on their own account, when there is a shortage. There are about 60 specialists on the New York exchange and the system dates from before the First World War.

In a given stock, a specialist may have buyers at \$45¼ and sellers at \$45½ – these are the best prices, that is, highest bid and lowest offer. A broker approaches and is quoted '\$45¼/\$45½'. The broker's client wants to buy 100 shares. He tries '\$45⅜' in case anyone in the crowd surrounding the specialist wishes to match this. If this fails, he raises the bid to \$45½ and the specialist calls out 'sold' and gives the broker the name of the first order on his book at that price.

At the start of the day, the specialist is faced with many orders – some at the closing market price, some at limit prices. His duty is to set a price as near as possibly to the close (to maintain an orderly market) and yet also match as many orders as possible. Sometimes the system works well in a crisis, sometimes not. On Monday, 26 September 1955, following President Eisenhower's heart attack the previous day, there was frenzied trading. Specialists, holding stocks worth \$50m, bought almost another \$50m to help stabilise the market. However, on 'Black Monday', 19 October 1987, the specialists were overwhelmed and for hours there was no trading in two key stocks, IBM and General Motors. In London, the market makers kept going but there were frequent accusations of not answering the telephone!

There is an important automatic electronic order execution service in New York, DOT (Designated Order Turnaround), which was introduced in 1976 to transmit to the trading posts orders of up to a given maximum size and to send back confirmation of completed orders. In 1984, this was replaced by SuperDOT, able to handle bigger volumes. This itself was integrated with OARS (Opening Order Automated Report Service) which collected and stored the opening orders each day. The system pairs buy and sell orders and specialists can quickly see imbalances and determine the day's opening prices.

In Amsterdam, the market is split between retail and wholesale. Retail orders go via the 'hoekman' who may match orders or take a position like a market maker. Wholesale orders go through an order matching system called AIDA. Banks and brokers can also advertise their desire to buy and sell via a system called ASSET.

Although the London SETS system is essentially order matching, in practice it is more of a hybrid system. Users are not obliged to enter orders via the system. London's culture for years has been one of market making. As a result, many institutions still telephone stock exchange members and ask if they want to buy or sell and take the risk. Sometimes the dealer will accept a large order at a protected price but attempt to better it by feeding it through the system in smaller batches or offering it to other institutions. These very large orders are called *worked principal orders* and publication details are delayed. Since currently less than half the orders are going via order matching for automatic execution, we can describe the SETS system as a kind of hybrid with characteristics of both order-driven and quotation-driven systems.

Inter Dealer Brokers

In some markets (for example, London), transactions between market dealers are facilitated by *inter dealer brokers* (IDBs). Their function is like brokers in money markets or foreign exchange. They publish (on computer screens) large potential deals at bid and offer prices, but anonymously. Another dealer may see the quotation and decide to make a trade. The transaction is carried out by the broker and the two counterparties never learn of each other's identity. The dealer who identifies a trade and indicates a willingness to conclude it, pays the commission and is called (curiously) the 'aggressor'. Anonymous order matching systems, like SETS, have dealt IDBs a severe blow.

Stock Borrowing and Lending

A dealer may sell shares or bonds they don't have, going 'short'. An alternative to buying the stock prior to settlement is to borrow it from institutions who will lend stock for a commission and pass over money (or other securities) as collateral. Typically, the stock is paid for and the money returned when the dealer actually buys the stock and returns it. This facility greatly assists the liquidity of the market.

On the other hand, dealers have to fund their 'long' positions. One way to fund them is to lend stock not needed and take the money to help fund other positions.

Thus stock lending may be done by institutions merely to enhance income, or may be done by dealers as a means of financing their position.

To complicate matters, although everyone calls it stock *lending*, in fact, the stock is *sold*, albeit on a temporary basis. In other words, the whole arrangement is the sale and repurchase agreement, or *repo*, which we met in Chapter 6. There it was a means of banks funding their liquidity by selling stock (temporarily) to the central bank.

This market is particularly large for bonds, although there is some lending of equities.

The language, as usual, is used loosely. Generally 'stock lending' is used where dealers want to cover short positions and is driven by borrower demand. 'Repo' is used where the transaction is to meet funding needs. The legal agreements for stock lending and repos are, however, different.

Bought Deals/Block Trades

Occasionally, very large share deals are executed called bought deals or block trades. The investment bank involved buys the shares using its own capital and hopes to sell them to investors at a profit. It can be very lucrative but also involves great risk.

It is usually a competitive process. In December 1995, for example, NM Rothschild held an auction for the sale of the UK government's remaining stake in BP. SBC Warburg won the business by offering £5.08 per share and later sold them for £5.13m making about £5m. The sales total was £500m.

Perhaps encouraged by this, the French government also selected NM Rothschild to hold an auction to sell the government's remaining stake in Total. The auction was held one Tuesday evening in March 1996. Crédit Lyonnais and Lehman Bros won by bidding to sell the stock at FFr326 each, a 2.4% discount to the market price. The shares were placed by 9.00 am on Wednesday morning and a commission of between 0.5% and 0.7% was believed to have been earned. The total proceeds were FFr3.1bn.

In March 1999, the German energy group, Veba, sold its 10.2% stake in Cable and Wireless – the biggest block trade in the European stock markets. 246 million shares were placed by ABN Amro at £7.35, raising £1.8bn, a discount of 11.5% to the latest stock price. ABN Amro was believed to have paid £7.24 for the stake, leaving a profit of £26m, about 1.5%.

It's not always easy, of course. Kleinwort Benson once attempted to sell a block representing Burmah Castrol's 29.7% holding in Premier Consolidated. They lost £34m!

Share Buy-Backs

An interesting issue is that of companies buying back their own shares. This is very common in the UK and the US. For example, in July 1996, National Westminster Bank bought back shares worth £450m and Barclays Bank bought back shares worth £470m. In 2002, GlaxoSmithKline bought back the first of two instalments of £42bn of its shares. The idea is to cancel the shares so that profit and dividend per remaining share are then enhanced. In France, however, it is common to buy shares back as a defensive move, either to support price or prevent a takeover. Under a new law passed in 1998, the AGM has powers to authorise a buy-back of up to 10% in the next 18 months. Once bought, the shares may be cancelled (subject to EGM approval) or allocated to employees.

Critics point out that if a company is unable to employ surplus capital profitably, this is a sad reflection on the business vision of the company's management and does not augur well for the company's prospects. Consequently, a share buy-back may actually result in a fall in the share price (this happened in the case of GlaxoSmithKline and has also happened to Reuters).

Share buy-backs were illegal in Germany until a new law of March 1998 permitting companies to buy back up to 10% of their shares in an 18 month period.

The BHF-Bank took advantage of this to buy back 3.4% of its shares.

In Japan, share repurchases have not been as common and have traditionally been frowned upon as a way of manipulating share prices. In any case, no more than 3% could be bought back. With economic recovery, many companies believe that their capital will be better spent on research and development. In spite of this, Toyota Motors bought back 1.2% of its shares, Komatsu 2% and Asahi Breweries 1.9%. Then, at the end of 1997, a new law increased the possible buy-back percentage to 10%.

SETTLEMENT

Settlement is the basic question of paying money and receiving stock or receiving money and delivering the stock. If the stock cannot be delivered without money being credited to pay for it, this is called 'Delivery Versus Payment' (DVP) and is the ideal. It is another recommendation of the G30 report on settlement.

Sometimes settlement systems are 'rolling settlement', for example, rolling 5 working day settlement. This means that a deal on Tuesday must be settled on the next Tuesday, a deal on Wednesday must be settled on the next Wednesday and so on. This is called 'T+5', that is, 'Trade Date +5'. The G30 report recommends rolling settlement systems and 'T+3' if possible. The US is T+3, Germany T+2 and France T+3 under their new 'RELIT' system (Règlement Livraison de Titres).

The alternative is the system of an 'account period'. For example, Paris has its Règlement Mensuel, which can still be used to settle if requested. The 'month' is the 5 last working days of the month plus the next month up to 5 working days from the end. All deals within this month are settled on the last trading day of the month. There is, however, also a cash market (marché au comptant). This is used for less actively traded stocks, all the second market, OTC and all bonds.

In New York, the Depository Trust Corporation (DTC) holds large blocks of stocks registered in its name for safe custody. Between the New York Stock Exchange and the DTC is the National Securities Clearing Corporation, which acts as a clearing function for the exchange and passes the transfers to the DTC. Net money due to or from a broker is settled daily by a single payment.

The UK had a fortnightly account system. Settlement day was a week on Monday, following the end of the two weekly account ending on the Friday. All member firms' deals were then settled as one net figure. The system was handled at the Stock Exchange and was called Talisman. It was to be replaced by a new system called Taurus, which would have involved rolling settlement and abolition of share certificates. However, after three separate start dates for the new system were announced and cancelled, the whole project was abandoned in March 1993. Its successor abolishes the use of share certificates, but only for professionals. The private investor is still able to use share certificates if they wish. The system is called CREST and is run by a new company – CREST CO – with the Stock

Exchange as one shareholder amongst many. It started operation in the second half of 1996. (Currently, CREST CO is merging operations with the Brussels-based Euroclear.) Where paper certificates no longer exist and transfer of ownership is on computer register only, this is called '*dematerialisation*'. The French *RELIT* system is of this type.

Italy dropped its monthly settlement system and moved to T+5 rolling settlement in February, 1996.

In general the trend is towards new rolling settlement systems and dematerialisation.

NEW ISSUES

Handling issues of shares of new companies coming to the market is very much the essence of a stock exchange.

We should, perhaps, begin by asking – why do companies go public anyway? There is a variety of reasons.

In the first place, the company may be seeking new capital for an expansion plan. This may be a more attractive way of getting the money than, say, bank loans or trying to attract more private shareholders. (If a company feels it is not yet ready to go public, but is looking for more capital, it may seek as a new shareholder a bank which specialises in this, and is usually referred to as a *venture capital* company.) In later years, if the company needs more capital, it can go back to the shareholders with a *rights issue* (which we discuss shortly).

Secondly, going public produces a price for the shares and a market. Without this, if one of the original private shareholders wishes to sell out and retire, there may be a problem. What price do we put on the shares? Who can afford to buy them? In addition, giving staff the right to buy shares through one of a variety of share purchase schemes provides a valuable incentive. It is also cheap for the company. To sell shares to the staff, the company usually creates new shares. The number is so small that any dilution of the share price is not noticeable.

Finally, in a takeover situation, the company can now offer new shares in its own company instead of cash to the victim company's shareholders. This can be very useful and is also very common. If the victim shareholders would prefer cash, institutions can be found to buy the shares, usually referred to as a *vendor placing*.

In general, there are two systems – the public offer for sale and the placing, or private placement.

In the case of a *public offer for sale* (an *initial public offering* in the US) the offer receives wide publicity and investors are invited to submit applications for the shares. If oversubscribed, some form of rationing or allocation must take place.

Usually, a detailed prospectus giving details of the firm's history and accounts must be produced. The issue is brought to market by a bank or stockbroker. They will advise on the pricing of the issue, will attempt to persuade the market of its merits and arrange *underwriting*. This means that, in so far as the investing public does not buy the shares, the group of underwriters undertake to purchase them. For this they receive a fee, perhaps 1½% to 2% of the value underwritten. The risk is spread widely and investment institutions will often participate, hoping to keep the fee and sleep well at night. 'Black Monday' in 1987 occurred in the middle of the UK government's privatisation of further shares in British Petroleum. The underwriters had to purchase the shares at the offer price and incur a considerable loss. Sometimes, if the market is seen to be weak, a planned issue is withdrawn. In September 1992, Commerzbank withdrew a planned offering of more shares worth DM600m due to the weak state of the market.

In the *placing*, the broker concerned contacts investment clients with the details of the offer and sells the shares without any public offering. The number of shareholders for a given sum raised is usually set at a minimum by local stock exchange rules.

The placing is much easier and cheaper from the administrative point of view and also saves underwriting fees. Other things being equal, firms may prefer a placing. However, there are usually local Stock Exchange rules on this subject. For example, in the UK, if the sum of money raised was more than £3m, a placing was not allowed. In 1986, this limit was raised to £15m and in 1991 more complex rules were introduced. These envisaged the possibility of a new issue which was part placing and part offer for sale, a 100% placing being ruled out if the amount raised exceeded £50m. In 1992, there were several new issues which were 50% offer for sale and 50% placing. However, from 1 January 1996, these rules were abolished and there is now no limitation on the amount that can be raised by a placing.

Sometimes we hear of an unquoted company taking over a 'shell' company. This is a company with few assets, profits in decline or non-existent and a low share price. The takeover company usually imposes its own name. It's a way of getting a listing without going through all the procedures of an official new issue.

Another possibility is for a company to be admitted to the list of shares which are being traded on an exchange by an *introduction*. This is typically a firm quoted on a foreign stock exchange which seeks an admission to the list of firms traded on a domestic exchange. Normally, no new money is being raised at that time. This became very common in the 1980s as part of the 'international equity' idea which we discussed earlier. The Japanese firm Toshiba, for example, is listed on nine European Stock Exchanges. Daiwa began to trade on 7 European Stock Exchanges simultaneously in April 1990. Volkswagen was listed on all four Spanish stock exchanges in June 1990 and Volkswagen and Bayer Chemicals became the first foreign companies to be listed on the Milan Stock Exchange in the same year. Daimler Benz became the first German company to list on the New York Stock Exchange in 1993. The National Bank of Greece listed on the New York Stock Exchange in mid-1999.

Foreign shares listed in the US would have a disadvantage if quoted and dealt in their own currency. There are also higher costs for investors in buying foreign shares and worries (in some cases) about receiving share certificates. As a result, many foreign companies' shares trade in the US as *American Depositary Receipts (ADRs)*. The receipt for one or more of a foreign company's shares is held by a trustee (often Morgan Guaranty Trust) and the receipt is traded rather than the shares themselves. For example, a BP ADR is worth twelve ordinary shares. The US investor avoids the inconvenience of collecting dividends and converting them to dollars. The sponsor bank takes care of this. The first ADR was issued in 1927 for the British–American Tobacco Company. There are some 2000 ADR programmes worth $400bn.

A more general theme is Global Depositary Receipt (GDR) which refers to using the same technique as ADRs for listing shares on exchanges outside the US. The first of these was issued in 1990 and they have proved very useful for emerging markets. For example, there were 24 GDR listings on the London Stock Exchange in 1998. Included were the first companies to list in London from Cyprus, Malawi, Malta, Romania and Tunisia. It brought the total of London GDR listings to 166.

There is also now the European Depository Receipt, launched by the Paris Bourse and Citibank in 1998, for issues in euros and cleared through the Paris Sicovam.

The Asian crisis naturally led to a fall in this type of issue in 1998. The Bank of New York estimated that ADRs raised $10bn in 1998 compared with $18bn in 1997. Although London had 24 GDR programmes in 1998 compared with 31 in 1997, they actually raised more money – £3.9bn as opposed to £2.6bn.

However, 1999 saw a revival. Citibank figures showed issues totalling $7bn in the first 6 months. After the Far East crisis of 1997, it was particularly interesting to see four Korean offerings. The largest ADR offering in the 6 months was from Korea Telecom – $2.5bn. In 2000, London saw new issues from companies as diverse as China Petroleum (£2.4bn) and the Indian software and business conglomerate Tata (£51m) contributing to an overall total value of new issues of £3590m.

RIGHTS ISSUES

Later, a firm may decide to offer the existing shareholders the right to buy some new shares in proportion to the shares they already hold. This is why they are typically called 'rights issues'. Across most of Europe, the law requires that existing shareholders have pre-emptive rights to any new shares issued for cash. (New shares may not necessarily be issued for cash – they may be issued in order to fund a takeover bid by offering them to the shareholders of the company to be taken over.)

In the US, shareholders' rights to new shares are not so firmly established. The whole question of these pre-emptive rights is controversial. Periodically, articles appear arguing that firms should be able to issue a block of new shares by auction without offering them first to the existing shareholders.

Although pre-emptive rights are common across Europe, one exception is Germany. In March 1998, Mannesman, the industrial conglomerate, issued new shares to the value of DM3bn without offering them to existing shareholders. In March 1999, Deutsche Bank was raising money to fund its takeover of Bankers Trust. It raised DM4bn by means of a rights issue to existing shareholders but also sold a further DM2bn of new shares worldwide on a non-rights basis.

Of course, the shareholders may be approached to waive their rights. When Midland Bank sold 14.9% of its shares by way of new shares to the Hong Kong and Shanghai Bank in 1987, they approached the existing shareholders for their permission.

The new shares will be offered at a discount to the existing shares, for example, an offer of one new share at $90 may be made for every three existing shares whose market price is $110. The discount is more apparent than real. The firm is regarded as having diluted the value of the issue by this offer of extra shares at a discount. An averaging or pro-rating now takes place as follows:

			$
3 existing shares	@ $110	=	330
1 new share	@ $90	=	90
Therefore each block of four shares		=	420
So 1 new share		=	105

When the shares are declared *ex-rights* (XR), the price will be $105 if the market price remains at $110. 'XR' means that anyone buying the shares does not enjoy the rights to the new shares. It now seems that the shareholder will not gain from taking up the rights in any explicit sense but will lose if they do not. They may have 100 shares at $110 per share and soon will have 100 shares at $105 per share!

They may not have the money to buy the new shares. Some shareholders sell some of their existing shares to buy new ones or the rights may be sold to someone else for a quoted premium. In the above case, the premium would be $15. The purchaser of the rights will pay the shareholder $15 and later pay the company $90, paying $105. The shareholder has shares at present for which each set of three are valued at $330 and will soon be valued at $315 – however, they sold the rights for $15.

The market price does not obligingly remain stable while the shareholders make up their minds. The premium for buying the rights thus goes up and down. What is particularly serious is if the rights price ends up above the market price. Suppose the market price in the case above falls to $80. How many people will wish to buy shares at $90 if the existing shares can be purchased for $80? This reminds us that a rights issue must be underwritten just like a new issue.

In 1991, in the UK, British Aerospace announced a rights issue at £3.80 at a time when the market price was £5.00. The announcement of poor profit prospects, however, saw the market price plunge to £3.60 as the market lost faith in British Aerospace. The underwriters took up 95% of the offering.

Rights issues are examined carefully by the market. The new money needs to be used wisely if profit per share and dividend per share are not to suffer. Sometimes, the rights issue is seen as positive and well received, sometimes as negative, the sign of a firm in trouble and the share price suffers.

SCRIP ISSUES AND SPLITS

Sometimes firms offer shareholders free shares in proportion to the shares they own. For example, they may be offered one free share for every share owned. This is the *scrip* issue. Alternatively, the shares are *split*. For example, every share, 'par' or 'nominal' value $1, is replaced by two shares, 'par' or 'nominal' value 50¢.

In each case, the market value of the share will fall to half of the previous figure. The idea is that markets recognise a broad range of trading prices for shares. With growing profits and dividends over the years, the share price increases. Sometimes, the market feels that the new price is inconvenient and deters small shareholders from buying. The theory is that shareholders are happier with 100 shares at $50 than ten shares at $500. If this doesn't seem logical it is because it is, in fact, quite illogical – it's pure investor psychology.

For example, the UK market likes share prices in a range, say of £1 – £10. Above this level, companies frequently do scrips or splits to bring the price down to a 'better' trading price, one which is thought to lead to a more widespread holding and more liquidity. Thus, in the autumn of 1998, the Logica share price was £20. They did a 4 for 1 scrip issue to bring the price down to £4.

In the US, the same idea prevails, but at much higher share price levels. On the Continent of Europe, too, shares trade typically at far higher prices than in the UK. When Paribas was privatised, for example, 3.8m applied for the shares and received just four each – but the price each was about FFr450. Switzerland is a place where, traditionally, the shares of the banks, pharmaceutical companies and Nestlé have traded at a price equivalent to several thousand dollars. However, the law, which required a minimum legal value of SFr100 per share, has been altered to lower this to SFr10 per share. In May 1992, Nestlé took advantage of this to replace each share, legal value SFr100, by 10, with legal value of SFr10 each. The effect was to lower the price each from SFr9600 to SFr960. Other large Swiss companies have followed suit. In Spain, the Bank Argentaria split its nominal value of Pta 250 to Pta 125 to halve the share price.

In the US, they get less comfortable when share prices exceed $100. Fast growing shares end up doing many splits. In January 1999, Intel announced its 12th split when the share price hit $137. In the US, buying in multiples of 100 attracts cheaper commission – the split makes this easier. In the same week, IBM and Microsoft also did splits.

We have seen from the above that shares typically have a 'par' or legal value which may not bear any relationship to the market price – IBM at $1¼, for example, or AT & T at $1. There is no minimum for the legal value either in the US or the UK. In Germany, however, there was a minimum legal value of DM50, but this has been lowered to DM5, which may be part of a move to a lower average price. A low par or legal value enables the company to issue more shares when it is first formed and gives it greater flexibility later.

The scrip issue does not change the par value but gives, say, one additional share free. This doubles the par value on the balance sheet and the money is taken from reserves. A split does not alter the *total* par value owned as, say, one share at FFr75 is replaced by three at FFr25 – the total par value on the balance sheet is unchanged, but the par value of each share is. Thus Barclays' 4 for 1 split in 2002 reduced the par value of each share from £1 to 25p.

Finally, let's note that a *reverse split* or *consolidation* is possible. Here, say, five existing shares are replaced by one new one whose par value is five times as high. This is for situations where the share price is so low that it suggests a firm in serious trouble. Again, it's simply psychology. For example, in June 1992, the British advertising group Saatchi and Saatchi carried out a 1 for 10 consolidation when the share price touched a low of 15p each.

SCRIP DIVIDENDS

A common practice in many markets is to offer a choice of cash dividends or more shares – the scrip dividend. From the firm's point of view, it saves cash as it's easier to create new shares than pay dividends. From the investor's point of view, if dividends are not needed as income, it's a way of getting new shares without paying share tax or broker's commission.

SECOND MARKETS

It is quite common to have a 'second market' for shares that do not fulfil all the requirements for a full official listing. Both France and Belgium have 'second markets'; the UK has the 'Alternative Investment Market' (AIM); Germany has the 'Geregelter Markt' and a third market the 'Freiverkehr'; Amsterdam has its 'parallel' market.

In addition to this, there may be an active 'Over the Counter Market'. Paris has its 'Hors Cote', the US the huge NASDAQ market; and the UK a market called 'OFEX'.

Usually, the key requirements that the second or third market firm may not fulfil are the number of years' trading record and the percentage of shares in outside hands. The general European rule, under the 'Mutual Recognition of Listing Particulars', is that 3 years' trading is needed for a full listing and for recognition of a firm already listed on another EU exchange.

In both Paris and London, for the official list, 25% of shares must be in outside hands. The rule for the Paris Second Market is that only 10% need be in outside hands. There were 272 firms on the Second Market in Paris and 524 on the AIM in London in 2000.

During the period 1998–1999, new markets in France, Germany, Belgium and Holland formed an alliance called 'Euro.NM'. The markets are Nouveau Marché (France), Neuer Markt (Germany), Euro.NM (Belgium) and NMAX (Holland). They have common members, common data feeds and the shares trade, and are monitored on a single workstation (but not on a common system). The Italian Nuovo Mercato joined in the Spring of 1999 and by mid-year there were 250 firms trading, with a total capitalisation of €59bn. Stockholm, Copenhagen and Zurich are expected to join later in 1999. This is providing severe competition for other secondary markets, such as the UK's AIM, with a total capitalisation of £14.9bn at the end of 2000. The alliance suffered a setback, however, when the Germans announced, in September 2002, that the Neuer Markt would close in 2003.

A consortium of US and European banks has formed a new pan-European market called EASDAQ, modelled on the US NASDAQ market. The aim was to attract high growth companies. 20% of the shares must be in outside hands. It began in late 1996, but by mid-1999 had only 43 companies listed with a total capitalisation of €21bn. In 2001, it was taken over by NASDAQ.

ANALYSTS' RATIOS

When a firm makes an initial public offering of its shares, how does it decide what price to ask for the shares? A simple answer seems to be 'divide the value of the company by the number of the shares'. The problem is that the value of the company is the share price!

Sometimes people suggest 'asset values' as a possible guide. However, on 1 October 1987 companies' share prices were a great deal higher than at 31 October 1987, after the market crash, and yet the assets were the same. In any case, some firms are quite valuable but have few assets. 'People' companies like computer software houses or stockbrokers are like this.

The fact is that price is simply what the market will pay. We must, therefore, look at what the market does pay for similar companies. Their share prices will all be different, which doesn't immediately help. There are two rewards for buying a share – dividends and an increase in the share price. Both of these depend on *profits*, so what we need to do is see how the price per share of comparable companies compares to the profit per share. We might find an overall relationship of, say, 10. That is, if the profit is $4 per share, the share price is typically $40. If our profit per share is $3, this suggests a price of $30. Let's make it $28 and persuade everyone that it's a bargain!

This relationship of share price to profit is the *P/E* – the Price/Earnings Ratio and the most famous ratio of them all. We've seen one of its key uses, to help us set a price initially. Each time new profits are announced, a new P/E is calculated and the share may seem cheap or dear now compared to its peers in the market sector.

Sometimes analysts look at the P/E for the whole stock market, and compare this with historic values to see if the market is overpriced or not.

Sometimes it is not easy to find the market sector. When the composer, Andrew Lloyd Webber, went public as the 'Really Useful Group', it was difficult to find anything comparable! In that case, what took place was the *offer for sale by tender*. Investors put in their various bids and the share allocation is decided accordingly. In that case, it was a 'striking price' tender, that is, everyone paid the same price.

As dividends are part of the reward for holding shares, the market looks at dividend income as a percentage of the share price. To avoid complications, the dividend is grossed up if it is normally paid net, for example:

$$\frac{\text{Gross dividend}}{\text{Share price}} = \frac{\$2.5}{\$50} = 5\%$$

This ratio is the *gross dividend yield* or, simply, the *yield*. It will be compared with the yield on other shares and with the yield on bonds in particular. Analysts talk of the *yield ratio* – the ratio between the yield on government bonds and the yields on shares. As shares may have capital gain, the yield is usually less than that on medium maturity bonds (although this has not always been the case). Typical P/E ratios and yields for key exchanges in September 2002 are shown in Table 7.7.

Table 7.7 *P/E ratios and yields, September 2002*

Exchange	Index	P/E	Yield
US	S&P Ind	47.2	1.58
Germany	FAZ	10.6	2.63
UK	FTSE 100	17.3	3.65
France	SBF 250	11.1	3.77
Japan	Nikkei 225	41.2	0.94

Source: *Financial Times.*

Looking at the dividend paid, we may want to see how comfortable the firm was when paying the dividend out of profit. Was all the profit used? How much profit is retained for growth? We compare the profit per share with the *net* dividend per share, for example:

$$\frac{\text{Profit per share}}{\text{Net dividend}} = \frac{\$5}{\$2} = 2.5$$

This ratio is the *cover*. If the profit is small but the firm feels it must maintain the dividend, the net dividend paid may exceed the profit per share. We say the dividend is *uncovered*. Clearly, it is being financed out of the reserves (that is, previous years' profits) and the firm's capital is being weakened.

At a time of recession, there is fierce argument about the extent to which firms should try to maintain dividends even if they are not justified by profits. Pension funds or insurance companies who need income to meet commitments are concerned when dividends are cut or not paid. Trustees of some investment funds will not allow investment in any firm which has passed a dividend in a given previous time period.

Finally, analysts look at *earnings per share* and use this as a record of the firm's performance. Problems arise when accounting conventions may allow (legitimate) massaging of the profit figure. Should extraordinary items for unprecedented events (for example, acquisition costs) be charged against profit for this purpose?

For the EU, trying to impose common national standards is a veritable minefield. A new British accountancy standard has been enforced but has incurred criticism from some quarters. At the same time, a book by a former UBS Phillips & Drew analyst on how firms legitimately 'massage' their accounts went into the bestseller list! (Terry Smith, *Accounting for Growth*, Century Business, 1991). This is just one of many controversial issues in this area and of course mis-stated profits at WorldCom, the hiding of debt at Enron and other recent accounting scandals have shaken investors' confidence and contributed in 2002 to continuing decline in world stock markets.

US STOCK MARKET – THE NEW PARADIGM AND THE BURST OF THE DOT.COM BUBBLE

The performance of the United States economy in recent years up to and beyond the millennium seemed to have broken all normal economic rules. The stock market also experienced a period of unprecedented expansion.

For three years the US GDP grew at 4% per annum with no sign of inflationary pressures. Consumer price inflation at the end of 1998 was 1.7%, the lowest for 20 years, and unemployment, at 4.2%, the lowest for 30 years. At this point (according to normal rules) labour shortages should have appeared and competition for labour have forced wages and inflation up. Instead of declining productivity as poorer quality labour is employed, productivity in the years 1997 and 1998 doubled.

People referred to this as the 'new paradigm' – an era in which the old rules no longer applied. They pointed to declining commodity prices, cheaper imports due to the strong dollar, high productivity due to technology and an intensification of global competition making companies reluctant to increase prices for fear of losing market share.

The Dow Jones responded in kind, rising two and a half times in the three years 1996 to 1998, and continuing to rise in 1999 – the only small blip coming with the

Russian crisis in August 1998. The number of US households in mutual funds rose from 10m to 40m. At one point Alan Greenspan, the chairman of the Federal Reserve, issued warnings about 'irrational exuberance', but then seemed to content himself with pointing out that share prices implied confidence in a very strong growth in corporate profits.

Would the old rules reassert themselves in the end? Those who wanted to spoil the party pointed out that the stock market rose threefold between 1925 and 1929 and everyone talked of 'a new era'. The market then fell 89% from its peak to a low point in 1932.

With the burst of the dot.com bubble in 2001 and accounting scandals in 2002, the markets have fallen around 40%, and the Dow having peaked at over 12,000 has fallen below 8000 in 2002. The FTSE 100 peaked at 6930 in December 1999, since when it has fallen to below 3700 in September 2002, a 6 year low. Now analysts are back to talking about historical yields and indicators, unsustainable growth in prices and unrealistic expectations – all with the benefit of hindsight!

EU RULES

Investment Services Directive

At the end of June 1992, EU finance ministers reached agreement on the final shape of the Investment Services Directive (ISD). This extends the 'single passport' idea seen in the Second Banking Directive. Stockbrokers in one country have the right to deal in the shares of any other EU country, without having to set up a local office or buy a local stockbroker.

The ISD took effect from 1 January 1996. From this date, firms are able to operate in any EU member state provided they are regulated in one of them. This operation is subject to local rules on conduct of business.

In addition, all exchanges and futures and options markets can trade throughout the EU. The effect of all this is to increase competition between the Union's stock exchanges and derivatives exchanges. Thus, from 1 January 1996, NatWest Markets began trading on the Swedish stock exchange but from their office in London. There was no longer any need to pay a local Swedish broker. Equally, the German DTB, the derivatives exchange, opened an access point in London for local members to do business directly with Frankfurt.

Capital Adequacy Directive

Alongside the ISD is the Capital Adequacy Directive (CAD). This has also provoked fierce debate. Where there is a universal bank tradition, like Germany, the banks were happy to cover the investment banking activity under commercial bank capital ratio rules. US and UK operators, however, not owned by banks, were strongly opposed to this. The rules require dealers to have a minimum amount of capital to back their transactions but taking into account the precise nature of the risk and allowing for hedging of transactions.

From 1 January 1996, the European CAD came into operation. Investment banks must allocate capital to cover the risks of losses through changes in market prices. The BIS ratios, as we have seen, only covered default risks for lending. Large banks were covering this risk anyway but have had to cover the costs of rewriting IT systems to follow the new rules and monitor exposures constantly. Since most countries had local rules to cover capital adequacy, the effect has not been too serious in terms of banks having to provide extra capital.

Mergers and Acquisitions

The EU agreed a Merger Regulation in 1989. This defined circumstances in which a merger would have a 'European dimension' and come under the rules of the EU, and when a merger would be decided by national bodies. In one case, in particular, the Commission vetoed the takeover of De Havilland, the Canadian aircraft maker, by Aérospatiale of France and Alenia from Italy (to the fury of all concerned). On the other hand, objections to the Nestlé takeover of Perrier had little effect and Nestlé and BSN of France now control 75% of the French mineral water market. In the UK, Airtours abandoned its bid for First Choice in June 1999, following objections from the regulatory authorities in Brussels.

The EU has abandoned the idea of a detailed takeover bid directive in favour of one which outlines principles with which local legislation must comply – for example, equal treatment of all shareholders. However, the problem was stalled for 13 years, despite a clear need for general principles to be adopted. In France, BNP made a bid for Société Générale and Paribas. The last two can (and did) deal in BNP shares but BNP cannot deal in theirs. Gucci, facing a hostile bid from LVMH, sold 40% of new shares to an ally, François Pinault. This was only possible due to lax takeover rules in Amsterdam, where Gucci is listed. One current compromise floats the idea of 'joint jurisdiction', where a company is listed in one country but registered in another (like Gucci).

Finally, in 2002, a new takeover code was agreed by EU lawmakers. It curbs companies' use of poison pill takeover defences and requires bidders and targets to treat all shareholders equally. Also, predators will be required to make a formal bid once their stake reaches a certain threshold. EU nations have until 2005 to implement the rules.

CHALLENGES TO TRADITIONAL STOCK EXCHANGES

As we have already mentioned, stock exchanges do not necessarily have a monopoly of trading. Rival order matching systems are common and assisted by the growth of electronic networks. Traditional brokers face competition from brokers like Charles Schwab who offer cheaper Internet trading.

In the UK, Tradepoint opened up in 1995 in competition with the London Stock Exchange. Initially, it was a failure and ran up losses of £30m. However, in a rescue package in May 1999, new partners took a 55% stake and revitalised it by putting their own trades through it. These new partners include Instinet, Morgan Stanley, Dean Witter, J.P. Morgan and Warburg Dillon Read. In addition, Tradepoint became the first foreign exchange to receive clearance to operate in the US from the SEC.

In the US, Electronic Communications Networks (ECNs) act as mini-exchanges. They include Instinet, E*Trade, Charles Schwab, Datek, Island and Posit (now operating in the UK). E*Trade took over Telebanc on June 1 1999 in a move to add value with advice and research. Even worse for the traditional exchanges, the SEC is considering recognising ECNs as official exchanges.

Some brokers have now set up links with them – Goldman Sachs, Lehman Bros and Bear Stearns. Eyebrows were raised in June 1999 when Merrill Lynch revealed plans to enter discount on-line broking using the Internet in direct competition with Charles Schwab. Merrill's Internet service offers a fee of $29.95 per transaction, far less than its normal commissions, but still in excess of other on-line discount brokers. The Internet is becoming a major factor now. It is estimated that 61% of trades with Charles Schwab go through the Internet. In the UK, Barclays Stockbrokers have launched an on-line Internet service, and the Swedish bank, SEB, has a very successful Internet operation and claims that 20% of its customers use it. Charles Schwab already operates in the UK and E*Trade plans to do so.

One reaction of stock exchanges has been to offer more flexibility with evening sessions. NASDAQ announced plans in May 1999 for evening trading on the NASDAQ 100 stocks only. The New York Stock Exchange is considering the same move. However, staffing costs will be a problem as overheads go up for limited revenue.

In order to have greater flexibility for raising capital, the London Stock Exchange went public in June 2000 and NASDAQ will do so in early 2003. The CME was the first major US market to float when it went public in December 2002 with a market capitalisation of about $1bn.

Other moves to cut costs include mergers with derivatives exchanges and mergers with other stock exchanges.

The key stock exchange and derivatives exchange have merged in the following countries: Germany, France, the Netherlands, Sweden, Austria, Switzerland and Hong Kong. The merger in Australia has been delayed by a rival merger offer put to the Sydney Futures Exchange.

In the US, NASDAQ has merged with the American Stock Exchange. A proposed further merger with the Philadelphia Exchange has not yet progressed any further. Equally, a proposed merger between the Chicago Board Options Exchange and the Pacific Stock Exchange has also fallen through.

In Scandinavia, Sweden and Denmark announced a common system, Norex, and expect to include Norway and Finland (although the latter may join the London/Frankfurt link instead). The new Stockholm system, SAX-2000, will be used, and trading, regulations, clearing and settlement will all be unified.

The big talking point in Europe, however, is a planned pan-European exchange spurred on by EMU. The first move was the announcement in mid-1998 that the London and Frankfurt exchanges planned to merge. Paris was understandably upset and began to talk of a rival merger with other European exchanges. Nevertheless, a meeting took place in December 1998 attended by the exchanges from London, Frankfurt, Paris, Brussels, Madrid, Milan, Zurich and Amsterdam. At a further meeting in May 1999, the six other exchanges signed a memorandum of understanding with London and Frankfurt. The long-term objectives included a single electronic trading platform, common trading regulations, and common access and trading hours. London and Frankfurt had already announced common trading hours and one or two minor trading details. All German company trades are now handled in Frankfurt, and UK company trades in London.

There were, however, severe problems to be overcome. Which trading system to use – London or Frankfurt? Which settlement system? (Crest, London's system, formed an alliance with the Deutsche Börse Clearing in May 1999.) Which indices will be used? How will ownership of the exchange be structured? Will the latter be based on turnover or capitalisation? Germany's share based on capitalisation, for example, would be about 15% but 20% based on turnover. So severe are these problems that the partners, in September 1999, announced an alliance rather than a new unified exchange, giving access to all exchanges on one screen with anonymous trading and a central counterparty. In 2001, plans for a merger between Frankfurt and London were abandoned and, in 2002, the LSE announced that it was purchasing a 76% stake in OM, the Swedish exchange (and previously an unsuccessful bidder for the LSE). Their plan is to create a new joint venture called EDX in London which will offer an extended range of equity derivatives products as well as OTC derivatives confirmation and clearing services.

While they deliberate, the competition is not standing still. Euronext was created in September 2000 as an amalgamation of stock exchanges in Amsterdam, Brussels and Paris, and with the goal of becoming a fully integrated, cross-border, European market for equities, bonds, derivatives and commodities. One major step towards this goal was the acquisition of LIFFE in January 2002.

SUMMARY

Strictly speaking, stocks are fixed interest securities and shares are equities.

Share indices are usually based on market capitalisation and calculated every minute.

In most economies, the major shareholders are investment institutions (pension funds, insurance companies and mutual funds) rather than private shareholders. The world's ageing populations will lead to a growth in funded pensions.

Mixed pools of shares are popular investments. They may be *closed-ended* (for example, UK investment trusts) or *open-ended* (for example, US mutual funds).

Order-driven dealing systems are those where orders of buyers and sellers are matched. Quote-driven systems are those where *market makers* quote firm bid and offer prices. Hybrid systems, like New York, involve elements of both types.

Dealers with *long* positions can lend stock to get collateral to fund their position and those with *short* positions can borrow stock (offering collateral) to match their sales. This is *stock borrowing and lending*. Very large deals are *bought deals* or *block trades*.

Sometimes firms buy their own shares back in order to cancel them and enhance dividends and earnings per share.

Settlement systems are usually *rolling settlement*, although settlement of all deals in a given trading period still exists (for example, France).

With new issues, shares may be a *public offer for sale* (or *initial public offering*). The alternative is the *private placing*, although sometimes a mixture of both is used.

An offer of more shares to existing shareholders is a *rights issue*.

A *scrip* issue offers shareholders free shares and a *split* divides the par value of the existing shares. The objective in both cases is to lower the price to improve liquidity. A *consolidation* replaces a number of existing shares by one new one to enhance the price. A *scrip dividend* is an offer of shares instead of cash dividends (optional).

As well as the normal market for shares, there may be a secondary market for newer companies who do not meet the requirements for a full listing. There may also be dealing outside the exchange – *over the counter* (OTC).

When a firm goes public, we look at the relationship between the price of similar shares and the profit per share to guide us as to the correct offer price of the new share. This is the *price/earnings ratio* (P/E). We also look at the likely dividend as a percentage of the share price to calculate the *gross dividend yield*. To check if the latter is achieved by giving away all the profit, we compare the profit per share to the net dividend to calculate the *cover ratio*. Finally, analysts look at the *earnings per share*.

From 1 January 1996, the EU *Investment Services Directive* took effect. This enables member firms to trade across all 15 markets.

Also taking effect from 1 January 1996 was the EU's *Capital Adequacy Directive*, which links capital to market risk.

In Europe, eight exchanges have formed an alliance as a possible first step to a pan-European stock exchange, while Euronext also aspires to be a pan-European securities and derivatives exchange.

In general, the future for traditional exchanges is under threat from Internet trading and the growth of *electronic communications networks* (ECNs).

Foreign Exchange and International Trade

8   Foreign Exchange

9   Trade Finance

10 European Economic
    and Monetary Union

8　Foreign Exchange

INTRODUCTION

The Market

Foreign exchange dealing rooms at times of peak activity resemble bedlam. Shirt-sleeved dealers look at computer screens, talk into several phones at once and yell to colleagues. They talk in the space of minutes to key centres – London, New York, Paris, Zurich, Frankfurt. The phrases are terse and mysterious – 'What's cable?'; '50/60'; 'Mine!'; 'Yours!'; 'Cable 70/80 – give five, take three'; 'tomnext'.

The foreign exchange market is international, open 24 hours a day, adjusts prices constantly and deals in huge sums. 'Five' always means 5m whether of dollars, yen or sterling. 'Yards' is a billion. Central bankers have now fallen into a pattern of doing a full survey of the size of the market every 3 years. 1986 showed a total world market which traded over $300bn every *day*. The 2001 survey showed a figure of $1.2 trillion – a huge increase. London is the biggest centre in the world, trading $504bn daily, with New York at $254bn and Tokyo $147bn.

Buyers and Sellers

Who is buying and selling all this foreign exchange? One's first thought is of importers and exporters. BIS calculate the daily value of imports and exports. The latter are $\frac{1}{32}$ of the value of daily foreign exchange dealing! What drives the market these days is huge capital transactions. Looking at buyers/sellers of foreign currencies we see:

❏　Importers/Exporters
❏　Tourists
❏　Government spending (for example, for troops abroad)
❏　Speculators
❏　Banks and institutions.

We've mentioned importers/exporters and the role of tourism and government spending is easy to understand and not crucial.

As exchange controls have been abandoned by major centres, pension fund managers, investment fund managers and insurance companies can invest in foreign equities and bonds. They then need the foreign currencies to pay for them.

Investors with spare funds will move money around freely. Convinced that Spain, Italy and the UK offered high interest rates together with low exchange rate risk due to the Exchange Rate Mechanism (ERM), they put their funds into these currencies. The head of research at Mitsubishi Bank in London, for example, estimated that free funds of some £40/£50bn flowed into the UK during 1985–92 attracted by high interest rates. As the ERM all but collapsed in the dramatic days of September 1992, the funds flowed out of the high yielding currencies as exchange rate risk became a reality once more. Amongst these investors could be corporate treasurers at multinationals trying to protect their overall position. Those with heavy dollar earnings might worry if the dollar weakened and move spare funds into euros. We saw huge currency outflows again in 1997 as Far East countries, like South Korea, hit trouble.

The banks not only deal on behalf of their customers but do proprietary deals of their own. They will 'take a position': that is, what anyone else would call 'speculate'. If dollars seem to be falling they will sell dollars and expect to buy them back more cheaply 30 minutes later. In September 1992, as the lira fell below its official floor in the ERM, dealers would buy knowing that the central banks would have to support the lira. As it rose to its official floor of L765.4 to the deutschemark, they would sell it again at a guaranteed profit. As they all sold, the lira would fall again and the process would restart.

During this period of turbulence, banks selling sterling and lira (which both eventually left the ERM) made tens of millions of dollars profit. One dealer at Bank of America who casually revealed his huge profits to a television reporter was later said to have been disciplined!

Bank Profits

Foreign exchange profits are important for the major banks. The US comptroller of the currency calculates that foreign exchange dealing accounts for half the profits made by the big commercial banks.

The risks have grown, too. Big corporate customers have become more sophisticated, some with their own dealing rooms; new capital ratio rules have increased the cost of foreign exchange exposures; counterparty risk has become a major worry; dollar volatility in recent years has become more unpredictable. As a result, the business is increasingly concentrated in a handful of major banks. The ten most active banks account for 50% of the market. Top traders according to *Euromoney* magazine are shown in Table 8.1.

WHAT DETERMINES EXCHANGE RATES?

Amongst economists, the most popular theory for explaining exchange rates is that of *purchasing power parity* (PPP). At its simplest, if a given basket of goods is priced at £10 in the UK and $20 in the US, this suggests the exchange rate should be £1 = $2. If the exchange rate is actually £1 = $1, then the Americans can buy a basket of goods in the UK at half the price it costs them at home and dollar imports will rise heavily, causing the dollar to weaken. As time goes by, one factor causing US goods to become either more or less expensive than British goods is inflation. If UK inflation is higher than the US, then they may sell less goods to the US, but if the sterling/dollar exchange rate moves in the dollar's favour, the cost to the Americans is the same.

At least, that's the theory. Like most economic theories, it raises serious problems in practice. To begin with, what should go in the basket of goods, since nations' purchasing habits are different? Again, many of the prices in the basket will be for goods and services not traded internationally anyway. It also assumes that the price is not distorted by tax differences (VAT or Sales Tax) and that there are no artificial barriers to trade, such as tariffs.

(The *Economist* has some fun periodically with its McDonald PPP: it compares the price of a hamburger in key world capitals and arrives at an exchange rate which it compares with the real one! It started as a bit of fun, but has inspired several serious studies – for example, 'Purchasing Power Parity Theory and the Big Mac', Federal Reserve Bank of St Louis, January 1996.)

Table 8.1 *Top 10 traders by % share of foreign exchange market – Euromoney poll, Spring 2001*

Rank	Bank
1	Citigroup
2	Deutschebank
3	Goldman Sachs
4	J.P. Morgan
5	Chase Manhattan Bank
6	Crédit Suisse First Boston
7	UBS Warburg
8	State Street Bank & Trust
9	Bank of America
10	Morgan Stanley Dean Witter

Source: *Euromoney* (May 2001).

If inflation in one country is consistently higher than in another, then the expectation is that the exchange rate will deteriorate in the country with the higher inflation. How do we persuade foreigners to hold this currency? Answer – by offering them higher interest rates than they can get at home. The higher interest rates compensate for the anticipated higher inflation rate. Thus interest rates enter the equation along with inflation and balance of payments figures.

The relationship between inflation and the exchange rate was nicely shown by Samuel Brittan of the *Financial Times* in an article in the issue of 9 October 1992 (using original figures from Datastream). Brittan plotted the declining purchasing power of the pound against the declining deutschmark/sterling exchange rate from 1964 to 1992. The correlation was striking. Underlying this is the fact that beginning with £1 in 1950, we needed £17 to buy the same goods in 1992. Beginning with DM1 in 1950, we only needed DM3.5 in 1992 to buy the same goods. The German consciousness of the risks of inflation reflects the horrifying experiences following the Second World War. In 1918, a loaf was 63 pfennigs and in November 1923, 200 billion deutschmarks!

The balance of payments is the difference between what a country buys and what it sells. It buys and sells physical goods and services. There are also the financial items called 'invisibles'. A French investment bank holds US government bonds and earns interest on these bonds. A German firm pays Lloyd's of London premiums for insurance. The balance between all the above items is the *current account*. Then there is the holding of assets – foreign securities, factories, land and so on, called the *capital account*. The balance of payments is said to always balance because any deficit on current account will be offset by a surplus on the capital account. Unfortunately, the figures don't always balance and so we have 'balancing items' to account for errors and transactions which cannot be traced. Sometimes, the balancing items are huge, reducing confidence in the figures.

If a country has a consistent deficit on the current account, the inference is that the country is not competitive and the expectation is that the exchange rate will weaken in the future.

Since trade sales/purchases only account for a small amount of foreign exchange daily dealing as opposed to capital movements, attention has switched away from PPP to the question of investments. Investors are looking for high real interest rates, that is, the return after taking account of inflation and currency risk. The theory is that investors will shift assets from one country to another according to the relative prices of international assets, expectations of inflation, expectations of exchange rate stability or volatility and actual exchange rates. This is the *portfolio balance model*.

In a way this is more attractive than PPP if we look at the sheer volatility of exchange rates. In January 1991, for example, the dollar had weakened dramatically – it was virtually $2 = £1. Within weeks, however, the dollar strengthened to $1.70 = £1. Had the price of a basket of goods changed in this period? Surely not.

The problem with all these theories is when artificial systems, like the ERM, interfere with market forces. For example, in October 1990, the UK joined the ERM with a target rate of DM2.95 = £1. Although UK inflation rates fell over the next 2 years and German rates increased, the UK had on average higher inflation in the period and lower productivity in manufacturing. In the middle of a severe recession, it was running an extraordinary deficit on current account suggesting structural problems and severe difficulties to come as the economy came out of recession. In addition, UK interest rates were barely higher than Germany in September 1992. While inflation then, on a like for like basis, was much the same as Germany's, investors' *expectations* were different. They were far more confident that Germany would get inflation lower than they were that the UK would stop it rising further. They also had greater confidence in the Bundesbank holding interest rates high (unpopular politically but the Bundesbank is independent) than in the Bank of England (not independent at that time) keeping interest rates high in the middle of a severe recession.

In spite of this, sterling moved over the 23 months within its ± 6% band compared to the deutschmark. However, sentiment that the pound was overvalued and would have to devalue grew stronger. Financial institutions and corporates holding pounds sold them. Speculators joined in. Finally, the leak that the Bundesbank thought that sterling should seek a new parity was all that was needed for the dam to burst. On Wednesday, 17 September, the UK government withdrew sterling from the ERM and saw the rate fall in 2 weeks from a level of about DM2.80 to DM2.50 causing the experts to produce their favourite quotation, 'you can't buck the market'. The Italian lira had a similar experience. This was followed by further turbulence in July 1993, when currencies like the French franc were attacked, leading to a fundamental change in ERM rules.

Finally, what we can't ignore in looking at exchange rate determinants is the sheer psychology of the markets – the 'herd' instinct, for example, which causes dealers to act in concert and for the market to frequently 'overshoot' when new data is released. Paul de Grauwe and Danny Decupere of the Catholic University of Leuven in Belgium produced a study of 'Psychological Barriers in the Market' in 1992. They found, for instance, that traders tended to avoid certain exchange rates, especially those ending in round numbers!

Perhaps because of psychology, there are forecasters of movements called *chartists* who plot historic price data and look for patterns and trends. They talk of upper (resistance) levels and lower (support) levels. If a level is broken, the chartists believe that the break will be decisive. Those who look at the underlying economic factors – interest rates, inflation, productivity, balance of payments – are the *fundamentalists*. The same two approaches are used in equity and bond markets. The chartists and fundamentalists often clash in battle, like Guelphs and Ghibellines in mediaeval Italy or Catholics and Protestants. In fact, all banks use a blend of both techniques.

BRETTON WOODS

In the post-war period up to the early 1970s, currencies did not fluctuate as they do today but operated on a fixed basis. The system was set up at a conference in Bretton Woods (New Hampshire, US) in 1944. The conference was attended by world finance ministers and major economists, like J.M. Keynes, from 44 countries. It was called to discuss the international financial arrangements that would apply after the Second World War. In particular, it set up:

- ❏ A system of exchange rate stability
- ❏ The International Monetary Fund
- ❏ The World Bank.

Exchange Rate Stability

Exchange rate stability was achieved by members adopting an external or *par value* for their currency, expressed in terms either of gold or of the US dollar. America had no choice but to adopt a par value for the dollar expressed in gold; the dollar was convertible to gold on demand at $35 per oz but all other members pegged to the dollar. This Bretton Woods System was, therefore, termed the *Gold Exchange Standard*, with the dollar being linked directly to gold and other currencies indirectly linked to gold via the dollar. Having adopted a par value, the central banks of member countries had to routinely intervene in the foreign exchange markets to keep their exchange rate against the dollar within 1% on either side of the par value: selling their currency (and buying the dollar) when it threatened to rise above 1%; doing the opposite when it fell 1% below the par value. The central banks' efforts to keep their currency at the agreed rate could be supported by the International Monetary Fund (IMF) – hence its relevance to these arrangements.

International Monetary Fund

The decision to set up the IMF was taken at the Bretton Woods Conference in 1944 but the Fund did not come into operation until 1946. Its headquarters are in Washington, DC. The prime object in setting up the Fund was to prevent any return to the restrictive international trade environment and erratic exchange rate fluctuations of the inter-war period. The Fund's main task was to preside over a system of fixed exchange rates. Ancillary to this, it provided borrowing facilities for its members, these also allowing trade deficit nations to embark upon more gradual corrective policies that would be less disruptive for trading partners.

When a member country had a balance of payments deficit, it borrowed from the IMF to finance it, as well as to obtain supplies of foreign currency with which to buy up its weak currency in the foreign exchange markets, in order to prevent it falling more than 1% below its par value. Thus, in this way the *borrowing facilities* function was ancillary to the stable exchange rate goal. When members exhausted their borrowing entitlement, they had perforce to adopt a new, and lower, par value. *Devaluation* (and revaluation) was possible but had to be carried out in discussion with the IMF, the latter having to be satisfied that a state of 'fundamental disequilibrium' in the member country's balance of payments did exist. Thus, although under the Bretton Woods system exchange rates were fixed, they were not immutably fixed.

For example, the UK, having sold every foreign asset to pay for the war, was in a weak position.

After the war it adopted (possibly foolishly) an exchange rate of $4 = £1. In 1949, however, it devalued to $2.80 = £1. Devaluation is always difficult. Governments cannot announce devaluations in advance as everyone will immediately sell their currency. As a result, they always deny any intention to devalue in the strongest terms. Then, they suddenly devalue. The result is that protestations about a determination not to devalue may, in the end, simply be disbelieved. When enough people disbelieve it, devaluation is inevitable due to the massive selling of the currency. The chaos in the ERM in September 1992 illustrates these forces at work.

Member countries had to pay a subscription to the IMF, related originally to their pre-war value of trade. This subscription had originally (but no longer) to be one quarter in gold, with the remainder in the member's own currency. In this way the IMF acquired a vast pool of gold and members' currencies, giving it resources to lend. *Borrowing entitlements* were basically 125% of subscription, although the needs of small-subscription countries, as well as the oil price rise of the 1970s, called for additional categories of borrowing facilities to be brought into being. IMF loans are conditional upon the borrowing country agreeing to adopt certain corrective economic policies, generally of an unpopular, restrictive nature.

In the late 1960s, there had been concern that *international liquidity* (the means of payment for international trade) would not keep pace with the volume growth in trade, thus exerting a deflationary pressure. A new function for the IMF was therefore brought into being, that of creating man-made international liquidity in the form of *Special Drawing Rights* (SDRs). These were credits created in the books of the IMF and allocated to members to pay for their balance of payments deficits (surplus countries accumulating SDRs). SDRs were first issued in 1971 but thereafter, with the fear now being one of inflation rather than deflation, further subsequent issues of SDRs have been limited. The value of an SDR is calculated daily, based on an average of the exchange rates of the world's major currencies. As Switzerland did not join the IMF formally until 1992, Swiss francs were not used.

The World Bank

The official title is the *International Bank for Reconstruction and Development* (IBRD). The IBRD began operations in 1945 and was initially concerned with the 'reconstruction' of war-devastated Europe. Nowadays, it is primarily concerned with helping LDCs to develop their economies. It makes loans for up to 20 years at rates of interest slightly below the commercial level, with repayment being guaranteed by the government of the borrowing country. The majority of these loans are for specific projects in the areas of agriculture, energy and transport. Recently, more generalised 'programme' and 'structural adjustment' loans have also been extended to aid less developed economies. The IBRD obtains its funds from members (the same 100 or so countries that are members of the IMF) as well as by the issuance of international bonds. The IBRD is a major borrower in the eurobond market. Under the umbrella title of the World Bank are two other institutions.

The *International Finance Corporation* (IFC) was set up in 1956 as a multilateral investment bank to provide risk capital (without government guarantee) to private sector enterprises in LDCs, as well as being a catalyst in encouraging loans from other sources. In the latter respect, the IFC is also concerned to stimulate multinational corporations' direct investment in LDCs, this being further encouraged by the Multilateral Investment Guarantee Agency to provide insurance against non-commercial risks.

The *International Development Association* (IDA) (1960) is the soft-loan arm of the World Bank. It gives interest-free loans for up to 50 years to the poorest of the developing countries. The IDA's resources come from donations from the rich members of the World Bank, with the US usually contributing not less than 25% of funds.

FLOATING RATES

By August 1972, there were huge pressures on the dollar, partly due to the cost of the Vietnam War. In August, the US authorities abandoned any guaranteed convertibility of the dollar into gold. An international meeting took place in Washington and attempted to hold the fixed exchange rate system together but the effort failed. The European Common Market was concerned that freely floating rates would upset the operation of the Common Agricultural Policy (CAP) and set up an arrangement known as the *snake*, designed to keep currencies within a band of ± 2¼%. The oil price rises of the 1970s put the arrangements under pressure and membership gradually dwindled.

The arrival of floating rates meant that central banks didn't have to intervene to the same extent and didn't need the IMF to help with intervention. However, nations still needed to finance their balance of payments deficits. The fact that these were often less developed countries (LDCs) with large international debts and seeking World Bank assistance has led some observers to comment on a confusion between the roles of the IMF and the World Bank and indeed, a certain amount of rivalry. We discuss this further in Chapter 15.

In this period of floating exchange rates, the dollar has proved to be a very volatile currency. Foreign trade as a proportion of GDP is much less for the US than for many countries and they seem to be able to live with wild fluctuations that would cause havoc elsewhere. It has implications for world trade that may cause international central banks to wish to intervene, and we shall examine this later in the chapter.

Sterling has not exactly been a stable currency either. Table 8.2 is an extract of dollar/sterling rates over the years 1972–2002.

Table 8.2 *Sterling/Dollar exchange rates, 1972–2002*

	Year	Sterling/Dollar rate $	
	1972	2.50	(year of floating)
	1977	1.75	
	1980	2.32	
Jan	1985	1.03	
Late	1985	1.40	
Jan	1991	1.98	
Mar	1991	1.70	
Aug	1992	1.98	
Jun	1993	1.55	
Jun	1999	1.60	
Jun	2002	1.52	

Our previous comments about the effect on an exchange rate of one country's higher inflation and lower productivity are dramatically illustrated by looking at the list of sterling/deutschmark exchange rates shown in Table 8.3 up until EMU in 1999 and its equivalent rate since.

Table 8.3 *Sterling/Deutschmark exchange rates, 1960–2002*

	Year	Sterling/Deutschmark rate DM	
	1960	11.71	
	1980	4.23	
Feb	1987	2.85	
July	1989	2.76	
Oct	1990	2.95	(ERM target)
Sep	1992	2.51	(Sterling leaves ERM)
Apr	1996	2.27	
Dec	1998	2.80	
Sep	2002	3.13	(equivalent)

We can see the efforts of the UK government in the 1980s to reduce inflation and increase productivity culminating in accepting the ERM 'straitjacket' in October 1990.

EUROPEAN ECONOMIC AND MONETARY UNION

Moves to European Economic and Monetary Union led to changes which had an important impact on foreign exchange markets – the introduction of the Exchange Rate Mechanism in 1979 and the adoption of a single currency for eleven countries, the euro, in January 1999.

These moves are so significant that they have a special chapter of their own (Chapter 10).

FOREIGN EXCHANGE RISK FOR CORPORATES

Types of Risk

Companies which compete in an international marketplace are at risk to changes in foreign exchange rates. These risks are of three types:

1. Transaction risk
2. Translation risk
3. Economic risk.

Transaction risk   This is the most obvious and common risk. A Swiss importer needs to pay for dollar imports in 6 months which are ordered today. If the Swiss franc weakens against the dollar, the imports will cost more. A Swiss exporter has sold goods to someone in the US to be paid for in dollars. By the time the goods are shipped and paid for, say in 9 months, the Swiss franc may have strengthened against the dollar, making the dollar earnings worth less money.

Most corporates will decide to reduce this risk by the technique called hedging. Our concentration in this chapter will be on this type of risk.

Translation risk   A French firm has overseas subsidiaries reporting profits in Swiss francs. It also owns land and property in Switzerland. If the Swiss franc weakens against the euro, the profits are worth less in euros when included in the annual report. The value of the land and property may be unchanged but, translated in euros, the assets seem to have lost value.

Should these exposures be hedged? This is a subject of huge controversy. Not hedging may distort asset values and earnings per share. On the other hand, hedging means spending real money to protect accountancy figures. In any case, sophisticated investors will take the exposure into account. Knowing that our French firm has a heavy exposure to Switzerland, they will adjust their view of the firm's prospects. If, however, the risk has already been hedged away, their view will be incorrect. It may be complicated by the fact that the French firm makes extensive purchases in Swiss francs, thus giving a natural offset of risk.

We can sum this up with the totally opposite views of two firms in not dissimilar businesses.

SmithKline Beecham, the former UK-listed pharmaceuticals group, made 90% of its profits outside the UK. The treasurer (in the *Financial Times,* 27 November 1991) argued in favour of producing less volatile earnings by hedging: 'stable and predictable earnings are more valuable to investors'.

The UK chemicals and pharmaceutical group, ICI, made 55% of its earnings overseas but did not hedge. Their treasurer (1991 *Financial Times* article) argues: 'Translation exposures do not have any immediate cash flow consequences yet any hedging activity will involve cash expenditure.'

Economic risk   This is by no means as obvious as the other two. Suppose a Dutch firm is selling goods into the US and its main competitor is a British firm. If sterling weakens against the dollar, the Dutch firm has lost competitive advantage. The UK left the ERM in September 1992. Sterling fell 15% against the deutschmark in a matter of weeks but the Dutch guilder did not. Obviously this is serious for the Dutch firm but it may not be easy to hedge such a risk. It does need to be considered as part of marketing and competitive strategy.

Transaction Risk – Forward Rates

Let's take a German computer software company which imports computers from the US, paid for in dollars. It resells them with its added-value services – software, installation and so on. A contract has just been signed with a German customer and two computers ordered from the US in order to fulfil the contract. In its own accounts, the German firm would use euros. The rate for the euro/dollar could fluctuate. The computers cost $100,000 and the exchange rate is $1 = €1.10. The cost is, therefore, €110,000. By the time the computers arrive and the German firm is due to pay for them (say, in 3 months' time), the dollar may have strengthened and the exchange rate changed to $1 = €1.25. The cost in deutschemarks is now €125,000. If the German firm costed the computers at €110,000 when making the sale, then €15,000 has just been lost from its profit. How can it prevent this happening?

This is, of course, the standard problem facing all importers and exporters. Importers pay later but don't know what the exchange rate will be. Exporters earn foreign currencies at a later date but equally don't know how rates will move.

One simple solution for the importer is to buy the dollars today at $1 = €1.10. The dollars are not needed for 3 months, so the $100,000 is put on deposit to earn interest. In 3 months' time, they are taken out of deposit and used to pay for the machine.

In principle, there's nothing wrong with this solution apart from the assumption that the importer has the €110,000 now to do this as opposed to having to find it in 3 months when, perhaps, his own customer has paid. However, there is another solution which is so common that this is probably the one that would be used. The importer buys the dollars from the bank *3 months forward* – the *forward* deal.

The bank is requested to provide $100,000 in 3 months in exchange for euros.

Today's rate (called *spot*) is €1.10. The bank may quote, say, €1.1055 for the 3 month deal. The importer now has certainty. The rate could depreciate later to €1.25 but the purchase of dollars will be made at €1.1055. It's a little bit worse than the spot rate but it has bought peace of mind.

The question is, how did the bank decide that €1.1055 was the correct rate? Does the bank have analysts studying key exchange rate trends and making a forecast? Do they have, in a discreet corner of the dealing room, a gypsy and crystal ball?

The bank is, of course, now at risk instead of the importer. If they do nothing, then in 3 months they face buying dollars at, say, a rate of €1.25 and only getting €1.1055 from their customer. Before, we suggested that the firm could buy the dollars today and put them on deposit. The bank can do the same. It can buy the dollars today at €1.10 and simply lend them in the interbank market for 3 months until their client needs them. The question is – what is the cost to the bank?

The consequence of their action is that money which had been in euros and earning interest (or borrowed – the argument is much the same) is now in dollars and earning interest. But suppose dollar rates for 3 months' money are 3% p.a. and euro rates are 5% p.a.? The bank has lost 2% p.a. (that is, ½% in 3 months) through being in dollars. It is what economists call the 'opportunity cost'. It has lost the opportunity to earn interest on euros and the cost is ½%. This will be charged to the client as a worsening of the spot rate from €1.10 to €1.1055. Thus forward rates arise *from the difference in interest rates in the two currencies concerned.*

We can try this argument from another angle. A rich American, with $1 million on deposit in the US earning 3%, sees that euro interest rates are 5% and moves into euros for 1 year to earn an easy extra 2%. The snag, of course, is that, if euros depreciate by, say, 5% against the dollar, then the original $1 million will later only be worth $950,000 and this loss has wiped out the interest rate gain. To prevent this, the American arranges to sell the euros (and buy back the dollars) 1 year *forward*. If the charge for this is any less than 2%, then our American has a locked in profit and no risk. This will apply to dozens of other Americans with spare funds. The result is that billions of dollars will flow into euros until the laws of supply and demand put up the cost of the forward rate by 2% and make the whole exercise no longer worthwhile. The activity of trying to make a risk-free profit by exploiting price discrepancies is known as 'arbitrage', but of course supply and demand eliminate the possibility very quickly – if indeed it arises in the first place.

As dollar interest rates are less than euro interest rates, we say the dollar is at a *premium* (and the euro at a *discount*). Notice, however, the effect of this on an *exporter* in Germany. This firm will, say, earn $100,000 in 3 months and ask the bank to quote a forward rate for buying the dollars from them and providing euros instead. What steps can the bank now take to avoid risk? As it's a little more complicated than our previous example, let's lay out the steps the bank can take:

Today
1. Borrow $100,000 for 3 months
2. Buy €110,000 with the dollars at today's rate of €1.10
3. Put the €110,000 on deposit for 3 months.

3 months later   1. The €110,000 comes off deposit and is sold to the bank's client for dollars
2. The client gives the bank the $100,000 earned from exports
3. The dollar loan is repaid with the $100,000.

The effect of this is that the bank has paid 3% p.a. interest on the dollars and earned 5% p.a. interest on the euros for 3 months (that is, gained ½%). The bank has now made money from the interest rate difference and the forward rate is *more favourable* than the spot rate.

(In all these examples, the question of bid/offer spreads has been ignored in the interests of simplicity.)

Where the dollar is at a *premium* to the euro this means that:

❑   For the *importer* the forward rate is *less* favourable
❑   For the *exporter* the forward rate is *more* favourable.

The importer may not be quite sure when they will pay for the dollars and ask for a forward purchase of dollars, for example, 'between 1 and 28 February'. This is a *forward dated option contract* and not to be confused with 'options' as such. (In today's market there is, in fact, nothing like this difference between US and euro rates, as you may be aware. For purposes of illustration, however, it is usually easier to pick figures which the beginner can easily understand.)

Transaction Risk – Options

Let's go back to the case of our German importer. The $100,000 needed for imports are bought forward at a rate of €1.1055. However, in 3 months, the rate is actually €1.05 and has improved from the euro point of view. The $100,000 could be bought spot for only €105,000. However, they can't be bought spot as the importer has already committed to buy forward at €1.1055. This illustrates a most important point about forward purchases:

The forward purchase protects against a deterioration in the rate but the forward buyer cannot now gain should the rate improve.

The importer will probably not worry about this, being happy to have protected the profit in the computer deal. Others may not take this view and argue as follows:

Today's spot rate is €1.10. I want protection if the rate worsens in 3 months to €1.25 – I still want to buy dollars at €1.10. On the other hand, if the rate improves to €1.05, I want to forget the above protection and buy spot at €1.05.

In other words, there are those who wish to have their cake and also eat it. The markets being advanced and ingenious, provide a means by which this can be done called *options*.

Options can become quite complicated when considered in detail. Happily, the principle is very easy. The importer does not commit to buy the dollars forward at €1.10 but pays for an *option* to do so. If, later, the rate has worsened, the importer takes up the option at €1.10. If, however, the rate has improved to, say, €1.05, the importer abandons what was only an option and buys dollars spot at the better rate.

This is clearly more flexible and advantageous than buying forward and naturally costs more (or who would buy forward?). The cost is called the *premium* and usually paid in advance. We can, therefore, say of options:

> *The option purchase protects against a deterioration in the rate but the option buyer can still benefit from an improvement in the rate. There is a cost – the premium.*

Where would the importer (or exporter) go to buy this option? There are two possibilities:

❑ Deal through a Traded Options Exchange, or
❑ Deal through a bank – called OTC ('over the counter') .

There are very few currency options contracts available in Europe on trading exchanges. This is largely due to the strength of the OTC market there. The biggest currency option deals are handled in the US at either the Chicago Mercantile Exchange (CME), also called the International Monetary Market (IMM), or the Philadelphia Stock Exchange (PHLX).

The characteristics of an exchange are that there are standard contract sizes and standard expiry months. If we take our German importer, he could go to either the CME or PHLX for dollar/deutschmark options and would find the terms shown in Table 8.4.

Table 8.4   *Dollar/euro options terms*

US EXCHANGE	*$/€*	*OPTIONS*
Exchange	*Contract size (euros)*	*Contract months*
CME	125,000	Jan/Mar/Apr/Jun Jul/Sep/Oct/Dec and spot month
PHLX	62,500	Mar/Jun/Sep/Dec plus 2 near months

The first problem for the importer is that €110,000 need to be covered and the contract size is €125,000 (or 2 × €62,500). The next problem may be that the expiry in 3 months is 18 February and neither exchange handles this expiry date.

The advantage of the standard contracts is that, being standard, there is plenty of competition for the business. In particular, the contracts can be sold back later, called '*trading the option*'.

Finally, the exchange protects contracts from default by the use of a body called a 'Clearing House', and we shall explain this further in Chapter 11.

Going to the bank, the terms can be tailored to the needs of the option buyer, for example, €110,000, expiring 18 February. The bank may also offer a number of variations on the deal (see below). However, the options cannot normally be traded and, if the bank is BCCI and crashes into liquidation, the contract is not guaranteed. In currencies the OTC market with the banks is huge. Perhaps this is because the bank may be helping the importer/exporter with general finance for trade anyway and it seems natural to ask them to handle the options business. In addition, the banks may construct attractive variations on the options theme, some of which have proved very popular. Here are three examples:

Breakforward   This was invented by Midland Bank. Here the client is offered a forward rate (at a rate not quite as good as the normal forward) but, at a predetermined rate, the contract can be unwound, leaving the client to benefit from a future favourable rate.

For example, a British firm needs to import dollar goods and buy dollars in 3 months. The forward rate is £1 = $1.89. The firm wants downside protection but feels that it is just as likely that sterling will improve.

The bank offers a 'floor' rate of $1.88 and a 'break' rate of $1.91. The effect is that, up to a rate of $1.91, the client will buy dollars at $1.88. Above $1.91, the client is freed from this obligation and can buy dollars at the spot rate less 3¢ (that is, the difference between the 'floor' and the 'break' rate which the bank is cleverly using to buy an option!).

Thus:

❏ Future spot rate $1.80, client buys at $1.88
❏ Future spot rate $1.91, client buys at $1.88
❏ Future spot rate $1.98, client buys at $1.95.

The firm thus gets almost complete downside protection but can benefit from a forward rate to a large extent. This leads naturally to participating forward.

Participating forward   Again, a 'floor' rate is agreed as is a participation level in future favourable rates. Let us say that the normal forward rate is $1.89, the 'floor' is $1.86 and the agreed participation in improvement above $1.86 is 80%. If the spot rate later is worse than $1.86, the client buys dollars at $1.86. If the rate is, say, $1.96, the client rate is based on 80% of this improvement. The spot rate is 10 points better than $1.86 so the client can have a rate 8 points better, that is $1.94.

Thus:

- ❏ Future spot rate $1.80, client buys at $1.86
- ❏ Future spot rate $1.91, client buys at $1.90
- ❏ Future spot rate $1.96, client buys at $1.94.

Again, the client has substantial downside protection but can also benefit to a large extent from an improvement in the rate. The client can discuss the desired participation level with the bank – the higher the level, the lower the floor rate!

Cylinder or Collar   This technique is identical to the 'collar' technique used in interest rate futures.

Again, a UK importer needs to buy dollars in 3 months. Let us say that today's spot rate is $1.90. The importer can come to an arrangement with the bank that the future dollars will be bought within a range of, say, $1.85–$1.95. (As a result, the technique is also called 'range forward'.)

- ❏ If the future spot rate is worse than $1.85, the client buys at $1.85
- ❏ If the future spot rate is better than $1.95, the client buys at $1.95
- ❏ If the future spot rate is between $1.85 and $1.95, the client buys at that rate.

The client now gets some downside protection and also some upside gain. Depending on the rates chosen, the cost may be small or even none at all.

How does the bank achieve the above end objectives for the client? The answer lies in very ingenious use of option techniques.

The whole question of option trading is treated in detail in Chapter 11.

FOREIGN EXCHANGE DEALING

Quotations

The foreign exchange dealer is surrounded by computer terminals giving exchange rates quoted by banks all over the world. The main information provider is Reuters but Telerate and Quotron are both very active. The rates quoted are 'indicative' only. For a firm rate the dealer must telephone and ask for a quotation for a given currency pair. The dealer merely asks for a quote and does not say if this is a sale or purchase.

The market has its own curious jargon for exchange rates, for example:

Cable	Dollar/Sterling
Swissy	Dollar/Swiss franc
Stocky	Dollar/Swedish Kroner (from Stockholm)
Copey	Dollar/Danish Kroner (from Copenhagen).

In London, even cockney rhyming slang is used. The Japanese yen rate is the 'Bill and Ben'!

As elsewhere in financial markets, rates are given as 'bid and offer', that is, buying/selling. For example, asked for a 'Swissy' quote, the reply might be SFr1.4250/SFr1.4260 or more likely '50/60' as the dealers are following rates every second of the day. If in any doubt, the enquirer will ask, 'What's the big figure?' and the reply is, '1.42'.

This means that the fellow dealer will *buy* dollars at SFr1.4250 or *sell* dollars at SFr1.4260. The 10 bp in the rate is the profit margin or 'spread'.

We can see this by following it through slowly. Suppose the dealer begins with SFr1.4250 and buys $1. Now the dealer owns $1 (they would say, 'is *long* of dollars'). On a second enquiry, the dealer sells the dollar at the selling rate of SFr1.4260. Now the dealer, having started out with SFr1.4250, has ended with SFr1.4260 after buying and selling dollars.

If this all seems terribly obvious, we apologise. The problem is that foreign exchange can be very confusing for the newcomer. For example, two currencies are involved, not one (as when buying bonds or equities in the domestic currency). Thus, if the dealer buys dollars at SFr1.4250, that is also the rate at which he *sells* Swiss francs. If the dealer sells dollars at SFr1.4260, that is also the rate at which he *buys* Swiss francs. So bid/offer is buy/sell for dollars. For Swiss francs it is best viewed as sell/buy.

It gets more confusing if we consider sterling. Here the convention is to quote a rate of *dollars for the pound sterling*, for example, the rate is given as $1.70. Everywhere else, we give a rate for each currency against the dollar. Asked to quote for 'cable' (sterling/dollar), the dealer quotes '60/70' or, in full, $1.7360/$1.7370. This time the buy/sell rate is in terms of *sterling*, that is, the dealer buys sterling at $1.7360 and sells it at $1.7370. In dollars, it's the sell/buy rate.

The result of this way of quoting sterling can be seen when we consider an importer who wishes to buy dollars. One importer is in Switzerland and the other in the UK. The quotes are (mid-point rates):

Dollar/Swiss franc	SFr1.50
Dollar/Sterling	$1.73

Later, the rates change to SFr1.55 and $1.78 respectively. For the Swiss, the increase gives a *worse* rate as they must give up SFr1.55 to buy $1 instead of SFr1.50. For the UK importer, the increase has given a *better* rate. For each £1 they obtain $1.78 instead of $1.73. (Notice that, for an exporter, the results would be exactly the opposite.)

Foreign exchange rates can be very confusing for the newcomer, unless these basic points are borne in mind from the outset:

The market is oriented to the dollar. The dealers quotes are normally given as an amount of the currency to the dollar and the bid/offer is buy/sell from a dollar point of view.

Sterling is the exception, typically quoted as an amount of dollars for the pound sterling. From the dollar point of view, the bid/offer is now sell/buy.

Cross-Rates

When a Swiss firm telephones their bank to buy Canadian dollars, the bank will buy US dollars with the Swiss francs and with the US dollars buy Canadian dollars. The market is wedded to the dollar and finds organisation easier and simpler if dealers go in and out of the dollar, even if some 'double counting' is involved. To attempt to deal directly between any pair of currencies would be too complex. The BIS survey of the London market (the world's biggest), in April 2001, found that over 90% of deals involved the dollar.

An exchange rate between two currencies, neither of them the dollar, is a *cross-rate*. If a dealer goes directly from Swiss francs to sterling, it would be called a direct cross-rate deal or *cross*. Due to the anticipated arrival of the euro, crosses between European countries became more popular. With the replacement of twelve currencies by the euro (for wholesale purposes), the figure has fallen.

Foreign Exchange Swaps

When we discussed the problem of the mythical German importer, we suggested that the bank, requested to *sell* dollars to its client in 3 months, might buy the dollars today and put them on deposit. For a client wanting the bank to *buy* dollars in 3 months, the procedure was more complex but involved borrowing dollars for 3 months, buying euros and putting them on deposit.

Whilst both techniques are quite feasible, they tie up balance sheet assets and liabilities. They impact on the banks' credit limits, involve counterparty risk and use up capital under capital ratio rules.

As a result, the problem is usually solved instead by the *foreign exchange swap*. Before going any further, these swaps have nothing to do with the swaps market for interest rate and currency swaps. The use of the same term can cause confusion. Many foreign exchange dealers simple call them 'forward' deals because that's how they handle forward requirements.

The swap is *one* transaction which combines *two* deals, one spot and one forward. In the first deal a bank buys a currency spot and in the second simultaneously sells it forward for delivery at a later date. The bank will, therefore, return to the original position at the future date. Thus, bank *A* may have £10m and enters into a swap with bank *B* for dollars:

1. Bank *A* sells £10m *spot* for, say, $20m to Bank *B*
2. Bank *A* sells the $20m *forward* for £10m in 3 months.

At the moment, then, bank *A* has $20m. In 3 months, bank *A* will exchange the $20m for £10m, returning to the original position.

Thus, the foreign exchange swap is a combined spot and forward deal.

When a bank commits to sell a customer a currency at a future date, there may be others wanting to buy the currency for the same date. However, while some deals will offset in this fashion, in most cases the dealer won't be so fortunate. If he has sold $2m for delivery on 20 March, he may find that he is due to buy $2m for £s on 30 March – leaving an exposure 'gap'. Alternatively, he is due to buy $s for £s on 20 March, but only $1m, leaving the dealer 'short' of $1m for 20 March delivery.

One way of handling the problem is to buy $2m today and put it on deposit until 20 March. This may mean having to borrow the £s to do it. This involves finding suitable lenders and borrowers and ties up lines of credit with other banks.

Instead it will be easier to buy $2m spot. The $s, however, are not required until 20 March, so the dealer now enters the *swap*:

1. The dealer sells the $2m spot for £s, returning back to a £ position
2. At the same time, the dealer sells the £s forward for $2m to be delivered on 20 March.

The counterparty to the swap that had £s originally is now sitting on $s until 20 March. If $ interest rates are lower than the £ the swap rate will reflect the difference in interest rates. Thus if UK interest rates were 6% higher than the US, then a 6 month forward deal would involve a *premium* of 3% (ignoring yield curve variations). If spot were, say, $1.80, then the 6 month forward premium would be about 5.40¢. The spot rate might thus be quoted as $1.8000/$1.8010 with a forward margin or spread of, say, 5.40¢/5.30¢ (or quoted as basis points 540/530). As the $ is at a premium, these rates will be *subtracted* from the spot rates (if at a discount, the rates would be added to the spot rates).

Thus, an *importer* wanting to buy $s for £s in 6 months will be quoted as follows:

Spot	$ 1.8000	
Premium	540	–

Forward rate $1.7460

An *exporter* wanting to sell $s for £s in 6 months will be quoted as follows:

Spot	$ 1.8010	
Premium	530	–

Forward rate $ 1.7480

The *importer* has a *worse* rate than spot as he only gets $1.7460 for £1 rather than $1.80.

The *exporter* has a *better* rate than spot as he only gives up $1.7480 to obtain £1 rather than $1.8010.

Thus the swap handles the request from a customer for a forward deal. It would also handle a situation where the dealer was 'long' in spot $s (and thus at risk) but 'short' of the same quantity for delivery in 3 months. He sells the $s spot for £s (and is no longer 'long' of spot $s) and sells the £s back for the $s in 3 months.

(Those who have very quick minds will see that, while the dealer is no longer at risk to changes in currency rates, he may be at risk to changes in interest rates. The cost of the swap is based on an interest rate difference between dollar/sterling of 6% p.a. But what if this changes to 4% p.a. or 7%? There is, indeed, a potential problem here but the solutions are outside the scope of an introductory book of this nature! Suffice it to say that there is a risk – market risk – which could result in losses if not hedged, and which will be taken into account by the risk management policies and practices of the bank as well as by regulators in setting capital ratios.)

Often swap deals are very short-term. Many are for delivery spot (2 days) but will be reversed the following day, called 'spotnext'. Others are for delivery the next day and reversed the following day, called 'tomnext'. It all adds to the horrible jargon of the markets!

Brokers

In these markets, extensive use is made of brokers. A dealer who is long on dollars and anxious to sell may not wish to reveal their position to others. The desire to sell, say, $50m for sterling at a given rate can be passed to a broker who will disseminate this information anonymously using computer screens or voice boxes. Another dealer, who finds this rate acceptable, may close the deal via the broker. The broker takes no risk. The clients settle directly and the broker takes a small commission.

A broker may quote 'Cable 70/80 – give five, take three'. Cable is sterling/dollar and the broker has a client who will buy £3m at, say, $1.7370 and sell £5m at $1.7380.

The new Reuters system, Dealing 2000/2, was released in mid-1992. This enables the computer system itself to match deals automatically and anonymously. Its progress is being watched closely. Fearful of Reuters acquiring a potential monopoly position, eleven banks funded a rival development via Quotron called EBS which was released in 1993. A third, similar, system is MINEX which was developed by Telerate and KDD of Japan.

By April 1995, there was very little doubt that the new electronic broking systems were having an impact. The EBS group bought out MINEX, which resulted in just two competitors. It is clear that conventional brokers were losing business. The Bank of England 1995 Survey showed, as we have said, that 35% of business was placed via brokers but, of this, 5% was already handled by electronic broking.

The 1998 survey showed that only 27% of business was placed via brokers, with 16% going to voice brokers and 11% to electronic broking. Voice brokers thus had 30% of the business in 1995 but only 16% in 1998. One unusual side effect was the fact that small banks began to use the broking systems, to some extent, instead of placing orders with larger banks. This electronic broking is so far only used for spot markets. However, in July 1999, the US company, Bloomberg, announced that it would join with the London-based voice broker, Tullett & Tokyo, to launch an electronic broking system for the forward market before the end of 1999. FX All now offers electronic broking to the corporate market. Brokers are also under pressure in the equity markets for similar reasons and we are now seeing mergers and takeovers.

Settlement

Getting paid is, naturally, crucially important. Doing the deal on the telephone is called 'front office'. Getting paid, reconciling accounts and so on is 'back office'.

In some systems, the dealer writes the details of the deal on a slip of paper. These are later encoded into the computerised back office system. In other cases, the dealer enters the deal into the computer system used for front office which prints a deal slip and holds the data electronically for transfer to the back office system.

A domestic bank thinks of its account with a foreign bank in the foreign currency as its 'nostro' account. For example, BNP Paribas thinks of its dollar account with Citibank in New York as its 'nostro' or *our* account with you. Equally, it regards Citibank's account with itself, BNP Paribas in euros as the 'vostro' or 'loro' account, that is, '*your* account with us'. This all goes back to those clever Italian bankers years ago.

The department dealing with settlement and reconciliation is thus the 'nostro department'. Agreeing our calculation of the value of the foreign currency account with the foreign bank's statement for the same account is 'nostro reconciliation', an important but tedious chore for which computer systems are used to speed up the process.

Banks today are most concerned about counterparty risk (even before BCCI!). For example, all spot deals are settled in two working days. What if we settle the foreign currency deal but the counterparty doesn't? The bankers call this Herstatt risk, following the failure, on 26 June 1974, of ID Herstatt, a German bank, to settle the dollar side of its transactions (6 hours behind) although the deutschmarks had been paid to it. This risk has led to the use of techniques called *netting*. The influential bank 'think tank', G30, produced an important report on settlement. Amongst other things, it recommended netting arrangements to reduce risk.

A system of bilateral netting of foreign exchange deals has operated in London for several years. The system is known as FX Net and involves about 16 banks.

Netting no longer requires the exchange of two payments for each pair of currencies dealt with. The two parties make or receive one net payment for each currency deal for each settlement date.

For example, suppose counterparty *A* and counterparty *B* enter into the four transactions for the same settlement date, as shown in Figure 8.1.

In the conventional way, each counterparty would process eight transactions each, paying away four and receiving four.

In the FX Net system, running accounts are maintained for each currency and settlement date and at settlement each counterparty would process three *net* deals, one for each currency. The running accounts would appear as shown in Figure 8.2.

Settlement of the net amounts occurs as each settlement date is reached.

Using conventional settlement methods, if we take the $ account, *A* will pay *B* $40m and *B* will pay *A* $20m. Taking the £ account, *A* will pay *B* £10m and *B* will pay *A* £5m. Suppose *A* defaults and does not settle? *B* will lose $40m and £10m. Under the netting, *B* would lose $20m and £5m. In other words, a key reason for net settlement is to reduce substantially the underlying risk of foreign exchange dealing.

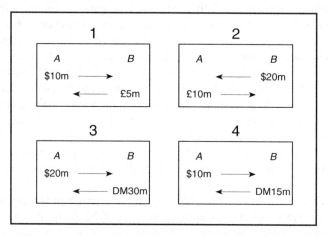

Figure 8.1   *Netting by counterparties*

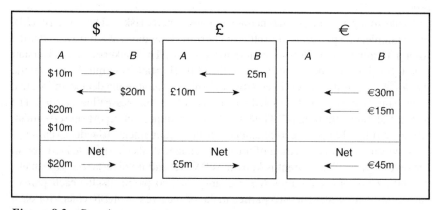

Figure 8.2   *Running accounts*

FX Net receives the counterparties' SWIFT messages (MT300) and at cut off time notifies the counterparties of the net amounts due with SWIFT payment instructions (MT202/MT210) and a SWIFT statement (MT950). The fact that gross details of transactions are sent as well as net details allows full nostro reconciliation to take place as required. (The SWIFT system is explained in Chapter 9.)

A multilateral netting system called Echo began operations in London in 1995, as did a similar system called Multinet in the US. Then, in March 1996, came the announcement that 20 major banks, 'the group of 20', were setting up a global clearing system to handle foreign exchange settlement which would operate in real-time. This will be an instantaneous settlement system in which payment by one bank is immediately offset by payment by another, eliminating Herstatt risk. With this announcement, Echo and Multinet merged, and later merged with the new system, called CLS Services. This became operational in September 2002, having completed trials in July 2002. It has 63 banks as owners.

ARBITRAGE

'Arbitrage' is a term that was first used in the foreign exchange markets. In the days when communications were not as good as today, one might find a disparity in rates quoted for the same pair of currencies. Perhaps the offer price for dollar/sterling in Paris is less than the bid price for dollar/sterling in London or any similar disparity in rates quoted by various banks. A currency could be bought in Paris and resold in London for an easy profit.

In general, arbitrage is taking advantage of any pricing anomaly. More arbitrage opportunities and more sophisticated arbitrage opportunities than ever before are being spotted due to the use of computers, often linked to constant feeds of live prices and using 'expert systems' techniques. At the same time, the paradox is that a dealer has to be quicker than ever to take advantage of an arbitrage opportunity, because everyone else is using computers too!

For example, a dealer may spot that another dealer's forward rate does *not* eliminate the difference in interest rates. As a result, perhaps the low interest rate currency is borrowed, sold for the high interest rate currency and this put on deposit for, say, 6 months. At the same time, to avoid currency risk, the low interest rate currency is bought back forward in 6 months' time so that the original loan can be repaid. The forward rate cost, however, is less than the interest rate difference leaving a risk free profit. This is called *covered interest rate arbitrage*.

Arbitrage can be found in any market these days, not just foreign exchange. As it is essentially risk free, it's good business if you can find it. All the banks employ arbitrage specialists who look for these opportunities, especially in the derivative products marketplace. The argument in its favour is that it keeps pricing efficient. In spite of this, arbitrage between equities and futures markets *(stock index arbitrage)* rouses great suspicions and is a subject of considerable controversy.

(One of the earliest records of telegraphic links was that between Rothschild's of London and Behrens of Hamburg in 1843 to exchange prices of securities, currencies and bills of exchange. Rich arbitrage opportunities for those quick off the mark!)

CENTRAL BANK SURVEYS

At the start of this chapter, we explained that global central banks carried out a simultaneous survey of their markets in 1986, 1989, 1992, 1995, 1998 and 2001.

Recent results in the major centres can be seen in Table 8.5.

The first point to note is the huge size of the figures. London trades 504 billion dollars worth of business each day and every day! The BIS, in Basle, collects all the figures and eliminates double counting (a deal done in London with a New York bank will be reported in both centres). The total figure in 1986 was just in excess of $300bn daily but by 2001 the figure was $1.2 trillion.

Table 8.5 *Central bank foreign exchange surveys – daily foreign exchange dealing*

Centre	1998		2001	
	Amount $bn	Share %	Amount $bn	Share %
UK	637	32.5	504	31
US	351	18	254	16
Japan	136	7	147	9
Singapore	139	7	101	6
Germany	94	5	88	5
Switzerland	82	4	71	4
Hong Kong	79	4	67	4
France	72	4	48	3

Source BIS (October 2001).

The second point is the pattern of growth. In London and New York, the 1986 figure had grown to between six and seven times as big by 1995, since when it has been comparatively stable. Many analysts and commentators expected the arrival of the euro and the location of the ECB in Frankfurt to cause a massive reduction in trading volumes generally, and in London in particular. Although volumes have dropped since 1999, there has been nothing like the huge decline some predicted. London has pretty well maintained its share at over 30% and Germany has not gained.

Trading in the individual currencies of the twelve member countries against the dollar accounted for 37% of total volume in 1998; dollar/euro trading now accounts for 30%. The Appendix to this chapter gives the breakdown of trading by currency pair. Note that the dollar is the main traded currency, featuring in 91% of dealing, followed by the euro (38%), yen (23%) and then sterling (13%).

Tokyo is an interesting case. We saw in Chapter 4, on Commercial Banking, that the Japanese have withdrawn a little from the international markets. Cross-border capital flows have slowed down. Trust banks in Japan, major players at one time, have been hit by the decline in trust fund investment. The fall in the Nikkei index after January 1990 and the collapse of property values has hit the market generally. Bank mergers have reduced the number of players and the BIS capital ratio rules in 1993 have made the banks more cautious as the Japanese system continues to be weak after incurring heavy losses in 2001.

One problem for central banks, intervening from time to time to support their currencies, is that the forces that can be marshalled against them are much bigger. If we look at the ERM crisis as it unfolded in August/September 1992, we see the Bank of England sitting on reserves of gold and foreign currencies of about $44bn. The trading in deals involving sterling, including cross-rate, amounted to some $79bn every single day. Even with the assistance of the Bundesbank, the resistance was simply swept away.

What we have seen in recent years is concerted action by major central banks acting in tandem and usually agreed at G7 meetings.

It all began at the beginning of 1985. The rise of the dollar was making USA exports uncompetitive and the pound/dollar rate was nearing parity. After a series of secret telephone calls, the world's major central banks hit the dollar simultaneously on Wednesday morning, 27 February. There was near pandemonium on the foreign exchange markets and within an hour the dollar had fallen 6% against the mark, from DM3.50 to DM3.30.

Intervention came again in September that year. The Group of Five (G5) major economies (later to expand to G7 and include Canada and Italy) met at the Plaza Hotel, New York on 22 September. A statement was issued that the dollar was overvalued, but although that seemed to be words only, it did the trick. On Monday 23 September, the dollar fell 3.5% without the central banks spending anything. The dollarmark rate was then DM2.70. Later, the central banks did intervene to reinforce their wishes and, by November, the dollar/mark was DM2.50. This has become known as the 'Plaza Agreement' and was, perhaps, the first international agreement on currencies since Bretton Woods.

If the Plaza Agreement seemed to mark a new milestone, this has not really proved to be the case. The central bankers met again at the Louvre in Paris (February 1987) and this time declared the dollar undervalued. It also announced a resolve to hold major world interest rates within narrow bands. This became known as the 'Louvre Accord'. However, this and several concerted attempts later to boost the dollar were not nearly as successful as attempts earlier to halt its runaway success.

Nevertheless, the US and Japan moved to support the yen in June 1998 and, for a time, moved the rate from ¥143 to the dollar to ¥136.8; by 2002 it was trading in the ¥120 – ¥125 range.

WHY LONDON?

The figures shown in the last section reveal London not only as the biggest foreign exchange market in the world, but by a considerable margin, as it accounts for 32.5% of world foreign exchange dealings. In view of the decline of the UK as an economic power and the weakness of the pound as a major currency, one may well ask why it is the major foreign exchange market.

There are, perhaps, four factors:

❏ *Time-zone*   London is well placed here. It can talk to Tokyo for an hour in the morning; the Middle East at about 11.30 a.m.; New York/Chicago at 1.30 p.m. and Los Angeles/San Francisco at 4.30 p.m. New York and Tokyo are in non-overlapping time zones.

❏ *Tradition*   London has a historical and traditional role as a major financial centre. There are over 500 foreign banks trading there and it has the infrastructure needed – accountants, lawyers, speciality printers.

❏ *Euromarkets*   The Euromarkets have large implications for foreign exchange. London's traditional role and its lack of protectionism led to the Euromarket business emanating from London and the huge population of foreign banks to which we have just referred.

❏ *English language*   English is the major language in international finance. The use of English as a first or second language is actually growing. This certainly helps London to score over Paris or Frankfurt. Indeed, the French insistence (at the highest official level) on the use of French militates against their desire to promote Paris further as an international centre.

SUMMARY

The foreign exchange market is huge, trading over $1 trillion a day in 2002 with London the biggest market.

The demand for foreign exchange arises from trade, tourism, government spending, international security trading and speculation.

Interbank business in London is 83% of the market by value and the top ten banks accounted for 50% of the market. Foreign exchange dealing accounts for half the profits of the big US commercial banks.

One economic theory for explaining exchange rates is *purchasing power parity* (PPP). Pricing the same basket of goods in two countries should result in the exchange rate. If a country consistently has higher inflation than another, its currency will tend to weaken compared with that of the country with lower inflation. The high inflation country will have to offer higher interest rates to persuade non-nationals to hold its currency. The theory that investors will shift assets according to factors like these is the *portfolio balance model*.

The post-war period of fixed exchange rates was agreed at a meeting in Bretton Woods in 1944. This also set up the IMF and the World Bank.

Foreign exchange risk for corporates has three elements – *transaction* risk, *translation* risk and *economic* risk.

Spot rates are today's exchange rates with settlement in 2 days. *Forward* rates are fixed rates for a transaction at a later date. They are determined by the difference in interest rates in the two currencies concerned. Worldwide, 60% of deals by value are forward and 40% spot.

The forward rate, being fixed, protects against the currency moving to the buyer's/seller's disadvantage, but they cannot benefit if it moves in their favour. This can be achieved by *currency options*. Options can be dealt on an exchange or over the counter (OTC).

Foreign exchange quotations are shown as a bid/offer rate. The dollar lies at the heart of foreign exchange dealing, as most transactions involve moving in and out of the dollar. Sterling and currencies which were linked to sterling quote so many dollars to the domestic currency. Other currencies quote a quantity of that currency to the dollar. A rate between two currencies, neither of them the dollar, is called a *cross-rate*.

The purchase of a currency spot accompanied by its simultaneous sale forward is the foreign exchange *swap*.

Brokers are active and link buyers and sellers on an anonymous basis. Electronic broking systems like Reuters 2000/2 and EBS are now being used.

A bank's foreign currency holdings with banks abroad are its *nostro* accounts. The foreign banks' balances with it in the domestic currency are *vostro* accounts. Bilateral *netting* of foreign exchange settlement is now common to reduce settlement risk. Multilateral netting is on the way, with a new real-time global settlement system due in 2000.

Arbitrage is taking advantage of an anomaly in rates to make risk-free profit.

Central banks carry out a foreign exchange survey every 3 years (2001 was the last occasion) with the results coordinated by the BIS.

Appendix

***Table** 8.A1   BIS Foreign exchange turnover by currency pair, daily averages in April, 2001 in billions of USD*

Currency pair	1992 Amount	1992 Share %	1995 Amount	1995 Share %	1998 Amount	1998 Share %	2001 Amount	2001 Share %
US$/€							352	30
US$/DM	192	25	254	22	291	20		
US$/FFr	19	2	51	4	58	4		
US$/Ecu	13	2	18	2	17	1		
US$/Other EMS	43	6	104	9	176	12		
US$/Yen	155	20	242	21	257	18	230	20
US$/£	77	10	78	7	118	8	125	11
US$/SwFr	49	6	61	5	79	5	57	5
US$/CAN$	25	3	38	3	50	3	50	4
US$/AUS$	18	2	29	3	42	3	47	4
US$/Other	48	6	72	6	172	12	197	17
€/Yen							30	3
€/£							24	2
€/SwFr							12	1
€/Oth							22	2
DM/Yen	18	2	24	2	24	2		
DM/£	23	3	21	2	31	2		
DM/SwFr	13	2	18	2	18	1		
DM/FFr	10	1	34	3	10	1		
DM/Ecu	6	1	6	1	3	0		
DM/Other EMS	21	3	38	3	35	2		
DM/Other	20	3	16	1	18	1		
Other EMS/ Other EMS	3	0	3	0	5	0		
Other currency pairs	25	3	30	4	31	5	27	1
All currency pairs	778	100	1137	100	1435	100	1,173	100

Source: BIS (October 2001).

9 Trade Finance

GENERAL PROBLEMS

One important aspect of global markets is, of course, international trade. If we consider the various problems which will arise in the export/import business, there are many ways in which banks can provide assistance:

1. *Payment services* The basic question of money transfers
2. *Collection of debts* The heart of the matter – how to ensure that we get paid
3. *Extension of credit* This involves ensuring that we get paid and the question of extending credit using, say, the bill of exchange
4. *Finance* This may be for the exporter to fund completion of the contract or for the importer to help pay for goods
5. *Foreign exchange* Sales/purchases of foreign currency spot, forward and by way of options, which are discussed in Chapter 8
6. *Trading guarantees* This covers many questions – quality of goods already paid for (importer), failure of chosen supplier to perform on award of a tender (importer), insurance against political risk, sudden withdrawal of export licences (exporter)
7. *Miscellaneous* This involves market intelligence, letters of introduction, correspondent banking facilities and similar services.

PAYMENT SERVICES

There are various ways in which the banks may arrange to remit funds:

❑ *Mail transfer* (MT) – instruction by letter
❑ *Telegraphic transfer* (TT)
❑ *SWIFT* – the Society for Worldwide Interbank Financial Telecommunication, is the bank-owned cooperative supplying secure messaging services and interface software to 7200 financial institutions in 197 countries. SWIFT helps its customers reduce costs, improve automation and manage risk. In addition to its 2265 member banks, SWIFT users include brokers, investment managers, securities deposit and clearing organisations and stock exchanges.

SWIFT scrl reported its network traffic grew 17% in 2001 to 1.5 billion messages, compared with, say, 812 million in 1997. On an average basis SWIFT is handling more than 6 million messages per day.

Securities traffic grew 28% in 2001. The securities sector represents 29% of SWIFT's total message volume. Securities messages are the second largest category of messages used by SWIFT's customers.

There are nine message categories distributed over four markets for which the share of business at end of 2001 is shown in Table 9.1.

Table 9.1 *SWIFT message categories and share of business, 2001*

Market	Traffic (000)	Share %
Payments	926	60.4
Treasury	108	7.0
Trade services	43	2.8
Securities	447	29.1
Others	10	0.7

Source: SWIFT.

The geographic distribution of traffic by region in 2001 is shown in Table 9.2.

Table 9.2 *SWIFT traffic by region, 2001*

Region	Traffic (000)	Distribution %
Americas	291	19.0
Asia-Pacific	180	11.8
Europe, Middle East, Asia	955	62.3
Others	104	6.9

Source: SWIFT.

❑ *International money transfer* (IMT) or *Express* IMT – modern terms for the mail transfer and telegraphic transfer
❑ *International money order* (IMO) – A UK bank, for example, may issue a cheque drawn on their New York office
❑ *Bank draft* – This will be drawn on a bank's home account or on their nostro account at a correspondent bank.

The last two documents are usually sent by the customer and not their bank.

COLLECTION OF DEBTS

There are methods which may not involve extension of credit:

- ❏ *Advance payment* This seems ideal but there are still problems. Suppose the advance payment is not received? What if the order is cancelled *prior* to sending the payment? Time must be allowed to clear the cheque/draft anyway. From the *importer's* point of view, the goods may not be shipped, or the wrong goods may be shipped, or the shipping documents may be wrong.
- ❏ *Payment on shipment* The exporter emails notice of shipment and awaits payment. The exporter could find themselves having shipped goods and yet the payment does not arrive. The bill of lading may give the importer title to the goods. From the *importer's* point of view, the goods may be found to be faulty or the wrong goods.
- ❏ *Open account trading* We despatch the goods and send an invoice marked 'payment within 7 days' (for example). Full of risk but quite suitable for circumstances where a valuable trading relationship has been set up and trust exists. This is very common in the US.

EXTENSION OF CREDIT

We now consider methods which involve extension of credit or cash on delivery but where we ask for a bank's help in collecting the money and guaranteeing arrangements to a certain extent.

Bill of Exchange

This is drawn by the exporter on the importer, with the latter agreeing to pay on demand or at a determinable future time the value of the goods to a specified person or bearer of the bill. This is explained fully in Chapter 5.

Sight bill or demand draft Immediate payment upon presentation of the bill and documents, with no required acceptance of the bill by the importer, as part of a documentary credit.

Usance, tenor or term bill Payable in a number of days or months, usually 'accepted' by a bank, the exporter then sells to a bill broker who holds to maturity or trades.

Documentary bill With documents (bill of lading, invoice, insurance cover and similar documents) attached.

Clean bill Without documents.

Documentary Letter of Credit

A bill of exchange is drawn by the exporter. A documentary letter of credit is opened by the *importer*.

There is an international code of practice for documentary credits set out in the International Chamber of Commerce's *Uniform Customs & Practices for Documentary Credits*.

(The International Chamber of Commerce was set up in 1919 to define the rules and norms by which trade is carried out. 60 national commissions make up its federal structure.)

The importer opens a documentary credit with his bank (*issuing bank*). This arranges for the issuing bank, upon instructions from the importer, to:

(a) make payment to the exporter (the *beneficiary*); or

(b) pay on or accept a bill of exchange drawn by the exporter; or

(c) authorise another bank (probably its correspondent bank in the exporter's country) to be the *advising bank*, which makes payment to the exporter or accepts his bill of exchange (thus becoming a 'documentary acceptance credit'). The advising bank may also be asked to be the *confirming bank*, to add its guarantee that the exporter will get paid if the issuing bank does not. (However, some countries, for example Iran, prohibit banks from opening credits on terms that require an advising bank to add its confirmation.)

All the above have to be backed by *stipulated documents*.
These documents include:

❑ *Transport documents*   Usually by sea under a *bill of lading*, which gives evidence that the goods have been dispatched, purport to be of the type and quality ordered and be properly transported. A copy of the bill of lading is the buyer's claim to possession of the goods when they arrive.

  With container traffic these days there may be a *forwarder's bill of lading* – not necessarily a document of title.

  If by air there is an *air waybill*, not however a document of title, merely acknowledgement of acceptance for delivery.

  If by road or rail there is a *carrier's receipt* or *railway receipt* and this is also not a document of title.

❑ *Commercial invoice*   Specifying quality, quantity and unit and total price.

❑ *Insurance documents*

❑ *SAD document*   Simplified customs form for the EU.

❑ *Other documents*   Certificate of origin; certificate of quality; health certificate; veterinary certificate; weight note.

There are potential problems with documents – documents missing, incorrectly completed or showing an invoice value different from that on the documentary letter of credit. The bank's staff check these and should see, for example, 'freight paid' on the bill of lading and insurance certificate if goods are sent CIF. Incorrect documents can cause delays at the port on landing and incur costs such as local storage.

Types of Documentary Credit

❑ *Confirmed credit* – when the advising bank also guarantees payment.
❑ *Revocable/Irrevocable credit* – *revocable* may be amended/cancelled by the issuing bank if the importer is not satisfied. This is obviously not usually acceptable to the exporter but may be suitable for selling to overseas subsidiaries where letters of credit must be used by local regulation. *Irrevocable* can only be amended/cancelled with agreement of the confirming bank and the beneficiary.
❑ *Sight credit, term or acceptance credit.*
Sight – the exporter draws a demand draft (bill) and presents it to the correspondent bank for payment.
Term/acceptance – the exporter draws a draft for a period of time (30, 60, 90 days) on the issuing or confirming bank.
❑ *Negotiation credit* – the confirming bank is instructed by the advising bank (if they are not one and the same) to negotiate the bill which is drawn on the advising bank. *Or* the bill may be drawn on the confirming bank who will accept it, making it a bank bill and therefore 'discountable'.
❑ *Standby credit* – to fall back upon if payment has not been made to the beneficiary by the other arranged methods.
❑ *Deferred payment credit* – payment made later.

Typically, in the Western world, all questions of import licences, exchange controls, insurance and documentation have been settled prior to issuing the letter of credit.

From the point of view of the *exporter* there are these advantages:

❑ Assurance of a payment or acceptance on shipping the goods.
❑ If an acceptance, then it will be a banker's acceptance and at best discount rates. Who pays the discount is a matter for negotiation!
❑ Generally, the reassurance of a bank (or banks) rather than just the importer's promises.

The *importer*, too, has advantages:

❑ No money will be paid until the goods are shipped and the required documents lodged.
❑ There may be time to pay, if a bill of exchange is involved. Again, acceptance will not be made until the goods are shipped.
❑ All formalities are complete before authorising the letter of credit.

There is, finally, the question of the relationship of the *bank* and the *bank's client* wanting to issue a letter of credit. The request to the bank for a letter of credit must be signed by someone in authority as it incurs obligations for the client (the 'accountee'). Links with the bank in this day and age may be *electronic*. The whole trade deal must conform with local import regulations and EU rules if the client is a member of that community.

From the *bank's* point of view, this is a contingent liability and affects existing credit agreements and limits. It is also an off-balance sheet transaction which needs capital under BIS capital ratio rules. The bank will probably charge the client a deposit and needs authority to debit expenses and charges. If a bill of lading is not used, the bank may require the goods to be at the disposal of the bank or consigned to the bank.

If the bank is the *advising* bank, it is responsible for seeing that the proposed credit is authentic.

Documentary Collection

The exporter ships the goods and presents the documents through a bank. The bank may be requested either to collect the payment in return for the documents or to see that a bill of exchange is accepted in return for handing over the documents.

The bank, however, is only using its 'best efforts' to collect the money or acceptance. The importer may still refuse the documents. If the goods have been shipped and the documents are *not* documents of title, the importer might even be able to collect the goods anyway. We may request the collecting bank to protect our interest in the event of default. If the importer doesn't pay or refuses the transaction, the goods (having been despatched) may have to be stored locally.

Effect of 1997 Asian Crisis

Prior to the Asian crisis in mid-1997 (see Chapter 15), much international trade had moved to an open account basis or was transacted through payment on documentary collection. The demand for confirmed letters of credit naturally increased after the crisis. Although this is more expensive for the exporter, it provided more secure cover for sales to countries like South Korea, Thailand and Malaysia. The bank issuing the confirmation would look at it on a case-by-case basis.

FINANCE FOR THE EXPORTER

The exporter may need finance while waiting to be paid other than that provided by, say, discounting the bill of exchange. Two possibilities are forfaiting and factoring.

Forfaiting This is traditionally associated with longer-term high value capital goods and construction projects. In the UK, London Forfaiting has a high concentration of deals in excess of £50m in value. However, others have also done a lot of 60 day business with £250,000 probably a minimum figure.

A bill of exchange or promissory note is bought 'à forfait', meaning *without recourse* to the exporter: that is, the purchaser forfaits all recourse to other parties. They look to the importer's bank to sign the bill or promissory note to guarantee payment and the bill/note will be unconditional. They can then sell the note/bill in an active secondary market. The major currencies are dollars, Swiss francs and deutschmarks.

For the exporter, forfaiting has the advantage that the finance is without recourse and has no effect on credit limits with their bank or any other. It is useful where export credit guarantees (or private insurance) are not available and, where it is available, avoids cash flow problems while waiting for a claim to be met. However, the forfaiter needs to be satisfied about client, country and political risk and the discount may be expensive. Also, they may not finance 100% of the value.

Factoring Factoring companies purchase trade debts of clients and usually pay 80% of the full value of debts due to be paid in less than 6 months. Normally, this is used for continuous rather than *ad hoc* business. The remaining 20% is passed to the client after all the debt has been collected. The factor runs the sales ledger and collects the money. Factoring can be with or without recourse. The latter can be very convenient, especially for export business, but is, naturally, more expensive. Frequently 'open account' terms are used. As well as a charge for providing finance, there is also a service fee for running the sales ledger and collecting the debt. This service fee varies from ½% to 2%. A variation on the theme is *invoice discounting*, in which the factor provides finance against invoices as before but the client runs the sales ledger and collects the debt.

The overseas agent of a factor will investigate credit status so that a quick report can be made to the factor, and the agent will usually underwrite the debt and deal with any queries locally. Factors may have their own offices abroad or be part of a network of independent factoring organisations. The largest such network is Factors Chain International (FCI), founded in 1968. It has 90 member companies in 35 of the world's main commercial centres. In the UK, the Factors and Discounters Association reported that 30,000 businesses with a total turnover of £90bn used their services in 2001. Factoring companies are often subsidiaries of banks – for example, in the UK, Barclays Sales Financing, HSBC Invoice Finance and Lloyds TSB Commercial Finance. The exporter has the advantages of dealing with a bank subsidiary, funding working capital on normal finance terms, not having to run the sales ledger and collect the debt and (in the case of non-recourse) peace of mind.

As stated, factoring is only provided for short-term debts and continuous sales of consumer items. In principle, it is similar to an overdraft.

While most factoring is *domestic*, international factoring is on the increase. The biggest markets using international factoring are the Netherlands, Germany, Italy, the UK, France, Belgium and the US.

Other finance   The exporter may require more general financial help than that merely required to bridge the gap while waiting to be paid – finance to produce capital goods, for example, that may take up to a year to deliver. Most large banks have departments which specialise in export finance and have 'packaged' schemes available. Sometimes some form of government aid or support may be available and the most important of these is insurance from a government export credit guarantee body (discussed later). If it is a large international project, then the term used may be 'project finance' with a syndicate of banks involved, and recourse is available only to the stream of funds from the project. The exporter, in some cases, may be interested in the question of aid to the *importer* to help purchase the goods. In a small number of cases, where factors are involved, the factor's overseas agent may get involved with providing finance to the importer also. On many occasions, however, a key component will be official sources of finance.

There are programmes from donors such as the World Bank, the EU and the African Development Bank. It is estimated that more than one third of sub-Saharan African imports are aid financed. Assistance is focused on countries implementing the economic reform programmes of the IMF and the World Bank. The paperwork and bureaucracy are formidable but payments are guaranteed and there is no currency risk.

In other cases, banks provide 'buyer credits' in conjunction with export credit guarantee insurance.

FOREIGN EXCHANGE (This subject was dealt with in Chapter 8)

TRADING GUARANTEES

The question of guarantees has been mentioned and the concerns of both exporters (political and currency risk) and importers (faulty goods or general non-performance of contracts). There is a series of schemes for trading guarantees other than export credit guarantees. These refer to guarantees backed by banks:

Bid or tender bond   This is required to support an exporter's offer to supply goods or a contractor's offer to carry out a service.

The bond safeguards a buyer against loss if the tender is awarded but the seller fails to proceed by signing the contract or submitting a performance bond.

A bid bond is guaranteed by the seller's bank and is usually 2%–5% of the value of the contract.

Performance bond   When the seller's bid is accepted, the bid bond is replaced by a performance bond, usually 10% of the value of the contract.

It is issued by the seller's bank, guaranteeing that he will supply goods (to the standard required by the buyer) or perform a service. If the buyer does not accept that goods are up to standard then they can claim under the performance bond.

Advance payment guarantee   The buyer pays the seller an agreed percentage of the contract price as an advance payment, which can be claimed back if goods/ services provided are not satisfactory.

Retention monies guarantees / progress payment bonds   Part of the contract price (usually 5%) can be held back by the buyer for a certain period to give time to assure himself that the goods or services supplied are satisfactory, or stage payments may be made on a similar basis.

These may be conditional or unconditional – for example, conditional on the seller admitting the fault or having won an arbitration proceeding or legal case. The bank must have a counter indemnity with their client, authorising debit of the said sum if money is paid under the guarantee. 'Unconditional' means that the bank will pay up simply on the signed statement by the buyer that the seller has failed in their obligation.

The bank guarantee may have to be paid *even if the bank's client goes into liquidation.*

Export credit guarantees   Government departments often provide exporters with facilities for insuring their shipments of goods against default by foreign importers and most other risks, except for normal marine insurance. Premiums are charged but the service is generally provided on a non-profit making basis. Such government departments do not themselves extend export finance but in providing insurance against risk encourage the banks to do so.

There are, however, also private insurers that will quote premiums for trade risk; for example, in the UK, Trade Indemnity. The UK's Export Credit Guarantee Department was founded in 1919. There is a distinction drawn between short-term projects, up to 2 years, and longer-term risks. The short-term end was located in Cardiff and called the Insurance Services Group (ISG). However, the government sold this in December 1991 to the Dutch insurer NCM. The new name is 'NCM Credit Insurance'. NCM also took control of the short-term export insurance in Sweden following the collapse of Svenska Credit.

The insurance protection is against non-payment, insolvency, withdrawal of import licences, problems due to foreign government decree and war and earthquake. Cover is typically up to 90%.

Given export credit guarantees, the banks are obviously happier to provide export finance and may arrange and administer the policy as part of the deal.

Other export credit guarantee organisations are:

❑ Hermes   Germany   (private sector)
❑ NCM   Holland   (private sector)

❏ COFACE   France   (state majority holding)
❏ SACE   Italy   (state majority holding).

An example of international cooperation here is seen in the case of the financing of the new international airport in the Portuguese colony of Macao. Export credits are supported by ECGD (UK), Hermes (Germany), Eximbank (US), EFIC (Australia) and COSEC (Portugal).

MISCELLANEOUS SERVICES

Export houses   These are market experts who know about shipping, insurance, quotas, licences, exchange terms and local conditions. They may:

❏ Handle all the paperwork and even promote sales abroad but the exporter is still the principal although the export house carries the risk
❏ Act for an overseas buyer – find a supplier, arrange shipment and insurance and confirm the contract on the buyer's behalf
❏ Act as an agent and buy goods and resell them but only against firm orders.

Confirming houses   Similar to export houses but will place an order for a buyer as a *principal* and will pay the exporter when the goods are despatched. May arrange credit for the buyer.

International credit unions   Finance houses and some banks have entered into reciprocal arrangements to arrange local finance to help an importer to import goods from a fellow member. An exporter, for example, may be asked by the importer of capital goods for instalment terms of payment. The bank may be able to arrange this through the partner in the credit union in the foreign company. The local bank/finance house will investigate and arrange finance – typically for machinery and capital goods generally. Examples are European Credit Union, Amstel Club, Export Finance International.

Barter/Countertrade   These arrangements are common where currencies are not convertible or subject to any restrictions preventing normal issue of export licences. Barter is a simple exchange of goods; countertrade is a wider term including things like counterpurchase and buy-back. Under these arrangements, exporters may agree to buy back goods from the importing companies, for example, the exporter of textile machinery must agree to buy back textiles. Alternatively, the exporter agrees to buy back goods in a more general way to a given percentage value of the exports.

For many years, Russia dealt with Finland on the basis that Russian oil purchased by Finland accumulated credits that could only be used to buy Russian goods. Other examples: car imports into Tunisia (Peugeot, VW) were only permitted on the basis that spare parts were purchased from Tunisian companies to a value of 50% of the cost of the car; Balfour Beatty in the UK won a contract for £2m in Malaysia on the basis that Balfour Beatty had to find buyers for tin, palm oil and rubber goods.

Barter and countertrade have now become a very big international business, with specialist companies like ICON International and Attwood Richards. For example, Keebler, a US biscuit company, was left with $1m of unusable packaging. Attwood Richards asked Keebler UK to fill the packaging with biscuits worth $14m for sale in markets where Keebler had no presence – Russia, Ukraine and the Baltic States. Keebler was paid in trade credits, eventually exchanged for packaging and shipping services. Attwood Richards also arrange barter for surplus seasonal goods – swimwear, beach umbrellas and golf clubs. Trade credits have also been used to buy office furniture, computers, cleaning services, hotel rooms and airline seats.

General   Banks also provide a host of other services in connection with export/ import business – market intelligence, credit status enquiries, letters of introduction, correspondent banking, translation, legal and accountancy facilities.

SUMMARY

Banks facilitate international trade with cross-border payment systems. The *SWIFT* system is the most important.

Simply sending an invoice to the importer and awaiting payment is *open account trading*.

Credit may be extended by the use of a *bill of exchange* which may be a *sight*, *tenor*, *documentary* or *clean* bill.

A promise by the importer's bank either to pay for the goods or to sign a bill of exchange on despatch is a *documentary letter of credit*, which may be *revocable* or *irrevocable*. The importer's bank is the *issuing* bank in this connection and the exporter's bank is the *advising* bank.

The exporter is the *beneficiary*. If the exporter's bank agrees to pay for the goods, even if the importer or the importer's bank doesn't, it is a *confirmed* letter of credit.

With *documentary collection*, the exporter's bank attempts to obtain payment by offering the shipping documents to the importer's bank.

Finance for export might be based on *forfaiting* or *factoring*. There may also be official help from development banks. Export credit guarantees, offered by governments or the private sector, insure against non-payment. The banks offer other guarantees such as *bid* or *tender bonds*, *performance bonds*, *advance payment guarantees* and *progress payment bonds*.

Miscellaneous services offered by banks include acting as *export* and *confirming houses* and assisting with *barter* and *countertrade*.

10 European Economic and Monetary Union

INTRODUCTION

The world is increasingly becoming one vast global market – general deregulation, the collapse of artificial barriers to trade, modern electronic communications – all have contributed to this state of affairs.

A supreme example of globalisation is surely Europe's Economic and Monetary Union (EMU). Twelve sovereign states, with a total population of 302 million, have accepted a single currency and central bank. The phrase 'cross-border' has become less significant as the EMU area moves (with limitations) to become simply one market. In many ways, it is the most dramatic political and economic development of our time. Hence this separate chapter, looking at this phenomenon in more detail.

We shall begin by examining the history of the European Union generally and look at its institutions, moving on from there to consider the history of previous monetary unions and the history of EMU and its new institutions in particular.

We shall then discuss the objectives of EMU. Why create it in the first place? What advantages should it bring? What are the problems? During this, we consider the effect of EMU (actual and anticipated) on the securities markets in their various aspects.

One country in Europe not yet a member is, of course, the United Kingdom, where a ferocious debate is taking place at this moment.

Finally, we look at the general arguments for and against the UK joining (while trying not to upset anybody!).

HISTORY OF THE EUROPEAN UNION

Early History

Most of us believe that the impetus towards European Union came in the post-war years after 1945. While this is generally true, the concept has a long history. Several people have thought of the idea of drawing Europe together by military conquest, from the Romans through Charlemagne to Napoleon. The general idea then was to maintain peace and provide defence against enemies.

Peace was certainly what the UK Quaker, William Penn, had in mind when he argued in 1693 for a European parliament and an end to the nation state. Jeremy Bentham also argued for a European assembly and Jean-Jacques Rousseau wanted a European Federation.

In 1814, Henri Saint-Simon actually produced a detailed scheme with a European monarch, government and parliament. He invented the phrase 'A United States of Europe', a phrase used later in the century by Victor Hugo at the Paris peace conference of 1849.

All these people, of course, were only on the fringes of political power and had little practical influence on what happened.

More important was the setting up in 1923 of a 'Pan-European Union' by an Austrian aristocrat called Richard Coudenhove-Kalergi. He argued for a European federation and, importantly, attracted as members several young politicians who later were able to wield considerable influence. Among these were Konrad Adenauer, Georges Pompidou and Carlos Sforza.

One key objective (as today) was to compete better in the world's economic markets. Interestingly, the UK was never regarded as a potential participant. No practical results were achieved, although the idea had general support.

1945

After 1945, things changed. Europe had been devastated by the third major war in less than 100 years. There was a widespread feeling that the nation state had no future. There was an awareness of Europe's weakened state economically, the dominance of the United States and fear of Russia and communism.

In 1948, the Organisation for European Economic Co-operation (OEEC) was formed to oversee the distribution of US aid. It had a Council of Ministers, with each state having one voice, and decisions needed a unanimous vote. After the widespread devaluations of 1949, the OEEC set up a European Payments Union in 1950 to act as a sort of central bank for intra-European trade and payments.

The OEEC was not a foundation stone. It had no political implications and limited economic power. It was still, however, a major exercise in Europeans working together. In 1960, it became the wider Organisation for Economic Co-operation and Development (OECD) which we have today, with membership from the US and Canada and, in 1964, Japan.

The Council of Europe

In 1947, an International Committee of the Movements for European Integration was formed and held a Congress of Europe in the Hague in May 1948. Several hundred delegates attended from 16 states. Delegates wanted a European assembly and a European court. A European movement was formed to carry on the debate and put pressure on politicians.

After the UK's unique position in the war, many looked to them for leadership here, but did not get it. The Attlee government was preoccupied with its own problems in implementing a socialist economy.

The idea of a European Assembly was, however, supported by many pro-Europe politicians, notably Paul-Henri Spaak of Belgium, and Robert Schuman, France's foreign minister.

In May 1949, representatives of the states agreed to set up a Council of Europe in Strasbourg to achieve ' a greater unity between its members for the purpose of safeguarding and realising the ideals and principles which are their common heritage and facilitating their economic and social progress'.

The Council of Europe met in August 1949, with a Committee of Ministers, meeting twice per year, and a Consultative Assembly. Paul-Henri Spaak was the first president.

No positive move towards European integration took place, and often the Committee of Ministers and the Assembly were at loggerheads. Nevertheless, the Council did useful work on human rights and founded the European Court of Justice in 1959. It also worked on coordinating policies in transport, civil aviation and agriculture. Again, Europeans were trying to work together.

The European Coal and Steel Community

In May 1950, Robert Schuman, the French foreign minister, produced the 'Schuman Plan', proposing a pooling of coal and steel resources. They were to be pooled and administered by a new supranational authority in conjunction with the various states involved. Tariff barriers would be eliminated gradually.

It is most important, however, to see the political motivation here. There was a recognition that stability and security in Western Europe rested on France and Germany coming together. Indeed, the initial proposal was for a Franco-German coal and steel pool with others invited to join (incidentally, the Council of Europe had made a similar recommendation earlier). It was also seen as the first step to political integration.

A specific plan was drafted by Jean Monnet, head of the French Planning Commission.

The Treaty of Paris, setting up the European Coal and Steel Community (ECSC), was signed in April 1951 and ratification by local parliaments took a further year. Members were France and West Germany with Italy, Netherlands, Belgium and Luxembourg – the Common Market's original 'six'. Although the Attlee government in the UK lost the 1951 election, the new government under Churchill (a supposed European) was no more enthusiastic about the ECSC than they were, to the disappointment of many dedicated Europeans.

People committed to a form of common future for Europe were now in positions of power – Schuman and Monnet in France, Adenauer in Germany, de Gasperi in Italy, Spaak in Belgium and Beck in Luxembourg.

It is very common for people in the UK to talk of a 'hidden agenda' behind EMU, namely some form of political federation. Certainly some UK pro-Europeans have played this aspect down, but the agenda has always been in the open. The founders of the ECSC wanted to foster economic expansion, growth in employment and a rising standard of living, it is true. They were, however, very clear about political motives – a check on Germany to reduce the risk of war and, ultimately, a form of political federation. Schuman's declaration said openly 'Europe must be organised on a federal basis' and also said that this was 'a first step in the federation of Europe'. That is not to say that people in the mass were in favour of this move but, like today, were led towards it by political leaders dedicated to the idea.

Jean Monnet was the first president of the ECSC. There was a Common Assembly of 78 members, a Council of Ministers and the new High Authority, whose supranational powers had caused a long debate before parliaments ratified the treaty. The first meeting of the High Authority was in 1952.

'All Roads Lead to Rome'

The ECSC was not a total success but did much useful work on trade discrimination and restrictive practices. Although nothing political was achieved, it had started a process of European decision making on matters of vital interest.

However, whatever aspirations some politicians may have had, Europe was not yet ready to make any dramatic move towards political union. A treaty was actually signed in May 1952 for a European Defence Community, but defeated in the French Assembly in August 1954 – France was alarmed at any idea of re-arming Germany.

The ECSC move led to discussions within the OEEC and the Council of Europe on cooperation in other sectors such as transport, agriculture, health, postal services and communications. Gradually, however, the 'six' felt that a number of separate organisations was not the way forward, but rather a single body to oversee integration of the economies.

The idea of some form of common market gathered strength by the mid-1950s, and the foreign ministers of the six met at Messina in Italy in the middle of 1955 to launch 'a fresh advance towards the building of Europe'. They agreed to set up a committee under Paul-Henri Spaak to report back on concrete proposals. The Spaak report was discussed at the ECSC Common Assembly in March 1956 and approved by foreign ministers of the six in May. The Spaak Committee then drafted two treaties – one for a European Economic Community (EEC) and one for a European Atomic Energy Authority. The six made it clear that other countries, especially the UK, could join. In March 1957, the two treaties were signed in Rome. The atomic energy initiative became known as 'Euratom' and was largely a failure. The same could not be said of the EEC!

The European Economic Community

By December 1957, the Treaty of Rome had been ratified by the six states, and the first meeting of the Assembly took place in Strasbourg in March 1958. The first elected president was Robert Schuman. Support had come from France, who saw in it export potential for its agriculture, and Germany, who saw the export potential for its industrial goods.

The treaty ran to 248 articles, supplemented by four annexes, thirteen protocols, four conventions and nine declarations. It emphasised that the problems of one member state would be the problems of all. The treaty was to remain in force for an unlimited period and could not be revoked.

The main objectives were expressed in economic terms – setting up a common market, ending price fixing, dumping, unfair subsidies and ensuring free competition. Behind it all lay the political motives. The treaty's preamble spoke of 'the foundations of an even closer union among Europe's peoples'. Walter Hallstein, the first president of the European Commission, said 'We are not integrating economies, we are integrating policies.' In 1964, Paul-Henri Spaak reminded the Council of Europe: 'Those who drew up the Rome Treaty ... did not think of it as essentially economic; they thought of it as a stage on the way to political union.' So much for the 'hidden agenda'.

Membership of the EEC meant a commitment to the free movement of capital and labour, a common investment policy and coordination of social welfare policies. Three funds were set up, a European Social Fund, a European Investment Bank and a European Development Fund.

The general institutions of the EEC are discussed in the next major section.

In 1965, the Commission absorbed the equivalent bodies in the ECSC and Euratom.

Progress continued over the next ten to eleven years in moving to a common market. A customs union was declared operational in 1968, with a single external customs duty and the abolition of all internal tariffs. 1968 also saw the commencement of the Common Agricultural Policy.

The 1960s generally saw the greatest tensions over the future direction of the Community. These concerned the extension of the EEC to other members and the question of the powers of the Commission.

Wider Membership

1961 saw Ireland, Denmark and the UK formally applying for membership of the EEC, followed by negotiations with Norway. However, the 1960s also saw a French government headed by Charles de Gaulle, who vetoed the UK's application in 1963 and again in 1967. What particularly incensed France's partners was that de Gaulle's 1963 veto was announced at a press conference and without prior consultation with the other governments.

A summit at the Hague in 1969 agreed on the principles for enlargement, and discussions re-opened with Ireland, Denmark, the UK and Norway. Treaties were signed in 1972 but a referendum in Norway rejected the idea, leaving the other three to join in 1973. The 'six' were now nine at last. Greece joined in 1981, and Spain and Portugal in 1986. The nine are now twelve. Finally, Sweden, Austria and Finland joined in January 1985, giving us the fifteen we have today.

The de Gaulle Stalemate

Apart from arguments with de Gaulle about accession of other members, a more serious dispute took place with France in the mid-1960s about the whole question of EEC powers as opposed to those of the members. Margaret Thatcher was not the first to question the powers of the Commission. They were also questioned by an equally dominant personality – de Gaulle.

In 1965, the European Commission, under Walter Hallstein, proposed that the EEC should have its own independent source of revenue and budget (instead of direct contributions from national treasuries). It was also proposed that the European Parliament should have more powers, especially over control of the budget. The third proposal concerned the setting up of a more formal agricultural policy. De Gaulle wanted the agricultural policy but not the first two. He was against them because they would increase the supranational characteristics of the EEC.

The community then faced its biggest crisis so far. De Gaulle attacked the powers of the Commission as taking away the powers of national governments. A federal Europe did not appeal to him any more than to Margaret Thatcher! To make things worse, the Treaty of Rome had envisaged a switch to majority voting for most cases after January 1966. De Gaulle was totally opposed to this. The French simply boycotted the Council of Ministers for seven months. However, this also meant no progress on the agricultural policy which France wanted. A compromise had to be found.

In Luxembourg, in January 1966, the six agreed that a state could continue to exercise a veto if it felt that its own vital interests were at stake. As a result, majority voting was *de jure* but not necessarily *de facto*. The Commission, in turn, agreed that it would consult more closely with the Council of Ministers and inform governments at all stages of any new initiatives.

The Hague Conference of 1969 was much more positive. It agreed proposals for the financing of the Common Agricultural Policy (itself finally agreed in 1968) and also the budgetary powers of the European Parliament. The latter had been discussing plans for direct elections and these began in 1979.

The Hague Conference also agreed on the principle of monetary union, to be reached by 1980. We discuss this more fully in the history of EMU in a later section.

The European Council

Periodically, heads of government had met to discuss issues affecting the EEC. The meetings of heads of state were institutionalised in 1974 by calling it the 'European Council'. This was a body which could resolve disputes, set new objectives and decide on future progress. It was outside the Treaty of Rome and not, therefore, subject to, for example, the European Court.

The whole question of the future for a more political union for the EEC was on the agenda in the late seventies and early eighties. This included the vexed question of majority voting. The European Council meeting of June 1983 ended with a rather extraordinary 'Solemn Declaration on European Union'. The Council saw itself as responsible for a general political impetus to the construction of Europe. There was fine rhetoric but not too much action.

However, the European Council meeting in Milan in June 1984 decided to set up an intergovernmental conference to discuss the future for the EEC and the question of majority voting. Their proposals, put to the European Council in December 1984, became the Single European Act.

The Single European Act

The Single European Act (SEA) set the target of a genuinely single internal market by the end of 1992. It aimed to sweep away all the obstacles that still remained to achieving a genuine single competitive market. In addition, it referred to new forms of decision making and legislative processes within the EEC, extending its scope to cover foreign policy and some matters of defence.

The economic aim of a single market, however, involved questions like tax, law, accountancy, national standards and social welfare as well as the question of frontiers themselves. In other words, we were back to politics.

On the question of the veto, it was agreed that this applied to the introduction of new members and the general *principles* of new policies.

The actual *implementation* of the policies in detail would be subject to qualified majority voting, in practice 54 out of 76 votes available at the Council. This was a very significant change, and one accepted by the arch anti-European, Margaret Thatcher.

The reforms for the European Parliament did not go as far as many people would have liked. Where the Council of Ministers had decided on a proposal by qualified majority, the Parliament could amend or reject the proposal. The Council of Ministers could then only override this by *unanimous* vote – a significant change, not totally appreciated at the time.

Finally, the SEA asserted that member states should formulate a European foreign policy and should work more closely together on defence issues.

After certain delays, the SEA was finally ratified by all parliaments by 1987.

European Free Trade Area

As an alternative to full membership of the EEC, the UK had raised the question of forming a free trade area within the Community, during the late 1950s. When this failed, the UK joined with Austria, Denmark, Norway, Portugal, Sweden and Switzerland in forming the European Free Trade Area (EFTA). Its aim was to work for the reduction and eventual elimination of tariffs on most industrial goods between the members. Special provisions were made for fisheries and agriculture. EFTA was launched in May 1960. It was not nearly as ambitious as the EEC, simply, as the name implied, a free trade area.

With the projected arrival of the single market, post-1992, many EFTA members were worried about its future. Austria, in particular, had decided to join the EEC anyway. As a result, they opened discussions with the EEC (by now simply called European Community – EC) about a European Economic Area (EEA). The two sides reached agreement in October 1991. Essentially, the EEA was a large free trade area with no internal tariffs but no common external tariffs. The EFTA states, for example, did not necessarily have to accept the Common Agricultural Policy (by then, of course, Denmark, Portugal and the UK were members of the EC anyway, but Iceland had also joined EFTA). The EEA came into force in 1993, but in rather unreal circumstances. Switzerland rejected the idea in a referendum in December 1992, and all the states except Iceland had either applied for full membership of the EC or were very near to doing so.

The Maastricht, Amsterdam and Nice Treaties

The most important decisions taken at Maastricht in December 1991 concerned monetary union, and for that reason are covered under that heading later in this chapter. However, once again, many people failed to notice that the treaty was in two parts – economic and monetary union and *political* union. We shall cover the latter aspects now.

The political section of the Maastricht Treaty decided on the following points:

❑ An inter-governmental foreign and security policy
❑ A concept of 'European citizenship'
❑ A central role for the principle of 'subsidiarity'
❑ A new 'social chapter' (the UK opted out)
❑ An increase in the powers of the European Parliament – co-decision authority with the Council of Ministers on certain subjects
❑ An inter-government framework for justice and home affairs.

There is nothing too dramatic, but political nevertheless.

Some of the perceived shortcomings of the Maastricht Treaty were redeemed by the Amsterdam Treaty, signed in 1997. Unlike Maastricht, the Amsterdam Treaty was solely concerned with political issues. The key points were:

❑ Safeguarding human rights, with penalties for states in breach
❑ Providing for the establishment of 'an area of freedom, security and justice in the EU'
❑ Gradually, bringing asylum, visas, immigration and external border control under common rules
❑ Allowing the UK and Ireland to opt out of the above two provisions
❑ Allowing the European Parliament co-decision policy within the Council over a wider range of issues than Maastricht

❑ Giving the Commission president greater powers in selecting commissioners
❑ Making promotion of high employment an EU goal
❑ Providing for a 'high representative' to put a name and face to EU foreign policy.

The Amsterdam Treaty came into effect in March 1999.

The Nice Treaty of December 2000 again did not involve EMU as such but was held largely to resolve issues caused by the prospective admission (at that stage thought to be from 2004 onwards) of twelve new members – Bulgaria, Cyprus, Czech Republic, Estonia, Hungary, Latvia, Lithuania, Malta, Poland, Romania, Slovakia and Slovenia. The key points were:

❑ Expansion of qualified majority voting while retaining vetoes in key areas
❑ Reallocation of votes to a total of 342, allowing for the new members
❑ A Charter of Human Rights
❑ A European Rapid Reaction Force
❑ An increase in European Parliament members to 738 when all new members have joined
❑ Changes in the composition of the European Commission.

However, all these splendid ideas suffered a setback when Ireland rejected the Nice Treaty in a referendum in June 2001! In spite of this, it was decided in December 2001 that ten of the twelve new applicants could still be ready for membership in 2004, Romania and Bulgaria being the exceptions. A date for the latter of 2007 is still a possibility. These ten will add 75m people to the EU's existing population of 375m. Romania and Bulgaria would add another 30m. Ireland voted again on 19 October 2002, and this time passed the Nice Treaty by 63% to 37%. The key question asked had been altered to reassure the Irish on neutrality in view of the Rapid Reaction Force. Once again, the reaction of the EU when faced with a setback was to move the goalposts!

Admission of the ten new members in 2004 was formally confirmed at the Copenhagen Summit in mid-December 2002. Much of the time of the meeting was taken up by the subject of Turkey, which was pressing hard for an early date to discuss its admission. Some countries (UK, Italy) were sympathetic, but others were not (France, Germany). In the end, December 2004 was set as the date to begin consideration of Turkey's entry, although the actual entry date is unlikely to be before 2010. In addition, a last-minute attempt to resolve the Greco/Turkish division of Cyprus failed and, at the time of going to press, the new entrant looks likely to be the 'Greek' Cyprus and not the whole island.

In theory, citizens from any of these countries can work anywhere in the Union. In practice, fears of cheap immigrant labour have caused most countries to postpone the free movement of labour until 2009 (Britain being an honourable exception). In addition, the potential increased cost to the CAP is such that payments to the new entrants will be phased in over ten years. Originally, the CAP was to be reorganised, resulting in lower payments to countries like France and Germany. However, these same countries have forced a delay in any such move.

The final hurdle? Each of the ten countries must ask its population to agree to entry to the EU. Anti-EU sentiment in some countries (Poland, Estonia) is such that this is not a foregone conclusion.

Most of the more recent developments in the EC (but now called the European Union (EU), following the Single European Act!) have concerned EMU. Before we look at this, however, we shall look at the institutions of the EU itself and then at the history of previous monetary unions.

THE INSTITUTIONS OF THE EUROPEAN UNION

The European Council

In a sense, this is not really an institution of the EU. From the early days, frequent 'summit' meetings of heads of government were called to resolve key issues of principle. At a summit in Paris in September 1974, it was decided to regularise these meetings under the name 'European Council' (not to be confused with the Council of Europe!). It consists of the heads of government with the President of the Commission entitled to attend. A decision to meet three times a year was amended to twice a year in 1985; the presidency of the meeting to rotate over the various countries of the EU every six months. It does not, of course, appear in the Treaty of Rome.

The Council of Ministers

This is the main political body of the union representing the elected governments of the 15 countries. They make the main strategic decisions, leaving the Commission to draw up the necessary directives. On some issues, each country has a veto.

The European Commission

This is, in effect, the civil service of the EU. They are the permanent officials. The President of the Commission (currently Romano Prodi) is picked by the Council of Ministers. The President, in turn, decides on the 19 individual Commissioners, with the usual horse trading to ensure that each country gets it fair share. The choice of Commissioners needs to be approved by the Parliament. The Commission prepares recommendations on broad macroeconomic guidelines and monitors member states' performance.

European Parliament

This is, of course, an elected body. Until recently its powers were limited, leading to complaints about the undemocratic nature of the EU generally. However, its powers have been strengthened by both the Maastricht Treaty (1991) and the Amsterdam Treaty (1997). Although a formal vote of censure failed, its criticisms of the Commissioners for a mixture of incompetence and fraud led to the resignation of all of them, including the President, Jacques Santer, in March 1999. This dramatic move was seen as a 'sea change' so far as the Parliament is concerned.

The powers of the Parliament are summarised below:

❑   The Maastricht Treaty gave the Parliament co-decision with the Council of Ministers in 15 areas. The Amsterdam Treaty increased this to 38 areas. The exceptions are tax, agriculture and EMU itself. In the 38 areas, the Parliament can amend drafts of the Commission, can reject them by majority vote or work with the Council on a compromise.
❑   They have the power to amend the draft budget prepared by the Commission, and also approve (or not) the Commission's handling of the budget.
❑   They have the right to approve or veto the appointment of the Commission's president and the Commissioners themselves. They can also pass a motion of censure on the Commissioners.
❑   They have the right to ratify any foreign treaties.

Ecofin

This body replaces the former EU Monetary Committee. It is the prime forum for macroeconomic policy and is responsible for broad economic guidelines. The finance ministers of all 15 states meet monthly. An agenda for the meetings is prepared by finance ministers, member central bank representatives and two members of the Commission. This body is called the *Economic and Financial Committee*. Where matters arise which concern the twelve members of EMU only, a smaller version of Ecofin consists of the twelve finance ministers, and currently goes by the popular name of 'Euro-X'. It is a political hot potato. The UK is against it and the French are strongly in favour (surprise, surprise!).

The European Central Bank

(Although the setting up of the European Central Bank is clearly part of the move to economic and monetary union, we discuss it here, together with the other key institutions of the EU generally. On paper at least, the European System of Central Banks includes the three non-members of EMU, as we shall see.)

There are technically no less than three terms here. There is the *European Central Bank* (ECB), which with the 15 *National Central Banks* (NCBs) form what is called the *European System of Central Banks* (ECSB). Note that this includes three countries which are not part of EMU. They do not, however, take part in the decision making regarding the single monetary policy for the euro area and the implementation of such decisions. The governing council of the ECB, however, to avoid confusion has introduced a fourth term – the *Eurosystem* – for the ECB and the twelve NCBs. Unfortunately, it has, perhaps, created further confusion, as even the technical press do not seem to be aware of this distinction.

There are two decision-making bodies:

❏ *The Governing Council*   This is the supreme decision-making body, and consists of the ECB and the twelve NCBs, that is, the Eurosystem. The Council adopts guidelines and makes decisions to ensure performance of the tasks entrusted to the Eurosystem. It also formulates the monetary policy of the EU – monetary objectives, interest rates and reserves.

❏ *The Executive Board*   This consists of the President, Vice-President and four other members. They are appointed by the governments of the twelve member states on a recommendation from the EU Council, after consultation with the Parliament and the Governing Council (in the first instance, the European Monetary Institute, the forerunner of the Eurosystem). The main responsibilities of the board are to prepare the meetings of the Governing Council, to implement the monetary policy that the Council has laid down and generally to be responsible for the ECB.

The president and vice-president serve for a minimum of five years and the other four for eight years, non-renewable. (To prevent all eight terminating at once, in the first instance there is a staggered system.) The first six appointments were:

❏ President – Wim Duisenberg (Netherlands)
❏ Vice-President – Christian Moyer (France)
❏ Otmar Issing (Germany)
❏ Tomasso Padoa Schioppa (Italy)
❏ Eugenio Domingo Solas (Spain)
❏ Sirrka Hamalainen (Finland).

Since then, Christian Moyer has been replaced by Lucas Papademos of Greece.

(A sordid argument about the first president resulted in a verbal compromise. Wim Duisenberg to resign after four years, making way for Jean-Paul Trichet, the French central bank governor, who would then serve eight years. However, later Wim Duisenberg said 'I may not go'! The whole episode hardly inspires confidence for the future of EMU. At the moment, Jean-Paul Trichet is due to take over in mid-2003.) However, as we go to press, there are doubts over this, as M. Trichet is facing a fraud trial following a financial scandal at Crédit Lyonnais. The trial began on 6 January, 2003. Alternative French candidates include Jacques de la Rosière, managing director of the IMF, and Christian Moyer, mentioned above. Non-French names include the German, Otmar Issing, the ECB's chief economist, or Antonio Fazio, the head of the Bank of Italy.

The basic tasks to be carried out by the Eurosystem are:

❑ To define and implement monetary policy
❑ To conduct foreign exchange operations
❑ To manage the official foreign reserves
❑ To promote the smooth operation of member systems.

The Maastricht Treaty stipulates that the ECB's main goal is 'price stability'. It also directs the ECB 'to support the general economic policies of the Community' but 'without prejudice to the objective of price stability'. The bank itself decides what price stability means.

The ECB has already decided that monetary policy will be based on a maximum inflation figure of 2% and a mixture of economic indicators including money supply. Inflation is based on a new harmonised index of consumer prices (HICP). It uses a narrower range of goods and services than most national indices and (for the technically minded) is based on a geometric mean rather than an arithmetic mean, to reduce the impact of sharp movements in a small number of prices. (In the case of the UK, the HICP usually produces a figure about 1% less than the local retail price index.)

All banks in member countries will deposit reserves with their central bank equivalent to 2% of their eligible liabilities. Gold is some 15% of the total reserves of gold and foreign currencies held at the ECB. Each central bank surrenders a percentage of its gold and foreign currency reserves to be held at the ECB. This percentage is based on a formula taking account of relative GDP and population. Whether gold should be held at all is a matter of some controversy these days. The UK Treasury, for example, has been selling off gold for three years. The UK's remaining 320 tonnes is only some 7% of gross reserves.

The total system is a decentralised one, as discussed in Chapter 6. The ECB sets three interest rates – a fixed rate tender or repo rate, a marginal lending rate and a rate at which deposits with central banks are paid. (Initially, these rates were 4.5%, 3% and 2% respectively.) The fixed rate tenders are carried out by the twelve central banks, who will also carry out any foreign exchange transactions called for by the ECB.

The monetary system is similar to that of the Bundesbank, showing the influence of Germany on the final decisions and the need to get the German public to agree to diminution of the power of the mighty Bundesbank. As Jacques Delors once said, 'Not all Germans believe in God, but they all believe in the Bundesbank.'

Nevertheless, various aspects of the Eurosystem have attracted criticism.

To begin with, this is the most independent and unaccountable central bank the world has ever seen. In the US, the Federal Reserve chairman has to appear before Congress every three months and knows that politicians could, if they wished, change the law. Equally, the Federal Open Market Committee publish minutes of their deliberations. In Germany, the law regarding the Bundesbank could be changed by a simple majority in parliament.

All this is totally absent for euroland, although the ECB must submit to questions from the European Parliament and publish annual and quarterly reports. The Maastricht Treaty explicitly forbids the ECB and its decision-making bodies to 'seek or take instructions from Community institutions or bodies, from any government of a member state or from any other body'. Any revision of the Treaty would require unanimity from all 15 states. In addition, Wim Duisenberg has ruled out publishing minutes for twelve years.

The system is also decentralised. The ECB lays down the crucial interest rates, but repos are carried out by the twelve central banks, who will also carry out any forex intervention.

Managing the currency has been divided from banking supervision. In any case, in only two of the twelve states is supervision in the hands of the central bank. In terms of voting, the twelve central banks have twelve votes as opposed to the six of the executive board. Could this lead to tensions later?

The ECB also has no role as 'lender of last resort'. Multilateral supervision is, in any case, a tough challenge (witness BCCI). If there is a crisis, is it solvency or liquidity? Suppose there was a cross-border merger – say BNP and Barclays, and the bank is in trouble – who bails it out?

The French, in particular, are worried about the lack of control of the ECB, and urged the creation of some form of supervising economic committee. This view did not find support. The bank has started out confidently enough. It publishes a full monthly report and it also resisted attempts by Oskar Lafontaine, the former German finance minister, to bounce it into premature interest rate cuts to stimulate higher employment – it won, he lost. Nevertheless, Paul de Grauwe, Professor of Economics at the University of Leuven, has concluded that the design of the ECB is flawed and will need to be changed. 'Failure to do so,' he says in the *Financial Times* of November 12, 1998, 'will jeopardise the whole European project of economic and monetary union.' We shall have to wait and see.

Perhaps we have to bear in mind Milton Friedman's comment on central banks. He suggested that they had two principal objectives: avoiding accountability on the one hand and achieving public prestige on the other!

The European Court of Justice

This was set up to interpret the Treaty of Rome and ensure that the original EEC institutions and member states were fulfilling their obligations under the Treaty. Originally, the Court was set up with six judges, one from each state, and a seventh selected by the Council of Ministers.

The Court gradually built up a body of case law. It repeatedly upheld the superiority of Community law over national law in an increasing number of sectors.

HISTORY OF PREVIOUS MONETARY UNIONS

We have many examples of previous monetary unions, especially in the last century. They are of different types and arise for diverse reasons.

Political Empires

The most obvious example is the existence of some form of political empire such as the Roman Empire, the British Empire, the Austro-Hungarian Empire and the Soviet Union. It is noticeable that when parts break away from the empire, the monetary union collapses. The newly independent parts want their own currency for three reasons: a) sovereignty and political symbolism, b) the ability to influence economic activity by altering interest rates and the exchange rate and c) insulation from direct foreign influence on the currency.

Political Unification

Another example is unions which arise from political unification. These are the ones which usually survive – Germany, Italy and the United States, where the Federal Reserve was finally established in 1913.

Voluntary Unions

There are also voluntary monetary unions, perhaps with more limited political ambitions. The Latin Monetary Union (1865–1926) was formed by France, Italy, Belgium, Greece and Switzerland. However, each state retained its own currency, tying it to the other states at a fixed exchange rate. Britain seriously considered joining the union in 1869 under Gladstone's government, but drew back in the end. Interestingly, the coins used had one side in common, the other being used for a national symbol (just like the current euro). The absence, however, of a central bank led to abuses in Greece and Italy, with excessive issue of banknotes. The French found themselves coping with 50 types of coin which were all legal tender. The excessive flexibility in the system led to its collapse in 1926.

A similar union was the Scandinavian Currency Union, 1873–1920, formed by Norway, Denmark and Sweden. It benefited from a more stable political and economic environment. Volatility of exchange rates, following suspension of the gold standard in 1914, led to the collapse of the union in 1920.

Smaller Unions

Paul de Grauwe of the Catholic University of Leuven has claimed that 'Not a single monetary union in the past came about because of a recognition of economic benefits of the union. In all cases, the integration was driven by political objectives.'

This is perhaps too sweeping a statement. The political motives of the Latin Monetary Union were fairly weak, although the union was not a tight one, as we have seen.

Small unions of a kind have been formed with economics to the foreground. This applies to the Belgium–Luxembourg Union (1923) and the West African CFA franc zone, formed by former French colonies. These are, of course, relatively small countries, but the unions survive.

Looking at the large unions which have survived – Germany, Italy and the United States – a strong political union is clearly a key element, and many believe that this must also be the case in the end for EMU.

HISTORY OF STEPS TO EMU

The Werner Report

As early as 1962, the European Commission had started discussing proposals for a single currency as a way of binding the original six countries together. Little progress was made, however, until 1969, when Willy Brandt revived these original plans. The theme was taken up in the Werner Report of 1970, which proposed a move to a single currency by 1980. The report was approved by European heads of state in 1971, but the collapse of the Bretton Woods system in 1971/72 stopped developments in their track. The 'snake' was set up in 1972 to align the European currencies to the deutschmark, with an allowed fluctuation of ±2¼%. The snake did not work well, especially with the oil price explosion at the end of 1973. The UK joined in May 1972 and left six months later. France and Italy joined, but left twice. The next move was the European Monetary System (EMS).

European Monetary System

This was set up in March 1979 and had three elements:

- ❑ The Exchange Rate Mechanism (ERM)
- ❑ The European Currency Unit (ECU)
- ❑ The European Monetary Cooperation Fund.

The ERM was the successor to the snake. This time, two bands of fluctuation were allowed – the narrow band of ±2¼% and the wide band of ±6%. Target rates for each currency against the others were established (the 'parity grid') and periodic realignments were allowed for. If rates moved near to their limit, the central bank concerned was expected to defend the currency by buying it and, perhaps, also raising interest rates. Currencies could be borrowed from other central banks to enable it to do this. By 1992, of the twelve countries of the EU, Greece was not a member, the UK, Spain and Portugal were members at the wide band and the other eight were members at the narrow band.

The ecu was calculated from a weighted basket of all European currencies (not just those in the ERM). It produced a common unit of accountancy and was used for all EU statistics, some currency dealings, some cross-border public sector invoicing within Europe and as a denomination for some Treasury bills and bonds (government and corporate). Clearly, the idea was that this laid the basis for a genuine future currency. If all countries in the ERM could move in time to the narrow band on a stable basis, this would make the transition to a single currency easier.

The European Monetary Cooperation Fund was actually set up following the Werner Report, but was effectively dormant until the EMS. Each country in the EU deposited 20% of their gold and foreign currency reserves and received ecus in exchange. The funds were held at the BIS in Basle. This was the *official* ecu as opposed to the *private* ecu, as used for Treasury bills and bonds. This central fund was only to be used for transactions between EMS central banks and named monetary institutions. Central banks obliged to intervene in the markets because of ERM rules could draw on an unlimited credit within the system. Apart from this, it had little practical use during the life of the system.

Changes to the ERM

In September 1992, the growing belief that a realignment was due and that sterling and the lira were overvalued led to great turbulence. The UK and Italy left the ERM, while devaluations of the peseta, escudo and punt followed. Further turbulence returned in July 1993, with attacks on the French franc and other currencies. In early August, a decision was taken to widen the bands to ±15% (except for the deutschmark/guilder, which remained at ±2¼%). These were black days for the ideal of monetary union.

The Delors Plan

The ultimate aim for Europe was Economic and Monetary Union (EMU). A blueprint was drawn up in 1989 by central banks chaired by Jacques Delors, President of the European Commission, and thus called the 'Delors Plan'. This set up three stages towards EMU:

❏ All members in the ERM; no exchange controls; achievement of a single market in financial services
❏ Setting up the European System of Central Banks (ESCB)
❏ Locked exchange rates; monetary policy controlled by ESCB; eventually, a single currency.

The Maastricht Treaty

This blueprint was broadly endorsed by the Madrid EC Summit in mid-1989, and mid-1990 was set as the starting date for Stage 1. The matter was further discussed at the inter-governmental conference which began in December 1990, and prepared for a treaty to be drawn up at Maastricht in December 1991. The Maastricht summit laid down a timetable for European Monetary Union as follows:

❏ End 1996, a decision on a possible EMU in 1997 if a minimum of seven nations could meet the convergence conditions (described later).
❏ By 1999, there would be EMU in any case if two nations were able to meet the convergence conditions.
❏ A European Central Bank to be set up six months prior to EMU, but a body called the 'European Monetary Institute' (EMI) to coordinate policies prior to setting up the Central Bank, and to be set up in 1994.
❏ Special protocols allowed the UK to opt out of a final move to a single currency, and Denmark to hold a referendum in June 1992.
❏ The convergence conditions were:
   a) Inflation rate within $1\frac{1}{2}\%$ of the best three nations.
   b) Long-term interest rates within 2% of the average of the lowest three nations.
   c) Currency within the $2\frac{1}{4}\%$ ERM band, and no devaluation in the previous two years.
   d) Budget deficit to GDP ratio not exceeding 3% and national debt not exceeding 60% of GDP.

The Danish referendum in June 1992 rejected the Maastricht Treaty by a narrow majority. Nevertheless, the other states decided to continue with the process of having the Treaty accepted by their parliaments. A French referendum in September 1992 narrowly voted in favour and the German parliament passed it in December, although this was challenged by the German Constitutional Court. Finally, after concessions, Denmark accepted Maastricht in a new referendum in May 1993.

The new European Monetary Institute (EMI) started operations in January 1994, located in Frankfurt. Sweden, Finland and Austria joined the Community on 1 January, 1995, and Austria joined the ERM. Later, Finland joined, Italy rejoined in November 1996, and Greece joined in early 1998.

The EMI laid down firmer plans for monetary union in November 1995:

1 January 1999	Start of monetary union, with locked exchange rates.
1 January 2002	Introduction of new notes and coins.
1 July 2002	The new currency to be legal tender.

The December Madrid meeting decided to call the new currency the 'euro' (not the ecu). The rates to be locked on 1 January, 1999, were decided at a meeting in May 1998, which also decided which countries would join the monetary union.

EMU Begins

The countries joining should have met the Maastricht conditions described above. Embarrassingly, Belgium and Italy, key candidates, had a national debt/GDP ratio well in excess of 100%. The budget deficit/GDP ratio of 3% was based on 1997 figures. Many countries used what could only be called 'creative accounting' to come below the 3% level. Such was the strong political will to have EMU, however, that these problems were ignored, and the system began as planned in January 1999 with eleven members – Austria, Belgium, Finland, France, Germany, Ireland, Italy, Luxembourg, Netherlands, Portugal and Spain. This left Greece, Sweden, the UK and Denmark outside. Later, Greece joined EMU making the eleven into twelve.

The permanently fixed rates for the euro against euro area currencies are shown in Table 10.1.

Table 10.1　*Euro rates against euro area currencies*

Country		€	Country		€
Austria	Sch	13.7603	Ireland	I£	0.787564
Belgium/Lux	BFr/LFr	40.3399	Italy	L	1936.27
Finland	FM	5.94573	Netherlands	Fl	2.20371
France	FFr	6.55957	Portugal	Es	200.482
Germany	DM	1.95583	Spain	Pta	166.386

As the rate for, say, the French franc and the euro, and also the Italian lira and the euro, are fixed, it follows that one multiplication gives us a fixed franc/lira rate, and so on.

No notes and coins were due until January 2002, but the euro was used for domestic bonds and eurobonds, as well as interbank transactions. It was also used for cheques or credit cards or any transaction where notes and coins are not used. Control of interest rates and monetary policy were in the hands of the new European Central Bank, which we described earlier.

Maastricht laid down a target budget deficit/GDP ratio of 3%, but said nothing about variations once EMU had started. This is covered by the so-called 'Stability and Growth Pact'. The position of the ERM now that EMU has started is 'ERM II'. We discuss both these subjects now.

Stability and Growth Pact

Further changes to the European Union were discussed at Amsterdam in June 1997, leading to a new treaty which became law in May 1999. Whilst at Amsterdam, heads of government discussed the question of control over excessive budget deficits once EMU had started. They agreed on a common code of fiscal conduct to uphold discipline in the management of government finances. Budgets are normally to be kept close to either a balance or small surplus. This should ensure that even in recession the maximum deficit/GDP ratio can be kept to 3%. Sound government finances are regarded as an indispensable requisite for macroeconomic stability. This common code is known as the 'Stability and Growth Pact'.

Technically, all countries in the EU are part of this pact, not just the twelve of EMU. All countries submit their forward budgetary plans to the Ecofin Council. This should enable early warning to be given of any slippage. Deficits in excess of 3% are only permitted in exceptional circumstances, such as a fall in GDP in excess of 2%.

The problem of sanctions for those who break the rules caused much argument, with the Germans wanting much tougher action than most other countries. It was decided that the Ecofin Council will formulate recommendations for correction, and measures must be taken within four months. The decision is taken by qualified majority, and the Ecofin Council could impose sanctions – a non-interest bearing deposit which might be converted later into a fine if effective action is not taken.

In April 1999, we saw the ECB issue a sharp warning that many governments risked breaking the budget limits agreed, and that safety margins were not sufficient.

Following this warning, we saw the pact in action in May 1999. Italy, whose forecast deficit was 2.0%, asked permission to raise this to 2.4%. Weak growth and high unemployment had led to this position. GDP was due to grow 1.5% in 1999. The Ecofin Council agreed to Italy's request, and many saw this as an ominous sign for the future. The euro then fell sharply on the forex markets.

Worse was to follow. Ironically, Germany, which had been so keen on tough action, found itself facing a formal warning for breaking the pact in February 2000. With the usual EU compromise, Germany said it would 'endeavour' to balance its budget by 2004. Otmar Issing, chief economist of the ECB, said 'if all other European states want the same treatment in future, the early warning system is useless'.

Then, in June 2002, Ecofin finance ministers criticised France for not balancing the budget. However, French finance minister, François Mer, refused to say that the country would be in balance by 2004, although they had promised to do so at the Barcelona Summit in March. Pressed again at the Seville Summit in June 2002, France agreed (reluctantly) to bring its budget 'close to balance' by 2004. Then, later in June 2002, Portugal admitted that its budget deficit as a percentage of GDP will probably be 3.9%, well above the so-called limit of 3%. In September 2002, the European Commission put off the deadline for members to balance their books to 2006 once it became clear that Germany, too, would breach the 3% limit. Jacques Chirac was reported as telling his finance minister to 'ignore the Stability Pact'; in October, Romano Prodi, the president of the Commission, described the Stability Pact as 'stupid' because the decisions made were too rigid.

Is the Stability and Growth Pact dead?

ERM II

On 1 September, 1998, the Governing Council and the Executive Board of the Eurosystem of Central Banks agreed on a text for the successor to the ERM. The Maastricht Treaty had had a condition that countries joining EMU had to have had a two year period in the ERM at the narrow band. The replacement of the narrow band by ±15% had led to a dispute. Most governments believe that this is still a prior requirement. This view is opposed by the UK, which argues that it has been overtaken by events. As departing from the ERM was part of a grave financial crisis in the UK, no government wants to be the one to suggest rejoining!

Nevertheless, what is called 'ERM II' has now been defined. The main change is that participating countries agree to maintain their currencies within a band of an agreed rate against the euro. The twelve central banks will intervene, if necessary, to support a currency, and loans are available to the participating countries from the ECB. These loans can only be drawn after first drawing on the country's own reserves. The loans are repayable in three months and subject to a ceiling on cumulative borrowings.

The bad news for the UK is that Denmark and Greece accepted the new rules and joined ERM II. Denmark's krona is being held within a 2¼% band and Greece's drachma was held within a ±15% band prior to joining EMU fully.

Key speeches by two ECB executive board members in March 2002, aimed at prospective new EU members, again stressed that a minimum period of at least two years in ERM II was a precondition for joining EMU.

Next Members?

Waiting in the wings to join the EU in 2004, and some time later EMU, are the Czech Republic, Estonia, Hungary, Latvia, Lithuania, Malta, Poland, Slovakia and Slovenia. There is also Cyprus, but facing a difficult political problem – is this all Cyprus or just the Greek-speaking area?

However, before all these countries can be admitted, we need a new deal on the Common Agricultural Policy, the budget, spending on poorer regions and an overhaul of the voting/decision-making process. Regarding the CAP, we must remember that many of these countries are farm intensive.

To join the EU itself, countries must meet all the rules and obligations of membership. The document recording these runs to 80,000 pages – banking laws, competition policy, state aid, veterinary inspection standards and so on. They also need efficiency in public administration to enforce the rules.

With the steps the countries themselves have to take, and the decisions to be taken by the EU on topics like the CAP and the voting process, the way forward will not be easy.

EMU Statistics

Some interesting statistics are shown in Table 10.2.

We can see that while the euro area is a very large trading block, it is still some way behind the United States, if bigger than Japan. The US has a bigger share of world GDP and a smaller public sector.

We see the euro area as having higher unemployment (9.9% as against 4.2%).

European companies (and Japanese) have tended to turn to bank loans for finance, as opposed to the US, where the capital markets are clearly much bigger.

Within the euro area itself, the market is dominated by Germany, France and Italy, who account for 72% of the total GDP. Germany alone accounts for 32%.

However, the IMF forecast for growth in 2002 is 2.2% for the US, 1.7% for the UK and only 0.9% for the euro area.

Table 10.2   *Key characteristics of the euro area (including Greece)*

	Reporting Period	Unit	Euro Area	United States	Japan
Population	2000	m	302	272	127
GDP (share of world GDP)	1999	%	16.2	21.9	7.6
Unemployment (% of labour force)	1999	%	9.9	4.2	4.7
General government expenditure	1999	% of GDP	49.0	31.9	39.9
Bank deposits	1999	% of GDP	80.0	41.0	134.5
Domestic debt securities	1999	% of GDP	89.8	178.0	157.9
Stock market capitalisation	1999	% of GDP	66.1	128.7	73.9

Source: *ECB Monthly Bulletin,* January 2001.

Payment Systems

The official interbank payments system for the euro is TARGET (Trans-European Automated Real Time Gross Settlement Express Transfer). After some controversy, access to TARGET is open to national central banks and participants in Real Time

Gross Settlement (RTGS) systems in non-euro area member states. These non-euro central banks must deposit a sum of money with the Eurosystem by 8.00 a.m. each day (for example, €3 billion for the Bank of England). This is to ensure the availability of intraday liquidity.

In addition to TARGET, there is a euro clearing system available through the Paris-based European Banking Association (EBA). It is, however, not RTGS but end of day netting (and thus cheaper).

There are also the individual national systems for clearing of these high value euro-based payments – EIL-2V and EAF2 in Germany, TBF in Francs and CHAPS-Euro in the UK. It is a sign of the huge international banking market in London that, by June 2002, 17% of TARGET volume was transfers from CHAPS-Euro, although the UK is not in EMU.

EMU – The Benefits

Having looked at the history and all the facts and figures, we are still left with the basic question 'why?'. What are the objectives of EMU? What advantages should accrue?

These issues split naturally into *economic* issues and *political* issues. Let us begin with economics.

One key argument is that the use of a single currency in twelve countries with a population of 292m will lead to more transparency of prices, and make it much more difficult to sell goods at a higher price in the Netherlands than, say, Italy.

Many studies have drawn attention to the disparity in motor car prices. Pre-tax differentials exceed 20%. A Bayerishe Landesbank study has shown that consumer prices in Austria and Finland are about 11% higher than those in Germany, France, Belgium and Portugal. On the other hand, prices in the Netherlands, Italy and Ireland are 8% lower than in those countries, and prices in Spain 11% lower.

A KPMG survey on pricing policy in March 1999 claimed that there was great scope for more uniformity of prices. Price variations in 31 standard consumer goods dwarfed any that could be explained by sales taxes and duties.

A Dresdner Kleinwort Benson survey published in June 1999 said that price convergence had already begun to put profits under strain. They pointed out that Europe's prices were much higher than those in the US in general retail, food retail and electronic and electrical equipment. They studied retail prices in nine principal European cities, and believed that corporate profits would be affected in as little as two to three years. (To be fair, there is little sign of this.)

If these views are correct, then greater price competition will lead to lower prices and more trade. With no worries about currency movements, it will be easier for manufacturers to move production to cheaper areas. There may be pressure in high cost countries for lower taxation and more flexible labour markets.

All the above are part of a wider argument that a single currency will make the euro area more of a genuine single market. There is supposed to have been a single market since January 1993. In many areas, especially finance, this is not so. How many cross-border life assurance policies are sold? Accountancy laws differ widely, cross-border banking and securities dealings are subject to varying local rules. Taxation is by no means uniform. With the growth of multinationals and increasing staff transfers, the need for pension reform is urgent, but it is not happening. In June 1999, the Spanish bank BSCH wanted to buy 40% of a Portuguese financial services group, Champalimaud. The Portuguese government moved immediately to block it. What happened to the single market? As if to confirm all this, a European Commission report, in August 2002, admitted that the single market was by no means a reality and that competing legal and regulatory frameworks pose almost insurmountable problems. Then, on 7 January 2003, the Internal Market Commissioner, Frits Bolkestein, complained that national laws and customs still prevent the running of a single market, and admitted that they are fighting more than 1500 legal actions against EU member states which are ignoring agreed legislation. One of the major causes of the problems is mutual distrust between member states of each others' laws, and a continuing protection of domestic business against competition.

So far, the introduction of the euro itself has not produced any new note of urgency. Another measure – the long-awaited European company statute needed to allow companies to incorporate under a single European structure of law – had reached a draft prospectus by the autumn of 2002, but faced many objections.

A more obvious example of the benefit of the introduction of a single currency is the saving to importers and exporters of buying/selling foreign currency. We saw in our foreign exchange chapter (Chapter 8) that there are spreads to be paid on spot and forward deals, and perhaps premiums if options are chosen. Not only is useful money now saved, but it is easier to look at the euro area as a single area. In particular, it streamlines European Treasury operations. Cash can be managed on a pan-European basis, saving currency and interest rate spreads and leading to greater efficiency.

Another area of cost saving for corporates is a reduction in the cost of capital. We know from the statistics that Europe has relied far more on bank finance than the US, which uses capital markets much more. In Germany, for instance, 40% of bond issues are public sector bonds. If Pfandbriefe (used for loans to local authorities) are included, the figure is nearer 70%. Prior to the introduction of the euro, fund managers and investors all over Europe were constrained by foreign exchange risk (and sometimes regulations) when it came to cross-border purchases. These constraints have now gone. If the euro area produces more of a single market in bonds and equities, then raising finance should be cheaper, to the benefit of the companies concerned.

There are also signs of a switch out of government paper into higher-yielding corporate paper, and that corporates are already using the bond markets more as a source of regular finance. We have seen this from issues by companies like Pirelli, Fiat, Lafarge and Telefonica. In October 2002, the ECB reported that the use of corporate debt, as opposed to equity or bank loans, had risen from 20% to 40%. This was put down to more foreign investors, greater liquidity and more integrated systems of trading. Europe is also getting more sophisticated, especially in the sphere of securitisation of assets, which we discussed in Chapter 6.

Equities are much less of a homogeneous market. We are, however, seeing the first moves to pan-European equity exchanges, which we described in Chapter 7. In addition, cross-border investment is on the move in equities as well as bonds. It is being driven by demographic factors (pensions) and, of course, the euro. In many ways, retail investors are leading the way here. Privatisation is also giving a fillip, with France's launch of Crédit Lyonnais followed by Ireland's success with its telecommunications authority. As independent shareholders increase, so will the frustration with rules that inhibit hostile takeovers, with the governments retaining a core shareholding ('noyaux durs') and the cosy German house bank system.

There is a common view that pension fund managers and others would stop looking at countries and look at market sector instead. However, we need to be cautious here. A study by the University of Liège, in Belgium, found that only four market sectors had high correlation across Europe – oils, pharmaceuticals, financials and consumer brands.

Of course, for fund managers there is still a basic question – what is Europe? There is the Europe of the twelve, the Europe of the fifteen and then Europe including Switzerland. Here is a country with two of Europe's biggest drug stocks (Novartis, Roche), two huge banks (Crédit Suisse and UBS), two of the world's biggest insurers (Swiss Re and Zurich Financial Services) and the world's biggest food company (Nestlé) – and it isn't even in the EU!

Interestingly, as well as bonds and equities, the syndicated loan market has also expanded in the euro area. We are seeing major acquisitions funded in the first place by a syndicated loan (for speed and confidentiality). Later it may be replaced by a bond issue. There has been Olivetti's bold and successful bid for Telecom Italia, Repsol's bid for YPF Argentina and Mannesman's bid for Omnitel and Infostrada from Olivetti – all financed by large loans.

In the *Financial Times* of 14 June, 1999, Graham Bishop, of Salomon Smith Barney, was quoted as saying 'companies all over Europe are merging and restructuring, and this is largely due to the effects of the single currency.'

Judged strictly as an economic venture, EMU will be a success if, over the coming years, we see countries benefiting from growing trade and investment, declining unemployment and low inflation.

All the above are *economic* benefits, but what of the *political* angle?

There are two key points here. One is the view that EMU will never work without tighter political union, whether we like it or not. The other is that political union is not merely necessary for EMU, but desirable in its own right.

On the first point, the argument is that there can never be a free market and full competition if the same goods can be at different prices in different countries purely due to value added tax.

Equally, how can there be full and fair cross-border competition between companies if some pay more tax than others? Payment of tax, in turn, depends on the definition of profit, which, to be fair, needs common accountancy principles. Finally, surely a company can be registered in 'Europe' rather than in one of the countries of the twelve?

Common taxes, common accountancy standards, common law – all this is very close to a political union.

Those who agree with the founders, like Schuman, Monnet, Spaak and so on, argue that political union is desirable if war is to be avoided and a single European entity is to bring justice and peace.

The Counter Arguments

Having looked at the benefits of EMU and its political implications, there are naturally those whose views are different.

Perhaps the most common counter-argument relates to the 'one size fits all' implication of the ECB, with its single interest rate and exchange rate. The fact that countries are at different phases in the economic cycle means that some may need high interest rates at the same time that others need lower ones. We had a perfect example of this as EMU started. Italy and Germany were growing GDP at 1.5%, while Spain and Portugal were growing at 3% and Ireland at a massive 7%. Irish interest rates prior to EMU were 6% and then fell to 2½% on entry with a later rise to 3%. Inflation took off and soon reached 7%, with little the Irish government could do about it. Other countries, on the other hand, might wish to stimulate the economy to increase growth. By the autumn of 2002, things were no better, with inflation in Ireland, Spain and Portugal in a range of 3% to 6%, and in Germany only 0.8%. The then ECB rate of 3.75% was far too high for Germany.

One response to this would be to change fiscal policy. However, this is limited by the Stability and Growth Pact. If a country is in recession, but interest rates are going up in EMU because others are in a boom, it could normally stimulate the economy by lower taxes and high government spending – but it no longer has the right to do this except within defined limits.

Ireland has the opposite problem – it should curb growth with higher taxes, but agreements with trade unions make this difficult. How is it to prevent rampant inflation in the euro locally?

Those in recession when interest rates are high may find that unemployment rises to socially unacceptable levels.

One result of all this is that the Stability and Growth Pact is coming under immense strain, as we have already reported.

In the *Times* of 8 December 2002, the economist Roger Bootle examined the progress of convergence in Europe. On unemployment, he found that the average difference between the rates in the twelve countries and the euro zone average was 3% higher than in 1990. France and Germany have unemployment rates of 9% and

10%, yet the Netherlands, Ireland and Portugal have rates between 2% and 5%.

On inflation there has been more convergence. In 1992, the average difference between member rates and the euro zone average was 2.5%, and in 2002, it was down to 1%. However, Germany and Belgium have inflation rates around 1%, while Ireland, Greece, Portugal and the Netherlands have rates around 4%.

Although the whole euro zone has the same interest rate, there is still the question of real interest rates due to varying inflation. In 1998, all countries except Greece and Portugal had much the same real interest rates. In 2002, however, Greece, Ireland, Portugal and the Netherlands actually had negative real interest rates. These countries need a higher nominal rate to combat inflation, but, of course, can't have one. Low inflation countries, like Germany and Belgium, have the highest real interest rates due to low inflation, but would like lower nominal rates to stimulate the economy!

Roger Bootle concludes that the system will move to equilibrium in the end as Germany, for example, becomes more competitive and the negative real interest rate countries will become less competitive.

If one state is in recession and one experiencing strong growth, one response is for labour to move from one to the other. Economists claim that a monetary union needs high labour mobility. After all, the US is a monetary union. Texas may be suffering where New England is prospering. This is where the euro area faces severe problems. The US has high labour mobility, the euro area very poor mobility. Of the 370 million people in the EU as a whole, only 5.5 million live and work in another country. In Germany, even to move from one federal state to another is a major decision. There is a fundamental and dangerous weakness here.

Another problem from 'one size fits all' is that different states react differently to changes in interest rates and exchange rates. In Ireland, for example, 80% of people own their homes, and variable rate mortgages are the most common. An interest rate increase has much more effect on consumers than in, say, Germany.

Looking at exchange rate changes, exports outside the euro area are 14% of the German economy but 24% in Belgium and Finland and 44% in Ireland.

To the above can be added what some people see as the weaknesses of the ECB and the Eurosystem, to which we referred earlier – its lack of accountability or any kind of control; the division of managing the currency from supervision; the possible struggle between the Executive Board and the Central Bank governors who could outvote them; the absence of a role for a 'lender of last resort' in the event of a crisis.

One of the key benefits which is claimed for EMU is the transparency of prices, which will lead to growing competition, higher efficiency and lower prices. Critics, however, point to the effect of varying VAT rates and, in particular, transport costs. Goods made in Spain which have higher transport costs will certainly not sell for the same price in Finland as they do in, say, Spain and Portugal.

The KPMG survey on pricing policy, to which we referred earlier, gives a perhaps extreme example, in the case of salt. Salt in Portugal is twelve times as expensive as it is in Italy, and three times as expensive as it is in the Netherlands.

Local production is small, forcing it to import. On the other hand, the Dutch produce more than they consume. The position is exacerbated by the fact that the Portuguese have the highest salt intake in Europe, which does raise the question of the effect on price due to varying international tastes.

In practice, the first few years of EMU have seen precious little sign of transparency of prices. When the twelve countries moved to the use of the euro and the dropping of domestic currencies in January 2002, it was hoped that the tendency to round up might be constrained by the transparency argument. In fact, a EuroStat study found record increases in the price of twenty categories of goods in the first three months of 2002. These increases ranged from 0.4% to as much as 14.3%.

There are great hopes for the euro area as a powerful, efficient, single market competing with the US and Japan. Many, however, point to severe weaknesses in Europe which are not currently being tackled.

One is high labour costs due to social security costs borne by employers. A Morgan Stanley Dean Witter study estimates social costs at 28% of hourly compensation in the US, and 45% in Germany. The hourly compensation in manufacturing in the euro area they estimate at 12% higher than the US. Another study shows Europe well behind the US in the use of IT, Western Europe spending 2.26% of GDP on IT as opposed to 4.08% in the US; white collar workers in the US having 103 personal computers per 100 workers as opposed to 52 in Western Europe.

Labour laws are much more inflexible in Europe than the US. In the latter, it is much easier to restructure and lay workers off. One's first humane reaction may be to see this as a bad thing, until it is realised that the alternative may be for everyone to lose their jobs as the firm is put out of business by global competition. It is much harder to sack people in the euro area than in the US, and yet the euro area has unemployment at 9.9% of the labour force, and the US 4.2%. In addition, as we saw from Table 10.2, government expenditure in the euro area is 49.0% of GDP and only 31.9% in the US. High government expenditure means high taxes. What makes things worse is that Europe is doing very little to change things. Italy is having the greatest difficulty in facing up to its pension problem, and the French government has implemented a 35 hour week. Unemployment in Germany is up to 4 million and growth in 2001 and 2002 of only 1%.

On the question of growing efficiency in capital markets due to the single currency, there is little doubt that this will take place, and that it has already started.

Even here, there are some reservations. The cross-border government bond markets are no longer affected by forex risk, but there is still the question of liquidity. Finland, for example, has a far better debt/GDP ratio than Belgium, and a better credit rating, but the spread of its bonds over Germany's are 24 basis points – the same as Belgium. This is simply due to lack of liquidity as Finland issues fewer bonds. It's a reminder that there's more to bond prices than foreign exchange and credit rating.

In the equity markets, the 'pan-European' stock exchange based in London and Frankfurt faced the massive problems outlined in Chapter 7 regarding trading systems, indices and regulation, and the plan was abandoned.

Many of the problems above will be worsened by enlargement. Presumably most of these countries hope that, having joined the EU, they will qualify in time for EMU; and perhaps the missing three will also join. The euro area of twelve countries is one thing, the euro area of, say, 25 might be another. There will be stalemate without majority voting, now a very contentious issue. If 'one size fits all' is a problem for the twelve countries, it will surely be much worse when we embrace Central and Eastern Europe and the Baltic States. Why stop there, anyway? Why are the former republics of the Soviet Union not considered? In addition, the exclusion of Turkey is purely political.

One assumes that the weaknesses in the single market, especially in finance, which we discussed earlier, will finally be resolved, but it does seem to be taking a long time. We have commented on the Portuguese government's attempt to block a Spanish bank taking a 40% holding in a local financial company. This is totally contrary to EU rules. On 12 July, 1999, the European Commission started a case against Spain and Italy in the European Court of Justice over their refusal to recognise engineers, architects and doctors from other countries.

In retail banking, there is a different mentality from wholesale. 'Savings regulations and fiscal laws continue to be efficient barriers to multinational retail banking activity' says Daniel Bouton, Chairman of Société Générale.

In the worst case, we might see the ECB hitting severe problems running euro monetary policy, with the euro weakening severely against other currencies. (It has, of course, been relatively weak ever since EMU started.) Unemployment has risen due to structural rigidities and government deficit levels have climbed. The enlargement issue may then be avoided indefinitely. Political pressure could build for the abandonment of EMU itself.

In an interview in late May 2002, Sir Alan Walters (former economic adviser to both Edward Heath and Margaret Thatcher) predicted that the euro would break up 'in five years' due to various economic and political pressures.

Even in this worst case scenario, however, it's difficult to see how EMU could be abandoned. Once countries have given up their currencies, including notes and coins, the effort to change back would be huge, even if all the legal problems could be solved. In the end, it may be that what holds EMU together and enables it to solve its problems is the fact that (in the famous words of Margaret Thatcher) it's TINA – There Is No Alternative!

Let us finish this particular discussion by looking at the words of that much-maligned thinker, Niccolò Machiavelli, in his work 'The Prince'. Referring to the introduction of something entirely new, he comments:

> '... there is nothing more difficult to take in hand, more perilous to conduct, or more uncertain in its success than to take the lead in the introduction of a new order of things. The reason is that the innovator has for enemies all those who have done well under the old conditions, and lukewarm defenders in

those who only may do well in the new. This coolness arises partly from fear of the opponents who have the laws on their side, and partly from the incredulity of men, who do not readily believe in new things until they have had a long experience of them. Thus it happens that whenever those who are hostile have the opportunity to attack they do it like partisans; whilst the others defend lukewarmly, in such wise that the prince is endangered along with them.'

The UK Position

The major EU economy absent from EMU is, of course, the United Kingdom. We shall finish by looking briefly at the arguments raging for and against.

The general arguments for joining EMU can be summarised as:

❑ Stability of the exchange rate.
❑ Lower foreign investment in the UK if outside. In recent years, 40% of foreign direct investment in Europe has come to the UK.
❑ The UK will progressively have far less influence on monetary and economic policy in Europe if outside. Frankfurt will gain, the City of London will lose. The ECB is already in Frankfurt, the LIFFE exchange has lost business to EUREX and EURIBOR is used as the reference rate, not EUROLIBOR.
❑ There will be savings on foreign exchange transactions.
❑ The UK is too small an economy to stay outside – it would gradually lose business and influence.
❑ As a matter of philosophy, the UK should join in this exciting historic venture and take its full place in Europe.
❑ The fear of federalism and political integration is exaggerated because in practice it will never happen.

Against this, the arguments range as follows:

❑ Stability of the exchange rate will only apply in the euro area. The UK will still have instability against the dollar, the yen and the Swiss franc.
❑ Decisions on foreign investment are not only influenced by currency risk – the UK has low labour costs, flexible labour laws and lower taxes than most of the euro area.
❑ The UK's GDP would only be 14% of the GDP of the euro area if it joined, and that is the extent of our probable influence – one sixth. Most currency transactions in London are not sterling anyway. LIFFE has already captured most of the derivatives business in short-term euro interest rates. London has 31% of world forex trading and Frankfurt only 5%. London trades 70% of the international bond market and has a far bigger OTC derivatives

market than the rest of the euro area. London has a pool of skilled labour, lower social taxes, the infrastructure of accountants and lawyers and the use of English as a language.

❏ Savings on foreign exchange transactions are useful but probably only ½% of GDP.

❏ The UK is small, but big enough to survive outside – look at Switzerland. 'One size fits all' would be a major problem with a business cycle out of line with France and Germany and the highest ratio of outstanding variable rate mortgage debt to GDP in Europe.

❏ The great new historic venture is not likely to succeed.

❏ EMU needs political integration to work properly.

The typical British attitude (rightly or wrongly) is summarised in the following quotation:

'We see nothing but good and hope in a richer, freer, more contented European commonality. But we have our own dream and our own task. We are with Europe, but not of it. We are linked, but not compromised. We are interested and associated, but not absorbed.'

This was written by Winston Churchill in an American periodical in 1930. In spite of the huge decline in British influence and power since then, it's probably still a fair summary of the attitude of many in the UK today.

SUMMARY

The origins of the European Union as it is today lie in the *European Coal and Steel Community* in 1952, a pooling of coal and steel resources in Belgium, France, Italy, Luxembourg, the Netherlands and West Germany. These six countries signed the *Treaty of Rome* in 1957 and began the concept of a common market and the *European Economic Community*. Its early institutions included the *Council of Ministers*, the *European Commission*, the *European Parliament* and the *European Court of Justice*. The motives were economic and political.

Enlargement of membership came later with the addition of Denmark, Ireland and the UK in 1973, Greece in 1981, Spain and Portugal in 1986 and Austria, Finland and Sweden in 1995.

In 1974, the periodic meeting of heads of state became the *European Council*. Today it meets twice per year, with the presidency rotating six monthly between the various states.

The *Single European Act* of 1987 (which began in January 1993) aimed to eliminate all final barriers to trade within Europe, and to establish a genuinely efficient and competitive single market.

The European Economic Community (EEC) had already been shortened to *European Community* (EC). With the Single European Act it became the *European Union* (EU).

The first moves to a single currency and monetary union were suggested in the *Werner Report* of 1970, proposing a single currency by 1980. Upheaval in the 1970s (the collapse of Bretton Woods and oil price inflation) prevented any progress.

The next move was the *European Monetary System* in 1979. This set up the use of the ecu as a common unit of accountancy, and also the *Exchange Rate Mechanism* (ERM) tying currencies to bands around a target rate against other currencies. The bands were ±2¼% or ±6%. By the end of 1990, eleven of Europe's twelve countries were members.

Attacks on currencies in the ERM in 1992 and 1993 led to a revision of the band to ±15% (except for the guilder/deutschemark rate, remaining at ±2¼%).

In 1989, a report by Jacques Delors, the Commission president, set out steps towards economic and monetary union. A treaty at *Maastricht* laid down convergence conditions, the setting up of a *European Monetary Institute* (EMI) in 1994 to precede the *European Central Bank* and the possibility of *Economic and Monetary Union* (EMU) beginning in 1999. It was later decided to call the new currency the '*euro*'.

Following detailed plans laid down by the EMI, economic and monetary union began on 1 January, 1999.

Initially, the euro was used for interbank and other wholesale purposes, with notes and coins following on 1 January, 2002. In the meantime, the relevant currencies were locked together in fixed exchange rates.

Eleven countries joined the new system – Austria, Belgium, Finland, France, Ireland, Italy, Germany, Luxembourg, the Netherlands, Portugal and Spain. Denmark, Greece, Sweden and the United Kingdom remained outside. (Greece joined later and so EMU now covers twelve countries.)

The European Central Bank (ECB) began operations in June 1998. It has six executive members who form the *Executive Board*. They meet with the twelve governors of the member states to form the *Governing Council*. This grouping of the ECB together with the twelve governors is usually called the *European System of Central Banks* (ESCB). However, the ECB has pointed out that legally this includes the four governors of the opt-outs, even though they play no part. It prefers to use the name *Eurosystem*.

To prevent excessive budget deficits, there is a *Stability and Growth Pact*, which limits budget deficits to a maximum of 3% in relation to GDP.

Those countries wishing to join EMU are expected to have spent two years in the successor to the ERM, known as *ERM II*. Denmark has joined this.

The EMU area has a population of 302 million people, as against 272 million in the United States, and it accounts for 16.2% of world GDP, as against the US which accounts for 21.9%.

The new interbank payment and settlement system for the euro is *TARGET*.

The objective of EMU is to produce a range of benefits – price transparency leading to more competition; a logical completion to the move towards a single competitive market; a saving in foreign currency transactions; a reduction of the cost of capital through more efficient capital markets – bonds, equities and derivatives. In addition, there is the desire for more political integration to make EMU work better and to produce a stronger and more peaceful Europe.

Critics, however, point to the problems of a 'one size fits all' policy in interest rates and currencies; the strains in fiscal policy that will emerge; the lack of labour mobility; some weaknesses in the structure of the ECB; the fact that full price transparency will not exist due to VAT and transport costs and weakness in Europe due to high social costs, inflexible labour markets and a large public sector. These problems will be worsened by enlargement of the euro area.

The major EU country not in EMU is the United Kingdom.

Those in the UK who wish to join want to continue to encourage foreign investment in the UK; to enjoy lower forex costs; to have greater stability of the currency; and believe that the UK outside would lose influence and the City of London lose ground to Frankfurt.

Others believe that the threat to foreign investment is exaggerated; that the lower forex costs are modest compared to the total picture; that there will still be currency instability against the dollar, yen and Swiss franc and believe that the London dominance in financial markets will not be affected. Finally, they believe the UK will suffer from the 'one size fits all' policy and fear greater political integration.

Derivative Products

11 Traded Options

12 Financial Futures

13 Other Derivative Products

11 Traded Options

DERIVATIVE PRODUCTS

Probably the fastest growing sector of the financial markets today is that of what are called *derivative products*. They are so called because they derive from another product. The buying of $1m for sterling is the product. The option to buy $1m for sterling later at a price we agree today is the derived product. Borrowing $1m at floating rate for 5 years is the product. A bank offering (for a fee) to compensate the borrower should rates rise above a given level in the next 5 years is the derived product – and so on.

In currency rates, interest rates, bonds, equities and equity indices there is volatility. Where there is volatility, there are those who believe they know what the next price movement is and back their judgement with money. We call them *speculators*. There are those who will lose money from a given price movement and seek to protect themselves from this. We call them *hedgers*. Both will use the derivative markets for this purpose. The interesting paradox is that one is using them to take risks and the other to reduce risks. Finally, there are those who perceive pricing anomalies and seek to exploit this. They are the *arbitrageurs*.

Thus, the three types of professional users of derivative products are:

❑ Speculators
❑ Hedgers
❑ Arbitrageurs.

Additionally, derivatives are being increasingly packaged with retail banking products to provide, for example, fixed rate mortgages or guaranteed investment funds.

Speculators are easy enough to understand but, before we look at hedgers and arbitrageurs, it will be as well to explain one of the derivative products first.

The two key products are *Options* and *Futures*. If readers can obtain a good working knowledge of these products, they are well placed to understand others (FRAs, Swaps, Caps) since they are simply variations on the options and futures themes.

This chapter will discuss options, Chapter 12 covers futures and Chapter 13 the remaining derivative products.

One last point. In Chapter 8, we mentioned that currency options could be purchased on a trading exchange or OTC, that is, direct with a bank or trader. While this was mentioned in the context of currency options, it is generally true that there are exchanges for traded options and financial futures but that these products can also be purchased OTC.

The advantage of a trading exchange is that there is plenty of trading liquidity, there are competing traders to ensure good prices, and there is the implicit protection against default provided by a body called the *Clearing House*. The disadvantage is that the products are standardised and may not suit the user's exact requirements. To take an example that we've already met, the cable contract on the Chicago Mercantile Exchange is based on multiples of £62,500. This means that if the amount required to be bought or sold for dollars is £75,000, then the product offered is not an exact fit.

The big advantage of OTC dealing is its flexibility. The product offered to the users can be tailored to their exact needs. On an exchange, however, it may be possible to 'trade' the product later – that is, sell it back to the exchange. Sometimes OTC products cannot be traded or, if they can, the user is very much in the hands of the seller for a price. This market is often accused of a lack of liquidity when it comes to trading even standardised products at a later stage. Finally, the user must consider the risk of default. If the seller is Deutsche Bank or UBS, we can be quite happy, but the US house Drexel Burnham Lambert crashed in February 1990 and defaulted on any OTC products outstanding. On the other hand, when Baring Bros defaulted on their obligations at the Singapore Monetary Exchange (SIMEX), no counterparties lost any money due to the operation of the clearing house.

In an effort to counteract the flexibility of OTC, some exchanges have introduced more flexible contacts themselves. In 1995, the Philadelphia Exchange introduced the possibility of tailored exercise prices and expiry dates. Similar moves have followed from other exchanges.

Let us turn now to the subject of options.

TRADED OPTIONS: EQUITIES

Calls and Puts

Traded options are standardised options which grant the buyer the right (but *not* the obligation) to buy or sell financial instruments at standard prices and dates in the future. A premium is charged for this right, and is usually paid when the option is bought.

Let us take a simple example. Suppose we look at a hypothetical UK company, XYZ Ltd, and the share price is £1.86. We may be optimistic and believe that the price may well rise to, say, £2.10 in the next 3 months. The option to *buy* a given quantity of XYZ Ltd shares at £1.86 in the next 3 months is very attractive. If we are right and the price goes to £2.10, we can use the option to buy the given quantity of shares at £1.86 and sell them again in the conventional way at £2.10. If we are wrong and the price falls or remains constant, we don't have to do anything as it was only an option, not an obligation. This is clearly a privileged position, and we must pay for it. The price we pay is the *premium* for the option. This right to *buy* a financial product later is the *call* option. We buy a call when we wish to gain from an increase in price later.

We may, alternatively, be pessimistic about XYZ Ltd and believe that the price of £1.86 will probably fall to £1.60 in the next 3 months. The option to *sell* a given quantity of XYZ Ltd shares at £1.86 in the next 3 months is very attractive. If we are correct, we can buy them later for £1.60 and use the option to sell them at £1.86. If we are wrong and the price rises or remains constant, we don't have to do anything as it was only an option, not an obligation. Again, we pay a premium for this privilege. The right to *sell* a financial product later is the *put* option. We buy a put when we wish to gain from a fall in price later.

Let's look at some figures. Suppose the call or put contract is for 1000 shares and that the premium in each case is 10p per share. We'll look at the call and the put in turn.

Call option   We have the right to buy 1000 XYZ Ltd shares within the next 3 months at £1.86 and pay a premium of 10p per share (= £100) up front.

XYZ Ltd share price later:

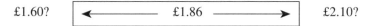

Suppose the price falls to £1.60 and we have come to the end of the 3 months. The right to buy at £1.86 is of no value as we can buy them at the market price of £1.60. The option will expire. There is no action to take – we just abandon our option. Our loss is the premium of £100 (which we've already paid). Notice that whatever happens, we *can't lose more than the premium*.

Suppose the price rises later to £2.10? Now, we can contact our broker, advise them that we are exercising our option to buy 1000 shares at £1.86 and ask them to sell them in the usual way for £2.10 (no further capital needs to be paid). We have made 1000 × (£2.10 – £1.86) = 1000 × 24p = £240. We paid a premium of £100 so the net gain is £140 or 140% (for convenience, dealing costs have been ignored).

The share price rose 24p from £1.86, a rise of about 13%. This rise of 13% generated us a profit of 140%. This effect is called *gearing*, which we met in Chapter 1 (the Americans call it *leverage*). In general, it's making a given sum of money go further. It's well summed up in the American expression 'more bang for your buck'! In Chapter 1, we looked at balance sheet gearing – making money go further by borrowing other people's money. This is another example. If we had bought 1000 XYZ Ltd shares, we would have paid £1860. We backed our view on £1860 of shares with just £100 premium. In addition (at least in theory) the remaining £1760 can be in the bank earning interest. The result, as in the above case, is that a small change in the price of the underlying asset (13%) may lead to a large percentage profit gain (140%). However, gearing cuts both ways. A small fall in price of just, say, 4% could result in 100% loss of our premium! Nevertheless, gearing is a big attraction in derivative products.

Put option   We now have paid for the right to sell 1000 XYZ Ltd shares within the next 3 months at £1.86 and pay a premium of 10p per share (= £100) up front.

XYZ Ltd share price later:

£1.60?   ◄─────── £1.86 ───────►   £2.10?

At this point the reader might wonder how we can buy the right to sell shares that we don't even own. We shall find that not only is this not a problem, it is part of the beauty of the put option!

Suppose the price rises to £2.10 and we have come to the end of the option period. We have the right to sell 1000 shares at £1.86. If we had the shares (which we don't), we could sell them on the market for £2.10. Our right is of no value and will expire, losing the premium of £100.

Suppose the price falls later to £1.60. We have the right to sell 1000 shares at £1.86 but don't actually own any. What we do, of course, is buy 1000 shares in the conventional way at £1.60 and use the option to sell them at £1.86, making 26p per share or a net 16p after deducting our cost of 10p per share. Our profit is £160 or 160% although the change in share price was only about 14%.

Option Writers

Who, in the first instance, sells us the XYZ Ltd shares at £1.86 when the market price is £2.10? Who, in the second instance, buys our shares from us at £1.86 when the market price is £1.60? The answer is the person who sold us the option in the first place, called the *writer* of the option. They took our premium and believed that it was a good price for the risk.

There are, thus, four possibilities in the option game. One can buy calls or puts and one can write calls or puts. The risk profile is quite different for buyers and writers:

	Maximum loss	Maximum gain
Buyers of options	The premium	Unlimited
Writers of options	Unlimited	The premium

Because the writers of options face unlimited risk, they pay a deposit, called *margin*, to the clearing house. When the deal is opened they pay *initial margin*. If the price moves against them they must pay more margin – *variation margin* – to cover their losses. If they go into liquidation, the deal is honoured by the clearing house.

Trading Options

In the above cases, we either abandoned our option or exercised it. On a trading exchange, there is the further choice of *trading the option*.

Let's illustrate this, and some of the real life complications, by looking at the prices that might be quoted for XYZ Ltd shares at any one time on the London International Financial Futures and Options Exchange (LIFFE). The exchange deals in the shares of about 70 UK companies and also offers options on the main share index, the FTSE 100 (to be explained later).

The position is more complicated than in our previous example:

❑ There is a choice of share prices at which calls/puts can be bought/written. They are called *exercise* or *strike* prices. There is a choice of dates for expiry of the contract. 3 dates are offered to a maximum of 9 months ahead.
❑ Options must be dealt in set multiples or standard contract sizes (typically 1000 shares on LIFFE, but varying by exchange).
❑ Options can be traded – that is, sold back to the market for a later premium.
❑ Having bought an option, it can be exercised at any time prior to the expiry date. This is called an *American* option. (It's nothing to do with America! Most options on European exchanges are American options.)

Let's first look at the matrix of choice and assume that we came to the market on 27 March and looked at options for XYZ Ltd (Table 11.1).

Table 11.1 XYZ Ltd, *call options, 27 March*

Market price	*Exercise price*	*Exercise expiry dates*		
		April	*July*	*October*
	180			
186	200			
	220			

Notice that we have standardised exercise prices of £1.80, £2.00 and £2.20 (in reality there might be several more, but these would tend to be the most liquid). None of them is the market price (£1.86) except by coincidence. We have a further choice of expiry in April, July or October – a maximum of 7 months. Had we come to the market on 1 February, we would still have seen April, July and October and hence, our maximum time horizon of 9 months.

There are thus nine choices and for each there is a quoted premium in pence per share. Suppose the premiums for all three exercise prices were the same? Naturally, we would pick the exercise price of £1.80 since we all like to be able to buy at the cheapest price. It will be no surprise to find that the premium for £1.80 is more expensive than that for £2.00 and much more expensive than that for £2.20. Again, suppose the premiums for all the three expiry dates were the same? Naturally, we would pick October to give XYZ Ltd the maximum time to go up in price. For the same reason, the writer of the option (who is not stupid!) wants a higher premium for October than April.

Let's look now at the full list of prices in Table 11.2.

On 27 March, the right to buy XYZ Ltd shares at £1.80 before an expiry in April costs 16p per share. For the minimum contract of 1000 shares this is £160. On 27 March, the right to buy XYZ Ltd shares at £2.00 before an expiry in October costs 21p per share. For the minimum contract, this is £210. Notice the gearing. To *buy* 1000 XYZ Ltd shares today would cost £1860.

Table 11.2　XYZ Ltd, *call options, 27 March*

Market price	Exercise price	April	July calls	October
	180	16	24	32
186	200	7	14	21
	220	3	7	12

Which of these nine options do we choose? There is no magic answer. It depends how strongly you feel XYZ Ltd is undervalued, how soon you think the price will rise, and how risk averse you are.

You could choose £1.80, already cheaper than the stock market price and October expiry, giving the largest time for XYZ Ltd to go up in price. It looks attractive but at £320 per 1000 shares is the most expensive.

At the other extreme, you could choose £2.20 and expiry in April. This is 34p dearer than the stock market price and there are perhaps only 4 weeks to the expiry date. It doesn't look attractive but it's cheap at £30 per 1000 shares.

Intrinsic Value and Time Value

The £1.80 option is already 6p cheaper than the market price of £1.86. We can argue, therefore, that the premium must be at least 6p. Suppose the premium was 4p. You would buy as many options as you could possibly afford and immediately exercise, buying the shares for £1.80 and selling for £1.86. An obvious profit of 6p for a cost of 4p. No chance! The market has a piece of jargon for this 6p – it's called *intrinsic value*. This occurs when the call exercise price is cheaper than the market price or a put exercise price is dearer than the market price.

The option premium for the April expiry is 16p. We know that it must be at least 6p and can see that 10p has been added to cover the possibility of XYZ Ltd going up in price prior to expiry. We call this the *time value* in the option. The exercise price of £2 is dearer than the market price and it has no intrinsic value (we don't use negative intrinsic value).

Breaking the premium down like this, into intrinsic value and time value, let's look at the £1.80 calls for April, July and October and the £2.00 calls for the same expiry dates in Table 11.3.

Table 11.3 *£1.80 and £2.00 calls for April, July and October*

Exercise price	Expiry	Intrinsic value		Time value		Premium
180	April	6	+	10	=	16
	July	6	+	18	=	24
	October	6	+	26	=	32
200	April	0	+	7	=	7
	July	0	+	14	=	14
	October	0	+	21	=	21

We can see how time value goes up steadily for later expiry dates.

Calculation of the Premium

Where does this time value come from? How are the premiums calculated?

Usually, in human activity, if we want to forecast the future, we start with the past: as T.S. Eliot tells us, 'In my beginning, is my end.' We look at the previous behaviour of the share price, say over the last 6 months, and project this forward using statistical techniques and laws of probability. These may suggest that there is a given probability that the XYZ Ltd share price in October will be within a given range. We look at the exercise price, the current market price, one or two other factors we don't need to go into, and the statistical calculations use the past behaviour to produce a theoretical or *fair value* for the premium. There may then be a question of whether the option writer believes that future price behaviour will be different, and also sheer demand and supply. If there are more option buyers than sellers, premiums will rise, and vice-versa. Experts will compare the market premiums with the fair value premiums and decide if the premiums look cheap or expensive.

These statistical techniques were developed in May 1973 when Fischer Black and Myron Scholes wrote a paper on the pricing of options in the *Journal of Political Economy*. The Black–Scholes formula, with one or two possible modifications, is still widely used to calculate premiums. Black and Scholes were professors at the University of Chicago and the timing was apt as the Chicago Board Options Exchange had started trading options in April 1973. A few years later, more professors appeared – Messrs Cox, Ross and Rubenstein. (They were also assisted by Professor Robert Merton. In October 1997, Scholes and Merton received the Nobel Prize for their work. Black was not included as the prize is never awarded posthumously and, unfortunately, Black died the previous year.) They produced a similar formula (one based on a binomial progression for those who understand such things). Other areas of probability theory are also used, for example, Monte Carlo simulation. The experts argue about the merits of one formula as opposed to another; for the lay person, the results are very similar.

In looking at the past behaviour of two shares, one may be much more volatile than another although the average price may be similar in each case. The more volatile share may produce higher or lower share prices later than the less volatile one and thus the premium will be higher.

Look at Figure 11.1.

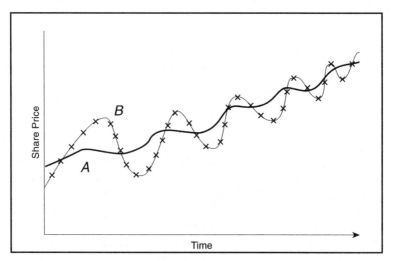

Figure 11.1   *Price behaviour of two shares, A and B*

For the writer of the option, share *B* is clearly more dangerous and risky than share *A*, even though the average price over time is much the same. Without knowing anything about statistics, we can accept that the option premiums quoted for share *B* will be higher than for share *A*. Those who understand statistics will be aware that this volatility is the standard deviation and a key element in the pricing formula. Experts will analyse market premiums to see the *implied volatility*. They will then decide if they agree with this figure, bearing in mind that future volatility may not be the same as past or *historic volatility*. These are advanced considerations that need not concern us in an introductory text. Be aware, however, that volatility is a big word in the options game.

Volatility is usually quoted as a percentage figure, for example, 20%. This would mean that, over 1 year, there is a 68% chance in laws of probability that a share price will be either 20% higher or lower than the starting price.

Suppose a share price is £1.00 and the volatility is 20%. The premium for a 1 year call option, the right to buy the share at 1.00 within the next year, would be 9.9p per share. If the volatility were 40%, the premium would be 17.1p.

(The above assumes 10% interest rates and 5% dividend yield, factors that are also taken into account.)

The Russian crisis of August 1998 is an example of how the volatilities of financial instruments can change. The Hong Kong and Shanghai Banking Corporation (HSBC) estimated the volatility of the UK's FTSE 100 index in July 1998 at 20%. Two months later, following the Russian crisis, it was 40%. Its range in 1995/96 was just 12% to 15%. In 2002, after two years of dramatic daily movements and large annual falls, the market is now estimating volatility of the FTSE 100 at 25%–30%. As option premiums go up as volatility rises, this means that just as people are looking for protection because the situation has become more uncertain, protection costs a lot more!

Exercise or Trade?

Going back to the XYZ Ltd prices on 27 March, let's assume that we bought a call option with exercise price £1.80 and expiry in July. Let's also assume that it's the minimum of one contract, that is, 1000 shares. The premium is quoted as 24 and so we will pay £240 plus broker's commission and a small charge for the costs of the clearing house.

(The premiums are actually quoted with a bid/offer spread so that 24 may be a mid-point representing a quote of 22/24. We will ignore this in the interests of simplicity.)

Let's move on now to 6 June in the same year. We can look at the current call option premiums in Table 11.4.

Table 11.4   *XYZ Ltd call options, 6 June*

Market price	Exercise price	July	October	January
	180	36	44	52
206	200	18	28	38
	220	6	13	24

We see that the April month has gone and been replaced by January, the next month in the series. We also note that the share price has gone up 20p and the £1.80/ July call premium is now quoted as 36.

If we are new to options, this might puzzle us. We could argue that, as the share price has gone up 20p, the right to buy at £1.80 must be 20p more valuable. If the old premium was 24, it should now be 44. To understand what is happening to the premium we must break it down into intrinsic value and time value and compare the positions on 27 March and 6 June. We can see this in Table 11.5.

Table 11.5   *Breaking down premium into intrinsic and time value*

Premium date	Market price	Intrinsic value		Time value		Premium
27 March	186	6	+	18	=	24
6 June	206	26	+	10	=	36

We can see that intrinsic value has gone up by 20 but time value down by 8, giving a net increase of 12. The time value is down simply because, at 6 June, there is less time left to expiry. If we need more time value for more time, as we saw earlier, then we need less time value for less time.

It is most important to grasp this. It means that there is an element in the premium, the time value, *which is steadily going down*, regardless of what is happening to the share price. There is an element, intrinsic value, which may be going *up* or *down* – that depends on the share price movement. Since we may *trade* the option, that is, receive the quoted premium, we must understand its behaviour.

Suppose we decide to take profit at this point, We have two choices – *exercise* the option or *trade* it. Let's examine each in turn.

If we exercise the option, we buy 1000 shares at £1.80 and sell them at the market price of £2.06, making 26p per share, ignoring dealing costs. As the option cost is 24p per share, our profit is 2p.

If we trade the option, we sell it back for 36p, today's quoted premium. As the option cost is 24p per share, our profit is 12p.

In the first case we make £20 and in the second, £120. Why was trading more profitable? When we exercise we buy at the exercise price (£1.80) and sell at the market price (£2.06). We have a term for this gap – intrinsic value. When we exercise we receive the intrinsic value, in this case 26p. When we trade, we receive the premium, that is, intrinsic value *plus* time value. The premium is 36 because 10p of time value was added to the intrinsic value. In other words, we are gaining from the protection built into the premium by the option writer. In fact, when we trade the option we *are* an option writer! However, as we previously bought the same option, we are not left with any outstanding position in the market. It follows that, at expiry, there is no time value and exercising the option or trading it will produce the same result. There is one final point regarding the time value. We have noted that it declines as time passes. However, this decline accelerates as we approach expiry. An option buyer may defer taking profit for several weeks, allowing the share price to rise even further. It may well be, however, that the time value declines faster than the intrinsic value rises and the total premium falls in value. This will be particularly true with a few weeks of expiry.

Other Terminology

We have noted the term 'intrinsic value' which is used when a call option exercise price is below the market price or a put option exercise price is above it. The option is also described here as *in the money*. If the exercise price is the same as the market price, we say the option is *at the money*. If the call exercise price is dearer than the market or the put exercise price cheaper we say the option is *out of the money*. Please note, however, that the use of standard exercise prices means that it is only rarely that one is the same as the market price. As a result, it is very common to call the at-the-money option the one which is *nearest* to the market price.

We described these LIFFE options earlier as *American* options, that is, they can be exercised at any time prior to the expiry date. The alternative is the *European* option which can only be exercised at expiry. We will give an example of this shortly. Typically, options on trading exchanges are American options but European options are quite common in the OTC market. Both options can be *traded* at any time on trading exchanges.

Options on Indices

Having looked at options on individual shares, we can now consider options on a whole share index, for example, S&P 100, FTSE 100, CAC 40, DAX and so on.

In principle, we can see that the idea has advantages. Now we can back a view on the whole market, not an individual share. Alternatively, we may be a market maker or fund manager owning all the top shares. The index might be a good way of hedging market risk. The practice of index options may be puzzling at first. One can readily envisage exercising an option and buying XYZ Ltd shares. What if we exercise the index option and buy the FTSE 100 index or the DAX? What exactly do we receive?

The contracts are *cash settled*. Since there isn't anything to deliver, the contract is settled by paying cash. The index must be regarded as a price. If a call option on the FTSE 100 index is bought at an exercise level of 6000, then money will be made if the level rises to 6100 because 'the price' is higher. If the option buyer exercises, buying at 6000 and selling at 6100, then 100 points have been gained. To turn this into money, we settle at £10 per point per contract. For one contract, the gain is $100 \times £10 = £1000$. For ten contracts, it would be £10,000, and so on. The premium paid would have to be deducted in the usual way to arrive at the net profit. Alternatively, the option could be traded in the way described earlier.

A fund manager with a holding of £30m in shares might be nervous of a fall in the market but not nervous enough to actually sell the shares. If an assumption is made that their holding of shares will behave in a similar way to the FTSE 100 (the correlation will be measured), then the manager could buy put options on the index contract. If the market falls, the puts will win some money to help compensate for the fall in the value of the portfolio.

How many contracts should the manager buy? Let us say that the index is at a level of 6000. If the contract is settled at £10 per point, then the whole index is $6000 \times £10 = £60,000$. As this is one contract, the total number of contracts needed to cover a portfolio of £30m is:

$$\frac{£30m}{£60,000} = 500$$

The manager buys 500 put options on the index at an exercise level of 6000 and pays the premium, say, £500 per contract or $500 \times £500 = £250,000$ in total.

(The premiums are also quoted as *index points*. In this case 50 index points. At £10 per point, this gives us a premium of £500.)

If the index falls 10% to 5400, the value of the portfolio of £30m is reduced by £3m. However, the manager could exercise the put option, that is, selling at a level of 6000 and buying at a level of 5400, making 600 points. Bearing in mind that the manager bought 500 contracts and that they are settled at £10 per point, the gross gain is:

600 points $\times £10 \times 500$ contracts = £3m.

From this we deduct the premium of £250,000 giving a net gain of £2.75m (ignoring dealing costs). This is a substantial compensation for the fall in the value of the portfolio of £3m. This is a classic *hedge*.

If the index rises 10% to 6600, the put option will expire worthless with the loss of the premium of £250,000. On the other hand, the value of the portfolio is now £33m not £30m, to help offset this loss. In particular, the manager is pleased that the portfolio was not liquidated due to nervousness about the market.

This is how options on an index are traded everywhere. At London's LIFFE, there are two FTSE 100 options. Both have a maximum maturity of 1 year but one is an American and one a European option.

The Chicago Board Options Exchange trades the S&P 100 at $100 per point (American). The Chicago Mercantile Exchange trades the S&P 500 at $250 per point and a mini S&P at $50 per point (both European and American). The Paris MONEP trades the CAC 40 at €1 per point as a European option.

In the US, the main markets for equity options are the Chicago Board Options Exchange, the New York Stock Exchange, the American Stock Exchange and the Philadelphia Stock Exchange.

In Europe, the main markets for equity options are shown in Table 11.6.

Table 11.6   *Main European markets for equity options (originally)*

Exchange	Country
Deutsche Termin Börse (DTB)	Germany (1990)
European Options Exchange (EOE)	Netherlands (1978)
London Traded Options Market (LTOM)	UK (1978)
Marché des Options Negociables de Paris (MONEP)	France (1987)
Swiss Options and Futures Exchange (SOFFEX)	Switzerland (1988)

In London, LTOM merged later with the futures exchange LIFFE; in 2001 LIFFE then announced it would be taken over by Euronext, which went ahead in January 2002. With the arrival of the euro it was clear that Europe could not sustain so many exchanges. The DTB and SOFFEX merged in 1998, calling themselves EUREX and forming a cooperation agreement with the Paris markets. On 1998 figures, EUREX passed LIFFE and became Europe's biggest exchange, and by 2002 was offering 41 contracts as compared with 27 on LIFFE.

This is not an exhaustive list and option markets have now been set up in virtually every major European economy. The contract size of 1000 shares in LIFFE reflects low UK share prices; a few options are dealt in smaller sizes, typically where the share price is very high. In the Chicago Board Options Exchange, it's 100 shares; in the MONEP, 10 shares; the DTB, 50 shares; and SOFFEX, only five shares, again reflecting the Swiss practice of high share prices!

Outside Europe and the US, important exchanges exist in Tokyo, Osaka, Singapore, Hong Kong and Sydney. The Singapore Exchange (SIMEX), which started in 1984, has done particularly well and has become the dominant player in the Far East.

TRADED OPTIONS: OTHER OPTIONS

Currencies

In this chapter so far, we have covered options on equities and equity indices. In Chapter 8, we discussed options on currencies and ways in which importers and exporters could hedge risk.

Having looked at the mechanics of options, let's return to the 'breakforward' option which we explained in Chapter 8. We showed that a buyer of dollars for sterling in 3 months might be offered a floor rate of $1.88 and a break rate of $1.91. If the spot rate in 3 months was less than $1.88, the importer will buy dollars at $1.88. If the spot rate later was better than $1.91, the importer could buy dollars at the spot rate less 3¢. Thus, if spot later were $1.98, the importer could buy dollars at $1.95 and thus benefit from an improvement in the rate while still getting substantial protection from any worsening. There is no cost to the importer.

The bank has bought a sterling put option at $1.91.

If the spot rate later is, say, $1.85 the bank exercises the option to buy dollars at $1.91 and sells them to the client at $1.88, making 3¢.

If the spot rate later is, say $1.98 the option is abandoned. The bank buys the dollars spot at $1.98 and sells them to the client at $1.95, again making 3¢.

The 3¢ cover the option premium and a profit margin. The client is happy with the blend of risk protection and profit participation and the bank makes a profit. A simple example of some of the clever ways in which options can be used.

Bonds

Options are also available on bonds. Many of the major exchanges trading equity options will also trade bonds.

Germany's DTB for example, trades the 5 year government bond and the 10 year government bond. London's LIFFE trades options on a range of government bonds – German, Italian, UK and Japanese. Here we have a situation where the German government 10 year bond is traded on both the DTB in Frankfurt and at LIFFE in London. Originally, London did two thirds of the volume, but in 1998 the DTB hit back and captured most of the business. In 1999, this bond, traded on EUREX, became the biggest derivatives contract in Europe (priced in euros).

In Paris, options on French government bonds are traded on the MATIF exchange. In the US, options on Treasury notes and bonds are traded on the American Stock Exchange, Chicago Board of Trade and Chicago Board Options Exchange. Options on 3 month Treasury bills are dealt on the American Stock Exchange and the Chicago Mercantile Exchange.

These bond contracts work in a similar way to the options on shares we described earlier. They can be used to speculate or hedge risk.

For example, the option on the French government bond on the MATIF offers standard exercise price levels, such as 108, 109, 110, 111. The contract size is €100,000 and the premiums are expressed as a percentage of the bond's nominal value to two decimal places. Thus, the March call at 110 exercise price may have a premium quoted as 3.25. In money terms, this is 3.25% of €100,000 = €3250. Each full 1% is €1000. If the bond price is 112, we can see that an exercise price of 110 has 2% of intrinsic value since it is the right to buy the bond at less than the market price. If the bond price rose to 114, the call buyer could make a profit of 4% = €4000 *less* the cost of the premium. If there is some time left to expiry, the call option buyer may trade the option and make even more profit. If the market price is 114, the right to buy at 110 has 4.00 intrinsic value plus an element of time value. Since the contract size is €100,000 a bond dealer wishing to hedge a portfolio of €10m, will need to deal in 100 contracts.

(The above explanation has been simplified. At this point, we have ignored the complication that the bond is called *notional* and that the option is an option to have the futures contract. This is explained in Chapter 12.)

Interest Rates

The equity, currency and bond options covered above can go to delivery. That is, we can use the option to actually purchase or sell the relevant equities, currencies or bonds.

We also met index options, which cannot go to delivery as there is no real underlying product. These are called *cash settled*. Interest rate options are of this kind. We cannot use the contract to borrow or lend money at a given rate of interest. Just as the index option was settled on the basis of a value per point of index change, so the interest rate option is settled on the basis of a value per 0.01% change in interest rates.

For example, the Chicago Mercantile Exchange trades 3 month Eurodollar interest rates. The contract size is $1m. Thus, with an underlying sum at risk of $20m, the options user would be dealing in 20 contracts. Each 0.01% of interest rate change will gain or lose $25 per contract. The option user buys a call or a put on a given level of interest rates and pays a premium. If rates change to the profit of the option user by 0.50%, the gain is $50 \times \$25 = \$1250$ per contract.

In the case of index options, the price per point is arbitrary. It is picked to produce a sensible contract size. In the case of the interest rate contract above, the $25 per 0.01% is not arbitrary but follows logically from the contract size of $1m. If the whole contract, that is 100%, has a value of $1m, then 0.01% has a value of $100. However, this is a 3 monthly contract, so the value is a quarter of this, that is, $25.

So far, the procedure for trading interest rates has seemed quite straightforward. The level of interest rate for 3 month Eurodollars is regarded as a price, like any other, and we either buy cheaper than we sell or face buying dearer than we sell, in which case the option is abandoned. Each 0.01% of gain on the price level wins $25 for each contract traded. We can either use the contract to speculate or hedge interest rate risk.

There is, unfortunately, a complication. This relates to the pricing of the contract. We might expect to see prices like 3.50%, 5.00% or 8.00%. What the market actually does is subtract the desired rate of interest from 100 to arrive at the price level of the contract. Thus an interest rate of 4.00% trades as 96.00 and one of 8.00% trades as 92.00.

Let's look at the effect of this pricing:

Interest rate	Contract price
10.00%	$100 - 10\% = 90.00$
9.00%	$100 - 9\% = 91.00$
11.00%	$100 - 11\% = 89.00$

Notice that as the interest rate goes *down* from 10% to 9%, the contract price goes *up* from 90.00 to 91.00. As the interest rate goes *up* from 10% to 11%, the contract price goes *down* from 90.00 to 89.00.

We met this reverse relationship before when we discussed long-dated bonds – interest rates down, bond prices up; interest rates up, bond prices down. The Chicago markets did start trading interest rates in the obvious way (in 1975). After a few weeks, however, the traders preferred to trade the contracts in the way we have just described. It suited bond dealers who were hedging risk and it suited the psychology of traders. After all, as a generalisation, higher interest rates are seen as bad news – equity and bond prices fall. It seemed logical that with higher interest rates, the contract price fell.

This means that the call/put logic we learned earlier must be reversed in the case of interest rate contracts. If you wish to gain from higher interest rates buy *put* options – the contract price will fall. If you wish to gain from lower interest rates, buy *call* options – the contract price will rise. Other than that, it's easy really!

Let's take an example. Suppose a US corporate has a $20m loan from the bank at floating rate and reviewed every 3 months. The rate is linked to Eurodollar LIBOR. Let us also suppose that the dates for the CME 3 monthly contracts coincide with the bank's rollover of the loan. The bank has just fixed the rate for 3 months based on Eurodollar LIBOR of 3.75%. The corporate believes that rates are due to rise and seeks a hedge using the CME contract.

As the contract size is $1m and the loan is $20m, they deal in 20 contracts. As they wish to gain if interest rates go up, they buy 20 *put* options for the next expiry at a level of 3.75%, that is, a contract price level of $100 - 3.75 = 96.25$. The premium is quoted as 0.30 and also must be interpreted at $25 per 0.01 per contract, the way the contract is settled. Thus 0.30 = $750 per contract and the corporate bought 20 contracts, paying $20 \times \$750 = \$15,000$.

Assume that at the expiry of the contract the Eurodollar LIBOR rate is 4.75%. The bank notifies the client that the interest charge is 1% higher on the $20m loan for 3 months – an increase of $50,000.

At the CME, the contract price is $100 - 4.75\% = 95.25$. The corporate bought 20 put options at 96.25, that is, the right to sell at 96.25. The contract is exercised by selling at 96.25 and buying at 95.25, a profit of 1% for each of 20 contracts. Since $0.01\% = \$25$ the gain is:

$$100 \times \$25 \times 20 \text{ contracts} = \$50,000$$

Deducting the premium of $15,000, the corporate has $35,000 to help meet the bank's extra interest charge of $50,000.

Suppose interest rates had fallen to 2.75%? The CME contract is not profitable and will be abandoned for the loss of the premium of $15,000. However, the bank notifies the corporate of a reduced interest charge for 3 months of $50,000. The corporate has bought protection from higher rates but can still gain if they fall.

This is the essential character of options to which we referred in Chapter 8 on foreign exchange. It is worth repeating.

The option purchase protects against a deterioration in the rate but the option buyer can still benefit from an improvement in the rate. There is a cost – the premium.

(Again, the complication that the CME contract is an option to have the future has been ignored.)

OPTION STRATEGIES

The experts in the option market will not content themselves with one position, such as buying a call at a particular exercise price and expiry but will combine several positions in order to carry out complex strategies.

For example, in the case of XYZ Ltd in equity options above, we might buy both a call *and* a put on the exercise price of £1.80 for July expiry. If the share price rises we win, if it falls we also win. Well, in principle at least. The problem is that two premiums have been paid. The call premium is 24 and the put might be 18, that is, 42 in total. Having paid 42 for a £1.80 call, the price must go up to £2.22 (£1.80 + 42) to break even and that ignores dealing costs. Having paid 42 for a £1.80 put, the price must fall to £1.38 (£1.80 – 42) to break even. In other words, this is a strategy for a very volatile situation. A sharp share movement is expected, either up or down. It might be that there is a takeover bid struggle. The bid will either fail and the victim's share price fall sharply or the bidder will come back with a higher offer and the opposite will happen.

The most dangerous situation for the buyer is if the price remains stable at £1.86. The call option will be worth 6p and the put will expire worthless. The loss is 42 – 6 = 36: for a single 1000 share contract, £360 lost out of the premium of £420. (This has ignored *trading* the option prior to expiry in order to cut the loss and take advantage of remaining time value in the premium.)

This is quite a well known strategy called the *straddle*. The straddle buyer expects a volatile situation; the straddle writer thinks they are wrong.

Another strategy might be to buy the July £1.80 calls and write the July £2.20 calls. The premium for the July £1.80 calls is 24p and for the July £2.20 calls, 7p. If the share price goes over £2.20 later, we have bought a call and also sold one at this level and so no further gain can be made, the purchase and sale will cancel out. However, we have offset the 24p premium for the £1.80 call by receiving the premium of 7p when we wrote the £2.20 call. Our net cost for a 1000 share contract is 24 – 7 = 17p per share or £170 instead of £240 had we simply bought the £1.80 call alone. We have reduced our possible loss from £240 per contract to £170 per contract and brought the break even point down from £1.80 + 24 to £1.80 +17. What we gave up to achieve this was any profit above a later share price of £2.20.

This strategy is called the *bull spread*. We give up some of our unlimited profit potential in order to cut cost and risk. It has become so popular that the Chicago Market offers this embedded in the option product. If we are pessimistic about XYZ Ltd, we do the opposite and buy the £1.80 put but write the £1.40 put – a *bear spread*.

There is no end to the permutations and variations on this theme. There are books on option strategies which will list a figure in excess of 50 possible strategies. Often they take their name from the shape of the graph showing the potential profit and loss from future changes in the market price, for example, the forked lightning, Mexican hat, Mae West, condor, butterfly and many others.

Look at all the variables there are to play with:

- ❏ Number of contracts
- ❏ Calls/puts
- ❏ Buy/write
- ❏ Exercise prices
- ❏ Expiry dates.

Apart from trading strategies like these, there are may other variations on the options theme. There is no place in an introductory text like this to mention them all, but we can cover a few just to give the reader an idea of the sheer ingenuity and imagination involved!

Some markets trade *share ratios*, that is to say not the share's absolute price and its movement but how it compares with others. For example, the Australian Stock Exchange offers contracts on leading shares (such as ANZ Bank, Broken Hill, News Corporation) based on the ratio of their price movement compared with the All Ordinaries Index.

Spread trading is similar, and is based on the difference between two prices. The Spanish exchange, MEFF, for instance, trades on the difference in yields between government bonds in Germany, Spain, France and Italy. Other spreads are *calendar spreads*, the difference between the option premiums for different expiry dates – for example, March and June. We may believe that the difference between the premiums will either get bigger or smaller, and trade accordingly.

There is also a class of options on the OTC market called *exotic options;* for instance *barrier options* which are very popular at the moment. The idea in this case is to cheapen the option premium by attaching some condition. Typically, the option may only be valid if the market price reaches a certain level or barrier (the 'knock in').

Suppose that today's price of a given share is £1.00. We may wish to sell shortly but are prepared to bear a loss down to 90p. We could buy a put option at 90p. A variation is to buy a put option at £1.00 which is only valid if the share price hits 90p – the 'knock in'.

Alternatively, we could buy a put option at £1.00 but agree the option is cancelled if the price ever hits £1.05.

If the price hits £1.05, we may accept cancellation of the option on the basis that prices are going up not down, and accept the risk for a cheaper premium – the 'knock out'. The risk is that having hit £1.05, the price falls later to less than £1.00.

Usually, the option is knocked in or out if the barrier level is reached at any time prior to expiry, and usually the options are European style. A refinement might be that the barrier price only relates to the closing price each day, not the price at any time during the day.

There are also, within the exotics list, *compound options* – that is options to have … another option! At this point, the brain begins to hurt, so let's leave it at that. You get the message. There are many exotics, and teams at banks regularly launch new variations; lookback options, digital options, binary options, up and unders, down and outs, ladder options, rainbow options and so on! Sometimes these endure and become relatively mainstream (like the lookback), sometimes they fade away. The Asian option, (where the strike price is the average over the option period) is now traded on the LME.

Computers are an essential tool to carry out the necessary calculations, produce the profit/loss graphs and control the total exposure contained in a trader's book of option deals.

Unfortunately, the activities of Nick Leeson, the Baring's derivatives trader who is alleged to have lost £860m and bankrupted the bank, have led many people to believe that derivatives trading is all about gambling.

It would be quite wrong to regard it all as simply sophisticated gambling. Risk management is a key topic today and options make their contribution. The description in Chapter 8 shows the ingenious use of options by banks to provide situations which are attractive to importers and exporters and which yield the banks a profit as well. Another possible tool is the *future* transaction, and that's the one which will be covered in Chapter 12.

SUMMARY

The users of derivative products are speculators, hedgers and arbitrageurs. The key products are *options* and *futures*. All the others (like FRAs and swaps) are simply variations on the same theme.

An option gives the buyer the right, but not the obligation, to buy or sell financial instruments or commodities at an agreed price and at an agreed future date or time period.

Options can be purchased on a trading exchange or over the counter. The exchange has the advantage of the protection of the *clearing house*, but the OTC market will more easily tailor a product to suit the user's needs.

Options to buy a given product at a later date are *calls*. Options to sell are *puts*. There are *buyers* of options and *writers* (sellers).

The price of the option is the *premium*, the price of the product at which the option buyer can exercise is the *exercise* or *strike price*. Options can also be *traded*.

The option buyer cannot lose more than the premium, the option writer cannot gain more than the premium.

To protect against default, the clearing house asks option writers for *initial margin* and, each day, *variation margin*.

If the option to buy or sell is at a price more favourable than the market price, the option is said to have *intrinsic value*. The balance of the premium is *time value*, which will fall as the expiry date approaches.

Trading the option will be more profitable than exercising if the option has time value.

A small percentage change in the price of the underlying asset leads to a large percentage change in the premium. This is *gearing*.

The premium is based on the past performance of the share price. The more volatile the performance, the higher the premium.

Options at a price more favourable than the market price are said to be *in the money*. If the price is less favourable than the market, they are *out of the money* and if the price is the same as the market they are *at the money*.

There are options on equities, equity indices, bonds, currencies, interest rates and commodities.

Combining option positions leads to options strategies such as a *straddle, bull spread* or *butterfly*.

Other non-standardised options are referred to as *exotic options*, for example, barrier options, lookback options, digital options, and so on.

12 Financial Futures

Background

Transactions very similar to options and futures contracts today have existed in commodity markets for hundreds of years. There was an astounding Dutch tulip bulb mania in the 17th century. As tulips became more and more fashionable, people bought tulips several months in advance of the harvest. As the price went up, the contracts at the old prices were more valuable and could be sold to other people without waiting to take delivery at harvest time. In the end, the government had to step in when more tulips had been bought than were actually in the ground and several people made large losses.

(For details of this and other amazing financial speculations, see *Extraordinary Popular Delusions and the Madness of Crowds* by Charles Mackay, Harmony Books.)

Commodity prices fluctuate and where there are fluctuations, we find speculators and hedgers. The harvest may be good or bad and the product is only available once per year anyway. It would be natural to buy or sell ahead of the harvest. As prices went up or down, some of these contracts became more valuable and could be sold on to other people.

Metals are not crops but prices do fluctuate and it takes some time to receive a consignment from overseas. The London Metal Exchange's 3 month contract came into use after the Suez Canal was opened and metals like copper and zinc could be shipped in 3 months.

The largest commodity markets in the world settled down in Chicago at the Mercantile Exchange and the Board of Trade. It was here too, that the modern futures contracts were developed. The Board of Trade opened in 1848 and the Mercantile Exchange in 1874.

Before looking at the mechanism of futures as opposed to options, let's look again at the hedging technique.

Hedgers vs Speculators

A hedger is at risk if a given potential price movement happens. Hedgers seek to create a profit from this price movement in another market so as to create a gain in partial compensation for the loss.

A sugar dealer may have sold sugar short for future delivery. That is, the dealer hasn't yet bought the sugar to meet these contracts. If the price of sugar goes up before the purchase is made, a loss will occur.

Let's look at the hedge diagrammatically in Figure 12.1.

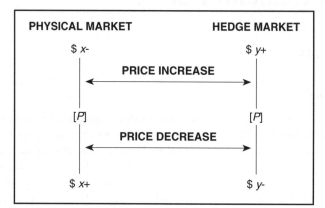

Figure 12.1   *Structure of a hedge*

If a given rise in the price of sugar will lose $x in physical trading, the sugar dealer could buy call options on sugar contracts at the Chicago Coffee, Sugar and Cocoa Exchange. This will create a profit of $y to, at least, offset the loss of $x in physical trading.

If the price of sugar falls, the dealer will have lost money on the call option but will be delighted because, having sold sugar short, even more profit is made on physical sugar trading. This explains why some traders with large losses may walk off the floor of the futures or options exchange and seem to be smiling. They must be hedgers. The price movement they feared hasn't happened. Speculators, of course, will have genuinely lost money.

This is a simple but most important principle, often misunderstood. It's worth repeating:

> *If hedgers lose money in the hedge market, they must make money in the market being hedged because the price movement they feared has not happened.*

We will find that futures, unlike options, involve unlimited risk. For the reason just explained, hedgers can accept this risk. Indeed, the bigger the loss on the futures hedge, the bigger the offsetting gain in the physical market.

There is another important principle – who is on the other side of the hedge? It may be another hedger but one whose position is the opposite – someone who will lose money if the price of sugar goes *down,* not up. This means that whatever happens to the price, both will get the hedge they are looking for. The broker will make a living, the exchange will make a profit and everybody goes home happy.

In financial markets, people are too quick to claim that it must be what they call a 'zero-sum game' – that is, what someone wins, someone else must lose. This is sometimes the case, but by no means always. There are usually plenty of opposite hedgers.

Those with loans at floating rate are hoping interest rates will go *down*. Those with investments at floating rate are hoping interest rates will go *up*.

It all seems too good to be true, and it is. The problem is that there won't be the same value of opposite positions except by a miracle. The hedger wants to do a deal and no one wants to say 'yes' or, at least, not at a reasonable price. That's where speculators come in. They provide the trading liquidity, so that trade hedgers can reduce the risk and do the deals they want. Usually, they are called *locals*, a term from the Chicago Markets, where more than half the membership is locals. Even the conservative London Metal Exchange, where no one can be a member unless they physically trade metals, agree in their literature that speculators play an essential role in providing liquidity. It's a new light on a term that most people regard as being totally pejorative.

Commodity Futures

A futures transaction provides an alternative to an option as a way of hedging risk. Its characteristics are different. A futures contract is a commitment to buy or sell a given quantity of an underlying product by a given date in the future at a price agreed now.

Let's note that a futures transaction is a *commitment*, not an option. If the price moves the wrong way, the option buyer can abandon the contract. As this is a privilege, a premium is paid. A futures contract cannot be abandoned in this way. Since no privilege is involved, no premium need be paid. For the same reason, a futures contract is riskier.

Options had calls, puts, buyers and sellers. Futures contracts only have buyers and sellers. To that extent, they are simpler.

Our sugar trader, worried about the price of sugar going up, could take a futures position in white sugar on the above-mentioned Chicago Exchange (or the exchange known as the LCE in London, now part of LIFFE).

Let us say that the trader commits to buy 100 tonnes of sugar by the next expiry date at $250 per tonne.

It is clear that if the price of sugar goes up to $280 a tonne, a contract that can buy at $250 a tonne has value and can create profit. That is not difficult to grasp but what people do find hard to understand is that the above trader hasn't the slightest intention of buying any sugar!

What happens then if sugar rises to $280 a tonne? The trader *closes the position* with the opposite contract – the trader commits to *sell* 100 tonnes of sugar by the next expiry date at $280 per tonne. The contracts are not settled in sugar but on the price difference of $30 a tonne, that is, our trader has gained $100 \times \$30 = \$3000$. This is to offset the trading loss which will result from having sold sugar short and being obliged to buy physical sugar at a higher price.

People tend to ask at this point – but what happens to the sugar? They have a vision of someone at expiry date trying to handle all the sugar that no one seems to want.

Let's realise that no one can contract to buy sugar unless someone contracts to sell. Equally, no one can contract to sell unless someone contracts to buy. If everyone closes their position with the opposite contract later (as we described above) there isn't anybody left at expiry, nor can there be.

If the sugar trader did not close the position, they would indeed buy 100 tonnes of sugar at $250 a tonne. But if they did remain open at expiry as a buyer, there must also be a seller with an open position. If there are three buyers left, there will be three sellers and so on.

The sugar is only the means to the end – the hedge or speculation. Either way, with the occasional exception, cash settlement is quite acceptable.

The fact that the contract *can* go to delivery, however, is crucially important. It means that the price of sugar in the futures exchange must relate to the real price of sugar. If it was cheaper, traders would use the futures exchange to buy it and sell it at profit in the cash market – arbitrage.

The contract is not an option, and we see the difference if we assume that sugar were to fall in price to $220 a tonne. If this were an option, the contract would now be abandoned – there is no point in buying sugar at $250 in order to sell it at $220. As a futures contract, the trader is committed to buy at $250 a tonne. The position is closed out by later entering the opposite contract to sell 100 tonnes of sugar at $220 a tonne, losing $3000.

This loss is not a problem. As the price of sugar has fallen, the short position in the physical sugar market is even more profitable as sugar can be purchased much more cheaply than it was sold. As we observed earlier, for the hedger a loss in the hedge market must mean a gain in the market being hedged.

Notice the symmetry in the futures contract – a rise in price of $30 a tonne gained $3000, a fall in price of $30 a tonne lost $3000. Options are not symmetrical because, when the price moves the wrong way, the contract is abandoned.

Finally, we now have two terms – forward and futures – which ought to mean the same, but don't.

❑ *Forward* is buying or selling for actual delivery at a future date at a price agreed now.
❑ *Futures* is similar to forward, but usually there is no intention to take or make delivery; later, the position will be closed with the opposite contract and settled in cash.

Forward is for those who want the physical commodity, futures for those who are speculating or hedging and happy with cash settlement.

Thus, we need futures exchanges where everyone realises what the end objective is. There will be formal contract sizes, fixed delivery dates and the guarantee offered by the clearing house. The latter will take margin (deposits) from *both* parties as both are at risk. All contracts are legally with the clearing house. *Initial margin* is paid with the first contract. If the contract moves into loss, extra margin, called *variation margin*, is debited on a daily basis but if the contract moves into profit, variation margin is credited. The major players will have what is, in effect, a bank account with the clearing house. The locals will arrange to clear with someone who is a full clearing member.

Financial Futures

If options and futures are essentially driven by price volatility, the only surprise is that it took so long to be applied to financial contracts. Looking at interest rates, currency rates, equity prices, equity index levels and bond prices, there is huge volatility and also huge risk for many of the parties involved.

As we have observed, a market in futures on currency rates began in the CME with the collapse of the Bretton Woods system. Options and futures on financial contracts spread to the CBOT, the CBOE, New York and Philadelphia in particular.

In Europe, the EOE opened in Amsterdam in 1978 and London's LTOM in the same year. LIFFE opened in London in 1982. Then came the Paris MATIF in 1986, the Paris MONEP in 1987, the Swiss SOFFEX in 1988 and the German DTB in 1990.

Let's look at LIFFE – the London International Financial Futures Exchange (now legally the London International Futures and Options Exchange Ltd due to the merger with the London Traded Options Market – LTOM – but still calling itself LIFFE).

There are three main types of financial contract – bonds, interest rates and equity indices, as well as commodities and even a weather future! There are futures on them all and options in some cases. As we will see, they are typically options to have the futures contract. The contracts are listed in Table 12.1.

(The German 'Bund' is the 10 year Bundesanleihen.)

Other than the FTSE 100, the options are options to have the futures contract. This doesn't make any difference if the buyer is trading the option but any exercise is into the futures contract. A key difference between this and a direct option is that, in the case of the direct option, having used (say) a call option to purchase the product, it can be sold at the market price. The seller of the option would have to purchase the product. If it is an option to have the futures, the buyer finds themself the buyer of the futures contract (a 'long futures' position). This can be left to go to delivery. The seller of the option is now the seller of the futures contract (a 'short futures' position). However, if they don't wish to physically sell the products they have time to close their position by buying the contract and letting someone else go to delivery. In the case of a direct option, they would have no choice. Most option contracts on futures exchanges are options to have the future.

Table 12.1　LIFFE contracts, September 2002

Contract type	Futures	Options
Bonds		
Long Gilt	Yes	Yes
German Government Bond (Bund)	Yes	Yes
German Treasury Note (Schatz)	Yes	No
Japanese Government Bond (JGB)	Yes	No
Short Term Interest Rates		
3 Month EURIBOR	Yes	Yes
3 Month EURO LIBOR	Yes	No
3 Month Sterling (Short Sterling)	Yes	Yes
3 Month Euro Swiss Franc (Euroswiss)	Yes	Yes
3 Month Euro Yen (TIBOR)	Yes	No
3 Month Euro Yen LIBOR	Yes	No
Swaps		
2 Year Euro Swapnote	Yes	Yes
5 Year Euro Swapnote	Yes	Yes
10 Year Euro Swapnote	Yes	Yes
2 Year USD Swapnote	Yes	No
5 Year USD Swapnote	Yes	No
10 Year USD Swapnote	Yes	No

Swapnote® is a registered trademark of Garban-Intercapital Management Services Limited (GIMS). GIMS is a subsidiary of Garban-International plc.

Contract type	Futures	Options
Equity & Equity Indices		
FTSE 100 Index	Yes	Yes
FTSE 250 Index	Yes	No
FTSE Eurotop 100 Index	No	No
FTSE Eurotop 300 Index	No	No
MSCI Euro Index	No	No
MSCI Pan-Euro Index	No	No
Equity Options on >75 companies	Yes	No
Planned for late 2002:		
Equity Shares in GBP (75 companies)	Yes	Yes
Equity Shares in EUR	Yes	No
Universal Stock Future	Yes	No

In addition, LIFFE trades in commodity contracts – cocoa, barley, wheat, coffee, sugar and weather as well as options on these items.

Source:　LIFFE.

From the last remarks, the reader will realise that in some cases, the contracts can go to delivery if the position is not closed out. The gilts contract size is £100,000. A buyer of 20 contracts can let the position go to delivery and buy £2m of gilts at the agreed price. All the bond contracts except the Japanese Government bond can go to delivery in this way. Prices will be kept in line with cash market prices or arbitrage will take place.

The FTSE 100 can't go to delivery (as there isn't anything to deliver) and the interest rate contracts can't go to delivery either, they can't be used to borrow money at an agreed rate of interest. This raises two interesting points. Since the contract can't go to delivery, what happens if a buyer *doesn't* close the position with the opposite sale? For the same reason, how do we know the price will relate to that of the underlying product in the cash market?

Any buyer or seller who doesn't close the position is automatically closed by the clearing house as the contract can't go to delivery. If the buyer or seller is letting the contract go to delivery, they don't need to take any action as the position will be closed for them.

The problem of correlation with the market price is solved by the convention that the expiry price is always the market price. The expiry price of the FTSE 100 is the average of the 81 Stock Exchange FTSE 100 values between 10.10 a.m. and 10.30 a.m. on the expiry day, the highest and lowest twelve values being excluded. (The index has a value every 15 seconds.) The expiry price of the short sterling interest rate contract is the average of the sterling LIBOR rate of 16 named banks at 11.00 a.m. on the expiry day, the highest and lowest four values being excluded.

Index Futures

In Chapter 11, we discussed options on share indices – S&P 100, FTSE 100, CAC 40, DAX and similar indices. Futures contracts are also available and make a good starting point, as we've already met options on the indices.

The futures contract is a commitment and there is no premium to pay, only margin to the clearing house.

An insurance company investment manager may be planning to sell £24m of shares in 3 weeks to meet claims for storm damage. The manager does not wish to sell at the moment as market conditions are poor. The worry about waiting, however, is that the market may fall in the next 3 weeks and the same quantity of shares raise less than £24m.

The answer may be a full hedge using the futures contract on the FTSE 100 contract. This is a way of locking in to today's index level without actually selling the shares.

The first question is – how many contracts? Cash settlement is based on £10 per point. If the index is 6000 then the whole index is valued at $6000 \times £10 = £60,000$. Since the value of shares to be hedged is £24m, then the number of contracts is:

$$\frac{£24m}{£60,000} = 400$$

The fund manager sells 400 contracts for the next expiry period. The first complication is that although the stock exchange index is 6000, the figure in the trading pit may be, say, 6020 (reflecting supply and demand, market expectations and certain technical factors). So our manager has 400 contracts to 'sell' the index at 6020.

Three weeks later the market is down 10% at 5400. The manager sells the shares at this level. For the same quantity of shares that might have been sold 3 weeks earlier, £21.6m is received not £24m, a loss of £2.4m.

The position in the LIFFE exchange is now closed. If the contract in the pit is being traded at a level of, say, 5430, the position is closed by buying 400 contracts at 5430. The gain is:

Sell contracts at	6020
Buy contracts at	5430
Gain per contract	590　points

The contract is cash settled at £10 per point, a gain of £10 × 590 = £5900. For 400 contracts, the total gain is 400 × £5900 = £2.36m. Thus, waiting 3 weeks lost £2.4m on the share sale but the LIFFE contract gained £2.36m.

An initial margin was paid of £2000 per contract and thus £2000 × 400 contracts = £800,000. However, as this was only a deposit to cover possible loss, this sum is returned. In addition, one can usually negotiate interest on initial margin.

There will be brokers' costs to pay and a fee to the clearing house. These might be about £4 per contract or a total of £4 × 400 = £1600 in this case.

If the index rose in the 3 week period, the contract cannot be abandoned, as in the case of options. If the index rose 10% to 6600, the futures position is now loss making. If the pit level is 6610, the position is now closed by buying 400 contracts at 6610. It is the opposite of the previous case:

Sell contracts at	6020
Buy contracts at	6610
Loss per contract	590　points

The total loss is:

£10 per contract × 590 points × 400 contracts = £2.36m

We commented before on the essential symmetry of the futures contract. A fall in the index traded of 590 points gains £2.36m but a rise of 590 points loses £2.36m.

Unlike options, the futures contract faces potentially unlimited loss. However, we are not talking here of a speculator but a hedger. When the investment manager sells the shares, the market is up 10% and the shares are sold for £26.4m not £24m. The gain of £2.4m offsets the loss of £2.36m on the futures contract. This is the point we made earlier in the chapter. For a hedger, a loss on the futures means a gain in the physical market being hedged.

Note one important point. Although the manager was protected against loss arising from a market fall, no profit can be made from a rise in the market.

Let's spell out this essential element in futures, as opposed to options:

Futures give the user protection from an adverse price movement but they cannot benefit from a favourable movement. Risk is unlimited but there is no premium to pay.

The manager could give up some of the protection to allow room for a gain should the market rise. Instead of selling 400 contracts, 200 could have been sold.

The effect would be that a loss of £2.4m due to a 10% market fall would be offset by a futures gain of only £1.18m. However, it follows that a gain of £2.4m due to a 10% market rise would be offset by a futures loss of only £1.18m.

The manager has a range of choices varying from not hedging a position at all right up to an attempted 100% hedge.

One final point. In the above case, there is an implicit assumption that the manager's mix of shares will behave in the same way as the market, that if the market fell 10% so would the mix of shares the manager is selling. It's not an unreasonable assumption but it won't be left to chance. Using computer techniques the manager measures the correlation between the volatility of the shares in the portfolio and the volatility of the FTSE 100 – it's called the *beta factor*. If the shares move in the same way as the index, the beta is 1.0. If the shares move by 90% of an index movement, the beta is 0.9. If the shares move by 110% of an index movement, the beta is 1.1. The number of contracts traded will be adjusted by the beta factor.

Bond Futures

In principle, bond futures are not difficult. The US Treasury bond contract in Chicago, for example, is based on an underlying value of $100,000. The smallest price movement, or tick, is $1/32$. If the contract is £100,000, then 1% = $1000 and $1/32$ = $31.25. If ten contracts are sold at a level 10 ticks higher than they were bought then there is a gain of:

$$10 \text{ ticks} \times \$31.25 \times 10 \text{ contracts} = \$3125$$

The contract need not be closed out but left to go to delivery. Certain days are *delivery days*. In the case of the Treasury bond contract and gilts, it's any business day in the delivery month. In the case of the German government 'Bund' contract, it's the tenth calendar day of the delivery month (if a working day). The decision as to which day is delivery day is made by the *seller*.

The principle, then, is not difficult but the practice is more complicated. Most bond futures contracts are based on a *notional* bond – that is, one that doesn't exist. Newcomers will find the idea of trading in a bond that doesn't exist very strange but the market takes it in its stride. The exchange makes available a list of bonds which can be delivered. The Treasury bond is a 6% coupon bond as the unit of trading. Delivery can be made from a list of actual bonds with 15 years left to maturity. If one of these is an 8% bond, an 8% bond is inherently more attractive than a 6% bond and has a better price. The exchange makes available a *conversion factor* which calculates the sales value which must be used for delivery purposes. If the contract is for a 6% bond with $100,000 nominal value, then an 8% bond can deliver $100,000 nominal to meet the contract specification but receive a higher price. There will be one bond in the list which is cheapest to deliver. The price in the trading pit will be based on this *cheapest to deliver* bond – if not, arbitrage between this and the cash market will take place. For example, someone will buy the underlying bonds, sell the futures contract at the current price level and actually deliver the bonds at a profit.

As a result, the list of bonds available for delivery is significant and the exchange will make changes from time to time. The German Bund contract traded on EUREX, for example, has become the most traded contract in Europe, reaching 700,000 contracts per day by mid-1999. The underlying basket of deliverable bonds is relatively small compared with these huge volumes. Although far less than 5% of bonds go to delivery, the market is nervous of this position and a possible 'squeeze' if a high percentage went to delivery. The bond contract is based on a notional coupon of 6%. There are suggestions that it should be lowered to 4% and the list of deliverable bonds raised. The French MATIF, faced with this problem, has made their bond contract multi-issuer – French, German and Netherlands governments bonds (all in euros, of course). It doesn't seem to have helped and they have attracted little business from EUREX.

Interest Rates

The interest rate contracts create valuable opportunities for those at risk from interest rate changes to hedge that risk. The LIFFE contracts offer short sterling, euro, Euroswiss franc and Euroyen interest rates. Rival euro interest rate contracts are offered at the other exchanges (MATIF, EUREX and so on), but LIFFE's 3 month euro interest rate contract is the biggest in Europe.

Interest rate contracts are cash settled – they cannot go to delivery. At expiry, any open positions are closed by the clearing house at the expiry price, which is always the market price. As we said in Chapter 11, the pricing of the contract is based on subtracting the implied rate of interest so that, for example, 10.00% is traded as 90.00.

The normal rule with futures is that the contract is bought in the first instance if a gain is to be made from a price increase. If a gain is to be made from a price fall, the contract is sold in the first instance. If a hedge is involved, then buying the contract is the *long hedge* and selling the contract is the *short hedge*.

Once again, interest rate contracts reverse the logic. To gain from a price increase, we *sell* the contract (because, if the price goes up, the contract level will fall). To gain from a price decrease, we *buy* the contract (because if the price goes down, the contract level will go up).

In Chapter 11, we used the example of a corporate with a $20m loan at floating rate related to Eurodollar LIBOR and reviewed every 3 months. To hedge interest rate risk, put option contracts were bought. The effect was that, when interest rates went up, the $50,000 extra bank bill was offset by a gain of $35,000 on the option contract. When interest rates went down, the $50,000 fall in the bank bill was only offset by the loss of the premium at $15,000. The option buyer still benefited.

Let's look at a futures hedge in the same circumstances. To keep it simple, we will assume that the interest rate level traded in the pit is the same as current real interest rates (since this was the assumption with the interest rate contract, we need to be consistent).

As the loan is $20m and the contract size on CME is $1m, then the corporate needs to deal in 20 contracts. As they wish to gain from an interest rate rise, they sell 20 contracts for the next expiry at a level of 3.75%, that is, a contract price level of $100 - 3.75 = 96.25$. No premium is paid but the initial margin is $500 per contract, so $20 \times \$500 = \$10,000$ is paid to the clearing house.

As before, we assume that at the expiry of the contract, the Eurodollar LIBOR rate is 4.75%. The bank notifies the client that the interest charge is 1% higher on the $20m loan for 3 months – an increase of $50,000.

At CME, the contract price is $100 - 4.75\% = 95.25$. The corporate's position is closed by buying 20 contracts at 95.25. The position is:

Sell 20 contracts	@	96.25
Buy 20 contracts	@	95.25
Gain per contract		1.00

Each 0.01% is settled at $25 so the gain is:

$100 \times \$25 \times 20$ contracts $= \$50,000$

There is no premium to deduct, so the bank's extra $50,000 interest is met by the gain of $50,000 on the CME contract (in the best of all possible worlds). As there was no premium to deduct, the futures contract has so far worked out better.

But what happens if interest rates fall to 2.75%? The bank notifies the corporate of a reduced interest rate charge for 3 months of $50,000.

At CME, the contract price is $100 - 2.75\% = 97.25$. The position is closed by buying 20 contracts at 97.25. The position is:

Sell 20 contracts	@ 96.25
Buy 20 contracts	@ 97.25
Loss per contract	1.00

The loss is:

$100 \times \$25 \times 20$ contracts $= \$50,000$

This is, of course, the symmetry in futures. A rise in interest rates of 1% gains $50,000, a fall in interest rates of 1% loses $50,000. The result is that the corporate does not gain from the fall in interest rates as the reduced interest rate bill is offset by the loss on the futures contract. Here options gained, as the contract was abandoned when the interest rate fell for the loss of the premium, allowing the corporate a net gain from the interest rate reduction.

Currency Futures

We commented in Chapter 8 on foreign exchange on the strength of the OTC market in currency futures. Currency options and futures closed in London in 1990. Very few are now traded in Europe.

The trading of the futures follows the lines we have explained in this chapter. The CME euro contract, for example, is based on €125,000 as the contract size and is quoted at an exchange rate of dollars per euro. A tick is 0.01¢ and is valued at $12.50. A contract can be bought at a dollar/euro exchange rate of $1.0384 and sold at $1.0484 – a gain of 100 ticks or $1250 per contract traded. Contracts can be left to go to delivery if required.

Some Problems of Futures Exchanges

In general, corporates are not enthusiastic about use of futures exchanges. The contracts are standard sizes, so a small corporate with a loan of $800,000 finds the interest rate contract size of $1m inconvenient. The expiry dates of the contract are unlikely to coincide with real life needs. Margin calls upset cash flow calculations and no interest is paid on variation margin in credit. For interest rate and currency contracts, the banks offer an attractive range of OTC products, some of which we will meet in Chapter 13.

For banks themselves, however, the exchanges have one key advantage – the security of the clearing house. At a time when counterparty risk is a major worry, this is increasingly a key benefit.

For fund managers, too, the index contracts provide secure, liquid trading and the chance to carry out asset allocation smoothly. Suppose a fund has £100m in assets. A decision may be taken to decrease exposure to equities by 2% and increase exposure to gilts by 2%. With one phone call, the fund manager can sell FTSE 100 index contracts to the value of £2m and buy gilts contracts to the same value. Over time and at leisure, the manager can progressively sell the equities, buy the gilts and close the futures position.

Open Outcry or Computers?

A major talking point at present is whether traders will continue to buy and sell in trading pits on a floor or whether the market will move to computerised order matching.

The large US markets are based on *open outcry* trading but the last European exchange to open on an open outcry basis was the Paris MATIF in 1986. The argument for open outcry is that it's the quickest way to trade high value standardised contracts. With computerised trading, however, the expensive floor is no longer needed and a firm audit trail is produced making fraud more difficult. (In 1989, 47 traders were indicted for fraud in Chicago following an undercover investigation by the FBI.)

The signalling in the pits usually follows the Chicago practice. There are three variables:

❏ Number of contracts
❏ Buy or sell?
❏ Price.

As in foreign exchange, only the last two digits of price will be quoted. If the interest rate contract level is 92.55, the price will be '55'. If the trader is buying, the hand begins away from the face and moves back to the forehead. The price is shouted with the hand away from the face and the number of contracts at the forehead. A buyer of 10 contracts at 92.55 will yell:

'55 for 10'

If the trader is selling, the hand begins at the forehead and moves away, shouting the number of contracts first and the price second:

'10 @ 55'

If there are no takers, the price may have to be moved up to 56 or 57 until a counterparty yells 'sold'! The two traders fill in dealing slips, the trades are matched by computer and matched trades are sent electronically to the clearing house.

The Chicago pits are very busy with frenzied shouting and pushing. The classic story is of the trader who died but couldn't fall over because the pit was too busy. Later, other traders who had lost on deals, filled in slips and put them in his pocket, leaving it to his insurer to pay up!

Computer systems are more boring, being based on order matching electronically. There is a CME/MATIF/Reuters system called GLOBEX. This is being used when the exchanges are closed, enabling them to continue trading and cross time zones with Europe and Japan. The CBOT already operates an evening session and the floor at the PHLX is open 18 hours per day.

It seems now that computer systems are winning and that open outcry is dying. CBOT has introduced a system – Project A – which runs both outside and alongside normal trading hours. The CME runs an electronic system – GLOBEX – in alliance with the MATIF and SIMEX in Singapore. While open outcry is still the norm at CME and SIMEX, it provides an electronic 24-hour trading platform. The CBOE announced in June 1999 that screen-based trading would shortly be introduced, although at first only to complement floor trading. The MATIF introduced screen trading in April 1998 alongside pit trading, but abandoned open outcry after just six weeks. The European Options Exchange (now called AEX) moved to screen-based trading, as did the Sydney Futures Exchange in 1999.

London's LIFFE seemed set to continue open outcry, and planned to move to a huge new floor in Spitalfields. Savage competition from the DTB in Germany, which took back all the Bund trading it had lost earlier, caused a change of mind. In June 1998, members voted to introduce electronic trading as soon as possible. The system – LIFFE Connect – was already under development and its introduction was accelerated. Intended at first for equity options only, its use was extended to gilts, other bonds and equity indices in April and May 1999, with interest rates to follow in September. In October 1999 came the announcement of the final closure of the floor in early 2000.

Another important move for LIFFE was the announcement, in August 1999, of a strategic alliance with the CME to link their trading systems and trade each other's short-term interest rate products in the euro and the US dollar.

Other competition for established exchanges has started to arrive. In the US, Cantor Fitzgerald and the New York Board of Trade have released a new electronic system to trade Treasury bond futures. Even worse, a group of entrepreneurs, financial trading firms and technology firms are launching the 'International Securities Exchange', an electronic exchange to trade options on 600 leading US stocks beginning in January 2000. Whilst it is still early days, the very threat of screen-based trading has had an effect, with both the CBOE and the American Stock Exchange cutting fees. It really does begin to look as if the days of open outcry are coming to an end, even if one of the world's oldest exchanges, the London Metal Exchange, decided in April 1999 to retain open outcry for 'the foreseeable future'!

Contract Volumes

The volumes in the major exchanges in 2002 are shown in Table 12.2.

Please note that these figures from *Futures Industry* magazine do not include options on individual indices. If they had, EUREX would be shown as the second biggest exchange after CBOT, with CBOE fourth and LIFFE fifth. The CBOE is the world's biggest exchange for options, trading options on 850 companies and 35 different equity indices. It took over the options business of the New York Stock Exchange in 1997.

('Millions of contracts' as a guide to size can, of course, be misleading, since it depends on the size of contract. The biggest percentage rise in option trading volume in 1998 occurred on the Paris MONEP, but it also coincided with a fall in contract size for individual stock options from 100 shares to 10. It also explains the very high volumes for Korea and Brazil.)

Table 12.2   *Global futures and options volumes, 2002, million contracts*

	Exchange	Total
1	Korea Stock Exchange	501
2	Eurex	241
3	Euronext	236
4	Chicago Merchantile Exchange (CME)	164
5	Chicago Board of Trade (CBOT)	95
6	Chicago Board Options Exchange	90
7	American Stock Exchange	65
8	New York Merchantile Exchange	44
9	International Securities Exchange	43
10	Brazilian & Merchantile Futures Exchange	36

Source: *Futures Industry*, July/August 2002.

SUMMARY

Futures trading began with crops which were only available once per year and whose price fluctuated.

Buyers and sellers might seek to reduce the risk of an adverse price movement by a *hedge*.

A futures contract is an agreement to buy or sell a product at a set price at a later date. Unlike options, however, it is a commitment. Speculators, therefore, are exposed to unlimited risk but hedgers can offset losses with profits on their physical positions.

Usually, futures contracts do not go to delivery. An opening contract to buy is closed by a later contract to sell; an opening contract to sell is closed by a later contract to buy. The position is cash settled. In contracts like equity indices and interest rates, delivery is not possible anyway.

A *forward* deal is one where the intention is to go to delivery.

A *futures* deal is one which is likely to be closed with the opposite and lead to cash settlement. They are traded on futures exchanges with set contract sizes, set expiry dates and the protection of the clearing house.

Futures exist on the same range of products as options although futures on equities are rare.

Many options contracts on futures exchanges are *options to have the future*.

Some exchanges use a trading floor and *open outcry*. Others use systems of order matching by computer. Order matching is now increasing at the expense of open outcry.

13 Other Derivative Products

INTRODUCTION

All the derivative products which we shall describe in this chapter are essentially options and futures in another guise. They are not, however, traded on exchanges but are OTC products. In addition, as interest rates, the price of money, lie at the heart of the financial markets, they are all about controlling *interest rate risk*.

FORWARD RATE AGREEMENTS (FRAs)

To begin with, we must consider the term 'forward/forward'. This is an arrangement between two counterparties to borrow or lend an agreed sum of money at an agreed rate for an agreed period which will not begin until a future date. For example, *A* will lend *B* $1m at 5% for 6 months commencing in 6 months, called '6 against 12' or simply '6 × 12'.

It may be that a corporate needs a bank loan of $1m in 6 months and is worried about rates going up. They ask the bank to quote a rate of interest now for lending money in 6 months for 6 months. This is rather like an importer asking a bank to quote a rate for buying dollars against deutschmarks in 6 months. In foreign exchange, we argued that the bank could avoid risk by buying the dollars today and putting them on deposit for 6 months until needed by the client.

In the interest rate market, if asked to quote forward/forward, the bank could equally borrow money at today's rates and put it on deposit until needed by the client. In the above case, the bank will borrow money for 12 months, deposit it for the first 6 months and then lend it to the client for the remaining 6 months. The rate quoted will depend on:

❏ The bank's cost of borrowing and return from lending
❏ The yield curve: if positive, the bank borrowing for longer periods costs more than borrowing for short periods
❏ The reinvestment of the interest it earns on the money in the first 6 months.

This is how such deals were actually handled until the 1980s, when other techniques were developed. The banks are not keen now to quote these forward rates since the borrowing/lending uses up the bank's line of credit with other banks and also the line of credit with its own customers.

The *Forward Rate Agreement* (FRA) is the bank's answer to the request for the forward/forward deal.

The FRA is not about borrowing money, but about a future level of interest rates.

The future level is compared to an agreed level and the agreement is settled on the difference between the two rates. The future level in the London market will be based on the LIBOR rate – in this case, Eurodollar LIBOR.

For example, the corporate arranges with a bank that the 'target rate' of interest for 6 months ahead is 5% on a notional principal of $1 million. If, in 6 months, interest rates are 5%, then nothing happens. If rates are 4%, the corporate pays the bank 1% of $1 million (but will have lower borrowing costs elsewhere). If rates are 6%, however, the bank pays the corporate 1% of $1 million to help offset their extra borrowing costs (see Figure 13.1).

This is 'accounting for differences', and has the advantage of less credit risk. The bank, for example, is not borrowing or lending $1 million, only accounting for the difference in rates from a target of 5%.

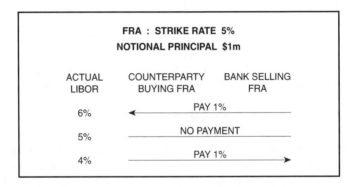

Figure 13.1   *Accounting for differences*

The corporate has fixed its rate for borrowing in 6 months in an indirect way. If rates go up, the corporate pays more for the money but is compensated for the extra cost by the FRA. If rates go down, the corporate will not benefit because the lower borrowing costs are offset by a payment under the FRA.

This line of explanation may well sound familiar. It's the same effect that was achieved by the interest rate futures transaction in Chapter 11. In selling the futures at 3.75%, the corporate was agreeing to settle on the difference between 3.75% and market rates at expiry. When rates were 4.75%, the corporate received 1% on the underlying contract value of $20m. When rates were 2.75%, the corporate paid the futures exchange 1% on the underlying $20m. The FRA is really an OTC future being arranged with a bank and not a futures exchange. It has the advantage of flexibility on both dates and amounts of money.

Typical FRA periods are '3 against 6' and '6 against 12'. This is because floating rates on loans and FRNs are revised at 3 month or 6 month intervals. A bank with a gap in its asset/liability management can thus close the exposure with an FRA. There will be a corporate market with corporates talking to their commercial banks for deals down to, say, $1m or £1m and a professional market, the banks between themselves, for typical sums from 50m to 100m and in sterling, yen, Swiss francs and euros.

How does the bank make a profit? The FRA is a product, like any other product, and sold with a bid/offer spread. Just as a market maker will buy shares and hope to sell them at a better rate, so the bank expects to buy FRAs at one rate and sell them at another. It will base the price for future interest rates on the deposit market yield curve or the prices of futures exchange contracts. Suppose that a '3 against 6' dollar FRA is quoted at 5.54/5.50. A bank will sell an FRA based on 5.54% but buy one based on 5.50%. If the rate at the 3 month date is 6%, the bank pays 46 basis points on the FRA it sold but receives 50 basis points on the one it bought. If rates are 5%, the bank receives 54 basis points on the FRA it sold but pays only 50 basis points on the one it bought (see Figure 13.2). Four basis points may not seem much for the administrative cost and the risk (*and* capital ratio for the risk) and it isn't. The market is very competitive and banks need to be totally efficient to make any money. As a result, the trader may choose not to offset the FRA with one in the opposite direction but believe they will receive more money than they will pay. This does, of course, now involve interest rate risk and risk limits must be set.

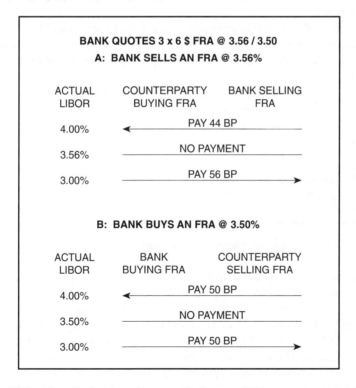

Figure 13.2   *How the bank makes a profit from an FRA*

(One technical point. With an FRA which is, say, in 3 months for 3 months, then the payment is made in *advance* of the second 3 month period. As a result, only the net present value is actually paid.)

It may be that an FRA buyer is unsure of the direction of interest rates. The FRA will protect against a rise in rates but no benefit will arise if rates fall. If this is unacceptable, the answer here is to pay for an *option* to have an FRA. If rates rise, the option to have the FRA is exercised. If rates fall, the option is abandoned. (Simple, really!)

The FRA solves the problem of an interest rate risk for one future time, but what about risk over, say, 5 years? For this we turn to *swaps*.

SWAPS

Comparative Advantage

Interest rate swaps exploit what could be described as arbitrage opportunities, and in doing so create a market in which others can hedge or speculate on the movement of interest rates.

It begins with the 19th century economist, David Ricardo and his 'Theory of Comparative Advantage'. Ricardo argued that two countries could benefit from international trade even where one made all products more productively than the second.

Let's take two countries, *ABC* and *XYZ*, and two products, *A* and *B*. The product rates per hour for *A* and *B* in both countries are shown in Figure 13.3.

	ABC			XYZ
Product *A*	100	Product *A*		50
Product *B*	100	Product *B*		70

Figure 13.3   *International trade – comparative advantage*

Ricardo argued that country *ABC* should concentrate on producing product *A* and country *XYZ* concentrate on product *B* and then trade. This is because, while country *ABC* is superior in both *A* and *B*, it has a great *comparative advantage* in *A*. Country *ABC*, thus, produces all product *A* and exports the surplus to country *XYZ*. The latter produces all product *B* and exports the surplus to country *ABC*. Both countries gain as *ABC* exploits to the full its comparative advantage in producing product *A*. This will become clearer from a study of the corresponding examples from the financial markets (see Figure 13.4 and the accompanying explanation).

We translate this now to borrowing rates instead. The two products become fixed rate finance and floating rate finance. The two countries become two companies, *ABC* and *XYZ*. Investors' perception of risk is not the same in the fixed interest rate market as it is in the floating rate market. Thus, company *ABC* may be able to borrow more cheaply than *XYZ* at either fixed or floating rate but the difference is not the same – that is, there is a comparative advantage to be exploited.

Company *ABC* can raise fixed rate finance at 7% or floating at LIBOR (really wants floating rate funds).

Company *XYZ* has to pay 10% for fixed rate borrowing and LIBOR + 1% for floating rate funds (really prefers fixed rate financing).

ABC can borrow cheaper than *XYZ* in both fixed and floating rate markets but has greater comparative advantage in fixed.

Therefore:

ABC raises fixed at 7% but agrees to pay LIBOR to *XYZ*. *XYZ* borrows floating rate funds at LIBOR + 1% but agrees to pay 8% to *ABC* (Figure 13.4).

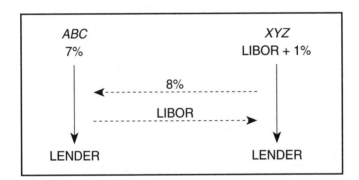

Figure 13.4 *Using the swap technique*

Thus:

ABC pays 7% fixed but receives 8% from *XYZ*. It pays LIBOR to *XYZ* but in effect is paying LIBOR −1%, less than if it borrowed at floating rate at LIBOR.

XYZ pays LIBOR + 1% but receives only LIBOR from *ABC*, thus costing *XYZ* 1%. It pays 8% to *ABC*, in effect paying 9% – but this is less than if it borrowed fixed at 10%. (This is another example of a technique that is not a 'zero-sum game'.)

ABC and *XYZ* are each saving 1% on their cost of borrowing by using the swap technique. This swap opportunity occurs because floating rate lenders do not distinguish between the credit standing of borrowers to the same degree as fixed rate lenders. We might imagine that if one borrower is AAA credit rating and one BBB, then the difference between the rates of borrowing, whether fixed or floating, would be the same. In fact, this is not the case. If lesser rated credits want to borrow at fixed rate instead of floating, then the rate is not quite as attractive.

Interest Rate Swaps

In our example above, the difference in rates was a considerable exaggeration on a real life situation. This was in order to simplify a concept that always seems complex to newcomers. The principle is the same even if the real life difference is only a matter of a few basis points.

There are, therefore, two aspects to an interest rate swap. One is simply that one party agrees to pay a fixed rate on a notional principal sum of money for a period of time and the other agrees to pay floating rate. In our FRA example (Figure 13.2) a counterparty bought an FRA at 5.54% from a bank. In effect they agreed to pay a fixed rate (5.54%) and receive a floating rate (LIBOR) from the bank. Thus the swap and the FRA are logically the same. Unlike an FRA, which was only for one future time period, a swap is for several time periods ahead, for example, 6 monthly rate comparisons for, say, 5 years.

The other element is a possible profit arising from the comparative advantage concept which we just described. Even without any 'profit' element, one party with a floating rate commitment may feel happier swapping into a fixed rate commitment.

The elements in the swap are:

❑   The fixed rate
❑   The variable rate
❑   The settlement periods
❑   The total maturity
❑   The underlying notional principal.

For example, the parties may agree that one pays 5.5% and the other pays Eurodollar LIBOR on a notional underlying principal of $50m. The swap is to last 5 years and the settlement periods are 6 monthly. That is, every 6 months 5.5% is compared with Eurodollar LIBOR and a net sum of money is paid over. If the difference was 1%, then 1% of $50m for 6 months is the sum to be paid over – $250,000. The money, however, is not in fact paid over until the end of the 6 monthly period, not at the beginning. That is because interest payments are paid in arrears. A bank, for example, sets the rate on an actual loan for 6 months at 5.5% but the interest is paid at the end of 6 months, not the beginning.

Making a Market in Swaps

How do these companies, *ABC* and *XYZ*, find each other? Obviously, with difficulty. So there is a role for banks to bring the parties together and take a piece of the action. In Figure 13.4, the bank could take 8% from *XYZ* and only pass on 7¾% to *ABC*. It could take LIBOR from *ABC* and only pass on LIBOR – ¼% to *XYZ*. *ABC* and *XYZ* will still profit from the deal but the bank now has ½% for its trouble.

The market began in 1982 and as it grew banks became prepared to carry out a swap just for one counterparty, pending finding another counterparty later. This is called a *warehouse* swap. The bank is prepared to 'warehouse' the swap until a counterparty can be found, in the meantime taking hedging action as we will explain later. It is called an 'unmatched swap'.

The swap, therefore, has simply become another product which the banks market with the usual bid/offer rates.

The bank may quote, for example, 5.80/5.75 for a 5 year dollar swap (Figure 13.5).

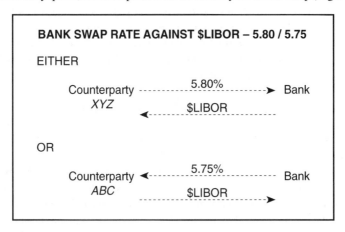

Figure 13.5   Bank swap quotation

If the bank stands in the middle between two counterparties (the matched swap), then the bank has no interest rate risk and a locked in 5 basis points profit. If LIBOR goes up, the bank pays more to counterparty *XYZ* but receives it from *ABC*. If rates fall, the bank receives less from *ABC* but pays less to *XYZ*. *XYZ* pays 5.80% to the bank and the bank pays 5.75% to *ABC*, keeping 5 basis points (Figure 13.6).

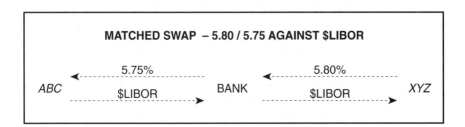

Figure 13.6   Using matched swap

The bank may have no interest rate risk but it does have counterparty risk. What if *ABC* or *XYZ* goes into liquidation and the bank is left with an unmatched swap?

Under today's rules from regulators, capital must be provided for this risk.

In providing a market in swaps the banks are exposed to risk until they can find someone who wants to do a swap in the opposite direction. In the meantime they can adopt hedging strategies:

❑ If the bank is at risk to a *fall in interest rates* (because it has lent floating and borrowed fixed), then it will buy fixed interest securities, whose price will rise when interest rates fall.

❑ If the bank is at risk should *interest rates rise* (because it has borrowed floating and lent fixed), then it can hedge in the *futures* market by selling an interest rate future, giving the right to borrow at prevailing rates of interest. When interest rates rise this right becomes valuable and the bank will make a profit on the futures contract.

(Notice the language used above. The bank receiving LIBOR and paying 5.75% can be said to have *lent floating and borrowed fixed* (and vice-versa).) Other language used is a reference to the 'payer' and the 'receiver'. This always refers to the fixed rate element.

Actual market rates tend to fall between the rates quoted for an AAA borrower and a single A borrower for borrowing for given periods of time. If $s, they are usually expressed as a given number of basis points over US Treasury bond rates for the fixed element. If £s, they are usually expressed as a given number of basis points over the gilts rate. The variable rate is Euro or domestic LIBOR.

Users of Swaps

Assuming that a 5 year dollar swap rate is quoted as 5.80/5.75, who are the users of these swaps? We find that the market talks of *liability swaps* and *asset swaps*.

❑ Liability swaps are simply swaps for borrowers of money
❑ Asset swaps are simply swaps for lenders of money.

The treasurer has a bank loan based on $ LIBOR (see Figure 13.7). Worried that rates will rise, he does a swap, changing the floating rate bank loan into fixed rate by this indirect route.

We can also envisage a situation in which a treasurer with a fixed rate loan could receive 5.75% and pay LIBOR, turning the fixed rate loan into floating rate. A further variation is possible. If the loan is, say, $100m, the treasurer can do the swap for only $50m – leaving half the money at fixed rate and half at floating (quite common).

Using the swap technique, a eurobond issuer may not only change the fixed rate basis into floating but create a profit margin of 10 basis points due to the general comparative advantage concept (see Figure 13.8).

What the issuer may well do is equalise the fixed rate payment and receipt and use the profit margin to cut the LIBOR rate (see Figure 13.9).

The issuer agrees to receive 5.65% instead of 5.75% and to pay LIBOR − 10 instead of just LIBOR. What we say is that the issuer has achieved 'sub-LIBOR funding'.

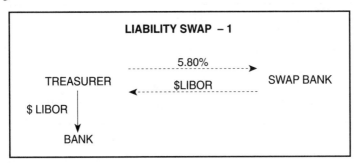

Figure 13.7 *Swap to change floating rate bank loan into fixed rate*

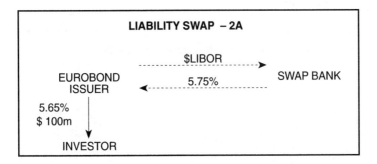

Figure 13.8 *Swap to change fixed rate bond into floating rate*

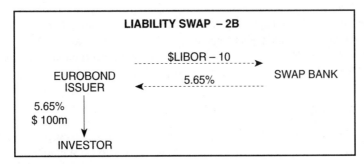

Figure 13.9 *Equalising the fixed rate payment and receipt*

The investor is receiving floating rate income based on $ LIBOR (either from a loan or FRN). Believing that rates will fall, the issuer swaps into a fixed rate return. We say that the investor has changed the FRN into a 'synthetic' fixed rate bond (see Figure 13.10).

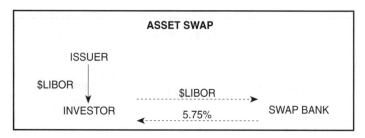

Figure 13.10   *'Synthetic' fixed rate bond*

Banks often buy fixed rate bonds from lesser rated corporates (that is, higher interest rates) to use for an asset swap to create floating rate income well above LIBOR (see Figure 13.11).

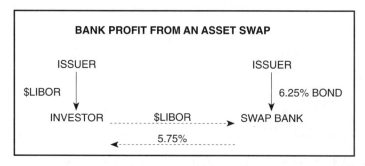

Figure 13.11   *Bank profit from an asset swap*

In Figure 13.11, the bank receives 6.25% from a bond but only pays 5.75% on the fixed leg of the swap. It also receives LIBOR and thus a total receipt of LIBOR + 50. It will probably 'package' the deal and pass it on to a fund looking for good floating rate income, the bank taking some profit while doing so.

Swaps and Futures

Swaps are really a strip of futures or FRA contracts lasting over several years. They are, of course, OTC with all the flexibility that that involves. When the corporate sold an interest rate future at 3.75%, we saw that the effect was the same as the FRA based on 3.75%. In the same way, selling an interest rate future at 3.75% is choosing to borrow fixed and lend floating (the alternative language we used for swaps). It's a swap (or FRA) for a single time period only. Equally, the buyer of an interest rate future is choosing to borrow floating and lend fixed – the other side of the swap.

Because the language and terminology used in FRAs and swaps is different from that used for futures, newcomers think of them as essentially different products when they are really all variations on the same product. They therefore have the essential characteristic of futures – that a hedger can gain protection from an adverse rate movement but will not benefit from a favourable one.

Futures are for 3 month time periods ahead (although we could book all eight quarterly contracts for the next 2 years – called a 'strip' of futures). FRAs are for one time period ahead but not necessarily 3 months and, again, a strip of FRAs could be purchased or sold. For periods of 2 years or more, swaps are more attractive. Most swaps are in the range 2–10 years. However, the former UK Halifax Building Society issued a 25 year bond which was said to have been swapped into floating rate for 25 years!

Other Swaps

A swap buyer may want a swap but only wish to commence in, say, 6 months' time. This becomes the *forward swap*.

In 6 months' time, the forward swap buyer's view of interest rates may turn out to be incorrect. The buyer is, however, committed to the swap. Another possibility, therefore, is to pay a premium for an option to have the swap later (just like the option to have an FRA). This is called by a curious piece of jargon – the *swaption*.

It may be that the notional principal in the swap is not constant but on a 'reducing' basis. For example, a swap based on a notional principal of $10m for 5 years but the amount of the principal is reduced each year. This could apply when the swap backs a loan of which some of the principal is constantly being repaid or a bond for which a sinking fund is being accumulated to redeem the bond. This is called an *amortising swap*.

The notional principal at risk might also vary but up and down rather than on a declining basis. This is the *roller coaster swap*.

There are swaps in which both parties pay floating rate, but on a different basis. For example, one pays Eurodollar LIBOR and the other pays 3 month US Treasury bill rates. This is the *basis swap*.

CURRENCY SWAPS

The swaps market began with currency swaps. It may be that a US-based issuer wants Swiss francs but is not well known to Swiss franc investors. A Swiss corporate or public body, well known in Switzerland, may want dollars but is not well known to dollar investors. The US issuer will have to pay a premium to raise Swiss francs and the Swiss issuer will have to pay a premium to raise dollars. The answer is for the US issuer to raise dollars, the Swiss issuer to raise Swiss francs and then swap the proceeds. This is the classic *currency swap.*

The first major case was in 1981, with the World Bank wanting a further Swiss franc issue and faced with paying a premium to persuade Swiss franc investors to hold even more World Bank paper. IBM wanted a dollar issue but faced the same problem. Salomon Bros arranged a swap. The World Bank raised the money in dollars and IBM raised the money in Swiss francs. Dollar investors were pleased to hold World Bank paper and Swiss franc investors were pleased to hold IBM paper. The two entities swapped the proceeds. On redemption (in 1986), they arranged to swap back at the same exchange rate.

In the meantime, IBM sent dollar interest payments to the World Bank who sent Swiss franc interest payments to IBM.

Again, as the market grew, banks took on unmatched deals and made a market in currency swaps. Sometimes, though, the bank can be lucky and match two investors coming to the market at the same time.

In September 1996, the European Investment Bank (EIB) and the Tennessee Valley Authority (TVA) came to the market at the same time. The EIB wanted 10 year D-marks and the TVA wanted 10 year dollars. However, the EIB could borrow in dollars 7 basis points less than TVA, but only 4 basis points less in D-marks. As a result, the EIB borrowed $1bn, the TVA borrowed DM1.5bn and they swapped the proceeds. It was a classic case of exploiting comparative advantage. In swapping directly, both parties also saved bid/offer spreads and reduced transaction costs.

CAPS, FLOORS AND COLLARS

Introduction

Sometimes, the user in this market may require protection in one direction only. For example, a corporate may seek protection from interest rates rising but seek to benefit should they fall. An investor, receiving money at floating rate, may seek protection from rates falling but seek to benefit should they rise.

This end objective can be achieved by interest rate options on trading exchanges. If the rate moves the wrong way for our market position, the option is exercised and compensation obtained. If the rate moves the right way for our borrowing/lending position, the option is abandoned and we benefit from better rates.

Exchanges, however, have drawbacks, as we have seen. The OTC market has responded with two flexible products to meet the above situations for borrowers and investors – the *cap* and the *floor.*

Caps

The interest rate cap sets a maximum level on a short-term rate interest rate. Buyers are compensated if the interest rate goes above a certain level (the strike level).

For example, the arrangement may be based on 3 months LIBOR and have a term of 3 years. The strike level is 5%, the revision of the rate is quarterly and the notional principal is $10 million. Thus, if LIBOR is 6% in 3 months, the seller pays the buyer 1% of $10 million for 3 months – say, $25,000 (see Figure 13.12).

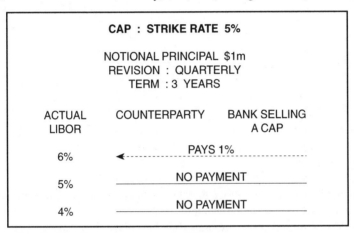

CAP : STRIKE RATE 5%

NOTIONAL PRINCIPAL $1m
REVISION : QUARTERLY
TERM : 3 YEARS

ACTUAL LIBOR	COUNTERPARTY	BANK SELLING A CAP
6%	◄------------ PAYS 1% ------------	
5%	NO PAYMENT	
4%	NO PAYMENT	

Figure 13.12 *Using the cap*

If rates are 5% or less, nothing happens and the cap buyer can benefit from lower borrowing rates. The fee is, of course, the option premium. The OTC cap can not only offer the precise dates we require but it is a continuous arrangement, like a swap, and not just for one time period ahead.

There are the usual variations on the theme that we associate with options. If the buyer is prepared to accept some interest rate risk, the strike rate in the above example could be chosen as 6%. This is 'out of the money' in options terms and the premium will be cheaper.

Floors

The interest rate floor is simply the opposite product. An investor, receiving income at floating rate, may buy a floor. This sets a minimum level to a rate of interest. The buyer is compensated if the market goes below this level (see Figure 13.13).

The terms could be exactly as described for the cap, but on the basis that payment is made if rates fall *below* the strike rate.

It may be that the user is fairly sure about interest rates for 1 year, but not thereafter. The cap or floor can be arranged to commence in 1 year's time – the *forward* cap or floor.

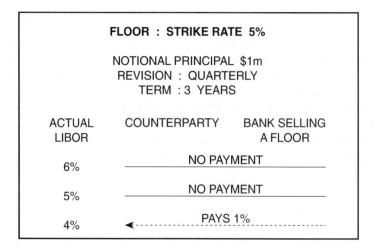

Figure 13.13   *Using the floor*

Collars

We will have seen from the above that the cap buyer pays a premium and receives payment if rates rise above a given level.

The floor seller receives a premium, but must make payment if rates fall below a given level.

Imagine simultaneously buying a cap at 6% and selling a floor at 4%.

The effect of this is shown in Figure 13.14.

The net effect is to lock into a band of rates – the *collar* – for the next 3 years.

If rates are between 6% and 4%, we borrow at the market rate. If rates rise above 6% we are protected. If they fall below 4%, we don't benefit. The effect of paying a premium and receiving one is that the cost is reduced. Rates can be chosen at which the two premiums are the same – the *no cost collar*.

This is an attractive device and very popular at the moment. All our other devices have turned around a given rate of interest. Here we select a band instead.

We have actually met this product before. It was in Chapter 8 on foreign exchange, and it was the 'cylinder' or 'collar' or 'range forward'. The future buyer of dollars will never have a worse rate than $1.85 per £ but never have a better rate than $1.95. It's just the same logic applied in a different market.

Caps, floors and collars are a series of interest rate options over a period of time. 2–5 years is the most popular range.

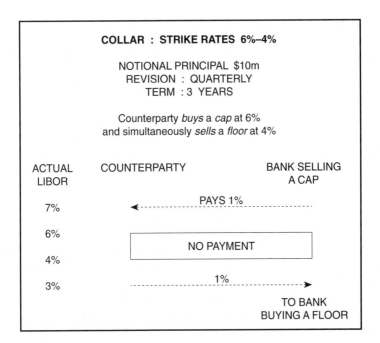

COLLAR : STRIKE RATES 6%–4%

NOTIONAL PRINCIPAL $10m
REVISION : QUARTERLY
TERM : 3 YEARS

Counterparty *buys* a *cap* at 6%
and simultaneously *sells* a *floor* at 4%

| ACTUAL LIBOR | COUNTERPARTY | BANK SELLING A CAP |

Figure 13.14   Using the collar

CREDIT DERIVATIVES

The most important recent technique in derivatives is the *credit derivative*. Whilst market risk has preoccupied derivatives, the Far East and Russian crises and earlier events have brought home the dangers of credit risk. The recent so-called Basle Committee decisions discussed in Chapter 2 are also focusing on more sophisticated control of credit risk.

In its broadest sense, a credit derivative is a customised agreement between two counterparties in which the payout is linked solely to some measure of the creditworthiness of a particular reference credit, and is thus largely independent of the market or other risks attached to the underlying contract. Contracts specify an exchange of payments in which at least one of the two legs is determined by the performance of the reference credit. Payouts can be triggered by a number of events, including a default, a rating downgrade or a stipulated change in the credit spread of the reference asset.

Credit derivatives (like other derivatives) split into futures-type contracts (usually swaps) and option-type contracts.

Although the products are relatively new, already the CME has introduced a product called 'Quarterly Bankruptcy Index' – with both futures and options available. This is clearly an attempt by an exchange to capture part of a very rapidly growing OTC market. The British Bankers' Association expects the market to reach $2000bn by end 2002 and $4800bn by 2004. London is the biggest centre, with around 50% market share and credit default swaps – protecting against default by a single counterparty – are the most popular product, accounting for around 45% of the market.

It is, of course, a very new product, and already there are siren voices pointing out that the correct pricing may not be properly understood, that there are unresolved issues around documentation and definitions and articles are beginning to appear on the 'hidden risks' in credit derivatives.

THE MARKET IN DERIVATIVE INSTRUMENTS

The BIS has carried out periodic surveys of the volume and value of derivatives contracts traded both on exchanges and on the much larger OTC market. The comparative figures for 1995–2001/02 in Tables 13.1 and 13.2 highlight the massive growth which has occurred in recent years. The markets have more than doubled in size, with huge growth in interest rate contracts generally and swaps in particular. Also notice the huge growth – nearly fivefold – in seven years of interest rate options traded on exchanges (Table 13.2). This increase in the market has been subsequent to Barings and other scandals, which led some commentators at the time to suggest that the derivatives bubble of the early '90s had burst – or at least that the growth era was over.

This growth in the market and the growth in sheer complexity have led the BIS and others to draw attention to the dangers of controlling the risks, and deficiencies in systems for controlling these risks.

To the usual counterparty and position risks we have to add legal risk and tax risk. The UK sterling swaps market was thrown into confusion by a decision that local authority swaps were illegal. Conflicting tax treatment in Australia and the US led to Westpac paying out an extra $80m in tax to the US authorities and cutting its dividend.

The outstanding example of the risk in derivative transactions was the collapse in early 1995 of the UK's oldest merchant bank, Baring Bros, alleged to be due to the activities of one trader, Nick Leeson. The bank's controls were woefully inadequate and management allowed one trader's activities to ruin the bank at a cost of £860 million. At Kidder Peabody, in the US, one trader, Joseph Jett, is alleged to have concealed losses of $350 million over a period of 2 years. The rogue trader at Daiwa in New York (who lost a similar sum to Nick Leeson) had apparently been concealing his mounting losses for eleven years! Mr Hamanaka at Sumitomo used derivatives allegedly to corner the world copper market, culminating in losses of around $2.4bn!

Table 13.1   *Global positions in OTC derivatives markets by type of risk*
              instruments

Instrument	March 1995	Dec 2001
Foreign exchange		
Outright forwards and forex swaps	8699	10,336
Currency swaps	1957	3942
Options	2378	2470
Other	61	
Total foreign exchange	13,095	16,748
Interest rate contracts		
FRAs	4598	7737
Swaps	18,283	58,897
Options	3548	10,879
Other	216	
Total interest rate	26,645	77,513
Equity-linked contracts		
Forwards and swaps	52	320
Options	527	1561
Total equity-linked	579	1881
Estimated gaps in reporting	6893	
Commodities / other		14,973
Grand Total	47,212	111,115

Source: BIS, May 2002.

Corporates, too, have incurred losses – Allied Lyons, Codelco, Metallgesellschaft, Procter and Gamble and Gibsons Greetings Cards were well publicised examples. The last two sued Bankers Trust and both settled out of court.

Perhaps we should not get this out of perspective. The banks lost enormous sums due to the LDC debt crisis, and also incurred large losses due to the global crises in the Far East and Russia. The bail out of Crédit Lyonnais, privatised in 1999, is estimated to have cost the French government somewhere between the equivalent of £10bn to £19bn (nobody seems quite sure!). The banks are owed £8000 million by Eurotunnel and haven't a hope of getting back more than half. This makes

Barings' £860 million loss seem less significant! These losses were incurred in bank lending, which we've had for the last 600 years. There aren't too many weighty reports on the risk in bank lending and yet reports on derivative risk have been written not only by the BIS but by the IMF, Bank of England, General Accounting Office (US), Federal Reserve and the G30 group of bankers.

Table 13.2   Exchange traded instruments – notional amounts outstanding in billions of US dollars

Instrument	Dec 1995	June 2002
Interest rate futures	5863	9415
Interest rate options	2742	12,477
Currency futures	38	48
Currency options	43	30
Stock market index futures	172	365
Stock market index options	329	1750
Total	9187	24,085

Source: BIS, 2002.

It's unfortunate that the intellectual effort required to gain an understanding of these products leads some people to dismiss it all as 'gambling'.

Suppose we have two corporates facing significant interest rate risk over the next 3 years. One buys certainty by doing an interest rate swap and electing to pay fixed. The other does nothing.

Who is gambling? Surely, it is the corporate that does nothing and leaves itself open to whatever volatility of interest rates comes along.

The paradox about these products is that the ability to use them to lay off risk means that bankers can *take* more risk. Insofar as they can take more risk, the more they can offer end users ingenious products which they find beneficial.

As the markets grow, there are more opportunities for laying off a growing variety of risks in an ever more efficient way. As a result, more and more end user products are being released which they find attractive.

This is the beneficial aspect of these markets. Of course, there are the gamblers (speculators) and the markets couldn't exist without them, but to dismiss it all as gambling is to make a serious mistake.

We are seeing this in the consumer markets, where individuals can now have fixed rate mortgages for up to 20 years, capped mortgages and an increasing range of exotic variations. These allow the individual to budget with peace of mind. Equally, investment products have been launched with a variety of guarantees, typically using options, to ensure that an individual is protected against a market downturn. This, again, allows the person in the street to know that their long term savings are not exposed to undue risk.

SUMMARY

Forward rate agreements (FRAs) are a way of fixing a rate of interest for a date in the future and for a given period of time (*forward/forward*).

The buyer is compensated by the seller if market rates on the given date exceed the given *strike rate*. The buyer, however, must compensate the seller if market rates fall below the strike rate.

Borrowers seeking protection will *buy* FRAs, investors will *sell* them. Banks make a profit through the use of a bid/offer spread.

Essentially, the FRA is the exchange-traded interest rate futures contract in the OTC market.

The FRA is for one forward period only. *Swaps* are agreements for many forward periods (for example, one per year for the next 10 years). Again, the market rate of interest (usually LIBOR) is compared with a given strike rate leading to a compensatory payment from one party to the other.

The buyer in the case of the FRA is usually called the *payer* in the swap (that is, the payer of the fixed rate). The seller in the FRA is usually called the *receiver* in a swap (that is, the receiver of the fixed rate).

The above are *interest rate swaps*; there are also *currency swaps*.

Profit may arise for both parties from the application of the theory of *comparative advantage*. Banks will make a profit through the bid/offer spread.

Swaps for those borrowing money are *liability swaps*; swaps for investors are *asset swaps*.

Swaps are essentially a series of FRAs. A swap starting at a future date is a *forward swap*; an option to have a swap is a *swaption* and a swap of two floating rates is a *basis swap*.

A borrower can be protected from an interest rate rise but still benefit from a fall using an interest rate *cap*; an investor can benefit from an interest rate rise but still be protected from a rise using an interest rate *floor*.

The combination of a cap and floor leads to a range of interest rates for future transactions called a *collar*.

Caps, floors and collars are variations on *options*.

Central banks carried out a survey of the OTC derivatives market in June 1998. Its initial estimate of the notional value outstanding was $71.5 trillion, but the replacement cost was estimated at just $2.58 trillion. The BIS estimate for the notional value outstanding of exchange traded contracts in mid-2002 was $24.1 trillion.

Interest rate derivatives accounted for much the largest category for both OTC and exchange-traded derivatives.

Insurance

14 Insurance

14 Insurance

BACKGROUND TO THE INSURANCE MARKETS

History

> *But ships are but boards, sailors but men: there be land rats and water rats,*
> *water-thieves and land-thieves, I mean pirates: and then there is the peril of*
> *waters, winds and rocks.*
> (*The Merchant of Venice,* Act I, Scene III)

Shylock is quite right and Antonio is soon to discover that an insurance premium is cheaper than a pound of flesh any day! While the history of insurance is lost in the mists of time, our modern history surely begins with marine insurance.

Shipowners would meet with rich merchants who would agree to jointly pay for any losses for a share of the premiums. A contract was drawn up and merchants added their name at the bottom. As they wrote underneath the text, they were *underwriters*. Apart from this, a group of shipowners might agree to raise a levy on all members and share losses between them. This principle continues today with the so-called 'P&I' club (see below).

Meetings in London for business took place in coffee houses. In 1688 we have the first mention of Edward Lloyd's coffee house in Tower Street. They moved to Lombard Street in 1691. Then, as now, information was power and, in 1734, they began a publication, *'Lloyd's List'*, which gave shipping information and also some financial data. It is still published today.

The insurance world in those days was as full of scandals as the world of stocks and shares. Just as the Stock Exchange was set up to bring respectability and rules so, in 1769, one Thomas Fielding set up a new organisation meeting in Pope's Head Alley and, in 1771, drew up a document setting up a ruling committee. A move to the Royal Exchange building in 1774 was followed in 1781 by the first constitution of Lloyd's. These were the early origins of the famous Lloyd's of London, of which more later.

Even earlier than Edward Lloyd's coffee house, the Fire Office Company was set up in 1680. The Amicable followed in 1706 and the London Assurance and the Royal Exchange Assurance in 1720.

The basic idea of insurance is the *sharing of risk*. Experience may suggest that, of an insurance population of buildings, 2% will have a fire in a given year. Dividing the anticipated claims by the numbers seeking insurance gives us the *premium* to be paid. Those who haven't had a fire have contributed to a pool to pay for those who have, while buying protection in case they were the unfortunate ones.

The Insurance Market

The biggest markets in the world by total premium income are the US, Japan, the UK, Germany and France. Premiums in the US in 2001 were $904bn, Japan $446bn, UK $218bn, Germany $124bn and France $114bn. The premiums for Europe as a whole totalled $762bn, of which the UK, Germany and France contributed 60%.

There are clear differences between life and non-life business. Non-life business is 50% of the market in the US, 39% in Europe, but only 20% in Japan. Taking life business only, Europe is the biggest market in the world, followed by the US.

Another way of looking at it is by market penetration, that is, as a percentage of GDP. Here, countries like South Korea and South Africa come out well. Of the industrialised countries, the largest by this measure are the UK, Switzerland, Japan and Ireland.

(Figures from Swiss Re *Sigma* publication No 6/December 2002.)

The main characteristic of the UK insurance companies is the international flavour of the business. This is discussed under the heading 'The London Market' later in this chapter.

Assurance/Insurance

Assurance is the cover for events which are certain. Since death comes to us all, life insurance (strictly speaking, 'death insurance'!) is providing cover for an event which is certain, only the timing being open to doubt. The study of the relevant statistics and laws of probability by a profession called *actuaries* leads to an accurate estimate as to how many of an insured population will die in a given year. As a result, it would be very unlikely that the claims would exceed the premiums. In other words, the company expects to make an *underwriting* profit. In addition, premiums are paid in advance and will be invested prior to any money being paid out. The second source of profit is thus the return on the investments. Ironically, interest rate risk will be more than mortality risk! Finally, people take out a life policy and perhaps do not change this for the whole of their life. As a result, the business is stable and can invest for the long-term. The nature of this business is such that it is natural for them also to invest funds to provide pensions in the longer term. We, thus, talk of the 'life and pensions business'.

The industry has been ingenious in working out variations on the theme of a simple life policy. One variation is *term assurance*. The life cover is for a given number of years such as 10 years. As death is no longer certain, the policy is cheaper. We can have heavier protection for a vulnerable period (a young family) than later.

Endowment policies add the element of investment. Life cover is provided up to the age of, say, 50 and if death has not taken place a sum of money is guaranteed. Often the 'life' element is only 10% of the premiums or even less.

Living assurance is a new type which has become popular in the US. This policy will pay out on the diagnosis of serious diseases such as cancer, heart disease, and so on.

Life policies can be with or without *profits*. The with profits policy declares bonuses annually (*reversionary*) and at termination.

A variation on this theme, which has become popular in many countries (US/Canada/UK/France), is to link the policy to mutual fund performance (*unit linked*), as the fund is usually divided into units (see Chapter 7).

Insurance is providing cover for events which may or may not happen: for example, theft, fire, accident, storms, and so on. Judging the probability of these events is much more difficult than judging the incidence of death and frequently claims exceed premiums – an underwriting loss. In recessions, for example, the incidence of arson mysteriously increases!

At times, too, premiums are driven down to uneconomic levels due to fierce competition. The industry is cyclical. It is not difficult to start up in insurance and, when profits are good, firms are attracted in until the extra competition produces losses. Firms then depart until profits rise again and the whole cycle starts once more. The 1980s and early 1990s were a very bad period for insurance, exacerbated by an extraordinary series of disasters – hurricanes, the Exxon Valdez spillage, and so on. Heavy losses were made, but then things settled down a little. Profits rose once again, new entrants came in and there was over-capacity in the industry, premiums fell and things were difficult, leading to a new spate of mergers. The events of 11 September 2001 changed things again. Premiums have increased considerably and we have moved to a new phase in the cycle.

The possibility of underwriting loss means that a good profit from the investment of the premiums is essential since this may be the only profit there is. To make matters worse, premiums are specifically renewed annually and the insured party may look around and decide to switch to another company, leading to less certainty regarding future income.

The investment policy of the insurance company, therefore, has to pay much more attention to liquidity than the investment policy of companies in life and pensions.

As a result of the two sides of the business – assurance and insurance – we find companies which do assurance only, insurance only and companies which are in both markets, called *composites*.

As well as public companies with shareholders, it is very common to find companies which are not public companies but are owned jointly by the policy holders. These are called *mutuals* and this is very common across all the Western markets, especially for life companies.

Regulation

The importance of insurance, and the fact that it is often bought by members of the general public, means that it is an industry which is closely regulated. The collapse of the Vehicle and General Company in the UK in 1971, for example, left 800,000 motorists uninsured overnight!

In the US, regulations are made by both the central government and the states themselves. In the UK, regulation is from the Financial Services Authority, in France from the Direction des Assurances and in Germany from a body called the BAV. In Japan, insurance is now controlled by the Financial Supervisory Agency, set up in 1998.

Regulations may cover general supervision, licensing, solvency ratios, accountancy practices and annual returns. They will also cover the question of compulsory insurance, such as third party motor insurance, public liability and so on.

Solvency ratio is similar to the concept of capital ratio in banking (see Chapter 2). In banking it was, in essence, a prudent relationship between capital and lending. In insurance, it is a prudent relationship between capital (shareholders' equity plus reserves) and premiums. Money spent buying *reinsurance* from others can usually be deducted from the premiums (up to a maximum figure), thus allowing the insurer to take more business. The rules are complicated and alternative calculations are often possible. Each country tends to have different rules but the EU single market regulations are imposing common minimum standards. Liquidity is important and the regulations may demand that part of the capital must be held as a *minimum guarantee fund*. In the US, if claims arise from risks written in London, they must be covered by a letter of credit.

Distribution

The question of the distribution channel for selling personal insurance is very important. It has led to insurers linking with banks to use them as a channel for selling policies (see Chapter 4) and banks buying or starting insurance companies.

Typical distribution channels are:

❑ Tied agents
❑ Direct sales staff
❑ Independent financial advisers (IFA)
❑ Part-time agents
❑ Brokers
❑ Telephone-based.

Tied agents are usually self-employed and sell only the policies of one company – Allianz, for example, has 43,000. They are also very common in France, where there are about 80,000.

A *direct sales force* is often employed, especially in assurance. In Japan, much of insurance is sold by a unique sales force of 'insurance ladies'.

Independent financial advisers will make recommendations from a range of products. They may charge a fee for their advice or simply take a commission on the policy offered from the company concerned. In the latter case, the possibility of bias towards high commission policies may lead to the 'independence' of IFAs being questioned. The UK has struggled with this problem in recent years and regulations forced IFAs to register with a 'Self-Regulatory Organisation' (SRO) and declare their commission on the recommended policy. Another rule called 'polarisation' ruled out combining the roles of IFA and tied agent in any way. For example, a bank manager might act as agent for the bank's mutual funds but act as adviser in other matters. This is not permitted. A seller of mutual funds and life policies must inform the prospective buyer in writing whether their status is that of IFA or tied agent. However, the Financial Services Authority has been looking at the possibility of altering the rules on polarisation, and from 2004 the strict division between independent advisers and tied agents will be abolished. Firms will be able to continue to describe themselves as tied agents provided that they offer the customer the option of paying a fee. Advisers will be required to disclose a menu of charges and fees prior to a sale.

Part-time agents are usually solicitors and estate agents who will handle personal assurance and insurance on a casual basis and take commission.

Brokers are very common in the US, the UK and the Netherlands. They are much more involved in commercial insurance for businesses than personal insurance. In so far as they do personal insurance, much of it is in areas like motor and household which are not especially lucrative. For the broker, it is the contact from which they hope to sell more profitable life and pensions business.

As elsewhere in financial markets, many mergers have taken place. The UK's last surviving independent broker of any size, Sedgwick, was taken over by Marsh & McLennan (US) in August 1998. Through a series of takeovers, the industry is now dominated by the US brokers Marsh & McLennan and Aon. These large brokers do not just do classic broker business – they also have consulting arms for pensions and employee benefits.

There is also a type of distribution called *industrial*. This involves calling door to door to collect premiums in cash. The term was used in the 19th century as it was regarded as insurance for people employed in the factories. In the UK, the Prudential was famous for its industrial sales force, giving rise to a cliché, 'the man from the Pru'.

Today this type of distribution is very expensive and is dying out fast in the US and Australia. The percentage cost of premiums collected is much higher than for other types of business. It suits some policy holders who manage their lives on a week to week cash basis! For others, sadly, loneliness is a factor. There will be someone to talk to each week even if it's only the person from the insurance company. Many companies are abandoning this type of business. The UK Prudential gave up taking new policies from January 1995, at which time it employed 8000 people visiting 1.6 million homes. It finally abandoned this business in 2001.

Lastly, mention should be made of the fact that company pension schemes (where they exist) usually provide life assurance cover automatically.

Telephone-based, as a way of cutting costs, is becoming very common. In the UK, this was pioneered by Direct Line, a subsidiary of the Royal Bank of Scotland, which now has three million motor policies, the largest private sector insurer in this market. They have now set up Línea Directa in Spain using Bankinter and similar bodies in Italy, Germany and Japan. Other insurance companies such as Axa and Zurich have followed suit as well as others in the UK.

Self-Insurance

As insurance is essentially a spreading of risk, the rising premiums in some market sectors have led to a growth in *self-insurance*. For example, municipal authorities with their common interests might form their own pool of premiums, especially for public and employers' liability.

For a single entity, a large multinational company, for example, self-insurance might simply involve putting aside an amount of money each year into a fund to build up a sum to meet given insurance risks. This could apply if the company felt that it was a much better risk than the general insured population of firms for a given risk and was paying excessive premiums as a result. It also saves on insurance commission and expenses.

In marine insurance, an association of shipowners will organise mutual aid for risks not covered under a marine hull policy. Each member will contribute to a pool to cover losses up to a given sum. Above this sum, reinsurance will be used (see below). These associations are known as *Protection and Indemnity Associations* or P&I clubs. There are 39 in the London market.

REINSURANCE

Definitions

Reinsurance is the form of insurance by which an insurance company can transfer to another company all or part of its liability for claims of a given type. This reduces the risk that excessive claims could seriously weaken the company.

The company transferring the risk is the *reinsured* and is also known as the *ceding* company. The company accepting the risk is the *reinsurer*.

The reinsurer may themselves pass on some of the risk to another company – this is a *retrocession* contract.

The reinsured company now has protection against excessive claims or a large accumulation of claims and can write more business than if it was standing 100% of the loss.

The amount of business it can take is limited by the solvency margin. The reinsured company can deduct premiums due to reinsurers when calculating this (although EU regulations restrict this to 50%).

Generally, reinsurance is divided into *proportional* and *non-proportional*.

Proportional and Non-Proportional Reinsurance

Proportional   The reinsurer takes an agreed share of the risks ceded in return for the same share of the premiums less a *reinsurance commission*. This latter is to offset commission paid to intermediaries and also the expenses incurred.

In the case of *quota share reinsurance*, the reinsurer takes an agreed proportion of all insurances of a given type written by the ceding company.

Surplus reinsurance occurs where the original insurer cedes the whole contract to a treaty where the original insurer bears some risk and the reinsurers the rest.

Occasional risks, not covered by the treaty, may be reinsured on a *facultative* basis.

Non-proportional   The reinsurers contribute to losses in excess of a given figure in return for a premium. This may be *excess of loss* or *excess of loss ratio*.

Excess of loss   Here the reinsurers agree to pay any loss in excess of a given figure up to a maximum stated amount. This may be on a *per risk* basis (that is specific to, say, a ship or building) or on an *event basis* (for example, a hurricane, and often called *catastrophe* cover). It is typically written in layers according to the risk of a 'hit'.

Excess of loss ratio   Here the excess of claims over an agreed loss ratio is reinsured. The loss ratio is the ratio of claims to premiums. For example, a reinsurer might cover 90% of losses above a loss ratio of 75% to a maximum of 110%. Suppose the premium income was $10m. A 75% loss ratio would arise for claims of $7.5m. A 110% loss ratio arises with claims of $11m. The difference is $3.5m. A reinsured might agree to cover 90% of this figure, leaving the reinsurer to bear some of the loss (an important principle).

Financial Reinsurance

This has three key features:

- ❏   A ceiling on the liability for the reinsurer
- ❏   A recognition of the time value of money
- ❏   A sharing of profits through premium rebates.

The first policies were the *time and distance* policies of Lloyd's syndicates in the 1970s. The reinsurer undertook to meet a number of future claim payments. The reinsured undertook to pay a premium equal to the net present value (that is, the discounted value) of the above payments. The reinsurer, in a tax haven, would make a profit by reinvesting the premium at a higher rate of interest than that used in the discounting calculation.

The reinsured was left with no responsibility for the correct investment of the premium and might still benefit from a rate of return it could not achieve by itself. There was no transfer of risk and the arrangement was purely financial.

Today's financial reinsurance contracts do involve a transfer of risk, for example, timing risk, that is, that claims payments may be made earlier than expected. They might also agree to cover a sum higher than that implied by the premium (*finite risk*).

Financial insurance contracts can be:

❑ *Retrospective* – the schedule of future payments is guaranteed in respect of business already written
❑ *Prospective* – providing cover for future losses on business currently being written
❑ *Loss portfolio transfer* – a transfer of liability for losses from policies already written up to a maximum figure.

The Reinsurance Market

Lloyd's (to be discussed below) covers reinsurance, as do many insurance companies. It is, however, a specialist international business rather dominated by specialist companies like Munich Re and Swiss Re, the world's two biggest. The German and Swiss firms are helped by being allowed to build up catastrophe reserves which can be offset against tax. In the US, high general catastrophe reserves are allowed – the tax position is much more favourable than in the UK.

As in most financial markets, consolidation has taken place. The US General Re, the world's third biggest, took a majority holding in Cologne Re, but was itself acquired by Berkshire Hathaway in 1998. Swiss Re bought Life Re (US) and Munich Re bought American Re.

The third largest resinsurer, by premium income, is Cologne Re, followed by Lloyd's, Allianz and the Zurich Group.

Reinsurance brokers also operate internationally and play a very important role in non-proportional reinsurance and also in handling unusual risks. Reinsurance broking is especially strong in the UK.

Financial reinsurance is a growing area and Zurich Insurance is probably the largest specialist. Its subsidiary is Centre Re and it has bought the Pinnacle company in Bermuda, which has underwritten many reinsurance policies for Lloyd's. Bermuda is the centre for financial reinsurance due to its tax free status.

The banks have also become involved in financial reinsurance and Bankers Trust have set up a subsidiary to handle this in Jersey (Channel Islands). J.P. Morgan and Marsh & McLennan have set up a joint venture catastrophe insurer based in Bermuda.

The excess of loss market was particularly badly hit by a string of disasters in the 1980s and early 1990s. This includes Hurricanes Gilbert, Hugo and Andrew; the Philips Petroleum explosion; the Piper Alpha oil rig disaster; the San Francisco earthquake; the Los Angeles riots; the Exxon Valdez oil spill; and the storms in Southern England in October 1987 and January 1990.

This spate of catastrophes has even led the Chicago Board of Trade to set up futures and options contracts for 'catastrophe insurance'! The latest development, however, is *catastrophe bonds*. Catastrophe bonds (first issued in 1994) are issued backed by a pool of insurance policies and designed to spread the risk. For example, Tokyo Fire and Marine issued $100m 10 year bonds in November 1997. They offered a high yield but the possibility of loss of some or all capital if Tokyo is struck by an earthquake in the next ten years. It is a further example of the idea of asset-backed securities which we discussed in Chapter 6.

It appeals to investors who are looking for a high yield for extra risk. In effect, investors are taking on the function of reinsurance, and most issuers so far have been reinsurance companies. This brings giant insurers into competition with investment bankers. Swiss Re and Allianz have set up capital market divisions, and Goldman Sachs has launched an insurance arm!

The idea has spread now into ordinary insurance, as opposed to catastrophe insurance. Hanover Re issued a bond in 1988 backed by ordinary life assurance policies, thus packaging the risk and selling it to investors who want higher yield but not the risk implied in catastrophe bonds.

THE LONDON MARKET

What people refer to as 'The London Market' consists of:

❑ Lloyd's
❑ The International Underwriting Association (IUA).

The IUA was itself formed in 1998 from a merger of the marine insurance body, The Institute of London Underwriters, and the corresponding organisation for non-marine insurance, The London Insurance and Reinsurance Association. The IUA has 117 members.

The London market enjoys a unique status in the insurance industry as the most important trading centre for risks from all over the world. It is a concentration of the biggest providers of insurance in one place, with brokers (142) as agents, the insurance companies (some 200) and Lloyd's syndicates as providers. Some 40% of aviation premiums world-wide and 60% of premiums for offshore oil and gas rigs are collected here. Apart from the Lloyd's brokers and IUA insurers, there are 39 P&I clubs specialising in the insurance of ships and cargo (cf. page 336 for P&I under Self-Insurance).

There is increasing cooperation between Lloyd's and the IUA to strengthen the appeal of the London market. There is a common standard slip and common terms, the 'General Underwriting Agreement' (GUA). In addition, there is now a common service company. Lloyd's own Policy Signing Office has merged with Xchanging and the equivalent IUA body to form 'Inssure'.

Lloyd's has always been particularly strong in international marine insurance and the time has come to consider this important body.

LLOYD'S

Organisation

Lloyd's of London is a special case and merits special treatment. The Corporation of Lloyd's (formed in the 1771 reorganisation) does not itself insure anyone. The council of Lloyd's lays down the regulations for members' financial status, provides premises and general central support services. The insurance itself is provided by individual members called *names*.

There are at present about 2490 names and they risk their personal wealth in providing insurance underwriting as they have unlimited liability. The theory is that, with unlimited liability, people will behave more prudently. The problem is, that with 2490 names and only 86 professional underwriters actually doing the work, controlling their actions is difficult. Much of the debate in Lloyd's over the last 20 years has turned on the question of giving the names more control, especially when it is borne in mind that in 1988 there were over 30,000 names! Most people will have read of individuals in Lloyd's having all their personal wealth destroyed (it even featured in a hugely praised play on Broadway and London's West End – *Amy's View*). This was because Lloyd's lost £8bn between 1988 and 1992 and, in these circumstances, unlimited liability became a personal disaster. Why did the names take such a risk? It was because, historically, it had been very profitable with generous tax concessions … or, if you want to be harsh, greed.

The actual underwriting is carried out by professional underwriters organised into 86 *syndicates* (in 1980, there were 437). Each syndicate is run by a *managing agency*, of which there are 49. As is often the case, they are dominated by the biggest (Ace, Limit, Amlin, Wellington) and the top 10 manage 50% of the capacity.

The syndicate runs for a year and is then reorganised. The accounts for that year are published 3 years later. For example, the accounts for 1997 were published in 2000. This allows time for claims to be made and settled. Even then, there may still be potential further claims, so these are reinsured so that the books can be closed – *reinsurance to close*. More recently, Lloyd's has proposed a move to 1 year accounting and we discuss this later.

Each name is looked after by a member's *agent* and they advise the members on the rules, risks and which syndicates to join. There are 20 agents.

Lloyd's will use brokers but only those who are the *Lloyd's brokers* (some 140). They have to be able to distribute premiums to several syndicates and collect payment of claims from several syndicates. There are also some direct sales, especially for motor insurance.

To facilitate dealings between underwriters and brokers, there is a central service provider, *Inssure*. This not only handles the distribution of money for premiums and claims but will also prepare the wordings of policies and check them.

The names must have personal disposable wealth of £350,000. They will deposit 40% of their maximum premium capacity. If the capacity is £1m, they will deposit £400,000. At this level, the risk will probably be spread over some 10/15 syndicates.

The big attraction for the aristocracy and wealthy sports and pop stars has always been the threefold opportunity for income:

❑   The investment revenue from the deposit
❑   The investment income from the premiums
❑   The share of underwriting profit.

In addition, the attitude of the tax authorities in previous years was not as strict as it is today.

Among the names are the Duke of Marlborough, author Jeffrey Archer, jockey Lester Piggott, golfer Tony Jacklin and former Prime Minister, Edward Heath. The late Robert Maxwell, too, was a name.

The names contribute 2.0% of premiums to a central fund for the protection of the insured and can themselves insure against excessive claims (although this has become more difficult and costly in recent years).

Lloyd's is run from the £160m Richard Rogers building which was opened in 1986. At the heart is the *room*. This is the area where underwriters sit on uncomfortable desks called 'boxes' and are visited by brokers seeking cover for particular risks. A broker gets agreement from a prominent underwriter (the 'lead underwriter') first – this is a *line* which is expressed as a percentage of the total risk. They then visit other underwriters (who will probably follow this example from one of their eminent colleagues) until they have enough 'lines' to cover the policy. Sometimes they may cover more than the required total to spread the risk further – say to 125%. In this case, each underwriter is scaled back ('signed down'). So, an original 5% would be scaled down to 4%. However, an original percentage is never 'scaled up' and there may be no change if there is an initial agreement for a 'line to stand'.

In the room is the famous Lutine Bell. This was salvaged by Lloyd's from HMS Lutine during the Napoleonic wars. In the days when communications were not as good as today, one ring was bad news (a delayed ship was lost) and two rings was good news (the delayed ship had arrived safely in harbour). It is now rung on ceremonial occasions only. The bell was rung when the Queen opened the building in 1986. In view of the many scandals which surrounded Lloyd's at the time, one wit asked whether it would be one ring or two! It was also rung on 4 September, 1998, when the Department of Trade and Industry approved the market's recovery plan – the Equitas vehicle (see below).

Lloyd's is run by the Lloyd's Council of 18 members – active names, non-active names, corporate members, the Chairman and Chief Executive and six others nominated from outside. There used to be a regulatory board and a market board, but these were replaced by the new franchise board in 2003.

The Chief Executive of Lloyd's is Nick Prettejohn and the Chairman is Lord Levene of Portsoken.

Lloyd's is a major centre for world reinsurance, of key importance for aviation insurance and marine insurance, and has pioneered policies for new risks such as AIDS and computer fraud. It has also always specialised in unusual risks such as multiple births, a famous film star's legs (Betty Grable, many years ago) and the world's largest cigar! Its reputation in the US was enormously enhanced by its prompt settlement following the 1906 San Francisco earthquake, in contrast to many other insurers.

Early Problems

From the late 1960s onwards, the operation of Lloyd's began to attract increasing criticism. The accounting information was weak (and prevented names from realising the true facts); managing agencies shared profits but not losses; some syndicates were exceeding premium limits; periodically huge losses arose; and finally, the ownership of managing agencies by brokers led to conflicts of interest.

Most of these problems were addressed by the Lloyd's Act of Parliament, passed in mid-1982 and becoming law in January 1983.

Before it even became law, Lloyd's was hit by massive scandals involving illegal transfers of money to offshore companies abroad. These transfers resulted in heavy losses, most of which had to be met by a special fund set up at Lloyd's. They led to a further change in which the outside members of the Lloyd's Council (nominated by the Bank of England) and nominations of the non-working names were to be in a majority. This was implemented in 1987.

Commercial Problems

The problems that hit Lloyd's in the late 1980s and early 1990s were commercial problems, partly due to poor underwriting rather than fraud.

The names have, of course, unlimited liability and began to find themselves facing huge losses, in many cases involving personal ruin.

This was particularly true in the excess of loss market (LMX). Here one syndicate reinsures the losses of another or of a company outside the Lloyd's market. At first, syndicates specialising in excess of loss were very profitable and attracted new and undercapitalised names. The old wealth minimum level of £100,000 had been kept at this figure for far too long and was only raised to £250,000 in 1990. Gooda Walker syndicate 290 went from underwriting capacity of £6.2m in 1982 to £69.4m in 1989. As the string of catastrophes occurred, to which we have already referred, names faced huge losses. Accusations began to be made that 'insiders' only put money into the safest syndicates and that some agents packed innocent names onto weak syndicates as cannon fodder. The insiders, however, put their money into safe syndicates, known as 'baby' or 'preferred' syndicates. In particular, there had been excessive passing on of reinsurance risks from one syndicate to another.

Members of the Oakley Vaughan syndicates brought a unique court case against the Corporation of Lloyd's itself, claiming that it had failed in its duty to protect the names. In June 1992, the High Court came to a decision. It was decided that Lloyd's had a duty to regulate the market and act fairly, but no specific duty of care to the names.

Another problem was caused by huge payments for compensation as a result of litigation arising in the US. The cases concerned pollution and asbestosis. In some cases, the law was even changed with retrospective effect. The uncertainties this created led to a large number of years' accounts being left 'open' – a highly undesirable state of affairs. Normally, the accounts are closed after 3 years by 'reinsurance to close'. If the value of potential claims is so uncertain that they cannot be reinsured, the accounts are left open. The names then face unlimited future claims on their resources.

The Rowland Report   David Rowland, Chairman of Sedgwicks, was asked to head a task force and produce a report on how Lloyd's could be a safer place for the names and respond to the latest difficulties.

Rowland made his report in January 1992. After allowing time for discussion of its revolutionary proposals, he then produced a firm business plan in April 1993.

The key elements of the Rowland proposals were:

1. Corporate members with limited liability to be admitted in 1994.
2. The formation of a new reinsurance company called Equitas, to which all the claims for earlier losses not yet settled would be transferred; this would enable a cap to be placed on names' losses.
3. A system like unit trusts to be set up to allow names to put money into a 'pool' of multiple syndicates.
4. The size of the Council to be reduced to make it more effective.

We must remember that the essence of Lloyd's had always been that of private members with unlimited liability. The admission of corporates with limited liability was a revolutionary change. Many new corporates were set up to trade at Lloyd's, usually via a quoted investment trust, spreading investment over a range of syndicates. Some larger investment trusts have bought underwriters and some underwriters have bought capacity on their own syndicates. For example, one of the largest corporate capital providers, Angerstein, has merged with one of the largest managing agencies, Murray Lawrence. Today, limited liability members provide 86% of the capacity at Lloyd's. (As well as corporates, individual names can change to a form of limited liability.) Outsiders are also buying in to Lloyd's – General Re has bought managing agency D.P. Mann, and Bermuda-based Ace has bought Charman Underwriting.

The second part of the above plan was the proposal to concentrate all old business into one new company and cap names' losses. All losses not settled up to 1992 were to be transferred to Equitas, but the names had to agree. The offer was put to 34,000 names who were affected. It was approved by 90% of the names by 30 August 1996, when the offer went unconditional. The DTI then gave the go-ahead for the Equitas plan and on 4 September David Rowland, Lloyd's chairman, rang the Lutine bell – not twice, but three times! Clearly, the hope was that the nightmare was over.

The plan puts a cap on names' losses prior to 1993 and enables an out-of-court settlement of claims. In addition, a new 'auction' system enables names to sell places on syndicates to others. These schemes, together with a pooling system for syndicates which operates like a unit trust, finally paved the way for the new Lloyd's into the 21st century.

In June 2002, Hugh Stevenson, chairman of Equitas, reported an accumulated surplus of £679m for the year ended March, a little lower than 2001 for 'technical reasons'. However, the solvency margin rose from 9.5% to 10.3% as a result of a significant fall in net claims.

Reserves for asbestos-related claims were increased by £3.2bn in the years 2000/2001, and he regards such claims as 'the greatest single threat to the stability of Equitas': Equitas paid out £269m for asbestosis claims in 2001.

In April 2002, Lloyds reported a loss of £3.1bn for 2001, nearly 30% bigger than its biggest deficit so far (1990). Of this figure, claims for 11 September (net of reinsurance) total £1.98bn. The results were reported for the first time on a pro-forma annual basis. On the traditional 3 year basis, Lloyds reported a loss of £1.9bn for 1999.

Chief Executive, Nick Prettejohn, pointed out that the number of syndicates was now 86, down from 179 in 1999. The bottom quartile is responsible for two-thirds of losses from 1999–2001. He explained that, over several years, the whole of non-life insurance had had poor results caused by excess capital, a high level of competition and increasing catastrophe losses. The outlook for 2002 onwards is better due to tougher underwriting standards, rising prices, higher deductibles and more rigorous terms.

It may be that Nick Prettejohn is right in this last assumption, as Berkshire Hathaway (the vehicle of the legendary US investor, Warren Buffet) has increased its investment in Lloyd's managing agencies several times in 2002.

In January 2002, the 'Chairman's Strategy Group' (CSG), acting on behalf of Council with consultants Bain and Co, put forward some far-reaching reform proposals. The CSG was set up with a specific objective which was to determine 'the future vision and strategy for Lloyd's which will maximise the wealth of capital providers to Lloyd's over the next ten years'. The key proposals were:

❏ Lloyd's to move to a formal franchise structure, with Lloyd's as franchiser and managing agents as franchisees, under a new relationship defined in a set of 'Franchise Principles'.

❏ The existing regulatory and market boards to be replaced by a new franchise board.

❏ Full annual accounting on the basis of the EU's new International Accounting Standard to be implemented from January 2005.

❏ A new mechanism for third party capital called the 'Single Reinsurance Syndicate' to be created.

❏ No new names to be admitted to the market from 1 January 2003.

❏ Existing names to cease trading as such from 1 January 2005.

The most controversial proposal was to end limited liability names by 2005. This would require a change to the 1982 Lloyd's Act and also the consent of the names, who declared their total opposition!

In July 2002, it was announced that Lloyd's was working on a compromise with the names. Attempts to agree on a price for a buy-out of their rights had totally failed. Like Mark Twain, rumours of their death are exaggerated. A change of status to limited liability also has nasty tax implications.

Lloyd's held an extraordinary AGM on 13 September 2002, and the CSG proposals were passed by an 80% majority. Although opposed by many names, the votes were weighted by underwriting capacity, which counted against them.

In November 2002, Lloyd's unveiled membership of its new franchise board, which started work in the beginning of 2003. It is led by Lloyd's new chairman, Lord Levene.

In spite of current problems, Lloyd's still has unique strengths:

❏ Underwriting skills – exotic risks that normal insurers will not touch.

❏ Security – premium trust funds of £13.5bn, capital requirements of members – £7.7bn, members' assets not held at Lloyd's but declared of £327m and finally, the central fund of £363m, backed by a five year insurance programme giving up to £350m in any one year.

❏ Global reach – Lloyd's is licensed to do business in 60 countries.

THE MARKET TODAY

The third edition of this book (2000) laid much emphasis on the spate of takeovers, mergers and alliances that had taken place in the previous three years. This activity seems to have settled down. The big issue in world insurance is the reaction following 11 September in the United States. The shock waves are still reverberating. It has led generally to losses of between $40bn and $50bn – easily the biggest ever.

So far, however, the industry has shown its ability to cope, including Lloyd's of London with net losses of nearly $3bn.

Global property and casualty rates were already on the way up, even before 11 September, but have now increased substantially. The catastrophic losses that might follow from a nuclear detonation or dissemination of, say, nerve gas, have led President Bush to urge Congress to approve a federal safety net for terrorism insurance. Prohibitively expensive premiums, claimed President Bush, were already leading to job losses.

As an example, the Golden Gate Bridge district in California had insurance against terrorism for a premium of $500,000, but has been offered a new premium of $1.7bn with reduced cover. They have decided to go for 'self-insurance' (discussed earlier in the chapter) on terrorist cover. Another possibility is to self-insure by forming a mutual with other companies in a similar position – the underwriting profit of the insurer is saved, but the mutual is exposed to more risk.

Meanwhile, re-insurers are generally not taking terrorism risk, and actuaries believe that at least three more years' of experience are needed to price this risk correctly.

In the UK, a similar crisis has hit the employers' liability business (compulsory for firms since 1969). Following a new culture of litigation, the increased costs of legal action against employers and higher court awards for damages, have led to rocketing premiums. It is affecting construction firms, quarries, mines and glass manufacturers – but also children's adventure playgrounds, go-kart tracks and semi-professional football clubs. At Lloyd's, the number of syndicates offering employers' liability insurance has dropped from twelve in 2001 to only three in 2002. A survey in mid-2002 by the British Insurance Brokers Association found that 60 commercial companies had gone out of business and another 60 were trading illegally.

Asbestos-related claims remain a key problem for everyone. Ten asbestos-related firms in the US had filed for bankruptcy by September 2002. They filed for Chapter 11 protection and segregated asbestos liabilities into a trust, clearing the way for a reorganisation of the company.

Munich Re has increased its reserves for such claims, and Allianz has added $750m into Firemans' Fund, its US unit, to cover asbestos-related claims.

Across the Western markets, the collapse of stock markets and an era of low interest rates have led to poor returns for the life business, and cast a dark shadow over pensions in particular. The pressure on solvency ratios has led to many employers in the UK abandoning final salary schemes and changing to pension schemes linked purely to fund performance. In August 2002, Royal and Sun Alliance announced a loss of £319m, a cut dividend and plans to shed 1200 jobs. It also announced the closure of its life operations to new business.

If the life business is no longer as attractive, what about general insurance? The overall view is that the current higher premiums make this business more attractive at the moment. At Lloyd's, syndicates have asked for permission to increase the maximum amount they can underwrite from £12.2bn in 2002 to £14.25bn in 2003 and, in December 2002, Lloyd's forecast a profit for the year of £1.8 billion. In addition, we have already mentioned that Warren Buffet is increasing his exposure to Lloyd's. However, the biggest syndicate, ACE, is decreasing its Lloyd's capacity from £900m in 2002 to £652m in 2003. They say that they see better opportunities elsewhere. Analysts see this as a sign that perhaps Lloyd's is too expensive, and point to Bermuda as an increasingly formidable competitor.

EU REGULATION

While some progress has been made with EU Directives on general insurance, progress with life assurance has been very slow. However, in June 1992, two key directives were finally passed – the Third Non-Life Insurance Directive and the Third Life Assurance Directive. These became law on 1 July 1994. From this date, insurers need only be authorised once, in their own country. This is the same 'single passport' idea that will apply in banking. However, marketing and selling practices will still be regulated by the country in which the insurance is sold. For example, cold calling is banned in Denmark and Germany.

There will still, of course, be problems with foreign insurers, especially at the retail level – language, distance, law, local support. Will policy holders wish to pursue a case in a foreign court? Following a European Court decision in 1992, it was ruled that a German, living in Belgium, could not claim tax relief from the Belgian government on insurance policies he was buying in Germany. For this and other reasons, the Chairman of Allianz said in October 1995 that the single market in insurance was a 'myth'! What was needed first was harmonisation of legal, tax and social security systems.

The 'Bureau Européen des Unions des Consommateurs' produced a report on comparative premiums in the life market. Using 100 as the cheapest cover, they produced the following figures:

Ireland	100
UK	102
Germany	118
France	151
Portugal	345

There is clearly scope for more competition!

SUMMARY

The biggest insurance markets in the world are in the US, followed by Japan, UK and Germany.

Assurance is cover for events which are certain (death). *Insurance* is cover for events which may or may not happen (accident, fire, catastrophe).

Offering insurance protection is *underwriting*.

Some companies do assurance only, some insurance only, and some (called *composites*) do both.

The equivalent of capital ratio in banking is *solvency ratio*.

The distribution of the insurance product is a key issue with the possibility of agents, direct sales staff, independent financial advisers, part-time agents, brokers and telephone selling.

Sometimes a large multinational or a group with similar interests will cover their own insurance – *self-insurance*.

Reinsurance occurs when the underwriter spreads the risk with other insurers or specialist reinsurers. There are various terms used such as *proportional, non-proportional, quota, share, surplus* and *excess of loss*.

A reinsurer may offer to reinvest premiums to provide future cover. This is *financial reinsurance*.

There are reinsurance companies, reinsurance brokers and a large reinsurance market at Lloyd's of London.

The so-called *London Market* consists of *Lloyd's* and the *International Underwriting Association of London* (IUA).

Lloyd's of London is an organisation of individual members called *names* who offer insurance. They have traditionally had unlimited liability. The actual underwriting is carried out through *syndicates* and syndicates are run by *managing agencies*. Names are advised by *members' agents*.

Syndicates run accounts for 1 year but they are left open for 3 and may then be terminated by *reinsurance to close*.

Lloyd's uses *Lloyds's brokers* and a central service provider, *Inssure*.

Lloyd's has faced increasing problems in the last 20 years. These have arisen from alleged fraud, careless underwriting, a disregard for the names' interests, huge claims due to pollution cases in the US and a string of natural catastrophes. This has all led to names facing huge losses.

In 1994, Lloyd's reorganised on the following lines:

❏   Allowing corporate membership with unlimited liability
❏   Setting up a system like unit trusts to pool money across syndicates
❏   Reorganising the Lloyd's Council
❏   Forming a new reinsurance vehicle called Equitas to which all claims up to the end of 1992 have been transferred; this will set a cap on names' losses.

In September 2002, Lloyd's agreed further changes:

❏ A formal franchise structure with a new franchise board to be set up.
❏ Full annual accounting to be implemented from January 2005.
❏ No new names to be admitted to the market from January 2003.

The EU has passed the *Third Non-Life Insurance Directive* and the *Third Life Assurance Directive*. These provide the single-passport concept that we have seen in banking but the results have been less than dramatic.

The Periodic Global Crises

15 Global Financial Crises

15 Global Financial Crises

INTRODUCTION

In January 1999, Stanley Fischer, deputy managing director of the IMF, spoke of 'the frequency, virulence and global spread of financial crises in the emerging countries in the last five years'.

He was referring to a variety of financial crises which occurred in those years, leading to inevitable 'rescues' by the IMF. The global world which we now have in finance may mean that the huge cross-border flows of money can be a destabilising influence when things go wrong, and lead to crises which threaten the world financial system itself. What Fischer was thinking of was the situation in Mexico in late 1994, in the Far East beginning in July 1997, in Russia in August 1998, in Brazil in late 1998 and general worries about Japan and China.

In considering this subject, we need to decide what actually happened, why it happened and whether anything can be done to prevent this happening again.

WHAT HAPPENED?

Mexico

The first crisis of any note in this series occurred in Mexico in December 1994. The new government of President Emesto Zedillo announced a controlled devaluation of the peso – 4% per year. Almost at once, money flowed out. Investors were worried about the current account deficit, high government spending and political instability. After lowering the official 'floor' of the peso by 15% on 19 December, the government let the currency float a few days later.

The foreign liabilities of Mexico were largely in marketable short-term paper. The inevitable IMF bail-out allowed holders of dollar short-term paper to escape, leaving holders of equity, long-term bonds and peso-denominated debt with losses.

Mexico is a major economy in Latin America and has a close relationship with the United States and its banks. After the 'LDC debt crisis' of the 1980s, Latin America had barely emerged again as a respectable borrower when these events happened. Readers may also recall that it was Mexican default which triggered the crisis in 1982 (see Chapter 6).

The Far East

Far more important was the series of events beginning in July 1997 and generally known as the 'Far East crisis'.

On 2 July, Thailand floated the baht, which had been linked to the dollar for 13 years. The baht plunged more than 17% against the dollar the same day. All the region's currencies fell – South Korea, Malaysia, Indonesia and even Singapore. Nervousness over investor losses and the effect on world trade led to a fall in major stock markets. The Hang Seng index in Hong Kong fell 25% in four days and, on 27 October, the Dow Jones fell 554 points – a fall of 7.2% in one day.

Tremors continued to run around the world. In November 1997, Brazil doubled interest rates to 43%. Korea stopped supporting the won and let it move into free fall. Thailand imposed exchange controls. On 27 November, Japan's fourth biggest securities house, Yamaichi, went into liquidation. In January, Indonesia suspended debt service payments.

The IMF stepped in during these testing months with a series of rescue packages – $17.2bn for Thailand in August, $42.3bn for Indonesia in November and $58.4bn for South Korea in December. There were worries about the amount of money the IMF actually had available. If the IMF wanted to have the same levels of funding in relation to the GDP of members that it had in 1945, its funds today would need to be three times as large as they are.

The IMF money was clearly needed. BIS figures show that bank lending to the area, at a figure of $22bn in the third quarter of 1997, turned to an outflow of $32bn in the last quarter!

The situation was nicely summarised in an article in the *Financial Times* on 26 April, 1999:

> *Investors piled into East Asia at the start of the decade with scant regard for risk.*
> *When the mood changed, investors belted in the opposite direction with equally scant regard for economic fundamentals. Small economies can be overwhelmed when large financial institutions make fractional adjustments to their global portfolios.*

Asia is a major trading partner for Japan, and the crisis heightened worries about the weakness of Japan's economy (to be discussed later). In April 1998, Moody's downgraded Japan's sovereign debt and in June the US and Japan took action to prop up the yen.

Commodity prices fell some 11% in the second half of 1997. Note that commodities are 60% of Chile's exports and oil is 40% of the revenues of the Mexican government. Asia and Japan have a 26% share of world trade. This is how financial contagion can spread.

We are already seeing some common themes. One is attempts to hold exchange rates, seen finally to be unrealistic due to economic weakness, political instability and other factors. This is usually exacerbated by weak levels of foreign exchange reserves, falls in commodity prices and poorly supervised financial systems.

Russia

Russia had funded its fiscal deficit by selling large amounts of government debt (especially Treasury bills) to foreigners. Continual fiscal weakness due to poor tax collection, corruption and inefficiency meant that investors were unwilling to continue to lend at this rate. On 17 August, 1998, Russia devalued the rouble and announced a 30 day moratorium on external debt servicing.

On 26 August, the rouble was effectively allowed to float. Russia had already had an IMF package of £21.2bn lent to it in 1996 and further loans were made.

On 31 August, the Dow Jones fell 500 points and had fallen 20% by mid-September, although recovery was swift and the market had resumed its upward progress by late October.

Foreign investors faced losses of at least $50bn following the Russian default. Banks in the City of London alone were estimated to have lost £7.5bn in 1998 as a result of losses in emerging markets, but especially Russia (Office of National Statistics).

In particular, a hedge fund called Long-Term Capital Management (LTCM) had large exposures and faced collapse in late September, but for an unprecedented rescue by the Federal Reserve. The chairman of UBS bank resigned on the revelation of large losses due to money at risk at LTCM, and even the Italian central bank had invested $250m of its reserves there! (The special case of LTCM and hedge funds generally will be discussed in the next section.)

On 29 September, the Fed calmed nerves by lowering interest rates by ¼% (the first time in three years) and by another ¼% on 15 October.

Russia's banking system was built following the collapse of communism, without the capital or credit skills needed for the long-term. At one point, 40 new banks were being set up each week, and Russia ended with 2500 new banks!

Negotiations are still taking place on the restructuring of Treasury bill debt and longer-dated bonds, the suspension of forward foreign exchange deals entered into and some dollar bonds issued by the Ministry of Finance.

The problem is that Russia's external debt is $200bn. At the same time, tax income is far below that which is necessary to service this debt (or do anything else, for that matter). Barter is now widespread. The Samara region is paying some of its bond holders in oil. The main diamond producer, Alrosa, has swapped rouble and dollar debt, originally the equivalent of $100m, into $40m of bonds secured against gem export revenues guaranteed by De Beers.

Very little has actually been done since the crisis to improve matters – hence the IMF reluctance to throw good money after bad.

LTCM and Hedge Funds

We referred above to the near collapse in September 1998 of Long-Term Capital Management (LTCM), described as a 'hedge fund'.

First of all, what is a hedge fund? LTCM started in 1994, but hedge funds have existed for many years and include well-known names like the George Soros fund, Quantum. Initially, they were collective investment vehicles, often private partnerships, that used various techniques to protect the value of the fund from price changes in securities and foreign exchange. Hence, the concept of the hedge. They also borrowed heavily and used the money to buy undervalued assets and enhance the performance of the fund by gearing.

Gradually, though, the emphasis changed to more outright speculative activities, for example a so-called directional strategy, betting on a particular currency or bond movement. Often sophisticated models would be used to spot undervalued bonds or currencies. Some would try to anticipate mergers and acquisitions, others would play the stock markets or try to exploit liquidation situations or companies in administration.

In view of the current speculative activity of these funds, the *Times* commented, in an article on 25 September, 1998: 'The term hedge fund is a lie, because the business of these funds is to take risks, not to cover them'.

In spite of its name, LTCM was not long-term at all, but was trying to exploit short-term situations with sophisticated arbitrage. In particular, they were leveraged to an astonishing degree. Borrowed funds were 50 times their equity capital, a gearing of 5000%!

They had large exposures to Russia, and some protective measures were invalidated by the suspension of forward foreign exchange deals in Russia. The Fed was worried that the collapse of LTCM would result in heavy losses for banks that had lent it money, and cause panic. The loans, it is true, were collateralised by holdings of, for example, government bonds, but if all banks start to sell these at the same time, liquidity dries up and prices collapse.

The Fed, therefore, coordinated a rescue raising $4.25bn with six major institutions – J.P. Morgan, Goldman Sachs, Morgan Stanley Dean Witter, Merrill Lynch, Deutsche Bank and UBS.

One effect of the Russian crisis and the near fall of LTCM is that investors world-wide became risk averse, and the price of non-investment grade bonds fell heavily.

The great irony of the LTCM incident is that it had on its board the Nobel Prize winning team of Scholes and Merton (specialists in risk management?), a former vice chairman of the Federal Reserve and John Meriwether of 'Liar's Poker' fame!

Perhaps the effect of hedge funds should not be too exaggerated, although they clearly play a role in exacerbating global crises. The IMF, in a study in May 1998, concluded that they were not to blame for currency crises (like Malaysia) because the money they control is too small compared with the general foreign exchange markets and central bank reserves ('Hedge Funds and Market Dynamics', May 1998).

Japan

The Japanese economy has been in trouble for several years, with poor or non-existent growth rates, a stock market collapse, a fall in property values and huge bank bad debts. It has also led to a weakening of the yen, which helps Japan to export more but makes imports more expensive. Sales to Japan are the equivalent of 12% of Malaysia's GDP and 6% of Indonesia's – hence the relevance of Japan's problems to problems elsewhere.

The banks kept weak firms going, the government kept weak banks going. Many firms had been borrowing excessively to invest in projects with low returns. In the middle of 1998, total bank debts in Japan were estimated at ¥80 trillion or 12% of GDP. As we have commented earlier, bank loans are a far higher percentage of corporate funding than they are in the US. For the future, Japan also faces the problem that pensioners will be the equivalent of 56% of the population within 20/30 years.

1997 saw the collapse of Yamaichi Securities (fourth biggest), Sanyo Securities, Nissan Mutual and Hokkaido Takoshoku, one of the top 20 banks.

The government finally decided to take more serious action and, in June 1998, formed the Financial Services Agency (FSA) to take over the job of supervising banks from the Ministry of Finance. In particular, its task was to force banks to face up to writing off bad loans with government financial help to enable them to do so.

It faced an early crisis with the collapse of Long Term Credit Bank, Japan's tenth largest by assets, which was nationalised, as was Nippon Credit Bank.

Also set up was a Financial Reconstruction Committee, which issued bonds to fund bank reform. It put forward credible restructuring plans which led to more mergers and alliances, for example that of Mitsui Trust and Chuo Trust in January 1999. In the same month, Sanwa Trust and Toyo Trust announced a 'comprehensive alliance'.

$62bn was injected into 15 of Japan's leading banks, who in turn wrote off $46bn of non-performing loans. By early 2002, the FSA pronounced the nation's leading banks to be in 'basically sound' health. However, early optimism that the banking system may have turned the corner now seems to be fading. After a brief return to profit in 2000–2001, the 121 Japanese banks in the world's top 1000 reported combined losses of $50.1bn, The top four banks alone incurred losses totalling $22.7bn. Many analysts believe that both the banks and the FSA are still not ruthless enough in writing off dubious loans from a weak corporate sector, and that further substantial loan write-offs are needed – meaning that it will be several years before the banking system returns to profit ... and almost certainly beyond the government target of 2004. The banking system therefore may be out of crisis but remains weak for the foreseeable future.

China

Throughout all these events, there have been persistent rumours of a Chinese devaluation. The fast growth of the economy has begun to falter and business conditions have become much tougher.

In particular, a regional development authority, Guandong International Trust and Investment Company, was forced to file for bankruptcy in January 1998, owing foreign banks more than $1bn. It was finally shut down in October that year. Foreign investors believed that either the government would compensate them or that they would, at least, get priority in any payments made from the asset values. Neither happened and, in consequence, foreign investment in China has now fallen, although there has not been any crisis so far comparable to the one in the Far East in 1997.

Brazil

Brazil, like Mexico and Argentina, had pegged its currency to the dollar to control inflation. However, confidence was falling by the second half of 1998, particularly with a fiscal deficit of 8% of GDP. A flight into dollars from August to September weakened the country's foreign exchange reserves. Attempts to set new floor levels for the real failed, and the IMF stepped in in November with a $41.5bn rescue package. Finally, Brazil floated the real in January 1999.

If there is any more cheerful note in the sad saga of events unfolded in this chapter, it is the fact that Brazil did not turn into the major crisis expected. The situation stabilised and then recovered with surprising rapidity. The spread over US Treasury rates of Brazil's bonds was 1000 basis points in January 1999. In April, Brazil issued a $2bn 5 year bond at a spread of 675 basis points and it was three times oversubscribed. Recovery, or just short memories?

Argentina

Mounting economic problems in Argentina in 2001 turned into crisis at the beginning of 2002, when the authorities were unable to maintain the peso/dollar exchange rate which had been pegged at par for over a decade. The collapse of the peg, and subsequent devaluation of the peso, left many corporations unable to repay debt taken out in dollars when it had seemed safe to do so. By March 2002, the peso stood at 3.75 to the dollar.

Problems originated in a deteriorating economy, with continuing high levels of Government expenditure and high levels of borrowing to finance this. As external investors perceived the risks, the cost of borrowing went up, creating a vicious circle. The twin problems of maintaining the dollar peg and also servicing debt from a growing deficit led a bond strategist at Nomura to comment in July 2001 'Something has got to give in Argentina. Either the economy will go further down the tube, or they will default.'

Tough political action was needed to curb the growing deficit of $132bn and qualify for IMF support. However, the austerity measures – pay cuts and tax rises – left many poor people struggling or destitute, and culminated in the riots of December 2001 and subsequent political turmoil. The authorities imposed restrictions on withdrawals to prevent a run on the banking system. As the peso continued to fall, in March 2002 the Government imposed limits on the purchase of dollars of $1000 for individuals and $10,000 for companies. At the same time, Metrogas (part owned by British Gas) said it would default on $425m in debt. In November 2002, the government paid only $79.2m to the World Bank against a scheduled repayment of $805m.

The outlook is bleak, with further defaults expected; higher inflation from the drop in the value of the peso and continuing social unrest effectively helping to undermine or circumscribe Government measures, while discussions and negotiations with the IMF continue.

WHY DID IT ALL HAPPEN?

Before we can begin to discuss what might be done to prevent all this happening again, we need to consider the causes of the crises in the first place.

Just as we shall see that there is no uniform agreement on solutions, so there is also some disagreement as to the causes.

Short-Term Capital Flows

What we do see is massive foreign capital flows into emerging markets, which leads to over-investment and excessive expansion of the money supply. As confidence falls, money is withdrawn. Many loans are short-term and subject to periodic renewal. They are then withdrawn in the event of a crisis. Since the loans are in a foreign currency, collapse of the domestic currency increases the real burden of repayment, itself leading to further losses.

A report by the Washington-based Institute for International Finance, in January 1999, calculated that net lending by banks to the 29 most important emerging markets accounted for 71% of the net increase in capital flows between 1993 and 1996. Between 1996 and 1998, net lending by banks accounted for all the reversal of net capital flows. The report shows that IMF rescues protect these lenders, leading to an issue called 'moral hazard'. They point out that if private sector lenders are punished financially, they may be less likely to lend on such a liberal basis in the future. The outflow of capital between 1996 and 1998 was the equivalent of 18% of the GDP of South Korea and 20% of the GDP of Thailand. These are massive adjustments.

IMF rescues guarantee a return to lending, but are these huge foreign currency loans desirable in the first place?

Paul Volcker's Views

Paul Volcker, a famous chairman of the Federal Reserve Board between 1979 and 1987, gave a speech on this whole subject to the International Finance Institute. The speech was printed in an edited version in the *Financial Times* in October 1998. It contains a nice summary of the causes of global crises:

The basic story is as old as financial capitalism itself. Success breeds confidence and over-confidence. Greed overcomes prudence. Then something unexpected happens ... to raise doubts. Fear becomes contagious. Individual self-defence helps spread distress. And if the excesses are widespread enough, a financial crisis becomes an economic crisis, which is where much of the emerging world is today.

The fact that the story is an old one can be seen from the following two quotations:

Every great crisis reveals the excessive speculation of many houses which no-one before suspected.

Baring Bros have of late been growing more speculative; they have taken up business which they ought to have rejected and they have enabled borrowers to obtain more money than ought to have been given them.

The first quotation is from Walter Bagehot in that wise book '*Lombard St*' in 1873.

The second is a comment on the Barings crisis of 1890, in a financial newspaper called '*The Statist*'. Although the story is not new, Paul Volcker points to two new factors. One is technological change, which means that capital can now move about the world with unprecedented speed. The second is the liberalisation of financial markets, the dismantling of controls which has swept across the world. This leads to a large number of countries whose own banking sector is small and vulnerable entering the financial market place.

BIS Warning

To be fair, the growth of the tiger economies prior to the crisis had been impressive, and may have led to over-exuberance on the part of the banks. The BIS annual report of 1997, however, warned of the credit bubble, pointing out that South Korea had $68bn of loans due to be repaid in one year. The warning of trouble to come was ignored. Indeed, the IMF annual report for 1997 welcomed South Korea's 'continuing impressive macroeconomic performance'.

In looking at the causes of the crises, there are several individual factors which all come together to produce a position which in physics is called 'unstable equilibrium' – one in which, if equilibrium is lost, the system at first moves further away from equilibrium (like a clock pendulum, for example).

Short-Term Capital – 'Hot Money'

One of these factors is the short-term nature of the loans and the fact that they are in foreign currencies, and that investment in stock markets has been short-term and speculative. Linked with this latter factor is the effort of many countries to maintain a fixed exchange rate. Allowing the currency to stay overvalued is risky, attempts to defend it foolish and, when they fail, the dam opens. Essentially, huge foreign debt is a risky way to finance economic development. We tend to think of funds flowing to emerging markets which have a low level of domestic savings and need foreign money in order to exploit opportunities. Curiously, in this case, many Asian economies actually had good levels of domestic savings.

Transparency

Lack of transparency also plays a role (as it did in the 1982 LDC debt crisis). In spite of some basic BIS figures, no-one seems to know the full extent of exposures in international lending and investment, and especially the effect of off-balance sheet exposures in the form of derivative products. An excellent description of the huge risks which may be concealed in derivatives can be found in '*F.I.A.S.C.O*' by Frank Partnoy (a former trader), (Profile Books).

We have new markets and techniques – the Euromarkets, junk bonds, securitisation of assets, derivative products, use of computers, the huge increase in forex volumes. Today's capital markets are *global*, but are supervised on a *national* basis. There is no official institution which is responsible for the global capital markets or capable of monitoring them on a worldwide basis.

Credit Control and Risk Management

Clearly, the banks themselves are not controlling their credit exposures very well. A BIS report on the LTCM crisis claimed that banks had compromised credit standards. The chairman of the BIS/G10 bank supervisors' committee, William McDonough (also president of the New York Federal Reserve), suggested that the solution to many risks was for the banks to raise their standards!

This, of course, raises the whole question of modern risk management techniques, which are much trumpeted and supposed to prevent these periodic crises and heavy bank losses. The banks relied on collateral in the case of LTCM but, in a given set of circumstances, many firms act together driving the market against them and triggering stop/loss limits again, which makes things worse. If markets are volatile, extreme movements are not necessarily rare. (For those who understand statistics, the criticism here is that the normal curve tails are much fatter than the models assume.)

IMF/World Bank Roles

There is, finally, some criticism of the role of the IMF and confusion between its role and that of the World Bank. Under the Bretton Woods fixed exchange rate regime, the role of the IMF was to help countries with temporary balance of payments difficulties. With the arrival of floating rates, much of the raison d'être of the IMF disappeared. Crises such as the LDC debt crisis in the 1980s saw both organisations playing a role, leading to disagreement. In 1988, for example, the World Bank announced a $1.25bn loan to Argentina when the IMF was withholding financial support! As a result, they agreed on a so-called concordat – the Fund to have primary responsibility for exchange rate matters, the balance of payments and growth-oriented stabilisation policies; the Bank to be responsible for development programmes and priorities. However, the handling of the Asian crisis generated fresh criticisms. One problem, as we mentioned earlier, is that the IMF doesn't have enough money. During the 1997 crisis, the World Bank had to support it with short-term liquidity. To any detached observer it is clear that only one body is needed. So far, neither set of officials has volunteered to give up their well-paid jobs!

Some commentators also criticise the IMF terms for a loan as too restrictive – weakening the countries concerned and slowing down longer-term recovery (rather like doctors in an earlier age, treating people simultaneously with blood letting and purgatives!). Having said that, the recovery in many of the emerging markets which we see in 1999 does not seem to support this argument.

THE SOLUTIONS?

One might think that it would not be that difficult for the world to devise solutions to prevent the re-occurrence of these global financial crises. In the widespread debate that has followed the crises of 1997, there have been many solutions suggested, but much scepticism about either their practicality or their effectiveness. Solutions have tended to centre round the factors we outline below.

Avoiding Fixed Exchange Rates

There seems to be widespread agreement that fixed exchange rates, or exchange rate 'pegs' (for example, pegging the currency to the dollar), are potentially dangerous. Market forces ultimately prevail (as they did in the ERM crises of 1992 and 1993, although we were not dealing with emerging market economies). The end result is sudden violent and destabilising movements. In spite of our reference above to 'widespread agreement', it should be noted that Paul Volcker, in the speech we mentioned earlier, believes that small, open economies do not have the breadth of financial markets to withstand sharp fluctuations in exchange rates anyway, and the Argentinian crisis seems to support this view.

Exchange Controls

Malaysia attracted a lot of attention with the imposition of some temporary exchange controls. Later, as Malaysia recovered, the Prime Minister claimed victory for this policy. This has led to a general discussion on the role of exchange controls. We should note at the outset that there are *inward* controls (restricting capital coming in) and *outward* controls (not letting people take capital out). Malaysia's controls were of the latter type.

In general, adoption of capital controls has attracted criticism. It is pointed out that this undermines access to capital markets, may increase the risk of inflation, and promotes a misallocation of investment. The limiting of foreign competition may allow mismanaged banks to survive.

In the case of Malaysia, some commentators suggest that this was, to some extent, a special case, in that Malaysia had a budget surplus, a high savings rate and relatively well regulated banks. It any case, the Malaysian ringgit had already fallen 40% when controls were introduced.

In spite of the almost universal criticism of exchange controls, there was one exception. Paul Krugman, a professor at MIT, writing in *Fortune* Magazine, has argued that the failure of the IMF to act in time has legitimised the adoption of exchange controls as a temporary measure. The country can stimulate the economy without risking the exchange rate.

Changes in Short-Term Loans and Capital

There have been many comments about the danger of funding long-term development with short-term foreign currency debt. Some admire the Chilean practice of a tax on such debt as a form of discouragement. Others, however, point out that, nevertheless, Chile suffered badly in the Far East crisis with the peso under pressure, foreign exchange reserves falling and interest rates raised to prohibitive levels. However, Barry Eichengreen, in an article in an Institute for International Economics publication *'Towards a New International Financial Architecture'*, strongly favours a tax on short-term foreign borrowing as pioneered by Chile.

Rescheduling the terms of short-term bank debt requires unanimity on the part of the lenders (there may be 50 of them). Many authorities believe that the whole process needs to be speeded up during crises.

Professor William Buiter (an economics professor at Cambridge) and Ann Sibert (economics professor at Birkbeck College) put forward an interesting suggestion in the July 1999 issue of *International Finance*. They propose a clause in all foreign currency debt agreements allowing it to be rolled over at a penal rate if the borrower's prospects have weakened – a sort of tax on short-term borrowing. The rate would be better for stable borrowers. This rollover clause would provide a discipline by forcing the market to price risk.

It does finally seem as though the markets themselves are responding to the losses and problems of recent years, and recent IMF data records a fall in private capital flows to emerging markets from some $120bn in 1997 to about $33bn in 2000. At the same time, foreign direct investment – long-term investment not withdrawn at times of market turmoil – remained constant. In parallel, the BIS commented on the steady withdrawals of money from global hedge funds from the end of 1998 onwards at the rate of around $2bn per quarter.

Precautionary Credit Line Facility

One proposal from the IMF was that countries with sound economic policies could be protected by the establishment in advance of a 'precautionary credit line facility'. The IMF would decide how much of this could be drawn at any time. The idea is that its existence would discourage a panic-stricken withdrawal of capital. The country, in applying for the credit, would have to show that it was the victim of 'contagion' – due to adverse developments in other countries.

However, the idea seems simply a variation of an existing IMF supplemental reserve facility! In any case, would not application to draw on the precautionary credit send a danger signal to the markets?

Greater Private Sector Role

During global financial crises we hear a lot about the role of the IMF and the World Bank. The IMF, in particular, is anxious to increase the role of the private sector. In a report in March 1999, the IMF was looking at the way in which its own efforts were undermined by destabilising private sector capital flows. It commented 'more needs to be done to create incentives and instruments for the private sector to remain involved'.

They want the banking sector to be more flexible in restructuring short-term loans and to allow an easing of the burden of debt if economic conditions are unfavourable. They also suggest that banks need better official communication with creditors on a regular basis.

Much more controversial is the suggestion that bond investors should bear some of the pain too. Default on bonds, especially international bonds, is very serious, triggers legal action and lowers credit ratings. The IMF is pressing for the restructuring of bond issues similar to the restructuring of bank loans. International bonds are an almost sacrosanct asset class – but why?

New IMF money is often used to meet existing bond payments. Since the bond holders are not penalised, we meet the 'moral hazard' question once again.

Many existing bonds have covenants requiring unanimity before the terms of payment can be altered. However, large sovereign bond holdings are scattered among perhaps thousands of investors, making agreement impractical. Retail investors, in particular, regard the bonds as 'safe'. Those who are against the restructuring of bonds (and there are many!) argue about the effect on future issues and the reduction of investors' general willingness to lend. Default would increase the cost of future issues and investors' general willingness to lend. This, argues the IMF, is exactly what *should* happen. Risk has its price. It would cause both borrowers and lenders to consider the contract more carefully.

The issue arose in April 1999, when the so-called 'Paris Club' of official creditors suggested that Pakistan renegotiate all private sector debt, including bonds. The really significant move, however, came in September 1999, when Ecuador became the first country to default on Brady Bond debts, with the IMF refusing a bail out. To quote the *Financial Times*, it sent 'a shiver of anxiety through global markets'. It's an important issue. According to Standard and Poors, sovereign bond obligations are now 70% higher than bank loans.

Financial Stability Forum

We commented earlier that crises are global but regulators arc national. At their meeting in Washington on 3 October, 1998, finance ministers and central bank governors of G7 asked Hans Tietmayer, President of the Bundesbank, to consult with appropriate bodies involved in international financial regulation and supervision, and report with 'recommendations for any new structures and arrangements that may be required'.

Hans Tietmayer came up with the idea of a new 'Financial Stability Forum', its first chairman to be Andrew Crockett, general manager of the BIS. Coming together in this forum would be a host of international regulatory and supervisory bodies – the IMF, the World Bank, the Organisation for Economic Cooperation and Development, the Basle Committee on bank supervision, the International Organisation of Securities Commissions, the International Association of Insurance Supervisors, the Committee on Payment and Settlement Systems and the Committee on the Global Financial System. (Cynics may be forgiven for wondering whether this enormous talking shop would ever be able to act decisively on anything!)

The idea is that this Financial Stability Forum would meet regularly to assess issues affecting the global financial system and report to the G7 finance ministers and central bank governors.

This idea was formally endorsed by G7 in February 1999, with a further suggestion that representatives of emerging nations be invited to attend the meetings. The first meeting was held in April 1999, and the forum set up three working groups to examine a) ways to reduce the destabilising potential of heavily leveraged institutions like hedge funds; b) measures to reduce the volatility of capital flows; and c) the impact of offshore financial centres on global financial stability and the enforcement of global prudential standards.

While there are those who greet the arrival of the forum with some scepticism, it is surely a step in the right direction. To quote Paul Volcker again:

There is an all too rare opportunity for real international reform. The world should seize the day.

Self Help

Finally, we should perhaps recognise that the world's financial powers can never totally eliminate financial crises. Each emerging market must learn to protect itself and learn the risks when opening up their economies. This means closely regulated banking, good foreign exchange reserves, sustainable exchange rate regimes, encouragement of long-term investment and discouragement of risky short-term capital flows.

SUMMARY

In recent years, a series of financial crises have hit various markets and have had a 'knock on' effect across the world.

These crises occurred in Mexico (1994), the Far East (1997), Russia (1998), Brazil (1998) and Argentina (2001). The Russian collapse resulted in the near liquidation of a large American hedge fund, LTCM. There were also concerns at the situation in Japan and China.

Hedge funds were originally collective investment funds which sought to protect the value of the fund with various hedges. More recently, they have become much more speculative and take large positions in the market using huge sums of borrowed money.

The IMF stepped in with a series of rescue packages for Mexico, Thailand, Indonesia, South Korea and Brazil. Negotiations with Russia are still continuing.

The causes of these crises seem to be a combination of various factors – large short-term capital flows in foreign currencies; sudden withdrawal of much of this money; attempts to prevent a fixed exchange rate failing, leading to a fall in the currency rate and a rise in the impact of foreign currency interest payments; poor banking supervision; lack of transparency of off-balance sheet commitments; and lack of any international financial supervision.

Ways to prevent crises happening again relate to many of the above points:

❏ Avoid fixed exchange rates
❏ Limit short-term capital flows in foreign currencies. Encourage more long-term commitment
❏ Speed up the process of restructuring loans
❏ Use a precautionary credit line from the IMF
❏ Involve the private sector more – banks and bond investors. Let them 'share the pain'
❏ Set up a world Financial Stability Forum to improve the supervision and monitoring of the world financial markets
❏ Encourage emerging markets to protect themselves more.

Trends in the Global Financial Markets

16 Key Trends

16 Key Trends

The total upheaval in global financial markets which began about the mid-1980s shows no sign of slowing down. We are in a period of rapid change brought about by deregulation, information technology and a changing economic and political outlook. A number of key trends continue to shape and reshape the financial world into new patterns.

It is the purpose of this final chapter to highlight a number of these recent and future trends.

11 SEPTEMBER

In considering this topic, it is important to try look at some of the trends and implications and not simply the immediate impact at the time on firms and markets.

Clearly, business continuance planning and managing operational risks, already important for Basle II, have been put further under the spotlight A study prepared for the New York City Partnership, a leading business group, about the impact of 11 September on the financial services industry, found several vulnerabilities in the system as a whole.

Among them were corporate back-up plans that did not include sites in different geographic areas; back-up plans that failed to consider that transportation could be disrupted; and energy and telecommunications infrastructures without alternative networks that could be put quickly into use. To reduce future risks, banks are looking to disperse staff over a wider area, not cluster them together. Morgan Stanley sold a planned new Manhattan office and, instead, purchased the former Texaco building in the suburbs north of New York; several thousand of its 14,000 staff will be transferred there. Goldman Sachs is planning to move 1200 staff working in equities across the Hudson River to Jersey City. The report also noted that financial markets were exposed to a few 'choke points' – key hubs such as exchanges, clearing firms and inter-dealer brokers, and pointed out that disruptions at those points triggered 'significant spillover effects for the rest of the financial services system'.

Equally, across both retail and wholesale banking we will continue to see a tightening up of both policies and practice regarding money laundering.

THE ECONOMIC OUTLOOK

The bull market of the '90s has turned into a prolonged bear market early in this new century, with major indices such as the Dow and FTSE 100 ending the year 2002 lower than they started for the third year in succession.

Banks have seen corporate finance activity reduce sharply, with a reduction in M&A activity and new issues in the TMT (Telecoms, Media and Technology) sector and generally. Bank profits have suffered as a result of this and will continue to be under pressure, as the general economic climate is characterised by at best uncertainty and at worst decline.

The period of low interest rates has had an initial beneficial effect on fixed income, with record volumes in many segments of this market in 2001. However, there is now a deteriorating outlook for corporate profits, uncertainty of the validity of accounting treatment post Enron and the biggest bankruptcy to date with WorldCom, both of which have led to credit ratings being downgraded. This, of course, then offsets the benefit of lower interest rates, making bond issues less attractive, as well as affecting the quality of the banks' loan books. Vickie Tillman, head of credit ratings at Standard & Poor's, said early in 2002: 'There hasn't been as diverse a credit crisis [as this one] in a decade'.

The slowdown will inevitably trigger further takeovers and mergers, as banks struggle to survive or try to achieve economies of scale. Other financial institutions face the same challenge. The closure of Germany's Neuer Markt in 2003 is likely to be one example of many exchanges and markets which have to merge to survive or otherwise disappear.

THE PENSION TIME BOMB

The pension time bomb discussed earlier is not new – the problem has been latent and predictable for a number of years. The 2001 census data for Britain shows that for the first time the number of people over the age of 60 exceeds the number of children below 16. The continuing slide of the stock markets is stoking the problem and creating a vicious circle in the industry. As share prices fall, insurance companies are required to sell shares to maintain their solvency ratios; as they sell, this pushes the shares even lower. Although the FSA is reviewing the solvency rules, the companies will still need to invest in order to generate returns. Does this mean that the insurance companies should invest elsewhere? The problem with this is that, if interest rates continue to remain low or are lowered further, yields are inadequate to meet the current or future payments to annuity holders. The Equitable crisis in the UK is a good illustration of this problem. With yields generally low there is no easy market-based solution. The pressure, therefore, can only translate into further efforts to drive down costs through internal measures, as well as more mergers. Equally, regulatory and policy changes are now inevitable, whether to raise the retirement age, give more incentives for personal pensions, or a mixture.

THE INTERNET

One important trend is the continuing impact of the Internet. The use of electronic trading is providing new distribution channels and shifting the balance of power to the consumer. For the user, the effect will be a cheaper and more efficient service. For the supplier, it will bring a new sales and distribution channel, but also exposure to new competition. The effects will be felt in all our financial markets – banking, bonds, equities, foreign exchange, derivatives and insurance.

In the US, direct debits and electronic transfer are rare – 77% of bills are still paid by cheque. Hence the relevance of the new service from Chase Manhattan, First Union and Wells Fargo, together with Sun Microsystems, to offer bill paying electronically.

Citigroup is combining with a Canadian software firm and a Finnish telecommunications company to offer a service which reformats Citigroup financial information for delivery to customers' mobile phones or Psion-type devices worldwide.

The Finnish/Swedish bank, Merita-Nordbanken, also claims that 44% of its active customers use its Internet service.

In the UK, one of the fastest movers is not a traditional bank at all, but an insurance company – the Prudential with egg. If cutting costs for banks is the opportunity, new competition is the threat.

ELECTRONIC BROKING

Regarding equities, we commented in Chapter 7 on the emergence of electronic broking, especially in the US, with systems like Instinet and POSIT and brokers like E*Trade and Charles Schwab. Research company, Forresters, calculates that 2.2m families trade on-line today and this will increase to 9.7m by 2003. The really important news here was the announcement by traditional broker Merrill Lynch (employing nearly 15,000 brokers) in mid-1999 of a new service via the Internet with fees far lower than usual. It's a fine example of 'if you can't beat them, join them.'

Charles Schwab and E*Trade have both arrived in the UK, and Schwab is signing up to 1000 new customers per week.

Charles Schwab is also now planning to offer a service in Japan through Tokyo Marine and Fire. The National Association of Securities Dealers is joining with the Japanese Softbank to offer on-line access to NASDAQ stocks in Japan.

One problem here is that a proliferation of suppliers leads to confusion and fragmentation. A user cannot know whether one specific order matching service is offering the best price. It's also a nightmare for the regulators.

Bonds have been an area that has been the slowest to respond to electronic order matching, but this is changing fast. A system started in Italy, called EuroMTS, to trade Italian government bonds, now covers those of France, Germany, Austria, Belgium, the Netherlands and Spain.

The big news here, however, was the announcement in mid-1999 by seven powerful investment bankers of their own system – BrokerTec. This trades on a global basis and has concentrated at first on US and European government bonds. They have also written to the world's biggest derivatives exchanges about an exciting project – delivering information on prices across the world on one screen.

There are now two Internet systems, Cognotec and Information Internet, which link end users of foreign exchange with the banks that serve them – no need to talk to sales staff. As with electronic broking, credit checks are carried out automatically.

In our foreign exchange chapter (Chapter 8) we mentioned that electronic broking for spot trades had hit the voice broking brokers badly. However, like bonds, foreign exchange is a market where, so far, the impact of electronic trading on traditional telephone traders and sales staff has been small.

In the derivatives market, open outcry trading is shrinking fast, with the CME and CBOT as the last major bastions. It can only be a matter of time. A *Financial Times* article, on 6 August, 1999, quoted one bank in London as saying that 65 staff had been employed at LIFFE, trading 150,000 contracts per day. With the arrival of electronic trading, there were now 18 staff trading 250,000 contracts per day. The figures speak for themselves.

The moves listed above show us the relevance of electronic trading for cross-border trading. Sitting at one screen with access to global markets, the world shrinks. However, for global trading to be truly successful we need more uniform clearing and settlement systems.

RISK MANAGEMENT AND DERIVATIVES

Slowly but surely, risk management systems are gaining in strength. Basle II is now extending the scope of capital adequacy by asking banks to address operational risk. Real Time Gross Settlement systems have become widespread, settlement is normally now delivery versus payment, paper is disappearing and settlement times reducing or moving to real time, along with an increase in netting. All this reduces risk.

In derivatives, we are seeing fewer corporate, bank or municipal failures (like Barings, Procter and Gamble, Orange County) and the market seems to be much more mature. Growth continues to be strong, both in established derivatives and in newer products such as credit derivatives. There remain worries about the 'value at risk' statistical models and the lack of transparency in OTC trading.

To take the first point, extreme conditions seem to make a mockery of the so-called '99% confidence levels'. Prior to the Russian crisis, this would have suggested a widening of the spread on bonds generally as 200 basis points maximum. After the crisis, they widened to 900 bp! Bankers Trust said that their value at risk model suggested that the value would only be exceeded on one day in 100. In the quarter ended 30 September, 1999, it was exceeded on four days. To be technical, the normal curve gives us the maximum loss 99 days out of 100, but not the loss on day 100. Another problem here is that models do not take account of the possible collapse of the hedge. In Russia's case, all forward rouble foreign exchange deals were suspended.

No model is likely to solve this problem, it's perhaps part of the move to avoid the global crises we described in Chapter 15.

Transparency is another problem. Long Term Capital Management had huge exposures to some 50 counterparties, but none of them knew of the overall exposure. The OTC market in derivatives is opaque, and some complex derivatives enable banks to overcome regulations on, say, foreign exchange exposure. Foreign currency exposures in Mexico were much greater than was generally realised, partly for this reason. Japanese banks have used complex bond derivatives to take profits now but push the associated losses out to, perhaps, 20 years. The Financial Supervisory Authority has finally had enough and imposed quite severe sanctions on Crédit Suisse in Tokyo.

Those who would like to know more are urged to read '*F.I.A.S.C.O.*' by former Morgan Stanley derivatives trader Frank Portnoy (Profile Books). It seems clear that this kind of transparency can no longer be tolerated by the authorities.

Under the heading of 'risk management' comes the question of global crises and their prevention. Much attention will now be paid to the new 'Financial Stability Forum'. Pessimistically, we may need one more crisis to really concentrate the minds.

EXCHANGES

Of one thing we can be quite certain, and that is the present spate of mergers will continue. We have become accustomed to bank mergers and alliances. We are now seeing this with derivatives exchanges (EUREX); stock exchanges (NASDAQ/ EASDAQ/American Stock Exchange) and across both (Euronext/LIFFE) and the LSE/OM.

In 2002, Brussels has announced a major shake-up of current regulations which restrict investors in many countries, including France, Italy and Spain to dealing through their stock exchange. Under the new proposals, investors will be able to trade shares freely with other banks or shareholders and bypass national exchanges. In London and Germany, where banks may already bypass exchanges, it is estimated that up to 15% of dealing is done this way. The added competition from this regulatory change will inevitably lead to further mergers amongst exchanges.

ASSET-BACKED SECURITIES

This is a market that has been tipped for explosive growth from as far back as 1986. It may be that sometimes we need a 'critical mass' to get things moving, but, suddenly, all over the globe, it's happening.

Chapter 6 shows the astonishing range of ABS securities that have been issued, with backings from pop record royalties, telephone calls, football season tickets and future export revenues.

One advantage to the issuer is balance sheet flexibility, the ability to make better use of capital. Another is access for corporates to cheaper funding. In particular, emerging markets can pledge future revenues from projects against bonds which make the project possible in the first place. Record volumes of new bond issues in the first quarter 2002 ($1300bn) were attributed by the Bond Markets Association to growth of asset-backed securities. In bond markets, this seems likely to be one of the key developments over the next ten years, as markets get used to the idea and some regulatory barriers are lowered.

SUMMARY

11 September   has highlighted both strengths and weaknesses in the financial system and the operations of banks.

The economy   The weak economic outlook is putting banks under further competitive pressure and will lead to more mergers and acquisitions.

Bear markets   Stock market declines are compounding the pension time bomb the insurance industry faces at a time of low yields.

The Internet   The Internet is providing new entrants, distribution channels and ways of doing business. It shifts the balance of power to the consumer, but exposes the supplier to new competition and the challenge of strategic change.

Electronic trading   This continues to change the role of traditional traders and sales staff and add competition for traditional brokers.

Risk management and derivatives   Control of risk seems to be slowly improving with new Basle Committee rules, the spread of real time settlement and the arrival of faster settlement times. Credit derivatives seem set to grow.

Mergers and cooperation   To the mergers and alliances of banks, we must now add those among stock exchanges, derivative exchanges, clearing houses and money brokers.

Asset-backed securities   The market has finally grasped the potential here and this will be a key feature of bond markets for some time to come.

Glossary

ABS	Asset-backed security – for example, a Mortgage Bond.
ACCEPTING	Signing a Bill of Exchange signifying an agreement to pay. Subsequent or alternative signature by a bank virtually guarantees payment.
ACCOUNT	For equity settlements, exchanges may have an account period, for example two weeks, one month, etc. with payment due on 'account' or 'settlement' day. The alternative is a rolling settlement system.
ACCRUED INTEREST	The interest accrued so far on a bond and payable by the purchaser. Quoted separately from the 'clean price'.
ADR	American Depositary Receipt – the form in which foreign shares can be traded in the US without a formal listing.
AIM	Alternative Investment Market – a new market for smaller companies' shares set up in the UK in June 1995.
ALPHA FACTOR	The element in a share price that reflects its individual performance as opposed to the market (which is the Beta Factor q.v.).
ANNUAL YIELD	See Flat Yield.
APACS	Association for Payment Clearing Services – controlling cheque clearing, BACS and CHAPS in the UK.
ARBITRAGE	Taking advantage of an anomaly in prices or rates in different markets – e.g. buying in one and simultaneously selling in the other.
ARBITRAGEURS	Those looking for arbitrage opportunities. Applied especially in the US to those trying to exploit takeover possibilities.
ARTICLE 65	Article of the Japanese Financial Code – prevented commercial banks from engaging in some investment banking activities (and vice-versa); now dismantled.
ASK RATE	See Offer Rate.
ASSETS	The side of the bank's balance sheet dealing with lending.
ASSURANCE	The business of life insurance and pensions.
ATM	Automated Teller Machine.
BACK OFFICE	Accounting and settlement procedures.

375

BACKWARDATION	When one market maker's offer price is less than another's bid – a clear opportunity for arbitrage!
BACS	Bankers Automated Clearing Services (UK).
BANK BILL	A Bill of Exchange accepted by a bank on the central bank's 'eligible' list. The central bank itself would rediscount a bill of this type. Also called an 'eligible' bill.
BARGAIN	Any Stock Exchange transaction.
BASIS POINT	One-hundredth of 1 per cent.
BEAR	A pessimist, selling securities in the belief of a falling market, hence a 'bear market'.
BEARER BOND	A bond payable to whoever is in possession – that is, no central register.
BED AND BREAKFAST	Selling shares one day and buying them back the next – at the end of the tax year to maximise CGT allowance or claim losses against profits.
BETA FACTOR	The effect of overall market movements on a share price (see Alpha Factor).
BID RATE	Rate of interest offered for interbank deposits. Generally, the dealer's buying price for equities, bonds, foreign exchange, etc.
BIG BANG	Deregulation of the UK Stock Exchange, 27 October 1986.
BILL OF EXCHANGE	A signed promise to pay by a receiver of goods or services and kept by the supplier. May be sold at a discount.
BIS	Bank for International Settlements (Basle). The central bankers' central bank.
BLUE CHIP	The most highly regarded shares. (Metaphor is from gambling casinos!)
BOBL	Short name for the short term German government bond contract on EUREX.
BOND	A certificate issued by a borrower as receipt for a loan longer than 12 months, indicating a rate of interest and date of repayment.
BOND STRIPPING	See Coupon Stripping.
BOND WASHING	Selling a bond prior to the ex dividend date to take a capital gain instead of receiving income.
BONOS	Bonos del Estado – Spanish government bonds.
BONUS ISSUE	A free issue of shares to existing holders.

BRADY BOND	Bonds issued as part of South American country debt reduction under a scheme devised by Nicholas Brady.
BRETTON WOODS	Meetings at Bretton Woods (US) in 1944 set up the World Bank, IMF and foreign exchange system for the period following the Second World War.
BROKER	An agent for buying/selling securities or intermediary for a loan or sale of foreign exchange.
BTAN	Bons du Trésor à Intérêt Annuel. French Government two and five year notes.
BTF	Bons du Trésor à Taux Fixe. French Government Treasury bills.
BTP	Italian Government bond (Buoni del Tesoro Poliennali)
BULL	An optimist, buying securities in the belief of a rising market, hence a 'bull market'.
BULLDOGS	Sterling bonds issued in the UK by foreign organisations.
BULLET REPAYMENT	The whole of a bond or bank loan is repaid at maturity (instead of staged payments in the last few years).
BUND	Short name for the medium-term German Government bond contract on EUREX and LIFFE.
BUNDESBANK	The German central bank.
BUY/SELL AGREEMENT	Like stock borrowing/lending (q.v.) or a repo except that the seller gives up all beneficial rights in the stock.
CABLE	Shorthand for dollar/sterling rate.
CALL MONEY	Money lent by banks to other banks or discount houses which can be recalled at noon each day.
CALL OPTION	An option to buy a share/bond/index/interest rate contract later at a price agreed today.
CAP	An agreement with a counterparty which sets an upper limit to interest rates for the cap buyer for a stated time period.
CAPITAL ADEQUACY	The need to maintain adequate capital to cover counterparty risk and position risk.
CAPITAL MARKETS	The market for medium- and long-term securities.
CAPITAL RATIO	The ratio of a bank's primary capital to a weighted value of assets (for example cash = 0 weighting).
CAPITALISATION	Market capitalisation of a company is the number of shares multiplied by the current price.
CBOE	Chicago Board Options Exchange.
CBOT	Chicago Board of Trade.

CERTIFICATE OF DEPOSIT	Issued by banks to raise money – strong secondary market. (Also Eurocertificate of Deposit.)
CGT	Capital Gains Tax.
CHAPS	Clearing House Automated Payments System – for electronic clearing of payments the same day (UK). Used for sterling and euros.
CHINESE WALL	A theoretical barrier between different sections of a firm to avoid conflicts of interest or insider dealing.
CHIPS	Clearing House Interbank Payments – electronic bank clearing system in New York.
CLEAN PRICE	Price of a bond not including the accrued interest element.
CLEARING HOUSE	Central body guaranteeing contracts in a traded options/ futures market place.
CLOSING OUT	For futures market – taking the opposite contract, for example, having previously bought 100 tons of cocoa for June delivery, the buyer now sells 100 tons for the same delivery (or vice-versa).
CME	Chicago Mercantile Exchange.
COLLAR	A combination of a cap and floor. Setting a band within which interest rates will apply, for example 10–12%, for a given period. Also used for currency rates.
COMMERCIAL BANKING	The 'classic' banking business of taking deposits and lending money, either retail or wholesale.
COMMERCIAL PAPER	A short-term security issued to raise money, usually by corporates. (Also Eurocommercial Paper.)
CONCERT PARTY	A group acting together (secretly) in a takeover situation, for example three people each buy 2.9% of shares to avoid no longer being able to hide behind nominee status.
CONNECT	A computer trading system at LIFFE.
CONSOLIDATION	Reorganising share holdings so that, for example, 10 shares at 10p nominal are replaced by one at £1 nominal.
CONVERTIBLE	A convertible bond may be converted later into equity, some other bond, or even a commodity, for example gold, as an alternative to redemption.
CORPORATE FINANCE	The department of a merchant/investment bank dealing with takeovers, mergers and strategic advice to companies.
COUNTERPARTY RISK	The risk involved if a counterparty fails to settle.
COUPON RATE	The annual rate of interest on a security noted on coupons issued with bearer bonds.

COUPON STRIPPING	Detaching the coupons from a bond and selling the coupons and the principal as individual zero coupon bonds.
COUPONS	Issued with bearer bonds to enable the holder to claim the interest.
COVER	The amount of dividend paid (net) divided into the amount of profit after tax available for distribution.
CREATION OF CREDIT	Banks' ability to lend money, facilitated by the use of notes and coin for a small percentage of transactions only.
CREDIT RATINGS	For example AAA, issued by companies like Standard and Poor's and Moody's to rate the level of security of a bond or note issue.
CREST	The new UK paperless equity settlement system which started in mid 1996.
CROSS-RATES	Rates between two currencies neither of which is the dollar.
CUMULATIVE	Applied to a Preference Share – if dividend is missed it is still owed to the holder.
CYLINDER	Name used for a collar in currency markets.
DEBENTURE	In the UK, a bond secured on assets. In the US and Canada, a bond not secured on assets!
DERIVATIVES	Products whose price is derived from the price of an underlying asset – for example if ICI shares are the underlying asset, an option to buy or sell them at a given price is the derivative. Applied to options, futures, swaps etc.
DIRTY PRICES	Bond prices including the accrued interest element.
DISCOUNTING	Buying/selling a security at less than face value.
DISINTERMEDIATION	Direct market borrowing or lending by companies without going through a bank. A bank is traditionally the 'intermediary' between depositors and borrowers.
DIVIDEND YIELD	The annual percentage return on a share price represented by the current dividend – usually gross.
DOCUMENTARY LETTER OF CREDIT	A documentary letter of credit is the written undertaking of a bank made at the request of a customer (for example an importer) to honour the demand for payment of a seller (for example an exporter) if terms and conditions are met.
DOUBLE	See Straddle.
DRAGON BOND	A Eurobond issued in Hong Kong or Singapore and targeted for primary distribution to Asian investors.

DTB	Former German Futures/Options Exchange (Deutsche Termin Börse), now EUREX (q.v.).
EARNINGS YIELD	Earnings per share (after tax) expressed as a percentage of share price.
EASDAQ	European Association of Securities Dealers Automated Quotations – a pan-European trading system which started in late 1996.
ECB	European Central Bank.
EFT-POS	Electronic Funds Transfer at Point of Sale.
ELIGIBLE BILLS	Bills of Exchange eligible for sale to the central bank when acting as 'lender of last resort'.
EMS	European Monetary System – general agreement on monetary cooperation. Included official use of the ECU, 20% of central banks' reserves held in a European Monetary Cooperation Fund and exchange rates of member countries kept within a stated range, one to another (ERM). Set up in 1979. Replaced by EMU.
EMU	European Economic and Monetary Union – a single currency area set up for eleven European countries on 1 January, 1999. Greece joined later, and notes and coins were included from 1 January, 2002.
EOE	European Options Exchange (Amsterdam), now known as AEX.
EONIA	Euro Overnight Indexed Average – average of overnight rates in the euro area.
EQUITY	General term for shares.
ERM	The interim exchange rate system for countries waiting to join EMU.
ESCB	The European System of Central Banks – the ECB plus the central banks of the EU, technically including those not in the euro area but who play no part in monetary policy decisions.
ESOPS	Employee Stock Ownership Plans (US).
EUREX	The futures/options exchange which combines Germany's DTB and Switzerland's SOFFEX.
EURIBOR	Interbank lending rate for the euro in the countries of the monetary union.
EURO	The name of the single currency in Europe's monetary union.
EURO LIBOR	Interbank lending rate for the euro in London.

EUROBOND	A bond issued in a market outside that of the domestic currency.
EUROCERTIFICATE OF DEPOSIT	See Certificate of Deposit.
EUROCOMMERCIAL PAPER	See Commercial Paper.
EUROCURRENCIES	Any currency held by banks, companies or individuals outside its country of origin.
EURONIA	Euro Overnight Indexed Average – average of overnight euro rates in the London Market.
EURO.NM	The Association of junior stock markets for smaller companies started by Paris, Frankfurt, Brussels and Amsterdam but with others joining.
EURONOTE	Short-term security denominated in a Eurocurrency.
EUROSYSTEM	The ECB plus the central banks of the participating countries only, not including those not in the euro area.
EXERCISE PRICE	The price at which an option can be exercised. (Also called strike price.)
FACTORING	Buying trade debts on a regular basis to assist cash flow – usually done by subsidiaries of banks.
FCP	Fonds Communs de Placement. French 'closed ended' fund.
FEDWIRE	Electronic payments system between Federal Reserve banks in the US.
FLAT YIELD	The annual percentage return on a bond taking into account the buying price, for example if £100 nominal worth of an 8% bond is bought for £50, the yield is 16%. Also called 'annual', 'running' and 'interest' yield (see Redemption Yield).
FLOATING RATE	A loan with the interest rate varied at agreed intervals, linked to a base rate, for example LIBOR.
FLOOR	An agreement with a counterparty which sets a lower limit to interest rates for the floor buyer for a stated time period.
FORFAITING	Buying export trade debts on a non-recourse basis to assist cash flow. The debts must be in the form of a Bill of Exchange or Promissory Note.
FORWARD CONTRACT	A contract to buy or sell a commodity or security for future delivery at a price agreed today.
FORWARD/FORWARD	1. An agreement to lend money at a future point in time for a given period of time, for example, in six months for six months.

	2. A forward foreign exchange deal not dated today but at a later date.
FORWARD RATE	A rate agreed now for a future purchase or sale of a currency. Derived from the difference in interest rates in the two currencies.
FRA	Forward Rate Agreement. An agreement with a counterparty which agrees on a stated rate of interest to apply to a notional principal sum at a future time to last for a stated time – for example, in six months for six months.
FRN	Floating Rate Note. An issue where the interest is at floating rate.
FRONT OFFICE	Dealing room system to facilitate buying and selling.
FSA	Financial Services Authority – the new financial regulatory body in the UK.
FUNGIBLE	Exchangeable – for example, a contract of one futures exchange may be identical with another. Can be opened in one and closed in the other exchange (or vice-versa). Also used for further issues of bonds on exactly the same terms (and accrued interest) as those issued earlier.
FUTURES CONTRACT	Similar to Forward but not expected to go to delivery as the position will be closed out with the opposite contract.
G7, G10, etc.	Meetings of international Finance Ministers – 'Group of 7', 'Group of 10', etc.
GDR	Global Depositary Receipt – a form in which foreign shares can be traded outside their domestic markets.
GEARING	Carrying out financial transactions on the basis of a deposit or borrowed money. US term is 'leverage'.
GEARING RATIO	Ratio of equity and long-term debt.
GENERAL CLEARING	Part of APACS – the normal 3/4 day cheque clearing (UK).
GILTS	Term applied to UK and Irish Government bonds. From 'gilt-edged' or virtually guaranteed. In general use for UK Government stock from the 1930s onward.
GLASS-STEAGALL ACT	Passed in the US in 1933, prevented Commercial Banks from engaging in certain Investment Banking business (and vice-versa); now repealed.
GLOBALISATION	The movement to integration of world markets regardless of national boundaries.
GREENSHOE OPTION	In the event of exceptional demand for a new issue, the issuer reserves the right to issue extra securities.

GREY MARKET	The market for sales of a security before the official market opens.
GROSS REDEMPTION YIELD	See Redemption Yield.
HAIRCUT	In a stock borrowing/lending agreement, the borrower passes collateral to a value in excess of the market value of the stock (to allow for the price rising). This excess is called a 'haircut'.
HEDGING	A technique for limiting risk. For example, if a price movement would cause loss, a purchase is made of an options or futures contract giving the opposite result; if a rise in interest rates causes loss, a position is taken with interest rate options/futures so that a rise in interest rates will yield a profit.
IDB	Inter Dealer Broker – facilitates deals between market makers who can deal in confidence and anonymity.
IMF	International Monetary Fund. Set up in 1946 to help nations in balance of payments difficulties.
INDICES	Like the S&P 500, the CAC 40, DAX, FTSE 100, etc.
INELIGIBLE BANK BILLS	Bills of Exchange accepted by a bank, but one not on the central bank's list (see Bank Bill).
INITIAL MARGIN	Initial deposit required by a Clearing House (as opposed to variation margin).
INSURANCE	If contrasted with assurance, this is business other than life insurance.
INTERBANK MARKET	Bank lending/borrowing one to another.
INTEREST YIELD	See Flat Yield.
INTERNATIONALISATION	See Globalisation.
INTRINSIC VALUE	The amount by which a call option exercise price is below the market price (or a put option exercise price is above it).
INTRODUCTION	A method of obtaining a Stock Exchange quotation. No new shares are issued. Usually they are foreign shares seeking a listing on a domestic market.
INVESTMENT BANKING	Banking implying a high involvement with securities – new equity issues, rights issues, bond issues, investment management, etc. Also advice to either party for mergers and acquisitions.
INVESTMENT GRADE	A credit rating of BBB (Standard and Poor's), Baa (Moodys) or better – that is, a high quality bond.
INVESTMENT TRUST	A company whose whole business is running a wide portfolio of shares. A 'closed ended' fund.

IPMA	International Primary Markets Association (for Eurobond dealers).
IPO	Initial Public Offering – American term for Offer for Sale.
IRREDEEMABLE	Same as perpetual.
ISDA	International Securities and Derivatives Association.
ISMA	International Securities Market Association.
ISSUING	Offering a security to the market in the first instance.
JOINT STOCK	Having shareholders.
JUNK BONDS	Specifically bonds with ratings of BB (Standard and Poor's), Ba (Moodys) or less. Generally high risk, high yield bonds.
KANGAROO BOND	An Australian dollar bond issued in Australia by a non-resident.
LCE	London Commodity Exchange – cocoa, coffee, sugar etc., now part of LIFFE.
LDC	Less Developed Countries.
LEAD MANAGER	Bank(s) taking a key role in a syndicated loan or issue of securities like Eurobonds.
LEVERAGE	American term for gearing or 'making a small amount of capital go a long way'!
LIABILITIES	The side of a bank's balance sheet dealing with borrowing – that is, deposits, formal loans from others. Also share capital.
LIBID	London Interbank Bid Rate. Rate paid by one bank to another for a deposit.
LIBOR	London Interbank Offered Rate. Rate charged by one bank to another for lending money.
LIFFE	London International Financial Futures and Options Exchange.
LIMEAN	Average of the LIBOR and LIBID rates.
LIQUIDITY RATIO	Usually a percentage relationship between a bank's liquid assets and its eligible liabilities.
LLOYD'S	The Corporation of Lloyd's provides insurance through pooling the resources of individual members (the 'Names') operating in syndicates.
LLOYD'S BROKER	Lloyd's will only deal with a 'Lloyd's Broker'.
LLOYDS REGISTER	Shipping classification society dating back to 1776.

LME	London Metal Exchange – deals in six non-ferrous metals.
LOCALS	Traders dealing for themselves as speculators.
LONDON CLEARING HOUSE	The main clearing house for exchange traded derivatives in London.
LONG	To be 'long' in shares, bonds or foreign exchange is to own more than have been sold.
LORO	Alternative term for 'Vostro'.
MANAGING AGENTS	Run and administer Lloyd's syndicates on behalf of the names.
MARGIN	The deposit required by a Clearing House.
MARKET MAKER	The dealers in stocks and shares as principals – that is, taking the risk in their own name.
MATADOR BOND	Peseta bonds issued in Spain by non-residents.
MATIF	French Futures Exchange (Marché à Terme International de France).
MEDIUM-TERM NOTES	A flexible facility to issue notes of varying maturity, varying currency and either fixed or floating – all within one set of legal documentation.
MEFF	Spanish Futures and Options Exchange in Madrid and Barcelona (Mercado de Futuros Financieros).
MEMBERS' AGENTS	Advise members on Lloyd's syndicates regarding tax, spread of risk, etc.
MERCHANT BANKS	UK term for Investment Banks.
MEZZANINE	Just as a mezzanine floor is a floor in between two others, so mezzanine debt is subordinated debt lying between equity and senior debt.
MIDDLE OFFICE	A general term for risk management systems.
MLA	Mandatory Liquid Asset – the charge for a sterling loan in the UK to cover non-interest bearing deposits at the Bank of England.
MLR	Minimum lending rate – the rate at which the Bank of England will lend to the banks. Only published as an 'official' rate in emergencies, for example January 1985 during the fierce run on sterling, October 1990 when the UK joined the ERM and the ERM crisis in September 1992. Now referred to as the 'repo' rate.
MOF	Multiple Option Facility. A revolving facility from a syndicate of banks permitting the raising of finance with various options – bank loan, banker's acceptance or commercial paper.

MONEP	French Options Exchange (Marché des Options Négociables de Paris).
MONEY BROKER	Intermediary putting borrowers in touch with lenders for a small commission.
MONEY MARKET	The market for money instruments with a maturity of less than one year.
MUTUAL	A bank or insurance company not a public company but owned by the members.
MUTUAL FUNDS	General name for pooled funds, such as investment trusts and unit trusts.
NAMES	Members at Lloyd's.
NASDAQ	North American Securities Dealers Automated Quotations – computerised dealing system for US 'over the counter' (OTC) trade outside recognised exchanges.
NATIONAL DEBT	The total of outstanding debt of the central government especially bonds and national savings.
NIL PAID	A new issue of shares following a rights issue on which payment has not yet been made. Rights can be sold 'nil paid'.
NMS	'Normal Market Size'. This is the classification concept which replaced the three classes alpha, beta and gamma. It is based on a percentage (currently 2½%) of an average day's trading. There are 12 bands and they are used to decide the minimum quote size and the maximum size for immediate publication of trades (UK).
NOSTRO	'Our' – the overseas currency account of a bank with a foreign bank or subsidiary.
OATS	Obligations Assimilable de Trésor. French Government bonds.
OFEX	An over-the-counter stock market in the UK.
OFF-BALANCE SHEET RISKS	Risks for bankers other than activities which end up as an asset on the balance sheet. For example, standby loans, standby letters of credit, derivatives generally.
OFFER FOR SALE	A method of bringing a company to the market. May be at a fixed price or by tender.
OFFER RATE	Rate of interest charged for interbank lending of money. Generally, the dealer's selling price for equities, bonds, foreign exchange, etc. Also called 'Ask' Rate or Price.
OPEN OUTCRY	Face to face trading.
OPEN YEAR	When an accounting year cannot be closed due to uncertainty about claims (the Lloyd's market).

OPTION DATED FORWARD RATE	A forward rate (foreign exchange), but the date is more flexible.
OPTIONS	The right but not the obligation to buy/sell equities, bonds, foreign exchange or interest rate contracts by a future date at a price agreed now. 'Traded options' means the options themselves can be bought and sold.
OTC	Over the counter market. Dealing outside a trading exchange, for example a currency option purchased from a bank.
OVERFUNDING	The issue of government bonds or Treasury bills not for immediate government borrowing needs but as an instrument of monetary control.
PAC-MAN DEFENCE	In a takeover situation, when the company which is the subject of a bid turns round and tries to take over the bidder!
PAR	The nominal value of a security, for example $1000 for US Treasury bonds or £100 for UK government bonds.
P/E RATIO	Ratio of share price to earnings after tax.
PERPETUAL	A security without time limit for redemption.
PITS	Trading areas in options, futures and commodity exchanges.
PLACING	A method of bringing a company to the market. The shares are placed with institutional investors and some private investors, that is, not 'offered for sale' generally.
PLAZA AGREEMENT	An example of international cooperation. Following a meeting in October 1975 at the Plaza Hotel, New York, international finance ministers agreed to take measures to reduce the exchange rate for the dollar.
POISON PILL	A device to frustrate a hostile takeover bid (US).
POSITION RISK	The risk involved in holding any financial market position (equities, bonds, currencies, options, futures, etc.) should the relevant rates/prices change.
PREFERENCE SHARES	Dividend is paid as a fixed percentage. They have preference over ordinary shareholders for dividend payment and in case of liquidation. Usually non-voting. (Preferred stock in the US.)
PRIMARY MARKET	Markets where securities are sold when first issued.
PRIVATE BANKING	Specialist banking services for high net worth individuals.
PROMISSORY NOTE	A signed promise to pay a sum of money.
PSBR	Public Sector Borrowing Requirement – excess of public sector spending over revenue.

PSDR	Public Sector Debt Repayment – excess of public sector revenue over spending.
PUT OPTION	An option to sell a share/bond/index/interest rate contract later at a price agreed today.
REDEEMABLE	Applied to a preference share or bond – may be redeemed by the issuer on terms stated at the outset.
REDEMPTION	Final payment to holders of bonds.
REDEMPTION YIELD	The gross redemption yield takes into account the gain or loss to redemption as well as the flat yield (also called yield to maturity).
REINSURANCE	Laying off the original risk with others.
RELIT	Règlement Livraison de Titres. French Stock Exchange settlement system.
REPO	Sale and Repurchase Agreement. Securities are sold but must be repurchased later.
RETAIL MONEY	High street deposits/borrowings.
REVERSE REPO	When the repo deal is initiated by the *buyer* of the securities.
REVERSE TAKEOVER	The acquisition by an unquoted company of a company whose shares are quoted and is often larger than the new owner. The new company takes over the quotation and imposes its own name. A way of getting a stock market listing.
REVOLVING CREDIT	A commitment to lend on a recurring basis on predefined terms.
RIGHTS ISSUE	An offer of shares for cash to existing shareholders in proportion to their existing holdings.
ROLLING OVER	Renewal of a bank loan with alteration of interest rate as per the agreed formula, for example LIBOR + 1%.
ROLLING SETTLEMENT	For example 'five working days' – that is deal on Tuesday, settle next Tuesday; deal Wednesday, settle next Wednesday, instead of all deals within a given 'account' being settled on a given day.
ROOM	The 'Room' is the area at Lloyd's where brokers meet underwriters.
RULE 144A	A rule of the US Securities and Exchange Commission (SEC) by which securities issued abroad can only be sold initially to qualified institutional investors.
RUNNING YIELD	See Flat Yield.
SAMURAI BONDS	A yen bond issued in Japan by non-residents.

SCRIP DIVIDEND	Offer of shares instead of a dividend (optional).
SCRIP ISSUE	Same as bonus issue.
SEAQ	Stock Exchange Automated Quotations – the system that came in with 'Big Bang' (UK).
SEATS	Stock Exchange Alternative Trading System. A dealing system for smaller companies' shares (UK).
SEC	US body controlling regulation of the market (Securities and Exchange Commission).
SECONDARY MARKETS	The buying and selling of a security after its primary issue.
SECURITISATION	The borrowing of money through issue of securities on international markets (in particular) instead of through a bank loan. Also, converting an existing loan into securities, for example mortgage bonds (see ABS).
SEIGNORAGE	The special profit central banks make from printing banknotes whose nominal value is well in excess of their cost to the bank.
SERIES	All options of the same class, exercise price and expiry dates.
SETS	Stock Exchange Electronic Trading System – the new UK order driven system implemented in October 1997.
SETTLEMENT DAY	When the money for a given trade is due to be paid (and the securities handed over).
SHARES	Shares are shareholdings in companies with reward by way of dividend – usually called equities.
SHATZE	German short-term Treasury issues.
SHELL COMPANY	A company with few assets, profits nil or in decline, and a very low share price.
SHORT	To be 'short' in shares, bonds or foreign exchange is to have sold more than have been bought.
SICAV	Société d'Investissement de Capital Variable. French 'open ended' mutual fund.
SIGHT BILL	A Bill of Exchange payable on acceptance.
SOFFEX	Former Swiss Options and Futures Exchange, now EUREX (q.v.).
SOFT COMMODITIES	Sugar, coffee, cocoa, etc. – as opposed to metals.
SONIA	Sterling Overnight Indexed Average – average of overnight rates.

SPLIT	Existing shares are reorganised ('split') into more shares, for example two shares @ 25p are exchanged for each one @ 50p (nominal values).
SPOT	Today's rate for settlement in two days.
SPREAD	Difference between a bid and offer rate. More generally between one rate and another.
STAG	One who applies for a new issue in the hope of selling for a premium – no real interest in the share.
STOCK BORROWING/ LENDING	Equity and bond traders may temporarily borrow or lend stock in exchange for collateral – especially useful for a short position. Although called 'borrowing/ lending', the stock is legally sold in UK law but not necessarily elsewhere.
STOCK EXCHANGE BORROWING/LENDING INTERMEDIARY	Someone prepared to act as a broker in matching the stock borrower and lender (UK).
STOCKS	Fixed interest securities, for example bonds, debentures, preference shares.
STRADDLE	A traded option strategy – simultaneous purchase/sale of both call and put options for the same share, exercise price and expiry date.
STRIKE PRICE	See Exercise Price (alternative term).
STRIPPED BONDS	See Coupon Stripping.
STRIPS	Stripped government bonds in the US – 'Separate Trading of Registered Interest and Principal of Securities'.
SUBORDINATED DEBT	A bond that, in the event of liquidation, can claim only after other senior debts have been met.
SUPERDOT	Automated execution system on the New York Stock Exchange.
SWAPS	Exchange of debt obligations between two parties, either exchange of currencies or fixed to floating rate (and vice-versa) and sometimes both. The latter applies to a notional principal sum and the agreement lasts for a stated time period.
SWAPTION	An option to have a swap at a future point in time.
SWIFT	The banks' international message switching system – Society for World Wide Interbank Financial Telecommunication.
SYNDICATE	Managers, underwriters and selling agents of a bond or bank loan.
SYNDICATES	Organisation of the names at Lloyd's. Each of the syndicates has their own professional underwriter.

TALISMAN	Transfer Accounting Lodgement for Investors Stock Management for Principals – the SE Computerised Settlement System until 1997 (UK).
TAP STOCK	In general, in bond markets further issues of a previously issued bond.
TARGET	Trans-European Automated Real Time Gross Settlement Express Transfer – the official interbank euro payment system for the euro area.
TENDER	A bank loan or new security is offered to dealers who must compete for the business. If settled on a striking price basis, all pay the same price. If offered on a bid price basis, all pay the price they bid.
TICKS	Smallest price movement of a contract, for example 0.01 or 1/32.
TIME VALUE	That part of an option premium which is not the intrinsic value.
TOMBSTONE	Formal notice in the press of a syndicated loan, bond issue, commercial paper programme etc.
TOPIC	Teletext Output of Price Information by Computer. The standardised display of SEAQ information (UK).
TOUCH PRICES	The highest bid price and lowest offer price for a particular stock or share.
TRADE BILL	A Bill of Exchange not endorsed by a bank and not eligible for rediscount at the central bank.
TRADE DATE	The date a trade is agreed, as opposed to settled.
TRADED OPTIONS	An option to buy or sell a share/currency/index/interest rate contract later at a price agreed today. This is a standardised market and the options can themselves be sold.
TRADEPOINT	A UK share trading system using computerised order matching. Began in September 1996.
TRANCHE	Further (large) issue of an existing bond to meet the needs of the market.
TRANCHETTE	Further (small) issue of an existing bond to meet the needs of the market.
TREASURY BILL	Issued by governments to raise money. Typically, three months, six months, 12 months.
UNDATED	Same as perpetual.
UNDERWRITE	When a group of financial concerns agree to subscribe for a proportion of a new issue to ensure its full subscription. The other use of the term is in insurance.

UNDERWRITER	Anyone offering insurance cover for a premium.
UNIT TRUST	A portfolio of holdings in various companies, divided into units which are bought and sold directly. An 'open ended' fund, for example, the French SICAVs.
UNIVERSAL BANK	A term for a bank that is equally engaged in commercial and investment banking, for example Deutsche Bank, UBS, etc.
USM	Unlisted Securities Market – a market since 1980 for companies that do not meet the requirements for a full listing. Ceased operation at the end of 1996 (UK). Replaced by the AIM (q.v.).
VARIATION MARGIN	Further amounts of deposit (debit or credit) calculated by a Clearing House.
VENTURE CAPITAL	Capital provided for high risks which would not normally attract conventional finance.
VOSTRO	'Your' – the domestic currency account of a foreign bank with a domestic bank.
VRN	Variable Rate Note. A floating rate note where the margin above LIBOR is not fixed but reset at intervals.
WARRANT	A certificate attached to a bond or security giving the holder the right to buy equity/bonds later at a set price. May be issued on its own without attachment, for example gilts warrants, currency warrants, CAC 40 warrants, Eurotunnel warrants, etc.
WHEN ISSUED	Grey market trading in government bonds prior to the regular auctions.
WHITE KNIGHT	In a takeover situation, a more acceptable bidder may be sought – the White Knight.
WHITE SQUIRE	Alternatively, key blocks of shares are bought by friendly contacts – the White Squire.
WHOLESALE MONEY	The borrowing and lending of large sums of money – usually between banks, large companies and the institutions.
WORKED PRINCIPAL AGREEMENT	A term used in London's SETS system, when a stock exchange member agrees to dispose of a large block of shares for an institution by buying/selling them in smaller parcels.
WORLD BANK	The International Bank for Reconstruction and Development. Set up in 1945.
WRITING AN OPTION	Selling the option. A margin is paid to the Clearing House.

XD	'Ex Dividend'. If a share or bond is marked 'XD', this means that the purchaser is not entitled to the forthcoming dividend/interest payment as the cut-off point has passed.
XR	'Ex Rights'. In rights issues, if a share is marked 'XR', this means that the purchaser is not entitled to the rights as the cut-off point has passed.
YANKEE BOND	A dollar bond issued in the US by non-residents.
YARD	Foreign exchange term for 1000 million.
YIELD	See Flat Yield.
YIELD CURVE	A graph showing the relationship between short-term and long-term yields for a given security or type of borrowing. Upward-sloping = positive yield curve; downward-sloping = negative yield curve.
ZERO COUPON BOND	A bond issued without interest payments but at a deep discount.

Index

A

ABS, Asset-backed Securities 132, 133, 152, 374
ACH, Automated Clearing House 71, 72
actuaries 346
ADP, actions à dividende prioritaire 135
ADR, American Depositary Receipt 184
advance payment 229, 235, 237
advance payment guarantee 235
advising bank 230, 231, 232, 237
agent bank 86, 87, 90
AIM, Alternative Investment Market 187, 188
Allfinanz 77
American Express Card 66
AMPs, Auction Market Preferred Stock 98
Amtliche Kursmakler 175
APACS, Association for Payment Clearing Services 71, 74
arbitrage 170, 210, 221, 222, 225, 296, 312, 356
Article 65 101, 104
assets 8, 26, 27, 28, 30, 35, 38, 88, 143, 146, 202, 216
assignment 88, 89
ATMs, Automatic Teller Machines 16, 62, 63, 64, 68, 69, 74, 75, 76

B

BACS, Bankers Automated Clearing Service 71
Bagehot, Walter 59, 360
Baker Plan 141
balance sheet 8, 10, 26, 27, 32, 35, 118, 132, 216, 275, 374
bancassurance 20, 77, 90
banco 13
bank draft 228
Bank of England 15, 16, 29, 30, 48, 49, 51, 52, 53, 54, 55, 56, 57, 59, 71, 84, 121, 124, 125, 140, 150, 203, 223, 326
Bank of France 47, 56, 60, 71, 128
Banking Act, 1826 49
Banking Act, 1924 47
Banking Act, 1979 49, 54
Banking Act, 1987 30, 49
banks
    clearing 25, 28
    commercial 15, 17, 24, 61, 65, 72, 78, 89, 91, 94, 99, 100, 101, 118, 124, 150
    cooperative 17, 18, 20, 76
    credit unions 17, 24, 39, 50, 236
    giro 17, 23, 24
    industrial 25
    international 9, 25, 38, 139
    investment 15, 17, 18, 26, 35, 61, 89, 91, 95, 98, 99, 100, 148, 150
    merchant 15, 18, 91
    national savings 17, 24, 25
    post office savings 24, 25
    private 15, 18, 59, 99
    public 25
    savings 17, 18, 19, 20, 62, 73, 109
    savings and loan associations 16, 19, 20, 50, 73
    state 25, 49
    thrifts 19
Bardi 13
barter 236, 355
basis point 82, 87, 107, 119, 316
Basle Committee 31, 32, 132, 323, 365
Bausparkassen 23
BCCI collapse 51, 219, 251
beneficiary 62, 230, 231
bid rate 118, 315
Big Bang 67, 98
Big Bang (Japan) 103
bill of exchange 5, 30, 79, 91, 92, 93, 94, 123, 124, 222, 227, 229, 230, 232, 233
    accepting 91, 92
    bank 94
    discounting 92
    documentary 229
    eligible 94
    sight 229
    tenor 229
    term 229
    usance 229
BIS, Bank for International Settlements 31, 38, 40, 51, 57, 64, 85, 122, 139, 140, 199, 222, 223, 232, 254, 324, 326, 360, 361
block trades 174, 180, 195
bonds
    asset-backed 127, 131
    bearer 127, 143
    bid 234
    bulldog 135
    catastrophe 339
    convertible 114, 134
    corporate 4, 89
    debenture 133
    dragon 148
    foreign 127, 135, 136, 166
    global 147
    government 4, 49, 55, 109, 113, 120, 121, 127, 155, 189, 265, 286, 356
    junk 96, 116, 127, 136, 137, 142, 361

kangaroo 135
local authority 127, 130
matador 135
mortgage 34, 102, 127, 131
performance 234, 235
progress payment 235
samurai 135, 136
tender 234
Treasury 125, 128, 141, 286, 301, 302, 316
yankee 135, 138
zero coupon 145
bonos del estado 125, 130
book-runner 86
bought deals 127, 180, 195
Bouton, Daniel 266
Brady Plan 141
Bretton Woods 58, 203, 204, 223, 253, 269, 297, 361
British Bankers' Association 81, 324
BrokerTec 372
BTAN, Bons du Trésor à Interêt Annuel 128
BTF, Bons du Trésor à Taux Fixe 128
BTP, Buoni del Tesoro Poliennali 130
building societies 22, 23, 62, 68, 73, 110
Building Societies Act 1986 22, 23
Buiter, William 363
bund 298, 302, 306
Bundesanleihen 128, 297
Bundesbank 16, 17, 47, 48, 52, 53, 54, 59, 84, 120, 128, 203, 223, 250
Bundesobligationen 128, 129
Bundesschatzanweisungen 128
Bundesschatzbriefe 129

C

cable 199, 214, 215, 218, 274
CAC, Cotation Assistée en Continu 172
CAD, Capital Adequacy Directive 33, 191, 195
Cahoot 70
call money 118, 120
cap 273, 320, 321, 322
capital ratio 17, 26, 29, 30, 31, 32, 33, 34, 82, 83, 84, 85, 88, 142, 191, 200, 216, 218, 223, 232, 311, 334
capitalisation 158
CATS, Computer Assisted Trading System 172
CBOE, Chicago Board Options Exchange 297 306, 307
CBOT, Chicago Board of Trade 297, 306, 307, 372
CCT, Certificati Credito del Tesoro 130
Cedel 142, 154
central bank reporting 34

certificate of deposit 5, 120, 121
certificats d'investissement 135
CHAPS, Clearing House Automated Payments System 17, 71, 72
CHAPS-Euro 71, 260
chartists 203
CHIPS, Clearing House Interbank Payments 17, 71
clearing house 71, 213, 274, 276, 281, 297, 299, 300, 302, 303, 304, 305, 374
CME, Chicago Mercantile Exchange 212, 274, 284, 286, 287, 288, 289, 297, 304, 306, 323, 372
CMO, collateralised mortgage obligations 132
co-manager 86
Cognotec 372
collar 147, 214, 320, 322, 323
commercial paper 5, 80, 84, 102, 115, 116, 120, 121, 122
commitment fees 82, 87
committed facilities 79, 80
confirming bank 230, 231
confirming houses 100, 236
consolidation 187
convertibles 5, 127, 134, 147
corporate bonds 102, 127, 133
Council of Ministers 268
coupon 111, 126, 145
coupon stripping 146, 152
covenants 84, 88, 364
cover 190
covered interest rate arbitrage 221
creation of credit 26, 28, 40, 52
credit card 16, 17, 52, 63, 64, 65, 66, 70, 73
credit derivatives 323, 324, 372
credit rating 33, 89, 364, 370
credit ratings 82, 114, 117, 136, 143, 313
CREST 154, 156, 181
Crockett, Andrew 365
cross-rates 216, 223
CTO, Certificati del Tesoro con Opzione 130

D

de Larosière, Jacques 140
debentures 5, 127, 133
debit card 17, 62, 63, 65, 67, 68
Debt Management Office 55, 127, 129, 154
dematerialisation 182
deposit accounts 61, 62
derivatives 10, 32, 98, 100, 103, 120, 175, 191, 193, 194, 221, 267, 273, 286, 291, 309, 324, 361, 371, 372, 373
see also options, futures, FRA, swaps, cap, floor, collar
devaluation 204, 205

Diners Club 66
discount rate 53, 120, 124, 231
disintermediation 142
documentary collection 232
documentary letter of credit 32, 93, 230, 231
  acceptance 229, 230, 231
  confirmed 231
  deferred payment 231
  irrevocable 231
  negotiation 231
  revocable 231
  sight 231
  standby 231
  term 231
DOT (Designated Order Turnaround) 178
Dow, Charles 160
DTB, Deutsche Termin Börse 285, 286, 297, 306
Duisenberg, Wim 251
Dutch auction 121
DVP, Delivery vs Payment 181

E

E*Trade 193, 371
earnings per share 190, 195, 208
EASDAQ 188, 373
EC (European Community) regulations 334, 336, 347, 373
EC, European Community 241, 245, 247, 269
  Amsterdam Treaty 245
  Bishop, Graham 262
  CAP, Common Agricultural Policy 206, 242, 243, 247, 258
  Copenhagen Summit 246
  Council of Europe 239
  Council of Ministers 247
  de Grauwe, Paul 203, 251, 252
  Ecofin 248
  EEA, European Economic Area 245
  EFTA, European Free Trade Area 244
  European Coal and Steel Community 240
  European Commission 72, 246, 247, 258, 268
  European Council 243, 247
  European Court of Justice 240, 251, 268
  European Parliament 59, 243, 244, 245, 246, 248, 268
  European Union 238, 247
  Monnet, Jean 240, 241
  Nice Treaty 245, 246
  Schuman, Robert 240
  Single European Act 244
  Treaty of Rome 138
ECB, European Central Bank 50, 222, 250, 251, 257

ECN, Electronic Communications Network 193
Ecofin 257
egg 70, 73, 371
Eichengreen, Barry 363
electronic broking 218, 219, 225, 371, 372
electronic purse 66, 67
EMU, European Economic and Monetary Union 50, 81, 207, 238, 246, 253, 254, 256, 259, 260, 265
  Delors Plan 254
  Duisenberg, Wim 50, 249
  EAF2 18, 260
  ECB, European Central Bank 47, 50, 125, 248
  EIL-2V 260
  EONIA 118
  ERM II 256, 258
  ESCB, European System of Central Banks 248
  EURIBOR 81, 119, 267
  euro 208, 256
  eurolibor 267
  EURONIA 118
  European Banking Association 260
  Eurosystem 249, 250
  Maastricht Treaty 50, 245, 248, 255
  Stability and Growth Pact 256, 257, 258, 263
  Trichet, Jean-Paul 47, 249
EOE, European Options Exchange 285, 297
ERM, Exchange Rate Mechanism 56, 199, 200, 202, 203, 205, 207, 209, 223, 253, 254
ESCB 254
Eufiserv 72
EURIBOR 267
euro 13, 18, 68, 72, 81, 89, 118, 119, 129, 133, 139, 147, 162, 208, 209, 210, 211, 216, 222, 223, 249, 256, 257, 258, 259, 260, 261, 262, 263, 264, 265, 266, 267, 269, 285, 298, 302, 304
Euro.NM 188
eurobonds 5, 26, 83, 95, 133, 135, 137, 138, 139, 142, 143, 144, 145, 147, 148, 151, 206
  callable 147
  dual currency 147
  medium term note 84
  puttable 147
  reverse FRN 147
  rising coupon 147
  zero coupon 145
eurocertificate of deposit 148
Euroclear 142, 154, 182
Eurocommercial paper 84, 148
eurocurrencies 137, 139, 142, 148, 149

eurodollars 138, 139, 287
Eurogiro 72
euromarkets 117, 127, 137, 139, 150, 224
 361
EuroMTS 371
Euronext 194, 285, 373
euronote 83, 84, 148
Europay 67
European Association of Savings Banks 19
EuroStat 265
events of default 87, 88
export credit guarantee 233, 234, 235
export houses 100, 236

F

facility fee 82, 86
factoring 101, 233
FCP, Fonds Communs de Placement 68, 169
FDIC, Federal Deposit Insurance Corporation
 16, 50, 51
Federal Banking Commission 16
Federal Banking Supervisory Office 16, 51
Federal Open Market Committee 50, 59,
 125, 251
Federal Reserve 16, 17, 50, 51, 57, 59,
 71, 101, 102, 125, 140, 252
Fedwire 71
financial futures 169, 273, 293, 297
 Beta factor 301
 locals 295
 long hedge 303
 short hedge 303
financial reinsurance 337, 338
 finite risk 338
 loss portfolio transfer 338
 prospective 338
 retrospective 338
 time and distance 337
Financial Services Agency (Japan) 16, 48,
 357
Financial Services Authority 17, 49, 51,
 74, 334, 335
Financial Stability Forum 365, 373
Finanzierungschätze 129
First Direct 69
First-e 70
Fischer, Stanley 279, 353
floor 147, 320, 321, 322
Fonds Deutsche Einheit 128
foreign exchange swap 216, 217
forfaiting 233
forward dated option contract 211
forward deal 209, 217, 218, 309
forward rate 209, 210, 211, 213, 217,
 221, 309
forward/forward 309

FRA, (forward rate agreement) 32, 98, 273,
 309, 310
Freiverkehr 187
Friedman, Milton 29, 251
FRN, Floating Rate Note 5, 6, 126, 143,
 144, 310, 318
front end fee 82, 86
Fugger 14
fundamentalists 203

G

G10, Group of 10 51, 58
G20, Group of 20 221
G24 58
G30, Group of 30 181, 219, 326
G7, Group of seven 56, 57, 58, 223, 365
GDR, Global Depositary Receipt 184
gearing 8, 88, 145, 275, 356
genusscheine 34, 135
Geregelter Markt 187
gilts 109, 129, 134, 154, 302, 305, 306,
 316
Glass-Steagall Act 84, 101, 102, 104
GLOBEX 306
Goldsmith, Sir James 97
Goodhart's Law 29
greenmail 97
gross dividend yield 189
gross redemption yield 111, 112

H

hedge funds 355, 364, 366
Herstatt risk 219, 221
Hors Cote 187
Hypotheken und Wechsel Bank 15

I

IBOS 72
Icahn, Carl 137
IDA, International Development Association
 206
IFC, International Finance Corporation 206
IMF, International Monetary Fund 53, 57,
 140, 204, 205, 206, 234, 361, 364, 365
Indices
 Affärsvärlden General 162
 American Stock Exchange 160
 ATX 162
 BCI 162
 BEL 20 162
 CAC 40 161, 283, 284, 299
 Comit All Share 162
 Commerzbank 161
 DAX 160, 161, 283, 299

Dow Jones 160, 161
Eurotrack 100 162
Eurotrack 200 162
FAZ 100 161
FT Ordinary Share 160
FTSE 100 161, 174, 277, 283, 284, 298,
    299, 301, 305
FTSE 250 161, 174, 298
FTSE 350 161, 174
FTSE Actuaries 161, 162
General Return 162
IBEX 35 162
KFX 25 162
Madrid SE 162
Major Market 161
MIB 30 162
NASDAQ 100 161
NASDAQ Composite 161
NASDAQ Industrial 161
NYSE 160
OBX25 162
OMX 162
Philadelphia Stock Exchange Value Line
    161
S&P 100 160, 170, 283, 284, 299
S&P 500 160, 284
SBF 120 161
SBF 240 161
SBF 250 161
SE All Share 162
Swiss Market Index 162
Swiss Performance Index 162
WBK 162
Information Internet 372
initial public offering 182, 188
Instinet 156, 193, 371
insurance
    actuaries 332
    assurance 332, 333
    British Insurance Brokers Association 346
    composites 333
    employers liability 336, 346
    endowment policies 332
    General Underwriting Agreement 339
    industrial 335
    Inssure 339, 341, 348
    Institute of London Underwriters 339
    International Underwriting Association 339
    International Underwriting Association of
        London 348
    living assurance 332
    Lloyd's *see* Lloyd's of London
    LMX 342
    London Insurance and Reinsurance
        Association 339
    London Market 332, 336, 339, 348
    minimum guarantee fund 334
    mutuals 333
    P&I clubs (Protection and Indemnity)
        331, 336
    self-insurance 336
    solvency ratio 334
    terrorism 346
    underwriting 332, 333
    unit linked policies 333
    Xchanging 339
interbank 71, 139, 259
interbank market 54, 81, 118
interest yield 111
international credit unions 236
international equity 159, 183
International money order 228
International money transfer 228
Internet 70, 78, 193, 371, 372
introduction 183
Investment Services Directive 35, 191
investment trusts 68, 102, 169, 343
invoice discounting 233
Island 156, 193
issuing bank 66, 230, 231

K

Kennedy, President 138
Keynes, J.M. 140, 203
Krugman, Paul 363

L

LDC (Less Developed Countries) debt crisis
    55, 83, 140, 141, 142, 206, 325, 353,
    361, 362
lead manager 86, 126, 142
Leeson, Nick 291, 324
Leutwiler, Fritz 140
leverage 8, 137, 275, 356, 365
Lewis, Michael 113
liabilities 26, 27, 35, 53, 88, 143, 146, 216
LIBID, London Interbank Bid Rate 119
LIBOR, London Interbank Offered Rate
    81, 119, 299
LIFFE, London International Financial Futures
    Exchange 120, 194, 267, 277, 284, 285,
    286, 295, 297, 298, 300, 302, 306, 307,
    373
limited recourse financing 82, 83
line of credit 79, 123, 217, 309
Lipton, Martin 97
liquidity paper 53
Lloyd's of London 202, 331, 340
    baby syndicate 343
    brokers 334, 340
    Equitas 343, 344, 348
    franchise board 342, 345, 349

Lloyd's brokers 340
Lloyd's List 331
Lutine Bell 341
managing agents 340
members' agents 340
names 340, 341, 342, 343
preferred syndicate 343
reinsurance to close 340, 343
Rowland Report 343
Single Reinsurance Syndicate 345
syndicates 340
the room 341
underwriters 331, 340, 341
loan agreement 80, 86, 87
loan margin 87
Loan Market Association 85
local authority bills 120, 121
lombard rate 53, 124, 125
Lombard Street 13, 331
London Clearing House 16
loro account 219
Louvre Accord 58, 223
LTCM, Long Term Capital Markets 355
LTOM, London Traded Options Market
    285, 297

M

M0 29
M3 29
M4 29
Maastricht 55
Machiavelli, Niccolo 266
Mail Transfer 227
market maker 10, 174, 175, 176, 178,
    283, 311
    gilt-edged 129
MasterCard 65, 67
MATIF, Marché à Terme International de
    France 286, 297, 302, 305, 306
McDonough, William 32, 361
Medici 13, 14, 91
Merger Regulation 192
Merton, Robert 280, 356
Milken, Michael 136, 137
Minitel 70
Modigliani–Miller 89
MOF, Multiple Option Facility 83, 84, 87,
    142, 149
Mondex 67
MONEP, Marché des Options Negotiables de
    Paris 284, 285, 297, 307
Monetary Policy Committee 49, 125
money market 3, 4, 9, 18, 40, 50, 61, 76,
    117, 118, 120, 124, 148, 167, 169, 170
money supply 28, 29, 52, 53, 54, 125,
    250, 359

Monnet, Jean 263
Moody's Investor Services 115, 142, 354
Morgan Stanley World Index 162
mortgage 64, 65, 77
Mortgage Credit Association 23
mutual funds 3, 24, 66, 68, 73, 76, 78,
    99, 150, 159, 163, 168, 169, 170, 335
Mutual Recognition of Listing Particulars 187

N

NASDAQ 158, 188, 193
NASDAQ, National Association of Securities
    Dealers 59, 157, 158, 161, 175, 176,
    187, 193, 373
National Association of Pension Funds 171
national debt 4, 55, 255, 256
negative pledge 88
netting 219, 220, 221, 260, 372
new issue 7, 95, 98, 128, 136, 163, 182,
    184, 185, 370
new paradigm 59, 190
NIF, Note Issuance Facility 83, 87, 142, 149
NMS 173, 177
no cost collar 322
non-competitive bid 153
nostro 225
nostro account 219, 221, 228
NSC, Nouveau Système de Cotation 172, 174

O

OARS, Opening Order Automated Report
    Service 178
OATS, Obligations Assimilable du Trésor 128
obligaciones del estado 125, 130
OECD, Organisation for European
    Cooperation and Economic Development
    32, 85, 239
off-balance sheet items 32, 84, 232
offer for sale 126, 182, 183, 189
offer rate 118, 225, 315
open account trading 229
open market operations 29, 52, 54, 124
open outcry 175, 305, 306, 372
OPMs, Opérateurs Principaux du Marché 120
options 32, 98, 212, 273, 274
    American 277, 283, 284
    barrier 290
    bear spread 290
    binary 291
    Black – Scholes 279
    bond 286
    break forward 213, 285
    bull spread 290
    butterfly 290
    calls 274, 275, 277, 278, 279, 281, 290

compound 291
Cox – Ross – Rubenstein 280
currency 212, 273
cylinder 214, 322
digital 291
down and outs 291
equity 284, 285
European 277, 283, 284
exercise price 277, 286, 290
exotic 290
fair value 279
index 283, 284, 287
initial margin 276
interest rate 287
intrinsic value 278
ladder 291
lookback 291
LTOM 283
participating forwards 213
premiums 274, 275, 276, 279, 280, 281, 282, 286
puts 274, 275, 276, 283, 290
rainbow 291
range forward 214, 322
share ratio 290
spread trading 290
straddle 289
strike price 277
time value 278, 282
up and unders 291
variation margin 276
volatility 280, 281
writers 276, 278, 279, 280, 290
OTC, over the counter 158, 181, 187, 194, 212, 213, 225, 267, 273, 274, 283, 290, 304, 309, 310, 318, 320, 321, 324, 372, 373
overdraft 64, 65, 78, 79, 123, 234

P

P/E, Price Earnings Ratio 188, 189
Pac-man defence 97
par value 110, 126, 151, 187, 204
participating bank 86
participation stock 127
payment on shipment 229
pension funds 3, 17, 99, 100, 109, 110, 130, 133, 150, 159, 163, 164, 166, 167, 168, 190
Perelman, Ronald 137
personal loan 64, 65, 70
Peruzzi 13
Pfandbriefe 23, 131, 261
PHLX, Philadelphia Stock Exchange 212, 306
placing 126, 182, 183

Plaza Agreement 58, 223
poison pill 97, 192
POSIT 156, 193, 371
praecipium 86
preference share 5, 31, 32, 33, 34, 127, 135
private placement 182
profit and loss account 28
project finance 80, 82, 87, 234
promissory note 92, 233
provisions 87, 115
Proxmire-Garn Bill 102
PSBR, Public Sector Borrowing Requirement 4
purchasing power parity 200

R

RAFT, Revolving Acceptance Facility by Tender 83, 142
Reed, John 78, 140
Règlement Mensuel 181
Regulation Q 138
Reichsbank 47
reinsurance 334, 336, 338
  catastrophe cover 337, 339
  ceding 336, 337
  event basis 337
  excess of loss 337, 342
  excess of loss ratio 337
  facultative 337
  financial reinsurance *see separate heading*
  non-proportional 336, 337
  per risk 337
  proportional 336, 337
  quota share 337
  reinsurance brokers 338
  retrocession 336
  surplus 337
Relay 72
RELIT, Règlement Livraison de Titres 181, 182
repo 124, 125, 149, 179, 250
reserves 27, 28, 29, 31, 51, 53, 56, 88, 124, 140, 141, 142, 187, 190, 223, 249, 250, 334, 338, 344, 356, 358, 363, 366
retail banking 17, 18, 25, 61, 64, 68, 72, 73, 77
retained profits 9, 27, 31, 40
retention monies guarantee 235
reverse split 187
revolving credit 81, 82, 86, 87, 123
Ricardo, David 312
Richardson, Gordon 140
rights issues 7, 8, 18, 33, 34, 68, 95, 98, 159, 171, 184, 185, 186
rolling settlement 181

Rowland, David 343, 344
RUF, Revolving Underwriting Facility
    83, 87, 142, 149
rule 144a 148

S

SAX-2000 194
Schatzwechsel 120
Schuman, Robert 241, 263
Schwab, Charles 193, 371
scrip dividend 187, 195
scrip issues 68, 186, 187
SDR, Special Drawing Rights 205
SEAQ, Stock Exchange Automated Quotations
    175, 176, 177
SEATS, Stock Exchange Alternative Trading
    System 176
Second Banking Directive 35, 191
securitisation 34, 132, 142, 262, 361
seignorage 53
SETS 157, 174, 175, 176, 178, 179
share buy-backs 180
shareholders' funds 8, 26, 27, 28
shell company 183
Sibert, Ann 363
SICAV, Société d'Investissement à Capital
    Variable 24, 68, 169
SIS, Système Interbancaire Suisse 72
SIT, Système Interbancaire Télétransmission
    18, 71, 72
smart card 66, 67
Smile 70
SOFFEX, Swiss Options and Futures
    Exchange 285, 297
SONIA 118
special purpose vehicle 34, 131
specialist 178
speculator 145, 199, 203, 273, 293, 294,
    295, 301, 326
splits 186, 187
stamp duty 174
Standard and Poor's Corporation 115, 116,
    117, 142, 160
standby credit 80, 81, 82, 86, 87, 231
stock borrowing 179
stock index arbitrage 170, 221
stock lending 143, 149, 171, 179
sub-participation 88, 89
Supercac 172
SuperDOT *see* DOT
SVT, Spécialiste en Valeurs du Trésor 128
Swapnote 298

swaps 32, 100, 144, 312
    amortising 319
    asset 316, 318
    basis 319
    CIRCUS 145
    currency 144, 216, 319
    foreign exchange 216
    forward 319
    interest rate 144, 216, 312, 314
    liability 316
    roller coaster 319
    swaption 319
    unmatched 315
    warehouse 315
SWIFT, Society for Worldwide Interbank
    Financial Telecommunications 221, 227,
    228
swingline 82
syndicated facilities 83, 85

T

Talisman, Transfer Accounting Lodgement for
    Investors and Stock Management for
    Principals 181
TARGET 18, 259
Taurus, Transfer and Automated Registration
    of Uncertified Stock 181
telegraphic transfer 227, 228
telephone banking 69, 75
telephone selling 334, 335, 348
term loans 80, 82, 86, 87
terrorism insurance 346
Third Life Assurance Directive 347
Third Non-Life Insurance Directive 347
TIBOR 119, 298
Tier 1 capital 31, 34, 36, 39, 135
Tier 2 capital 31, 34, 135
Tier 3 capital 33
Tietmayer, Hans 48, 365
TIPA-NET 72
titres participatifs 135
tombstone 139
tomnext 199, 218
touch price 176
tracker funds 170
traded options *see* options
Tradepoint 156, 193
Treasury bills 5, 27, 28, 30, 53, 54, 55,
    107, 120, 128, 154, 169, 286, 319
Treasury notes 125, 128, 286
Treaty of Rome 241, 243, 251

U

UCITS, Undertakings for Collective
  Investments in Transferable Securities
  68, 170
uncommitted facilities 79
undated 126, 129
Uniform Customs & Practices for Documentary Credit 230
unit trusts 68, 169, 343

V

variable rate note 33, 34, 98
vendor placing 182
Videotex 70
Visa 65, 67
Volcker, Paul 57, 140, 359, 360
vostro account 219, 225

W

warrants 134, 147
when issued 130
White Knight 97
White Squire 97
wholesale banking 17, 61, 79, 89
winner's curse 130
World Bank 53, 57, 58, 143, 147, 204,
  205, 206, 225, 234, 320, 361, 364, 365
Wriston, Walter 139, 140, 151

X

XD, ex dividend 114, 154
XR, ex rights 185

Y

yard 199
yield 110, 120, 189
yield curve 108, 109, 217, 309, 311
yield to maturity 112